# JOURNALS
# MID-FIFTIES

## By ALLEN GINSBERG

### Poetry

*Howl and Other Poems.* 1956.
*Kaddish and Other Poems.* 1961.
*Empty Mirror: Early Poems.* 1961.
*Reality Sandwiches.* 1963.
*Angkor Wat.* 1968.
*Planet News.* 1968.
*Airplane Dreams.* 1969.
*The Gates of Wrath: Rhymed Poems 1948–1951.* 1972.
*The Fall of America: Poems of These States.* 1973.
*Iron Horse.* 1973.
*First Blues.* 1975.
*Mind Breaths: Poems 1971–1976.* 1978.
*Plutonian Ode: Poems 1977–1980.* 1982.
*Collected Poems 1947–1980.* 1984.
*White Shroud: Poems 1980–1985.* 1986.
*Cosmopolitan Greetings: Poems 1986–1992.* 1994.

### Prose

*The Yage Letters* (w/William Burroughs). 1963.
*Indian Journals.* 1970, 1990.
*Gay Sunshine Interview* (w/Allen Young). 1974.
*Allen Verbatim: Lectures on Poetry, Politics, Consciousness* (Gordon Ball, ed.). 1974.
*Chicago Trial Testimony.* 1975.
*To Eberhart from Ginsberg.* 1976.
*Journals Early Fifties Early Sixties* (Gordon Ball, ed.). 1977, 1992.
*As Ever: Collected Correspondence Allen Ginsberg & Neal Cassady* (Barry Gifford, ed.). 1977.
*Composed on the Tongue* (Literary Conversations 1967–1977). 1980.
*Straight Hearts Delight, Love Poems and Selected Letters 1947–1980*, w/Peter Orlovsky (Winston Leyland, ed.). 1980.
*Howl, Original Draft Facsimile, Fully Annotated* (Barry Miles, ed.). 1986, 1995.
*The Visions of the Great Rememberer* (with *Visions of Cody*, Jack Kerouac). 1993.
*Journals Mid-Fifties 1954–1958* (Gordon Ball, ed.). 1995.

### Photography

*Photographs* (Twelvetrees Press). 1991.
*Snapshot Poetics* (Chronicle Books). (Michael Köhler, ed.). 1993.

### Vocal Words & Music

*First Blues*, Cassette tape (Folkways/Smithsonian Records FSS 37560). 1981.
*Howls, Raps & Roars*, 4CD Box (Fantasy). 1993.
*Hydrogen Jukebox* (opera) with Philip Glass, CD (Elektra/Nonesuch). 1993.
*Holy Soul Jelly Roll: Poems & Songs 1949–1993*, 4 CD Box (Rhino Records). 1994.

# ALLEN GINSBERG

# JOURNALS MID-FIFTIES
## 1954–1958

### Edited by Gordon Ball

Harper Perennial
*A Division of* HarperCollins*Publishers*

The Library of Congress has catalogued the hardcover edition as follows:
Ginsberg, Allen, 1926–
    Journals mid-fifties / by Allen Ginsberg ; edited by Gordon Ball.
        p.    cm.
    Includes index.
    ISBN 0-06-016771-8
    1. Ginsberg, Allen, 1926–   Diaries.   2. Poets, American—20th century—Diaries.   I. Ball, Gordon.   II. Title.
    PS3513.I74Z473   1995
    818'.5403—dc20
    [B]                                                                                     94-39143

ISBN 0-06-092681-3 (pbk.)
96  97  98  99  00  PS/HC  10  9  8  7  6  5  4  3  2  1

# Contents

# Acknowledgments

In the course of the past dozen years, as the material in these pages slowly took shape as a book, my debts as editor have grown larger than space allows for a complete listing of all individuals who've been of aid. I thank most of all my wife, Kathleen, for giving with generosity, acumen, and wisdom whenever I asked for assistance or advice. I'm likewise grateful to my daughter, Daisy, for tolerating her father's time in his study, for hours on end, with old notebooks and new transcriptions.

My debt to Allen Ginsberg is considerable, from his extending this opportunity to work to his making himself available virtually every time I needed to review with him portions of our labor. In the office of Ginsberg and Associates, Bob Rosenthal, Jacqueline Gens, Peter Hale, Gina Pellicano, Althea Crawford, Brian Graham, and Vicki Stansbury have been thoughtful and communicative. At HarperCollins, Terry Karten has been patient beyond reason, and Ashley Chase has offered much helpful advice; at the Ginsberg Special Collection, Butler Library, Columbia University, Bernard Crystal and staff have always been of help; as have Bonnie Hardwick of the Manuscripts Division, Bancroft Library, University of California at Berkeley; and Richard C. Fyffe of Special Collections, Homer Babbidge Library, University of Connecticut. Bibliographer Bill Morgan has, to my amazement, never seemed to mind my asking for assistance. His help has been extremely valuable.

Shigeyoshi Murao, Peter Orlovsky, Jack Shuai, Lucien Carr, Yves Le Pellec, Barry Miles, Robert La Vigne, Gerald Nicosia, Ann Charters, Michael Schumacher, James Grauerholz, John Sampas, David Stanford, Donald Hall, Robert Jackson, and Noël Riley Fitch were responsive to queries and requests. At Naropa Institute, Laban Hill, Susan Bonoy, and Doug Trotter made some preliminary transcriptions of journal pages. Sue Wallace provided clerical help early on. The Pryor Research Fund of Tougaloo College and the Research Committee of Virginia Military Institute provided summer funds. Within VMI's Department of English and Fine Arts, I owe a special debt to Professors John Leland and Alan Baragona.

Assistance from the staff at Preston Library, VMI, including most especially Elizabeth S. Hostetter, Wylma P. Davis, Marjorie Camper, and Janet Holly, has been skillful and generous.

GORDON BALL
August 1994

# Meditations on Record Keeping by Poet, Transcribed by Editor

*Recorded August 8, 1984, Varsity Apartments, Boulder, Colorado*

All this time [San Francisco, from 1955] I realized we were involved as a community with a historical change of consciousness and some kind of a cultural revolution. It was similar to things I had read about when I was in grammar school and high school, about people being burned at the stake for new ideas or strikers being attacked by the police, Ludlow Massacres; it seemed like a reminiscent situation where there was some noble effort to enlighten the populace and improve community consciousness and make a step forward, particularly, say, with ideas, with the psychedelics, with religion, with spiritual consciousness in America, Whitmanic consciousness; and the opposition seemed so cruel and unnecessary that I thought it would be a good idea to keep track of it all. Because I thought it was really in some respects a contest between further liberation or 1984 authoritarianism, police state; that it was creeping police state or creeping socialism-libertarianism. And so I thought for the benefit of posterity to keep a record of everything—don't lose any information.

So I began collecting every single scrap of paper from the newspapers that had to do with the word "beat" or "beat generation," to keep a sociological archive that would be as complete as possible, since I was near the center of a whirlpool of energy. And to keep a record of the literary history and the interrelationship of literary people and groups and communities, 'cause that seemed an old American tradition. And I had read Robert McAlmon's book *Being Geniuses Together,* which is a great record of the twenties, and I was interested in Hart Crane, Black Sun Press, and read a little Fitzgerald. . . .

One of the first things I did when *Howl* came out was to send it to Natalie Barney, who was an old lesbian in Paris, friend of Gertrude Stein and Caresse Crosby. I'd made connections with William Carlos Williams, and during the late fifties went up to the Museum of Modern Art's library and read through all the magazines that Williams and Nathanael West edited, *Contact* magazine from the early thirties—and went back and read *transition,* and sort of investigated the history of avant-garde modernism in writing from Dada days onward. And ours seemed to me part of that stream, the politics and the sociology of it, the literary aura of it; and the resistance to it seemed connected with the larger social-psychological-political structure of America. And I realized it was crucial to fight against censorship, 'cause we were actually liberating literature from censorship with all the books from '58 to '62, the *Howl* trial in '57 and then the *Naked Lunch* trials—after all, we hadda publish *Naked Lunch* in Europe, not America. And we had censorship on *Junky* going back ten years, Kerouac's huge *Visions of Cody* couldn't be printed complete in the late fifties on account of Laughlin was afraid of a legal fight, so he had to print only a limited edition of a hundred pages.*

So there was real censorship, so I realized we were going through a big social transition, a cultural revolution, and people were either making fun of it, not realizing its importance, or interpreting it in a Marxian way, like the Los Angeles–Venice group, so that it was necessary to keep some kind of archive or history of it, so that people in later generations would understand it, especially in case of a rollback, in case of a swinging of the pendulum back toward reaction and the reimposition of censorship particularly. So I had the idea of getting the word "fuck" into the high school or college textbooks, once and for all breaking the barrier in the official archives, so they could never erase that again. You know, they'd have to burn books in order to erase

---

* According to Ann Charters, this small 1959 printing included a New Directions insert stating that the excerpt was from Kerouac's favorite novel, "which is considered unpublishable at present." See her *A Bibliography of Works by Jack Kerouac 1939–1967* (New York: The Phoenix Book Shop, 1969), pp. 18–19. Illuminating commentary appears as well in Gerald Nicosia's *Memory Babe: A Critical Biography of Jack Kerouac* (New York: Grove Press, 1984), p. 562.

the literature, and to erase the impulse and to erase the mentality, and erase the sense of liberty and adventure and inquisitiveness and amusement and humor.

Simultaneous there was this growth of the problem of drugs, the corruption and involvement of the police in the whole drug racket, and the complete hallucination of the official "drug" setup. One of the first public breakthroughs re drugs was an early 1961 TV program with Mailer, Ashley Montagu, and others, where we said we'd all smoked pot and we thought the law should be changed.* That realization was another historic demystification or change.

Back in '58 there was also the increased growth of the military. I wrote a long article† in '59 in the *San Francisco Chronicle* saying that (with a $54 billion military budget in mind) we were headed toward some kind of police state or military-industrial-police state as a real sort of threat, but I wasn't seeing it in Marxist terms, I was seeing it in Whitmanic New Consciousness terms. So I began prose writing about "new consciousness" in the late fifties: formulating the relation between New Consciousness, expansion of poetic forms, breakthrough of new cultural forms, breakthrough of new social forms—and new society, new consciousness, new politics.

I saw all that at stake and thought best to keep a record: in my own writing but also just sort of an archive. So after I milked the notebooks for poems, I just kept hold of the notebooks for whatever I had in it, though I didn't keep like a historical record of conversations—that wasn't my function; I thought Kerouac had done that, historical record of scenes, conversations, characters, and persons. He had covered that and I couldn't possibly compete with him; the best I thought I could do was just keep a record of my own changes of self-nature and perceptions—you know, intermittent perceptions, spots of time. So my notebook is thoughts, epiphanies, vivid moments of haiku, poems, but not a continuous diary of conversations like Virginia Woolf, or Anaïs Nin, or Boswell.

---

* The John Crosby Show, Metromedia Network, February 12, 1961. For further details, see Larry Sloman's *Reefer Madness: A History of Marijuana in America* (New York: Bobbs Merrill, 1979), p. 217.

†"Poetry, Violence, and the Trembling Lambs," in *Poetics of the New American Poetry,* ed. Donald Allen and Warren Tallman (New York: Grove Press, 1973), pp. 331–33.

So I have this giant mass of archives which I kept around the house until 1968. And then moving into the Lower East Side slums, still being poor up till the sixties, to a place that had a sixty-dollar rent—it was a firetrap. I realized I had all my files, letters, early manuscripts stashed there and in my attic in Paterson, and it was time to unload them . . . also fearing intrusion of police, police bust and things like that, because around '65 there were some drug agency attempts to set me up for a bust in my house. So I tried to move it all out of the house, and moved it up on loan deposit to Columbia Special Collections, packing everything in used manila envelopes. And from '68 to maybe 1980, because of various misunderstandings with Columbia Library and with Gotham Book Mart, none of that material was sorted and filed, so it was really impossible to retrieve stuff. I finally realized that naturally librarians were not itemizing and indexing stuff that they hadn't bought, and that Gotham Book Mart was not going through it in detail, itemizing and indexing for their appraisals, and I heard rumors that some stuff was mislaid or missing—photographs, manuscripts, or first editions— maybe pilfered, I wasn't sure, and I didn't have any record of particulars I had up there. It wasn't until about 1982 that I had enough money to begin archiving material properly, and then Bill Morgan came in as bibliographer and began going through the entire material, and then Miles went through for biography. I'd had secretaries up there looking for stuff, and I'd sent everything up in boxes divided into "Manuscripts," "Letters," "Ordinary Mail," and "Literary Mail," but had no index. So it wasn't until about 1982 that I had an apprentice from Columbia, who went in and made a beginning survey. . . . Also with Bob Rosenthal, from 1976, I had a working relationship with a long-range permanent secretary who was literarily inclined, whom I could trust for literary judgment, who could organize going into the stacks to begin unearthing what was really there. When we worked on our last book of journals, I didn't really have a complete list, and I still don't have a complete list of what's up at Columbia—that won't be ready for another year or more.* So the

---

* Bibliographer Bill Morgan completed a catalog list, including all journals, by 1987. However, additional bibliographical work with Ginsberg material at Columbia continued until transfer of Ginsberg's entire archive to Stanford University, September 1994.

stray material from early fifties and from '59 to '60, up till the trip
to South America, January 1960—stray leaves and stray manu-
scripts and stray independent writings on pieces of paper and a few
stray notebooks and pocket notebooks—still have to be located,
whatever I don't have in my house. The instigation for getting
things together, finding all these old notebooks, was the advantage
of having apprentices at Naropa during mid-seventies, late seven-
ties, and early eighties, who were beginning to type the whole mass
of material up. 'Cause I hadn't had any typing done since 1965, by
Aileen Lee (who'd typed Burroughs' *Yage Letters* and *Queer* back in
1953). She typed a mass of material from '65 through '67—it was
ten years before I got back to the *huge* Sisyphean task of getting the
materials typed.

So then I began retrieving things from Columbia, and after
that I had to organize the retrieval, and then I organized files in
New York. And I don't do this all by myself, I can't do it all by
myself, 'cause I wouldn't have time to write and read. And I didn't
have enough money to *hire* secretarial help until about mid-
seventies, and pay a regular wage. I wasn't making enough money,
literally, to do that, and what money I was makin' earlier, from '68,
was going into the Cherry Valley farm,* at least six years there.

So this [*Journals Mid-Fifties*] results from increasing coherence
of what's archived.

---

* In 1966, once Ginsberg began receiving some income from poetry
readings, a modest foundation, Committee on Poetry, Inc., was estab-
lished to give small extra monies to other poets and artists. By 1968
C.O.P., Inc. purchased, as an artists' retreat from the city, an old farm-
house without electricity, situated a few miles from Cherry Valley, New
York.

# Editor's Note

The printed text of this volume of journals draws on material entered by Allen Ginsberg in twelve notebooks and related separate pages from June 1954 through mid-July 1958. In terms of his major poems, it represents the period from his entering the Bay Area, where within approximately a year he'd write *Howl*, through his first trips to the Arctic and to North Africa and Europe, when he made brief early notations that would culminate several years later in the completed *Kaddish*.

Though these notebooks are presented here as a single entity, the editing has involved considerable interleaving between one journal and another, and sometimes yet a third. Thus this volume represents the drawing together and interleaving of entries from such sources as: tiny red breast-pocket spirals from Paris 1958, recording names and addresses side by side with secret conversations and poems; a 9½-by-7½-inch accountant's calendar book kept on Ginsberg's Bay Area desks or bedside tables for midnight or light-of-day entries rich with ballpoint poetic theorizing and trial verses, as well as love's torments. There was also a small green hardbound issued by the U.S. Government Printing Office and used by the poet in uniform as he sailed toward the Arctic in summer 1956, entering exquisite descriptions as well as meditations on humanity, suffering, and God; a sizeable but handy hardbound with maroon elbows reinforcing the cover, containing early versions of some major works written in Europe mid-1957 through 1958; a paperback Série Velin Standard of fine blue and white graphed pages containing early notes on the death of his mother—some of the rough steps on an irregular path that would finally lead to one of his greatest poems.

Portions of the summer 1954 entries, as well as some from late 1955 and the beginning of 1956, appeared previously in *Journals Early Fifties Early Sixties* (New York: Grove Press, 1977, 1992). Incorporating considerably more material, this volume fills in that earlier text's chronological gaps 1954–1958. This is the third collection of Ginsberg's journals to see print, the first being his

*Indian Journals,* which presented entries from early 1962 (where *Journals Early Fifties Early Sixties* left off) through mid-1963.

In the Ginsberg Special Collection, Butler Library, Columbia University, independent bibliographer and archivist Bill Morgan has organized and cataloged over three hundred separate journal notebooks kept by Ginsberg from 1937, when the poet was eleven, through 1985 [see note, page xiv]. Within this immense collection, no diminution of Ginsberg's journal production is evident: there are sixteen notebooks begun in 1960, six of them over a hundred pages in length; there are fifteen begun in 1982, ten exceeding a hundred pages. Not only has there been no diminution: the poet, coming downstairs for breakfast one morning last spring, returning his Montblanc pen to his oxford-cloth breast pocket, remarked to my wife, "I'm writing more in my journals now than ever."

The text of this volume of journals has been lightly pruned and shaped by author and editor for general readability, clarity, and style. A great deal of abstract, subjective, and repetitious "maunderings," as Ginsberg has termed them, have been blue-penciled, though sufficient sample has been retained to give readers a large taste of such solitary ruminations. In general, an entry has been selected for print if it provides one of the following: biographical information about the author; literary/historical information about the author and/or his contemporaries; aesthetic interest or value in itself.

There is inevitably an element of approximation in the chronological ordering of entries, since the diarist can sometimes misdate an entry; often doesn't date successive entries, which can be months or even years apart; uses more than one notebook at the same time; and uses one notebook intermittently over a period of years. To ensure that each entry is placed in its chronologically correct position, author and editor have made use of the following: the author's memory, the memory of friends, manuscripts other than journals, the correspondence (published and unpublished) of the author and others, biographies of the author, biographies of Kerouac and Burroughs, Kerouac's fictional chronicles and other literary and nonliterary sources, and, finally, common sense.

Eccentric or nonstandard capitalization, punctuation, or

other mechanical/grammatical departures are sometimes re-
tained in order to reduce the sense of distance from the author's
actual notebooks felt by a reader of the printed page. Notation is
made when a draft of a published poem appears in the journal
text. If there is essentially little or no difference between journal
entry and published version, the notation (and, typically, the open-
ing line or lines) is all that appears. Poems included in Ginsberg's
*Collected Poems 1947–1980* (New York: Harper & Row, 1984) are
identified by the abbreviation CP and appropriate page numbers.
References to Ginsberg's and Orlovsky's *Straight Heart's Delight*, ed.
Winston Leyland (San Francisco: Gay Sunshine Press, 1980), use
the abbreviation SHD. Except when Ginsberg quotes other
sources, or when otherwise indicated, ellipsis periods represent
elision from the journal entry.

Ginsberg's diary entries are extensive under certain condi-
tions (for example, during his wholehearted efforts in early 1955
to cement a relationship with Peter Orlovsky, and during much of
his time aboard ship in Military Sea Transport Service in 1956) and
are infrequent under others (for example, during most of his first
stay in Morocco and travels in Europe, spring and summer 1957,
when he was quite active both in writing letters home and in taking
photographs). Obviously, what he does by day, and by night, can
determine whether or not he keeps up with a daily record. Readers
will also note an absence of entries for approximately a month
around September 1956, followed by infrequent entries from later
the same year through Ginsberg's settling into Paris in the fall of
1957. In compiling this volume, both poet and editor have at-
tempted to locate all relevant material, but it is, of course, possible
that a notebook from that period remains unretrieved, missing, or
no longer extant. Within the pages that follow, gaps are noted
editorially as they appear, with suggested alternative reading
sources.

GORDON BALL
August 1994

# I.  June 1954–September 1955

San Jose –
San Francisco

# Introduction

The years immediately preceding those represented in these journals were, as the author once remarked, "the consolidation of what later became known as the Beat Generation, in terms of the initial writing and many major works."* Jack Kerouac had been writing "exhaustively," having completed *On the Road*, *Visions of Cody*, and *The Subterraneans*, and begun *Book of Dreams*, *Some of the Dharma*, *Maggie Cassidy*, and *Visions of Gerard*. William S. Burroughs had started putting on paper some of his first routines, including "The Talking Asshole" and "Dr. Benway." Gregory Corso had begun the poems in his first collection, *The Vestal Lady on Brattle*.

And Allen Ginsberg had emerged "out of a slough of despond," several years beyond his outpatient days at the Psychiatric Institute, had worked in market research, and had recently, since mid-1953, been making a modest living as copyboy for the *New York World-Telegram*. He and Kerouac and Burroughs had experienced the "psychedelic amusements" of peyote; Kerouac had introduced him to Buddhism; and he had begun reading numerous volumes on Chinese and Japanese art at the New York Public Library.

Ginsberg and Burroughs had edited the latter's 1953 correspondence for part of what would be published as their *Yage Letters*, as well as the manuscript of the later book *Queer*. The poet had finished his "preliminary, early" verse volumes, *The Gates of Wrath* and *Empty Mirror*, and gone on to larger works, including that manifesto on the independence of the imagination "The Green Automobile." At this time, however, as he would proclaim on the 1956 dedication page of *Howl and Other Poems*, "All these books" of the Beat writers, excepting Kerouac's first novel, were "published in Heaven." For in spite of his characteristically determined efforts as amateur agent for the works of his friends, Ginsberg had suc-

---

* The bulk of background information in this and the two other sectional introductions, as well as all quotations not attributed to the journals themselves or other sources, are from the editor's interviews with Allen Ginsberg at Naropa Institute, August 7–9, 1984.

ceeded in getting only Burroughs' *Junky* published, "under de-grading circumstances as a paperback side-by-side with a narcotic agent's book on being a narc." And of his own verse efforts, "I hadn't written anything *that* good, certainly nothing striking enough to put out in New York as an unknown writer—though Williams thought he could do something."

In the fall of 1953, less than a year before these journals begin, Allen Ginsberg was sharing his New York apartment with William S. Burroughs. Burroughs was in love with him, wrenchingly. Ginsberg himself had begun to despair of his worka-day market research–copyboy existence, as well as of his limited results in getting friends published. Consequently, he decided to leave New York and go off to Mexico, or "out into the world," planning thence to visit Neal Cassady and, eventually, Europe. Cassady had often invited Ginsberg to stay with him at home in San Jose, and so in June 1954, six months after departing New York, Ginsberg crossed the border back into the United States. It was his first time in California, a land he'd read of in Kerouac's manu-scripts and letters. With a sense of foreboding about American militarism (as expressed in the closing of "Siesta in Xbalba"), a "happy, open feeling" at finally getting to California, and the rec-ognition (also expressed in "Siesta") of a "future, unimaginable God"—the future itself as a god—he returned to a new part of his native land.

His weeks at the Cassady household,* as the early pages of these journals painfully and vividly show, were no worse than might have been expected. Ginsberg's attachment to Cassady was per-haps as strong as Burroughs' to Ginsberg; he'd been in love with Neal since their first meeting, eight years before. They'd had an on-again, off-again involvement, but in the intervening years Cas-sady's situation had changed dramatically: he was now not only a husband but the father of three small children.

Neal now remained typically though irregularly aloof. Gins-berg, full of anguish, having no job, knowing no one else in San

---

* Part of this time, Neal was away from home on railroad work (work that Allen himself applied for), a day or two at a time. At least once, as these journal entries suggest, Allen visited San Francisco with Neal, as well as going in on his own.

Jose, turned—fortunately for us—to his journals: they were his friend, counselor, psychotherapist, profession . . . as well as his composition book. He entered poem after poem, prose passage after prose passage: the frequent crossings-out echo his torment. When on an August morning his dream of an erotic encounter with Neal at last began to come true, Carolyn Cassady discovered Ginsberg, fully clothed, making love to Neal in Allen's bed. Within days, Allen had packed his bags and was delivered to San Francisco by his outraged hostess, who handed the virtually indigent poet twenty dollars. Ginsberg, who later called this rift a "two-day upheaval," continued to see Neal fairly often in the days that followed as Cassady stopped in town on railroad work. In that two-month San Jose interval, full of romantic conflict, Ginsberg had written some of his finest love poems of the period, including "Song" and "Love Poem on Theme by Whitman."

Ginsberg entered San Francisco with little money and, outside of a letter from William Carlos Williams introducing him to Kenneth Rexroth, few personal contacts or occupational prospects. Thus as San Francisco journal entries commence, Ginsberg, from an inexpensive room at the Hotel Marconi, near the intersection of Columbus and Broadway, declared himself "Back alone in a Hotel and once again the great battle for survival . . . and no job [in the] offing."

Yet despite the apparent odds, Ginsberg "almost immediately" landed a market research position with Towne-Oller Associates, and equally quickly found a girlfriend, Sheila Williams. Soon he joined her and her small child in a large Pine Street apartment on Nob Hill, "which was the classy area, overlooking San Francisco's downtown valley and the Drake Hotel." Twenty-two years old (six younger than Ginsberg), Sheila was a small brunette who by day wrote advertising copy for the May Company, a large San Francisco department store. By night, she was a jazz singer; musicians Paul Desmond and Joe Albany were among her friends.

Ginsberg's own work at Towne-Oller on Montgomery Street—San Francisco's Madison Avenue—involved "marketing studies of toiletries on the front counters of supermarkets, correlating them with money spent on advertising campaigns by toothpaste companies or Johnson & Johnson baby powder and baby oil." He later termed it "the best job I'd had in the regular commercial wheel": before he quit the following May, his salary was $450 a month and he had a secretary.

Even in the fall of 1954, he appeared, outwardly, to have perhaps "everything." Ginsberg depicted himself in one journal poem, awaiting Sheila in Vesuvio's Bar, as

> . . . thoroughly
> beautiful
> Dark suit—dark eyes
> no glasses,
> money in my wallet—
> Checkbook abreast—
> Toward an evening
> of fucking and jazz

But soon he would confide his homosexual experiences to Sheila, and she inopportunely broke off their relationship; soon, he has recalled, she seemed to want him back.

Following an argument with her one night, Ginsberg wandered into an area he came to know as "Polk Gulch," centered around Foster's Cafeteria and the Hotel Wentley at Polk and Sutter. In Foster's he met the painter Robert La Vigne, and later that night went to his house nearby, where he first "met," on canvas, the twenty-one-year-old Russian-American Peter Orlovsky, recently discharged from the army and now taking classes at San Francisco City College. Orlovsky was living with La Vigne, but the two were breaking up their relationship, and one evening in Vesuvio's Café, as Ginsberg recalls, "La Vigne arranged for me and Peter to get together. But then he got upset, after we did." Journal entries during the next several weeks are intense, not only with the considerable pangs of Ginsberg's love for Orlovsky but with his working his way through the karma of the complex situation that included Robert and Sheila.

By this time—late 1954—Ginsberg had reconnected with Kenneth Rexroth, who was holding weekly salons in his home. He'd also met Robert Duncan, who was teaching a class at San Francisco State; Jack Spicer, at Duncan's house; and Michael McClure, who was taking Duncan's course. Before his departure for his brother's

East Coast wedding in mid-December 1954, he'd "gotten some distant acquaintance with the San Francisco literary scene" and moved into La Vigne's, joining Peter.

Soon after returning West, Ginsberg left La Vigne's for a nearby small hotel, where, in ambiguous amorous torment, he recorded extensive passages of interior monologue. His first entry for the new year (1955) begins, "The first time in life I feel evil." In just over a month, he and Peter would take a ground-floor apartment, with separate bedrooms, at 1010 Montgomery Street, on the edge of North Beach, several blocks uphill from where he'd continue another season in market research.

Meanwhile, Ginsberg was undergoing psychotherapy:

> . . . I was complaining all the time, I was depressed. And I thought that I should do something about my sexual orientation—or explore it, in any case. 'Cause during the fifties when I was going to psychothcrapy I began making it with girls a lot. . . . I was encouraged to do that.

Likewise, Ginsberg had seen early on the essential limitations of his lucrative workaday world. In a journal entry in the fall of 1954 he'd observed:

> Standardization and mechanization and control of the individual psyche seems now a fait accompli here. . . .
> Spiritual activity or Art a strictly sideline deal and not a centrally important goal.
> . . . things run on a routine of unspiritualized mediocrity and when anyone with any special insight tries to become a part it is a torture.

Luckily for the poet, Langley Porter Hospital was at the time the equivalent of his familiar Columbia Presbyterian Psychiatric Institute: a tony, "open and liberal" place where the patient-friendly psychiatry was a world apart from the sort practiced in many other hospitals of the day. The good influence of Langley Porter culminated with the now well-known response by Dr. Philip Hicks when Ginsberg explained that what he really wanted to do was stop work, write poetry, spend days out of doors, visit museums and friends, and cultivate his own perceptions and visions. Asked Dr. Hicks, "Well, why don't you?"

* * *

Ginsberg, who began his first journal at age eleven, had in recent years given considerable space to problems of poetics and aesthetics and composition. The first hundred or so pages of these notebooks, in fact, contain several entries whose recognitions are crucial to the writing of *Howl.* The entry dated October 17–18, 1954, for example, after Ginsberg had been in San Francisco less than two months, reveals his first sight, on peyote, of the Sir Francis Drake Hotel as "A tower in Hell," the visual base for what becomes "Moloch" in Part II of his first great poem.

In an entry dated March 31, 1955, he reported on a practice that he will begin to refine with the first part of *Howl* that summer: his own recent tendency, in revising, toward "small groups of lines as in 3-line stanza, begun however before reading the Williams late forms." Seeing the lines as "not yet free enough," he called for "expansion to a large form." As shown in Ginsberg's *Howl: Original Draft Facsimile,*\* the poet wrote the first draft of Part I of that poem in long verses consisting typically of triadic "ladders"; after the final draft, that three-part structure disappears from the layout, as each verse "strophe" realizes the "large form," or a variation of it, anticipated March 31.

Essential to the syntax of the entire poem are the perceptions noted in a sequence of entries on ellipsis (in Ginsberg, the juxtaposition of one entity with a second, dissimilar one, without connective), which was triggered by a visual "jump cut" at the end of his dream of the late Joan Burroughs in early June 1955.†

The principle and practice of ellipsis (demonstrated, to point to one conspicuous example, in the phrase "hydrogen jukebox" of Part I) is so central to the syntax of *Howl*—which itself

------

\* *Howl: Original Draft Facsimile, Transcript & Variant Versions, Fully Annotated by Author, with Contemporaneous Correspondence, Account of First Public Reading, Legal Skirmishes, Precursor Texts & Bibliography*, ed. Barry Miles (New York: Harper & Row, 1986; HarperPerennial, 1995).

† The poet has elsewhere (Reader's Guide, *Journals Early Fifties Early Sixties*, p. xx) claimed that it was "the crucial discovery of haiku, and ellipsis in the haiku, which really serves as the base in *Howl*"; it's also clear from these entries that another influence for Ginsberg's juxtaposition (or "parataxis") is this dream of William Burroughs' late wife.

revolutionized the syntax of American poetry—that the poet names it in the climactic manifesto explaining his method at the end of the poem's first part. Moreover, he's reported, the ellipsis of the dream

> fitted in with the studies I'd been doing way back at Columbia with Meyer Schapiro on space, the "little sensation" of space in Cézanne. And it was the space b e t w e e n my questioning Joan ["what kind of knowledge have/the dead?"] and the sudden answer with another image . . . all of a sudden seeing a tombstone as an answer . . . the visual image as an answer, rather than a linear, verbal explanation. And the sensation, in the dream, of worlds revolving. Sort of some transshifting gap of time. Or a gap of time transcending my question.

Over the next few days, as these journal entries reveal, Ginsberg examined the role of ellipsis, in Cézanne but also in numerous major poets before himself, from Shakespeare to Williams: taken as a whole, these several pages constitute a primer on the subject.

Ginsberg sent a copy of the resulting poem, "Dream Record: June 8, 1955," with comments on ellipsis, to Kenneth Rexroth, who chided him for being too academically theoretical and challenged him, as Ginsberg recalls, to "do something original." The result, in a matter of weeks, was *Howl.*

Having vowed eternal love to each other months earlier in a dramatic, transcendental moment at Foster's, and with their commitment to prove basically secure for well over three decades, Ginsberg and Peter Orlovsky spent Ginsberg's last night in San Francisco together at the end of August. Ironically, it was their first full night of lovemaking, which is detailed in pages 160–63. The next day, Allen, whose recently written poem would very shortly make him relatively famous "from bridge to bridge," as Rexroth predicted, moved to a quiet, thirty-five-dollar-a-month side-street cottage in Berkeley and enrolled in graduate school.

## Early June 1954, Southern California

Hills (North Mex.) like the brown brows of whales.

\* \* \*

L.A.—taking crap in L.A. Greyhound station—shoeshine boys with radio dominating throne of shine, loud mambo in tile room, big talking back & forth about six bucks.

> Shine shave washup
> Soap and towel
> Who want a shave
> Clean your suede
> Shine your shoes

\* \* \*

## Sketch Coffeeshop

Triangular vee-shaped coffee shoppe centralized on that narcotic raison d'être main counter, brown leather chairs on stationary brown stands turned this way and that—"Hey! here's Eliot"—with the mirrors of futurity o'erhanging all: pie, Eliot, fluorescent lights, a hatbox.

The immediate counterman a thin man an intellectual but dumb with glasses and shyness—an embarrassed half fairy sharing the spotlite with a Puerto Rican who because he is of the other race, a shade mixed in Africa, retains all virility tho his hair is curled & oiled and his cast of face feline effeminine—yet withal a man of the tropic, full of secret viciousness and catlike sweetness naiveté.

Facing them over the modern art arrangement of small forms of tiered coffeecups, milk nozzles, aluminum teats and black & chrome orangesqueezers vertical to the counter shelf like a Klee or Mondrian are the healthy boys and nattily painted women of the tileworld vision—all the kids—grown and with all the affectations of maturity—The balding thin but boyish assistant producer comes in and greets the familiar stuffy waitress "Hey Irish are you making eyes at me," heads for the back of the shop for an end-of-counter heart-to-heart with (behind the pillar) *who?* I can't see through that mighty mirror—and returns to talk to the older sister radio star—their friend joins them—he broadshouldered and a clunk but happy full of rhythms to the Muzak pizzicato bouncing softly thru the air so that as he sits down & unlooses his belt from his loafers his heels jump in time, toes to the counter-footrest.

—To the present moment a half hour later the previous by recollection not observation.

* * *

## In Riverside

Hollywood sight shrunken empty & run down can feel the name already lost its world magic. I dreamed party sat next Chaplin couch I was going to ask "What tourist sights you recommend?" but he started to ask "You all want to hear my next story?" and Shields* interrupted to take all to another room. I got mad having had couch with Chaplin then.

## L.A. June 8

Now I'm older and it isn't melancholy in the solitude . . . loving
drunken naked apartments . . . only a few flashes of that
shivering life . . .
One moment of tenderness and a year of nerves and intelligence,
one moment of actual fleshly tenderness . . .
As for the future now I am free . . . for no new love has been made
. . . after these last human stations . . .

* * *

As now I am 28 for the first time older than I've dreamed of being. The beard a joke, my character with its childish core a tiring taste . . . I could dismiss the Allen with grim pleasure, yet am saddled with myself, the experience of the last ten years, the whole taste from kid-hood—childhood in apartments in Paterson.

To break with that pattern entirely—
Must find energy & image & act on it.

---

* Karena Shields, A.G.'s hostess for several months preceding in Xbalba, Chiapas, Mexico.

# June 12

The Visions—if of my own making or hallucination I am at best, them, godlike.

\* \* \*

—3 Great deaths   Cannastra Joan   At last I have forgotten his name—D. Kammerer.\*

\* \* \*

Of an eternity we have a number of score of years. . . . I have had several months near joy, and of that perhaps one day doing what I inmost want and of that a minute of perfection . . .

Pershing Sq.: Suddenly in the middle of downtown black ant traffic & little buildings, the little banana grove on the corner of hill. There is this big block park on model of Mex town—except it has green flat rectangle of grass with benches all around in sun— hardly any shade—and an outer perimeter for walking without benches, but you can sit on concrete steps—all the old types, something different from Bryant Park, because they all look respectable & there's no one young, all look clean & model with low palms all around & plaintain leaves with bursts of tropic artichoke energy sprouting up on the sides—and a few high palms too.

\* \* \*

Sitting here in a car
        Nausea in my heart
& hollow throated
        Crucified by my feelings
Grasping & craving
        for an outside force
                of love

---

\* William Cannastra (d. 1950) lost his balance leaning out of a subway car window; Joan Vollmer Burroughs was shot by William S. Burroughs in Mexico City accident 1951; David Kammerer (d. 1944) molesting Lucien Carr was stabbed to death.

Moon's hid yet will rise
in 30 days to its completion
shining out on woods & streets.

\* \* \*

With Neal, First nite visiting S.F.:

The Geary Hotel—on the sideboard—ring, watch, glasses, pack of trick cards, ashtray, Bhaghavad Gita, & postcard. After sleeping with Neal.

I slept all afternoon, after 2, bewildered by the plenitude in which I felt disappointed. Nausea, out into the cool, chilly almost, nite for first walk down Theater bar Geary St. & chic looking S.F. first impressions. [Kearny St. with Al Sublette later days.\*]

Turkish Baths S.F.: Jack's Polk Street
Ellis St. Baths Mason & Taylor on Ellis

## San Jose, California

The possibility of neuroticism growing automatically out of certain family alignments—A family of 3 men; the third boy queer. A family of 3 women, the third girl queer.

Recalling my incestuous relation with my brother in fantasy; and also with father. The nights when I slept in their beds thru puberty.

\* \* \*

## Credo

1. The weight of the world is love.
2. The mind imagines all visions.
3. Man is as far divine as his imagination.
4. We go create as divine a world as we can imagine—must go on interpreting & recreating the given blank world (since not to imagine is not to eat) according to most extreme absolute of divinity we can conceive.

---

\* Al Sublette: African-American seaman, jazz aficionado, friend of Kerouac and Cassady, staying at Hotel Marconi. The bracketed note is a later addition by Ginsberg to this passage.

* * *

Jack's isolation like mine is sad & frightful mainly the blind alleys of money and love but life is not over, and much to be written and much to be respected in all of us not just for being humanity but for having tried and actually achieved a thing namely literature and also possibly a certain spiritual eye at this point.

And Neal who has money & love is desperate at the gate of heaven for he is unhappy with his existence, now he is seeking in his soul.

As for Bill he thinks he is lost.

Lucien* knows his way but may have a period of having to expand his spiritual horizon in order to accommodate the depth and height of possibility & this may yet be preceded by the appearance of a prison in his soul.

* * *

[Draft of "Song," CP 111–112:]
And the warm bodies shine
together in the darkness . . .

* * *

[Draft of "In back of the real," CP 113:]
Back of the real R.R. yard, S. Jose, in view dim of the white foothills beyond, in the foreground a factory with serried U for roofs—a flower on the hay on the asphalt—the dread hay flower perhaps, a brittle tough black stem like a vine, a halo of brown spikes like Jesus crown, several dozen, an inch long each, corolla of yellowish dirty spikes, and soiled & dry in the center cottony tufts sticking out like a dry shaving brush that's been lying under the garage for a year—yellow, yellow flower, and flower of industry, tough spikey ugly flower—but it has the form of the great yellow rose in its brain; it's a flower none the less—so brittle on the bench the wind keeps taking it away from me where I sit near the shack in

---

* Lucien Carr, journalist, friend of Allen Ginsberg since Columbia 1943.

the sunlight writing, & rise up no more to run after it. This is the flower of the world, ugly, dirty, worn brittle dry, yellow—incredible manifestation of the lifespring of the bud. —Thistles.

\* \* \*

All of us in our cities places working miracles of routine out to give a continuity of soul, a human continuity & meaning—the vision come when vision & reality meet & mate.

\* \* \*

Stonestown—A bright new sign 20th Avenue where maybe 2 years before it was a swamp—A great Walgreens with Budget euphuisms. In the bus out to S.F.—an advt. of a man sitting in an absolute chair by an abstract wire table drinking an abstract Coke out of an abstract straw; reading an abstract magazine with abstract prose illustrated by abstract cartoons.

—To sit in abstract chairs & read Dickens—

He wears glasses and has his hair cut short, abstract style, wears blue abstract loafer shoes and pants of abstract black style.

\* \* \*

## The Dream June 27—Sat. Nite

In the bathroom, N. in bathing suit, naked and alone, I sat down on couch with him, not looking, and in a movement together we touched hands, and then I felt the pressure as he enfolded my hand & clasped it frankly, I think I looked at him & put my arm round his shoulder, and he leaned over and put his head on my chest and took me around with his arms—Exaltation (what is the precise word for the sensation of love acceptance?)—the dream wandered, I went out of the bathroom (we were on a couch) and I went into the living room where my family was sitting propped up—happy at a dinner table, all faced one way: I spoke to my aunt Clara young Hannah, and bent down & kissed my grandmother—returning to the closed bathroom where N. was hiding—And combed hair out of my mouth—as I began pulling out the hair, I realized how long and tangled into my gullet it went down, as I pulled it broke & I grasped for more—thinking possibly that all along it was this that had been causing my debilitation.

. . . Creating out of myself the strength to continue in some kind of force, some kind of uncanny care—though I have nothing to give actually but a cheerful spirit now and hands for dishwashing—to give force for my own & others' pleasure—to learn to give love without despairing of the consequences.

As tonight, too poor and sordid for notation, I waited while Neal played abstract inhuman chess*, waiting for him to finish through seven games while Carolyn had at last returned and we were perhaps for one of the first times free to do whatever we had in mind, in mine, make it, and in his, sudden wordless retirement—I wish now I had spoken rather than waited, after I arranged the shades, turned down the lights, prepared a place on the couch.

Once again I've maneuvered myself into a frustrating idealistic situation where I am reduced to pathetic beggary.

My greatest fear perhaps is of the world outside this haven where I'll have to work and struggle with no goal in mind.

What do I want? Not this side street of conflict—And would it make any difference if I slept with N., to Carolyn?—But the rejection as tonite is deeply fixed in the situation.

Even a few moments with Neal—the attainment is bound to be short-lived due to his responsibilities and the apparent impossibility of it as a life situation—me living here hanging on him like a sick junkie.

Does he even want me here, now? She does perhaps as long as I am not too intimate with Neal. The waste of the chess game time, for me. Better perhaps look around for a Frisco job and room, escape this situation where I am often unhappy and troubled, it is a baffling position I am in. I live under the hope that Neal is as yet baffled by the problems as I am. But what can he do?

I feel myself sacrificing part of my being to him—and he has sacrificed money and some time & attention to me, given it, but no sacrifice of being or self, not much sign of interest except in offhand and patronizing ways, except at a few moments of tenderness that are hard fought for and accidental rare infusions of

---

* Likely, with neighbor Dick Woods, friend Al Hinkle.

pleasure into my otherwise bad-feeling starved routine here. But dare I by principle like some crazy character in Dosty. demand a return sacrifice?

I feel like a strange idiot, standing there among wife & children all to whom he gives needs of affection and attention, aching for some special side extra sacrifice of attention to me—as if like some nowhere evil beast intruding I were competing for his care with his own children & wife and job which seems to occupy energize bore & tire him.

\* \* \*

I can sleep with Neal, sleep with Carolyn, sleep with no one, and stay. Or sleep with both and no one alternately amid confusions. Or I can end this mad triangle, all three of us blocked, by leaving.

The problem furthermore of the difference between my night dream of N. and the actual moment of embrace as the other night where the confidence went far and yet despite my pleasure & relief, almost dreamlike, the release was not as direct and overwhelming in joy as the dream-feelings that are not false since I can feel them down there in dreams—

The essentially mad idea of trying to stay in this artificial situation.

\* \* \*

I know Neal understands all this knows all this; but what does he want? He says, do what I want—He does not encourage me in the situation and I again wonder what can I hope for from him. I feel I am all on the wrong track emotionally in expecting active sexual love from Neal to begin with—Would he be actually happier and relieved if I gave up finally and left him alone? What Karma has he with me, if I have no deeper erotic Karma with him than friend, helper & helped? Does he want all the morbid attention? If not I have the energy strength yes to make out otherwise; I will not suffer beyond my bearable load, but I would be unhappy awhile & adjust. So he has freedom. So have I. So what is the issue here. Must try to resolve it with him before it drags itself out and I get lost in confusions and imagined rejections.

In a way he is really a bastard inviting & rejecting, making things so unclear, leaving me hung up when he knows my habit so well, unless he just wants it resolved & given up by me under his care & aegis—on the other hand, his offers, his carnality at moments, his future acceptances, his plight of sexual starvation leads me to hope I am welcome.

## Serenade

How later I know I will regret the words I have pored over blindly, sifting and testing my thoughts for their coin.

The bank is bankrupt and the inflated currency is worthless in a ruined land. The bomb appeared intolerable, light and radiance, and afterwards the grey world appeared as a ghost.

Useless to belabor the reality. The poems are mad. Useless to practice a secret design. The skull is vacant. The flesh is a shell. The heart's consumed no phoenix.

How waste is the language and broken the thought—shadow flesh, third thoughts of the grave, obscure ravenings of spectral fright, the inward flame and darkness of the damned.

Rimbaud and Yeats already bid adieux (Circus Animal's Desertion) to these regrettable hallucinations.

I curse the ignominy of my being. Time to cut the throat of this fat rhetoric.

* * *

Dedicate New Book if any ever to Williams.

* * *

Don't tell me the truth
I want to be lied to—
Besides I know it all,
down to the smallest thought
constructed hour by hour
in city, in jungle, in train,
in subway, bus and plane.
Year after year remembered,
night after night dreamed.

## Dream July 6

We are all sleeping on the ground and C—— is there—we have sheets or thin blankets over us but are separate, my father & brother next to me—C—— and I touch but my father-brother could see—we move over away a bit but still the same trouble. We are a little cold & are trying to get together for warmth of body length contact under his cover. We try under a stair but that's too open finally it is time to get up & so we go in the narrow bathroom overlooking NYC—by this time we have a sort of new understanding but I don't trust him yet—nor he me. I reach down to blow him, he says OK but me standing up, I go to, but he already has sunk down taking down his thin shorts revealing half his cock, he says no fucking around as last time—in sentimental touching any other part of the body, no more kissing thighs just pure suck the head of it, I start to, and I see as I put my lips to it he's white in the head, he's ready, he comes in my mouth, a lot of come and his cock's big I don't get it all in my mouth just the head we get up I get ready to go out, to go. We were next to the toilet seat on the floor.

He says "By god we might as well go out"—suggesting that since it's all gone thru without hitch we can maybe make it on the town as before. I am ready to go back for my shorts, but he hands me a pair of his shorts to wear, with a flourish, but doesn't comment on the significance.

The city, an apartment in the Bronx El area we would visit.

## July 11, '54

Fortunately art is a community effort—a small but select community living in a spiritualized world endeavoring to interpret the wars and solitudes of the flesh.

\* \* \*

Love. He is our deepest self. Mysterious, actual, delightful and sorrowful at once, full of gentility and imprudence, a beneficent spirit, a god acting thru human masks. He is the same in all, neither man or woman. We all have the same sense of bottom self. He is the solitary.

Thus love others as the self. We are incorruptible. . . . The god survives. Love is complete. There is more than can be given. None is wasted no love is amiss none goes astray none perishes. . . . It never lacks because it is All. It comes on the mind in visions. Watch for it coming! It enters the house of the body without your seeking.

## July 14

That in some respects I have a purer love of people than in 1946 when Chase called me "Sacerdotal."
Certainly am less attached.

* * *

A house not built by human hands and a house built by human hands. I stand under the ceiling of both, natural and supernatural. The flash or impression of this as I lie on the couch.
The supernatural house may be the oft hinted platonic house. Or the suggestion of dream unreality of the natural house, as in Buddhism.
Therefore these suggestions by the unconscious noticing of an impression are not sufficient, what is needed is an *actual* vision to get the meaning.
When it comes I will know that I have been preparing for it since 1949 visions—that is to say the main theme of my thought has been in preparation for understanding or achieving a moment that is to come.*
I am on a bus—it turns out to be not the bus but one of a train of buses with soldiers following the main ones, I pass up front (Atotanilco bus).

* * *

A dream letter from John Holmes,† containing statements of new found principles—

---

\* It never came. —A.G., 1976
† John Clellon Holmes (1926–1988), novelist and friend of Kerouac and Ginsberg.

"  'A Shropshire Lad' was written under a cloak rag or shroud.

"The social organization which is most true of itself to the artist is the boy gang" (not society's perfum'd marriage).

* * *

Walking up dark streets Venice*—like Paterson after a fiesta or fireworks with Louis† and others, him explaining my artistic conscience or wotnot I skip ahead he taunts me with my eagerness to see the rest ahead of the street "No I've never seen this before" referring to the beergardens bars and bldg—"Nacionalista Mexicana" as we pass the high square white block-tower of "Bograts" ahead downtown, but as we approach, "Left," says Gene & Louis & we go down a dark alley instead of downtown which leads to the next phase of our living quarters toward the Eastside—we been coming up from Haledon Ave.—a great plaza near Eastside H.S. I am returning from—dark swept open football field.

Wandering around trying to get in library and gym— Drama class at Bennington—I come upon the library—I wander around in thru sections like at Paterson or N.Y. Museum Nat. Hist.—a lady at a desk to one side, fellows of indeterminate type like middleaged dark fags standing around gossiping—I have no card—walk on thru—a large door closed—the stairwell to the basement opening out on football field, the long corridors of the basement as at Columbia passageways football field like bullring empty I finally come to the drama gym or barn or Shed—A band at the entrance—much going on inside past the band I can't get,

---

* This dream and the one that follows are examples of Ginsberg's "room dreams," a familiar feature of his dream life over decades. A room dream typically involves a sense of disorientation on the part of the protagonist (usually Ginsberg) as he searches for what is known, "home," secure, stable, domestic, familiar and familial. Ginsberg himself interprets these dreams as "Bardo" experiences, confused wanderings after death, with loss of the familiar body. The room dream is discussed at some length in the "Reader's Guide," pp. xxv–xxvii, that introduces *Journals Early Fifties Early Sixties.*

† Louis Ginsberg (1895–1976), poet and teacher, father of Allen and Eugene (1921–), the "Gene" in this entry.

too many people working—one at the mike, near the piano near the door, is reading off note on a symphony concert—I am going up a big hill in Paterson also Columbia as in another dream of Morningside Heights where I lived in a room & Gene lived in a room, same room with my bed up in the right inner corner up on a partition shelf and a balcony inside room near the front window and walking around on Riverside interminable and 92nd St. (Thalia movie house) to Gene's & my house. Earlier a scene on ferry, the great giant ferry of Futures and fascism, I am crossing the vast Hudson & we get under the high wall concrete thousands feet high other N.Y. side of river in small (big) ferry on way across black waters long wide river miles across—Much mystery and scope to the border under the protective wall before N.Y. skyline heights & road complexities—in this dream I walking up 125th st. Bway to get to Columbia and on street I run across a few of the characters of the Shed Drama giving their spiels of the concert or inauguration—one man like Noel dark tho giving his spiel from memory, another further up as I pass a restaurant hid by River St. Gypsy curtains on way, to where a small moonfaced junky girl is giving her spiel into the radio portable mike in the snow near Barnard Furey Hall near chem-astronomy-physics bldg.

* * *

[Draft of "Love Poem on Theme by Whitman," CP 115:]
I will enter the bridebed of the beloved . . .

## Dream July 20, '54

enter room there's uncle Abe lying back on his back on a table shelf stuck out from the wall height of chest a partition between sections of the room lying there on his back with the boys talking all dressed up and as I enter to inquire one or the other for the hipsters whoever I'm looking for as I go knocking from cubicle to cubicle as I went knocking after cousins Gene & Eddie, he sits up, Abe does, and I notice a roach in his hand, he's a T head I realize, somewhat shocked also by disparity of ages between him &

my friends who are his friends—I had set out looking for someone
in particular, a Keck* or someone here in Frisco—

I descend a stairway, small narrow slum stairway like in 1930s
slum pix, and look in the mailbox to see the bulb has been removed,
remembering upstairs that a bulb had blown out & no one could
find a replacement, too cheap to buy a new one, they took the
necessary downstairs light & stuck it somewhere upstairs

—We are in some city or town and I am discussing with others
the return from Africa of Eugene or cousin Judy—apparently Judy
wants to marry Eugene or vice versa—the family is in the room,
there is a long couch I am spread on it or sitting showing the letter—
I express contempt and disapproval of her—Judy—I go on but they
don't understand, I wind up saying, "but what I mean is, she's
*crazy*"—this word received with some resentment or silence, I feel
embarrassed as if I am trying to put something over on them
perhaps projected or untrue, what are my motives in objecting to
the marriage—I feel uneasy.

Recent dreams bringing in associations with other earlier
central tho fugitive dreams—in this case the constellation men-
tioned on previous pages involving subway platform also—

Wanderings and flight to obscure apartments in Brooklyn—
or the recollection of wandering up and down the wrong streets à
la Lower East Side looking for the street doorway to the slum flat I
am destined to head for, finally winding up on topfloor flat where I
stand & look outside at city, people are looking for me? but don't
remember what took place in the apt.

Recall before sleeping recollection of traumatic time when
my *whole* sensation of life and feelings toward Louis changed
when I was *what*, 13? or earlier in regard to him fainting at
288 Graham Ave. and the letter from his amour girl friend I
found in wastebasket and Eugene & I pieced together—this re-
garding my tendency also to live with families like I was child with
ma & pa together trying to get pa's (Lucien's or Carolyn's)
attention.

---

* Bill Keck, bohemian compatriot from early 1950s, alluded to in
*Howl* ("who . . . rose up to build harpsichords in their lofts"); see also
*Journals Early Fifties Early Sixties*, pp. 5–7.

And also the above just reminded me that Liz Lehrman* was in the dream—I talking to her she has returned from the rotten orient—south seas area—I ask how did you get out there, what do?—she is a little heavier like Judy—is it she who is crazy (as Lucien said) who wants to marry Gene?—And my mother having been crazy I see a relationship of associations in the dreams.

Kerouac
c/o Carolyn Blake (his sister)
Box 31-A, Route 4, Rocky Mount
N. Carolina

* * *

Boccaccio, *La Fiammetta*—The exposition of the voice of Jealousy page 3 of chapter IV.

## Re: "Xbalba"

A reordering of the stanzas needed in the poem, some formal equality of stanzas, or alternation of stanza forms—

An interior order in each stanza someway apparent—syllable, accent, or quantity, or general weight of lines intuitively felt—What measure within the stanza, in the line?

Perhaps the concept of *line* is at basic root. Break up the line?

into emotive or meaningful or musical complete images or abstractions or sensations—whole, each, however.

Except for purposeful variations on the meaning.

Re-form lines in terms of concepts or/and units of words conjuring up a sensation (images).

* * *

---

* Liz Lehrman: Lucien Carr's girlfriend, early 1950s; a painter, friend of Larry Rivers, Nell Blaine, and other "Intra-Subjectivist" artists living on West 21st Street. —A.G., July 1, 1993

To inquire of self & others, Neal—the actual psychy and physy of the come, the orgasm—anal distribution or outlet of pelvic reflex energy.

* * *

Lower levels—I want to be your slave, suck your ass, suck your cock, you fuck me, you master me, you humiliate me, I want to be tied and whipped, spanked on the behind over knees, want to be made to cry and beg and weep for love.*

## Dream

Sitting in the Eastside park have to take a hip trip by bus far down the valley for spaghetti—I see the paintings by Jack from Russian Hill of the Mts. aiming toward the east. There in tent-fold of the earth Salt lake, Butte, Denver, etc.—they are colored chalk or crayon drawings.

I go to restaurant to get bus tickets to get two orders of spaghetti from some town 2 hrs. away but when I inquire it's 2¾ hrs away, the lady says, and she's behind the restaurant counter (as counter at Los Gatos) she serves up the spaghetti, I think, for me. Tho the plate has a little potatoes creamed, tomatoes & something else small portions no meat (Carolyn serves so) so I say have you spaghetti? She says no but we have Napoleon & Fritti—some other Italian type spaghettis—so I order that, thinking to save myself the long trip back—

Return to the loft to find a nice looking young man tall boy lying on bed with his poem spread around on the sheet him naked talking to another hip old man in chair in the cluttered loft as Frankel's in Hoboken—I look at last page of MS. It is poetic but early verse and not pointed like more mature Corso say I lay down with the boy & put my arm around him to read his poem moving over the bed under the big feather quilt, have to move my leg touching his to turn, his touches me, like Hal C——, how pleasurable this is—fragment ends here.

Then I am walking with the old lady (the Signora Shields)

---

* See "Please Master," CP 494–95.

thru the park, we come to a wooded section near the tennis court—the big trees there, some planted, some flower or fruit trees poorly planted, or not taken care of—a big room, we are in the City Council meeting, La Guardia is there the meeting wants to break up, but I sit in my folding chair by the wall of the long narrow room in the center saying how bad the city is run, and La G. pays attention, refers me to the Commissioner who is absent or knows nothing, I keep up the attack on the planting poorly of the trees, but suddenly am unsure of my facts—taken from the Signora— and she's there to back me up, she's used to dealing with business-men so she should be trustworthy—(writing I realize the boy is only a dream and I am sad for it is truly left to unconscious life, not the real person shining)

The argument continues, I see the politicians commission-ers—and on the back of all the politicians' pants is a stamped white notice, as on the backs of dress pants borrowed—the statement "Boro of Water Commissioners LaGuardia Reign City Hall 1954" etc. or whatever.

\* \* \*

Nathanael West wrote true surrealist novels—must read the sources, *Cocteau.*

In French—To read him & to also read Proust. Cocteau in San Jose (Public Library).

\* \* \*

My first novel will be a local work—Paterson Revisited, say, with W.C.W.'s letter in mind—to recreate Paterson in *my* own image to experiment with a different approach or style.

—The job would be beyond my means, for the present, however there is always hope for the Future. I might write him: I am the Trotsky with no dogma in your party.

Politics is also beyond my means—though what a hilarious chapter that might make, visions of mayors, of evenings of fire-works and speeches, the politics of the library board and school system, congressional races (auto races too from the rock near the stadium)—

The night the congressman won and lost in the same midnight—he got hysterical (Did they steal the election, the republicans?) (With the aid of the Press—Paterson News and Morning Call, the tough brute editor—the cowardly old woman editor on the Call and echoes of Jersey City Mayor Hague beyond) The night that Joelson, the last would-be congressman, lost, a great dumb union crusader wept (and what liberal Communist mysteries behind)—

Include Communist meetings of the '30s—though I do remember the man in front of the City Hall with his apocalyptic songs and speech*—his ghost appears in what garden? What park?

—We remember in addition the depression seen thru the eyes of the child, bankfailure and wage cuts. Saw no fighting—but I passed out anti-Hague pamphlets in New Jersey at 12 in maybe was it 1938 and then I saw the passion and characters of that war.

Therefore a poem, the history of my wanderings and accomplishments in the Great City and otherwhere, and various returns—

and perhaps return for a Judgment (In Inferno? or the clear world?) (or remotely heaven)—Thru all eyes of vision, another vision of Paterson.

Visions of Paterson, or The Shrouded Stranger of the Night—Paterson in Heaven—or Paterson thru the eyes of one who knew it well—

## Reading June—'54

Age of Anxiety—Auden
Folded Leaf—Maxwell
Kant—Selections
B. Russell—Selections from Hist. of Phil.
S. Anderson—Winesburg, O.
Quarterly Review of Lit.—British Poets (Durrell's Sappho)
Gore Vidal—The Judgment of Paris

---

* See *Kaddish* II ("Narrative"), CP 217:
(... where the Evangelist preached madly for 3 decades, hard-haired, cracked & true to his mean Bible—chalked Prepare to Meet Thy God on civic pave—

or God is Love on the railroad overpass concrete—he raved like I would rave, the lone Evangelist—Death on City Hall—)

## July

Céline—Mea Culpa & Semmelweiss
Gertrude Stein—Paris, France; Autobiog. of A. Toklas
Gina Cerminova—Cayce System Book
Wm. Cayce—Extracts from Readings (psychic)
Cassady, N.—Fragments of Autobiog. reread
Stein—Things As They Are
Horney—Our Inner Conflicts
Céline—Last half of Journey to End of Night (finally finished after
    10 years) I had reserved it for later pleasure. Will get hold of
    Guignol's Band, which just came out in English (Summer '54)
Proust—Cities of the Plain—part, first chapters Vol. II
Eliot—Selected Essays to 1932
Bhagavad Gita—Isherwood tr.
poems—in Understanding Poetry Brooks & Warren
Plato—Symposium
Encyclopedia Britannica articles on Hermetic types and sects
Eliot—4 Quartets—Idea of Xtian Society
Pound—Pisan Cantos, XXX Cantos
H.D.—Collected Poems (1925)
e. e. cummings—
An Examination of Pound—
A. E. Coppard—a few stories (The Silver Circus)
The Invisible Man—R. Ellison
Flee the Angry Strangers—Geo. Mandel
Pavannes & Divagations—Pound
Vita Nuova—Dante (Rossetti tr.)
Boccaccio—Fiammetta
Rimbaud—Season in Hell

\* \* \*

August 1 1954 San Jose California 1047 E. Santa Clara St.—Neal on
the couch-divan in the living room on Sunday afternoon hand
raised before his eyes in the light before the French window—
holding a religious pamphlet.

> An attack on the human intellect—
>     "The Jar in Tennessee" (Yvor Winters essay)

* * *

That ill constructing fabulous
        dinosaur of the mind,
had little intellect
        under the giant palmates
        in the Arboretum.

    We live in
    glass houses.
Don't throw bombs!
Very witty, very pretty
Said the connoisseur
        of savage styles.
He lives in limbo in an apartment
            in Paris
Surrounded by his stacks of wood,
his paintings and piano
            notebooks, essays
—excellent cook, withal.

The latest jazz exhibits darker flesh
warring with pure thought.

The world's gone black on us,
I conclude: as a historian,
it's an asiatic age
        to come—
Malay, Chinamen, Jap
        Siberian
Thibetan, Hindustani—
Buddha, Amok, Zen
and Zarathustra
        and the Golden
Drums of orient caves—

* * *

To avoid
    where rhythm and thought of a fragment
        run on one line to another in broken

lines
they must be *indented*
To indent *separate* thoughts & rhythms the *same*
    as run ons is mistake
      This distinction is one basis for discrimination of
typography

Free verse musical variation "no norm
    to depart from"—Winters' idea*

Find: conception of line allowing appreciable variation—line
allowing freedom of personal thought-rhythms as they
    occur and still be in some way comparatively measurable.
      So far mine is typographical definition
      Balance by intuitive sound not enough without
        rule to *refer* to.

Base line
    Indent for qualification
      qualification of qualification
Lines measured according to conceptual content.
Principles of thought-rhythm have not been measured
    and used, consciously recognized.

I've been consciously excluding metaphor from my poetry
for fear it will be contaminated by meaningless references to
archaic rhythms & ways of thinking in abstract verse.

* * *

---

* As presented in "The Influence of Meter on Poetic Convention,"
in *Primitivism and Decadence: A Study of American Experimental Poetry* (New
York: Arrow Editions, 1937), p. 120.

# Notes on "The Green Automobile"*

    Notes on the Solitary Soul
        Totally separate ideal world
            purely product of Imagination

    The green automobile goes forth with the
        speed of an idea
        outside Time boldly.
    To free imagination from contamination
        of a mode of reality
    Set myself at the wheel—
        To reride changeless vias of the past
        & raise its memory above the vanishing
            state

        dedicate my soul to yours
            no thought else but the angelic
        supernatural excess of Time—

        We shared a soul—
        shrewd in the mind of Time

            * * *

    And the night and the diner
        neon real light
    and the complete failure
        of all sensual dreams
            of Colorado.

        Conversations of the chauffeur & porter
    on the grass
        on a quiet street in Denver.

---

    * One draft of "The Green Automobile" (CP 83–87), recorded on Cassady's tape machine, which A.G. was then using, was issued 1994 by Rhino Records, in four-CD compilation *Holy Soul Jelly Roll: Poems & Songs 1949–1993*.

*  *  *

You make it hard for me
          to communicate
the moments slip by
          me, waiting as before
It seems for a second
          near to tears
a lifetime wasted—
          turned to trash
chess, silence
          metaphysics
Till I turn my thoughts
          from my heart
To these vain
          communications.

You are
          lying on the couch
familiar incarnation
          in the room
as before in my dreams

Where is your soul
          for this time
is it lost, does it wander
          some deserted street
or is it standing
          under the light,
arm raised to speak,
          fervid word
rising up from the breast
          and choked upon the tongue?
No—you are not
          there under the light—
a sad anticipation
          that must turn away
Unsatisfied from the
          blue figure on the couch
But here is the moment,

before us now
moving in silence
beyond our desires.

I'm too choked to speak.

\* \* \*

Syllabic rhythm as in XXIII ["Rigamarole"] Williams' *Spring and All* first 7 couplets—4 syllables is easy for ear to pick up: an 8 syllable couplet with each line varied as need be. To pick up on syllabic *rhythm.*

| and insects sting | 4 |
| while on the grass | 4 |

| the whitish moonlight | 5 |
| tearfully | 3 |

He sets up more or less a metronome of 4 syllables first lines thereafter and varies each second line, and then sets the 4 syl. line at end of each couplet, changing base. In syllabic measure, is it important or not that syllable units coincide with integral phrases? As

and sleepers in ⌣ / ⌣ /
the windows cough ⌣ / ⌣ /
or with regular accents as above?
The Red Wheelbarrow's verses count with symmetrical balance:
4-2 / 3-2 / 3-2 / 4-2

\* \* \*

# Thoughts Before Pissing

Now that we know all about
Reality, let's
forget about it
—its solitude, its labor
(on the railroad), its loneliness,
its automobiles
on the barren streets
and the ever faster
eclipse of the years

> Last night I dreamed
> an old lover welcomed
> me back with shining eyes
> and warm kisses
> arms round my shoulder
> then lay down with me
> embraced on his couch

\* \* \*

## Dream August 6

Examination by Barzun & Trilling\*—they cant do much for me now, too late for me to learn manners and take a place in the world—We told you then, we'll do what we can but your role is so limited now, your poetry so bad, or specialized.

Then as I leave thru the dark alleys I am attacked by a knife mugger—I would fight him for my one treasure, my watch—and the situation as Trilling and Barzun say had been typical of my fatal irresponsibility.

## Dream August 7

Visited C.'s apartment, he looking a bit younger un-mustachioed and more baby face—and he welcomed me back—I had stayed away overlong—saying "Well god dam sweet allen where you been?" and I said "But why haven't you been here reporting & to see me?" and I said I didnt want to call because you'd think well there he is old Allen sad in his apartment no one to call and talk to the useless nut now he's calling and wants to keep up the face of sympathy—No no" said C. "I have been lonely for you—I miss you" as I lay down on the couch with my arm about his shoulder and we kiss—he actually in the dream somewhat happy at least I've returned to complete his affection.

\* \* \*

---

\*Jacques Barzun and Lionel Trilling were well-known liberal arts professors at Columbia University during Ginsberg's matriculation.

[Exercises to] Try: Classical Quantitative meters:

| 1 | Tribrach | ˘ ˘ ˘ | Molossus | – – – |
|---|----------|-------|----------|-------|
| 2 | amphibrach | ˘ – ˘ | amphimacer | – ˘ – |
| 3 | bacchius | ˘ – – | antibacchius | – – ˘ |
| 4 | choriamb | – ˘ ˘ – | antichoriamb | ˘ – – ˘ |
| 5 | dochmiac | ˘ – – ˘ – | antidochmiac | – ˘ ˘ – ˘ |

iamb      ˘ / ˘ / ˘ / ˘ /
Trochee   / ˘ / ˘ / ˘ / ˘
Dactyl    / ˘ ˘ / ˘ ˘ / ˘ ˘ / ˘ ˘
Anapest   ˘ ˘ / ˘ ˘ / ˘ ˘ / ˘ ˘ /

Stress accents here stand equally for quantity—but in practice to approach quantity only if this is workable, switch to using ˘ / instead of ˘ – :

1. Tribrach ˘ ˘ ˘  ˘ ˘ ˘  ˘ ˘ ˘  ˘ ˘ ˘
Molossus /// /// /// ///
2. Amphimacer ˘ ˘ / ˘ ˘ / ˘
Amphibrach / ˘ // ˘ // ˘ // ˘ /
3. Bacchius ˘ // ˘ // ˘ // ˘ //
Antibacchius // ˘ // ˘ // ˘ // ˘
4. Choriamb / ˘ ˘ / / ˘ ˘ / / ˘ ˘ / / ˘ ˘ /
Antichoriamb ˘ // ˘ ˘ // ˘ ˘ // ˘
5. Dochmiac ˘ // ˘ / ˘ // ˘ / ˘ // ˘ / ˘ // ˘ /: Rebel, slaves rebel!
Antidochmiac / ˘ ˘ / ˘  / ˘ ˘ / ˘  / ˘ ˘ / ˘  / ˘ ˘ / ˘: marvelous money!

Antichoriamb ˘ // ˘ ˘ // ˘ ˘ // ˘:
    An old eagle, a blind eagle, who waits hungry . . .
Second epitritus / ˘ // / ˘ // / ˘ // / ˘ //: Slaves, rebel slaves!
Glyconic—immemorial harmonies (octosyllabic meter)

* * *

So foul a dream upon so fair a face,
And the dreamer lying in that starry shroud
—Melville's "America," last lines (in stanza III, of four)

\* \* \*

## America*

I'll sing of America and Time,
for as I lay in my bed alone one night
I ruminated with my secret soul
                    in ancient rhetoric,
"Inspire me tonight with a dreamlike poem
foretelling in rapt naturalistic forms
the fate of this country I hide in
penniless and lovelorn waiting for the barren
doom of my own days:
                    Illuminate your tragic
wisdom, my darkest deepest countryman,
reveal in shorthand and symbolic images
the paradigm of fortune for United States;
witness the downfall and roar of daily life,
in riches and despair amid great machinery,
lacking miracle of heart, in habitude to the substantial
trashy world, its dreams and miseries of steel,
for all the natural fatness, universal toys
prayed for, granted and betrayed:
                    let the unknown,
unknowable, shapeless and foreboded future be once
limned clearly, particularized in thought and set
down solid for the eye to wonder and receive, so I can
salvage some remnant of the truth
of all society out of my solitary craze—"
Dark America! toward whom I close my eyes for prophecy,
and bend my speaking heart!
                    Betrayed! Betrayed!

-----

    * One of several versions of this poem, which was first written in the summer of 1954. Not long after writing *Howl*, Ginsberg typed up the poem above, thinking to use it as a proem to *Howl*, retitling it "Howl for Carl Solomon." It is under the latter title that a manuscript of this poem is quoted from by James E. B. Breslin in *From Modern to Contemporary: American Poetry, 1945–1965*, Chicago: University of Chicago Press, 1984, p. 96). An early version of the poem published as "America" (CP 146–48) appears in this volume on p. 207.

* * *

## America & Siesta

> What begins as hatred of lovers,
>    hatred of wildness and delight
> —the agonizing competition among steel
>    structures
> and races up elevators
>    and watching of the clock
> —whose only respite and steam valve escape
>    is drunkenness and drugs & jazz—

ends in self conscious isolation in the dark outward teeming world—the oceans which were adventure become a wall—We've failed, in history, we'll go down under to great change—Can't imagine the future of America except become more barbarous, formed and ruled by fright and un-generosity in alien world where we're young happy prince of the world no more but an old shrewish nervous ulcerous has-been—and if the Atom bomb becomes a reality on us as we've already loosed that impossible apocalypse horror on Japan we can expect nothing but terror and twisted steel and starvation and anarchy and dog eat dog.

Only the reality of the bullet and respect for the obscure traditions of the Unknown and divinity's harsh laws—more pertinent, bloody holes in my skull, torn ligaments and eyeballs—keep me from suicide, from killing the personal shape of the flesh—

* * *

Neal & Allen [notes on conversation about Kerouac]
N. "Nothin' is nothin' " except every little thing that affects *him.* Well Jack is really sort of a fool. The reason he always disliked me is that I kept calling him on it. But the real trouble is you could never make *him* believe that, i.e., he's always being *misunderstood.* Fundamentally because . . .

There is always a black hair in tea, it's never any good unless you find a hair in it.

A. I didn't realize that Jack's self-pity was so akin—so imitative—of Wolfe's which fucks up Wolfe's books. Even to the very language of brooding, mysterious swirls and red October afternoons.

N. No one feels as much as they do they're alone.

A. Death of Father and end scene in Sax is so naturally very true and full of feeling, where does he get off being a fool?

N. But I don't think we've put the finger on his foolishness. For one thing it comes to downright eccentricity at times, bullheaded.

A. As Bill and you often complain, [Jack says] "Oh don't bother I'll build a little gas jet through the wall and get a hot plate."

N. He refuses to receive graciously. What the hell do I care about his shyness? I'm afraid he's too old now, too set in his ways. His only hope is to really convince himself that nothing is nothing. But I don't think he'll be capable of doing that.

A. "It requires a great effort—"

N. Besides he's too smart. Deep down he knows everybody loves him but he just can't accept it because he knows that would put a demand on him so he acts surly and he's a bore—just like me.

I can receive all day but I can't give back.

He knows he can't give back consistently so he doesn't want to receive.

Well he really did in Denver there that time. (Start the blankness.) Misunderstanding. I don't remember. What does Jack need, that's the important thing. Nothing haw haw after all "nothing is nothing."

Well I don't know anybody could ever penetrate that lard ass. Even if nothing is nothing it would still be quite a struggle.

I'm just wondering how many incarnations ago I was a woman. Oh sure I've been a woman, all of us have been a woman. Next lifetime, in 3 lifetimes I'll be a female whore. You've already been a real queer. I want to beat the 97 times.*

---

* Probably meaning to accelerate the progression of the hundred reincarnations necessary for his purification/redemption according to some prophecy by psychic Edgar Cayce. —A.G., May 25, 1993

A. Then he (Mel) and Jack got into a conspiracy against me; I've always found it hard to forgive of Jack, though easy to Mel, since so much was expected of them both, but with Mel the road was much more bitter.

* * *

## Dream [*August 10*]

Neal was in the room getting dressed rapidly, putting on white shirt to go out to the racetrack—it was Saturday night—he had spoken of the race—I came in his room—he was putting his shirt on over his shorts—and fixing his collar in the obscurity. I said "If you don't mind I would like to go with you to the auto race tonight may I?" He looked at me impatiently and I expected him to object and felt crushed and said again "I didn't mean to displease or bother you if you don't want me to come—It was just the question did you want me to ask, ought I come?"—he saw my hurt and took me around and kissed me on the lips—I kissed him back and then we put our arms around each other—I began to relax and gave way to my heart kissing and we sank down on the bed, and I felt wave of feeling passing out of my lips from inside my heart and stomach & solar plexus passing into him, shocks of waves of feeling of love pain & pleasure which he felt, and pressed his lips to me harder and more tender until I began to moan, high feminine like moans and small cries with the feeling passing out of me until I suddenly broke away—

Carolyn was coming into the door as I went to it foreboding and her entrance frightened me so that I jumped and fell on the slippery floor softly in my socks near the crib—We went out and I lay down on the couch with her and she held my head and I thought she was angry so explained about the door and she said "And there was the Baby, Johnny, in his crib didn't you think of that?" I said no, I hadn't realized it was there—Neal had disappeared—I was worried how I would tell her I was going to the races with Neal—it would have meant too much intimacy between us for her she would be angry and then I shuddered & woke—

I was in my room in my own bed alone and I was relieved that I was not in the situation of quarreling with her but unhappy to lose the bliss of feeling, and realized I was dreaming still however, and so lunged in spirit out of bed around the corner thru the door floating thru the living room to the sun room where there was an eerie frightening green light of ghosts in the air where I floated, and I sat on the couch, becoming more frightened of the series of dreams in which I was held captive unable to move my arms until with a thick cry half groan half scream I moved my thighs and woke finally to lie & ponder if I was awake, and realizing that I was, I opened the light and wrote this down— glory to the moment of loosing the small cries of love in Neal's arms kissing him, memory of a moment of a dream in which I discover the truth of feeling there in my soul waiting liberation— which will never come.

* * *

Hip my hype
hop my hat
kiss my head
pay my hap.

## PM of 17

Dream—Trying to get N to screw me, he was hard but not enuf, couldn't get it in, tried to cooperate, in my room.

* * *

Wyatt's sonnet "I freeze and burn" in mind. That's done in a classic way but doesn't catch the aspect of the sensual reality of the love attachment when it becomes involuntary and haunting as in dreams, though even consciously banished.

O it is impossible he's too hemmed in by family and job to be free, too occupied to be occupied.

I stare at his children like a madman in a ward—bewildered by my long-lived ambition toward possession of his life. That is painful but what sharpens the pathos is the fact of his indifference to Carolyn too.

That kind of love of mine is a *sickness*—must be cured. I can't stand it—too painful the dreams and then the daily longing and obscene lonely nites I spend grieving and dreaming and making love to shadows of bodies—Take this for the sincere lament of a lovesick queer.

It's the *feeling* I don't want to sacrifice, it's the actual blest passion that's torment so ungratified so disregarded or joked with—Am I nuts?

I lie in longing languor on the couch, I can't read unless I force myself. . . . I dream beautiful sexual dreams and wake up burning with ardor and tenderness—It's a physical anguish—I let it go on—I should *leave leave* it, finish it, kill it, burn it out, forget it, banish, destroy, nullify, ignore—Strength! to kill the whole affair.

and to be free for what vapidity, what lackluster—who besides us has the good to match and companion—but he's killed the good, I can't stand battering him with complaints. God knows what mystery he has at soul! God knows and save and help him with his own explosion. I can't follow the hidden sweetness he has. I can't see the light in him. It's in there somewhere burning hidden by his flesh by his eyes and moving hands. I can't get to the love. I can't get to the heart. I can't be humble enough, I can't be patient enough, I can't be strong enough, I can't suffer enough to feel his love.

And by dear god it's Love, sweet holy blessed love, old sacrament and sanctity, god-fathered and god-blessed love. I can't change the basic lust for it's a holy ache that cant be obliterated in life—only made barren in memory, forgotten—

He respects feelings when they do flash out—feeling the continual ecstasy of love for him that I do as if all out of proportion to the poor physical person he has to be—A terrific continual concentration on him—I torture self daily going through these ecstasies of affection, gusts of knowledge and respect for his real vibrancy, but there's nothing I can do—till he creates a moment of life, now unhappily remote—I never felt such sadness.

Smitten by his human loftiness and pain—dragging himself out to work in big shoes.

* * *

    Outs from the situation
        this ecstasy confounded with its object
        —Strength—turning aside

to a new creation . . .
I may pray but must not pine.
My beating heart beats on
      a moment of love!
A moment of desolation!
            what sweetness I felt!
These feelings are *real.*
            And must say farewell.
And with farewell,
      What weight lifted
And what gaiety?
      A moment
of illumination!
—irrational sadnesses
      leave me alone—

I'll be alright. I miss the joy—Lost! . . . What mysterious
secrets are kept! How little what's there can get across to us—
would we were more angels! . . .

      ah, leave me alone
            human angels
            I've had enough!
            I know you're there.
            I can't grieve
            forever love!
            I can't love
            forever.

            . . . it's over*
      the crisis is over.
      I feel better—
      Could I feel worse?
      Tonite's delight
      in pure Idea
      follows the desolate
      day's particulars—
      and tomorrow morning

_____

* Ellipsis periods appear in the journal entry.

when I wake
ah heaven! what bliss
I'll have tasted
—all my own dream?
all my own self made
sensation?

what painful hours
might we spend trying to be angels
to discover after all
that heaven is imagination,
our two painful bodies broken down
struggling with an invisible
      idea—
in a dark room on a bed.

* * *

I can't bear to think
what pleasure I'd embrace
if any these strong dreams
were enacted in this bed

with our naked bodies
meeting our naked souls
in actual passion
innocent of time

conceived in the mind
born in the flesh
the sweetest tenderness
known to the living.

## Conclusion

I've so idealized Neal I've given him in my imagination capability for any angelic shape and feeling including perfect love in accordance with my own being and since he hasn't this chimaeric ghostlike protean capacity of infinite spiritual-sexual-material variability I'm doomed to disappointment in my fantasies. I counted too much on that Quality of Genius I glimpsed in him of which even I'm not capable and have consistently misinterpreted in him—A free Genius of which he has no inkling and would be anguished to recognize if he realized it was my serious secret.

You see I keep expecting miracles and expecting so much of him, Cassady, that sometime I expect him to *create* this imaginary world for real and out of his infinite godly mercy.

I know this may prove to be totally alien to his awareness or interest or even curiosity.

A little common sense here (last page) to illustrate that I *know* where I am but still gamble saintlike that if we knew how great god was, we'd give divinity.

> Better accept what is—this last vision of Neal
> —and of myself as a crazy fantasist
>           of his perfections
> —perfected to my own mad purposes,
> Genius to my depraved body
> and potential genius of my unthinkable
>           metaphysical Idea—
> The spectacle of such love
> half secret, half spoken
>      the whole written down
> in the long ledger of the decade—
> abstract fragments,
>      fragments of dreams,
> fragmentary physical descriptions
>      days' and nights'
> wildness solitary or mutual—
>
> You might think me crazy if I confessed
> what I hoped for—
>      could I even define it,
> would I dare break up
>      the solid play
> "and phalanx of particulars,"
>      cards and dice and chess
>      his children, wife,
> devotion, attachments such as they are?
>      —to claim a mystical union

Drawing blood
      deeper than children's lives
outlasting progeny—because eternal
—for I did see in scx
or sexual joy,
or in pure human joy
a flash of the eternal

Let us say I was inspired
      with an honorable madness

"Divine frenzy" none the less divine,
yet none the less frenzied,
      unredeemable
for our railroad wife reality.

Let's say, It's my idea of you
      not you yourself
        I love.
I get mixed up between
      what I wish and know

Now it's time to paint consciously that imaginary picture—a monk so inhuman, so religious, so dostoyevskian, so queer, concerned for metaphysical sake with the particular, with gleams of pathos & saintly compassion, practically an image of *myself*—and yet more perfect, being more a man, more suffering in life, and more stoic and self-depossessed than I am, all that bumhood jail and orphanage and physical prowess sexuality, car genius and many loves scattered around the landscape, as well as the prose—

I've gulled myself with this image, beating you on the soul with it, battering unconsciously at your soul—perpetrated this madman in your household for two agonized months.

The only question that remains, what are you now? A railroad T-head with passion for chess, cock crazy as you define yourself before lapsing into silence.

I mean also there's something good about my kind of madness, keeps us from being beasts or that worse creature the perfect husband of the wife's sullen image.

You poor depraved maniac,
        you'd run to Frisco and grab a nigger whore,
You'd get drunk on beer—yet
        you're allergic to alcohol
And lick some 3 buck cunt in Tracy,
        and vomit in the streets
You've taken on male dwarfs
        and grey fat old mothers
in your hearse-like stationwagon
        on Mission street
Your bed squeaks nightly
        in the Stanley hotel,
& in brakeman's flops
everyone knows who's in cubicle 5 alone
You leave handkerchiefs
stained with the milky perfume
of your loins by my bedside,
        all over the house
in your car, in hotels
        over the peninsula
from Watsonville to Oakland—
and go jerkin off in dreams
        in the caboose—
spied on by old men
        in black uniforms—
You even! oh most utter misery
give your virgin body to—
Oh Woman of abomination!
Your damned white dirty shrew's
hellfish mouths—I write
this on the toilet seat—
the images of this love
        are true and sad
—yet visit my bed rarely. . . .

* * *

——                          Juventius since 1946 we've
eye                                 loved each other on Earth
on                          And now it's 1954, I see
reader                                  the turning of our lives
——                          much like the pages
Eternity                              of an ancient book . . .
exists
in
a
moment
of
consciousness
a
wink
of
god

                    *  *  *

## Abusive Poem

          You lie around the house
               all day naked under
          a yellow bathrobe
          jiggling yourself
               into an idle fingered hardon
                    while we talk
          humid cigarette and sweat
          smell of late come
          when I catch you in my room
          alone, feigning sleepiness
          I hope
          someday you'll be able
                    to fuck yourself
          and come to terms with love
               crying in joyful absorption
               or shudder and suffer

in the cold horror of rejection
  I feel
    when you're in my bed.

Not that tears and cocksucking
    aren't sweet
Not that you haven't dragged me
   into my room for your pleasure
—but you might as well put in
    at least one sweet glance in secret
while I'm bending sightless in blind prayer
   over your loins
    to your god Priapus.

* * *

I'm not berating your abuse
  of your own beauty
—God knows I'm forced to it myself
   with a vengeance, inspired by your example—

* * *

## Translation—Catullus

Let's live, my Lesbia, let's love & value
rumors of senile severities not worth
pretty pennies to us. Suns set and suns rise
again, we with brief light rise only once then
set in earth our night is perpetual sleep.*

* * *

Aug 20—Last nite the dream (Aug 10) came true in general structure except the part about floating in green lite, the actual kiss. Carolyn bitter and mad. Leaving Neal's house—or decided to, gave my word but depressed and frightened—*depressed* by the affair—much reminiscent of the sensation of unbearable horror

---

* Notes for translation of Catullus' V ("*Vivamus, Mea Lesbia, atque armemus . . .*") August 1954; reassembled May 24, 1993. —A.G.

in the bus with Naomi from Lakewood as child—feeling irreconcilable antagonism she feels, my confusion as to whether I do hate her and the consequences of dislike—the consequences in sum of the event—and the consequences of Neal's marriage, children and this disordered nagging. Also the future consequences of Neal & my relationship to be studied—as yet it seems an insoluble problem, an equation.

Elements of the equation:

1. Getting a place in S.J. to be near Neal
2. Going up to dread Frisco for same (prefer no Frisco till I am finished with [Xbalba] book?)
3. Stay with the Hinkles?* an outside chance . . .
4. Return East? No.

Feel I should somehow really *try* to propitiate her but know no general terms to do so—she's violent, seemingly unpropitiable—unless could be shown that her situation is *not* the result of my intrusion. Resentment against her picture of matters, her accusations and cold lacerations. Feeling of guilt toward her (the view that I am an extraneous pervert interloper) (before her eyes). Sincerity of my feeling for Neal. Realization that marriage breakup would be tragic for him. Realization that probably marriage is already too far gone & corrupted. Realization that I have no hope of life-gratification in Neal.

Fact that she is definitely antipathetic to any active friendship between me & Neal in action & in my dreams; now is willing to force the issue. How far? Forbid all intercourse? How unrelenting is her stand?

How far can she force Neal—as she has forced me? . . . Likely in immediate result he will *be* forced to take no active stand but be passive in circumstances. There is no stand for me to take in the house short of deceiving her or completely limiting Neal & my relation more than already naturally done by the 2 of us. Deceiving

---

* Al and Helen Hinkle, prototypes of Ed and Galatea Dunkel in *On the Road.* Al's descriptions of California railroad work had spurred Cassady to move there. Ginsberg visited the Hinkles several times while at the Cassadys'.

her impossible as would be unsuccessful in long run and also would breed instinctive hate on both sides. She adamant, I must go anyway. *Always* looked on me as enemy.

Neal must be passive in this situation as only way for him to hold together the reality of marriage and children consequences.

I don't aspire to carry him off so there is really no final contradiction except as she makes it one & reacts in fright or antipathy or ignorance to my role.

It was she who proposed she be included in the friendship.

I will make an effort to resolve this with her before I leave once I have the independent means to back up my assertions.

One must (as I have not) be aggressively forceful in making her cut the accusations & generalized guilt-making and give her the facts without hesitating—I'm afraid she'd get hysterical, unable to accept possibility of this sort of view, have some deep traumatic nervous collapse? Fear of uncontrollable emotional violence in her.

\* \* \*

Aug 20—Carolyn is a *charnel* that will stain Neal into total insensibility.

And with all the anxiety—fatigue in my back, constant sense of grating reality—Neal playing chess all night with Hinkle & Richard Woods, with Baby (earlier vision of John A.* as Cupid in his arms with Babe buttocks)—he wouldn't give me much strength or support for decision or determination—adamant & withdrawn even evasive as to where I should go.

It has not yet occurred to me that what C. avers is true, I am not in love with Neal but my idea. A strict conception of X empathy—that doesn't exist in him, there is no spiritual correlation, or "emotional" even. That, finally, he "rejects" or is indifferent to me. His gen'l actions so bespeak.

\* \* \*

A Masque—*The Interlopers*—Three characters: she I he
    "There is as much beauty in the human body"
The plot: Who does he love? Who *loves*?

---

* I.e., John Allen Cassady (1951–).

* * *

Her speeches—"Deeper than stomach ever was"
        "That's not a man"
        "Trying to break up my marriage"
        Lifts mask in Death: "I'm Reality—I suffer the
        consequences"

* * *

This—and the infatuation of the Green Auto—a lesson on the consequences of allowing my mind to fatten on its own images.

* * *

This second evening after crisis I am oppressed by perspective of the normalcy of her complaints—my own actual misconduct here. Should I say the *Justice* of her complaints. My deepest thought is: they will undergo the consequences of their mutual cruelty. Neal has been cruel to me.

We do not reincarnate, it's but a crude symbol of the fact that everyone has always been everyone—we are all the same person in myriad forms—the point is to be that universal person in the incarnation you are born in—recognise that unity and all it means. Achieve consciousness as that Person, of the great Person. I have striven to bring that person to consciousness between us & unify us in that, since you seemed most near recognition, but it seems a hopeless effort.

The person lives in us and then we perish. What perishes is an embodiment of the person, who never dies. He is like time— the present dies, becomes past, but Time never dies in the continuum.

* * *

That I love someone who doesn't love me. This realization dawns like waking from a dream, but like someone for whom the day is full of dreamy troubles I lie in bed in sleep unwilling to pull off the covers and open my eyes to the bare walls.

* * *

Or that my infatuation with Neal has no basis in fact. Like Catullus' sickness. Does he want me to love him? Does he need etc. or do I only need the illusion. And here to begin to define the word *love* that I've used—certainly a state of mind an obsession and sickness attributing all sorts of emotional sympathies and empathies to him that don't exist but I imagine they do. It sickens me. This egotism which "recognizes no boundaries of self" and

don't write down ideas you don't know the meaning of.
Staring in this space which
    I had filled with sensation
    of "love" realizing that what I attributed
    to myself, my own feelings of love
doesn't even exist
        leaving me wondering what feelings
            I actually have.

Alternatives of hate etc. He snubs my overtures. He makes me suck his cock. He orders me around. He makes me subservient. He is indifferent & it's a lot of bullshit & trouble, a weight on his head this farce.

My "loving" is a deception? Suddenly a flash of sex in my belly & loins.

* * *

## San Francisco

Monday Aug 23, 1954—Back alone in a Hotel and once again the great battle for survival—Hotel Marconi, Frisco—$14 (+20) in pocket, Vic lushing with me, appointment with Chronicle on Wed. and no job [in the] offing.

* * *

Dream unrecorded in time—Neal breaks whole leg & put out of commission.

\* \* \*

How sweet to be finished with Neal. The pain of masochism and the absolute angel gone.

(The absolute angel comes and goes.)

\* \* \*

Milton on Time—Isn't there in this accentual verse a *major* accent in each line, one central syntactical thought word which serves as the axle of the line? A major breathing emphasis, the *point* word of the line?*

\* \* \*

>Whether Allen is done with
>>his life in this life
>or returns to survive his sufferings
>>with another body
>to perfect an immortality for love—
>>Whether Neal will return to Allen
>in this body or another
>>I cannot say.
>Allen and Neal will be Angels together—
>>or another Allen and another Neal.

\* \* \*

"Wanna make a couple bucks?" "Well no, not right now—I'll be back in an hour or so—or I'll see you another day." I heard the conversation thru transom in the dark carpeted hall. Bob B. old-looking 26 yr. drunk wandering in the corridors. In my room earlier "C'mere"—"I'm here" I say. "I know but I want to talk to you," he sitting on my bed. From Salt Lake.

Later that night met Neal—It had been *he* responding to the fairy (Bob B.) in the hall. Told me his Rorschach reading—

---

* The fourth and tenth syllables are stressed in each line. —A.G., October 4, 1982

prepsychotic sexually sadistic with "Deluded" ideas of Reality. Trying to make dykes in the bar 12 Adler Place.

The party with Sheila Williams—Then with Sublette & Cosmo, we got arrested on vagrancy & spent a night in jail.*

A series of essays (short and pithy) on social subjects, taking all parts or stands & coming to conclusions

1. American destiny and the Fall of America. Thought control:

2. Drug and penal laws bad. 3. Communist laws bad. 4. Sex laws.

5. Jobs. Job hunting horrors. 6. National art—movies and TV.

Standardization and mechanization and control of the individual psyche seems now a fait accompli here.

The direction of public control is definitely not conducive to a good life.

The unsatisfying domestic marriage job orientation etc. solution—not offer enuf spiritual activity.

Spiritual activity or Art a strictly sideline deal and not a centrally important goal.

Here I am, the idea is, at my age and degree of maturity of experience completely stalemated in relation to social organization. Mainly it is a lack of sensitivity on part of employers—things run on a routine of unspiritualized mediocrity and when anyone with any special insight tries to become a part it is a torture.

Neal's madness makes me think I'm mad to be so attuned to it. A new poem to Neal on his entering the condition of madness.

Realization of the total masochism I feel toward Neal—and curiosity as to how far he can be pushed sadistically. This the core of the vow. Master-slaves—to be each other's master and each other's slave they lose human self-limitation gaining eternal bond-

---

* I.e., found sitting peaceably in a North Beach coffeehouse when police decided to search it in the middle of the night, they were taken to jail because of officers' suspicion that the foot powder belonging to bohemian colleague and poet Cosmo might be heroin.

age (transcending separations and departures, marriages and fortune).

Unless a man is continuously occupied in the creation of a form material or intellectual modeled after the immaterial eternal form which he either creates or perceives in his own soul . . . he cannot live alive, he's just a dead object floating in space . . .

\* \* \*

# Reading August 1954 (San Francisco)

W. C. Williams—Complete Collected Poems
Li Po Translations—Obata
Catullus Translations—Wm. A. Aiken
Ez. Pound—ABC Reading
F. R. Leavis—Revaluations in Poetry (parts)
Van Doren—Anthology of World Poetry (parts)
Stephens' Travels in Yucatán Vol. I
Karl Vossler—Medieval Culture Vol. II (parts)
W. C. Williams—The Build Up (Novel)
L. F. Céline—Guignol's Band
Sophocles—Philoctetes (Jebb tr.)
Shakespeare—Troilus & Cressida
Chandler Brossard—The Bold Saboteurs
Sister Mary Barry—Analysis of Eliot's Prosody (Catholic U.)
Eliot—Early poems
T. S. Eliot—Essay on Milton (1948? 50?); The Confidential Clerk
Glenn Hughes—Imagism & the Imagists
Catullus—Cambridge Latin ed. & Horace Gregory translations
Tibullus
Encyclopedia Britannica articles relating to verification, rhythm,
    etc.
W. C. Williams—The Desert Music
Rexroth, K.—A few plays & Early Poems
Marlowe—Ovid's Elegies Translation (skimmed)
Gide—Corydon
Cézanne—Biography by John Rewald
Keats—Odes & random shots
Milton—Shorter poems
Jack Lindsay—Catullus translations

* * *

The contents of Peter DuPeru's* bag left on my bed beside a white & black box of Smith's Cough Drops—¼ loaf of bread—Miracle Whip Salad Dressing—Fungi Rex Powder (athlete's foot). Book—*La Société Française au Dix-Septième Siècle,* an account of Fr. society in the XVIth Century from contemporary writers—edited for the use of schools & colleges etc by T. F. Crane, Am. Prof. Romance Lang. Cornell, Putnam's NY 1889. *Gryll Grange* by Thos. L. Peacock. And various articles of clothing—khaki, levis, pants, a bottom of wet papers & photos of people in armchairs near pianos—2 pks matches folded together—the wet dustjacket of *Historical Architecture* by Hugh Braun—a grey envelope from Crocker Nat. Bank "We enclose our check payable to your order representing weekly payment for yr. support & maintenance due today"—Amt. (in box below)—"18.75"; a little note in French in 5 numbers in strange handwriting—a U.P. Newspix card of admission to S.F. Motor Sports Show (#444)—another note in French written thick pencil crosswise on red-ruled paper.—address on wet paper of a Foreign Liaison Section person in Tokyo (female) with Jap address as well. A piece of cardboard torn—An ad, it is "Rubber Tippe," torn in a 4th of its depth & totally meaningless keepsake except it's yellow & blue with thick fine black print. Other side "Compa— with any o—"—New round ball rubber tip." Rent receipt for Aug. 1—It's now Sept. 7—for a Mr. D. Teuber Rm # signed by Maria Orloff for $6.25. A large pink pawn ticket for $2 for a pair shoes brown. New washed, a *wet* pair underpants awkward white style—a bottle of Red Lotion unidentified (hair?)—canopener puncher—soap bar, equally unidentified spray deodorant, big green plastic bottle—wet pink shirt—a blue transparent plastic cup. A wooden clothespin—blue plastic handled rusty bladed Schick razor, horrible gooey rust still wet like brown mud blood. A length of orange rubber enema pipe folded in round with no nozzles—just the pipe. Another Crocker 24 week statement of payments varying from $25.00 to $10.00—mostly all $18—for

---

* Peter DuPeru was a certain kind of archetypal bohemian, appearing in cameo as Richard de Chili in Kerouac's *Desolation Angels* (New York: G. P. Putnam, 1960), pp. 126–27.

Peter Lambert DuPeru Broadway Laguna Residence Club 1998
Broadway—Guardian of the Estate of P.L.D. "For completion of
necessary records we shall appreciate acknowledgement of these
payments by the execution & return of duplicate pay voucher" (of
the enclosed dup etc.). Book: pocket—*Four Great Historical Plays
Shakespeare.* An enamel funnel—5 inches high, black rimmed. A
red pamphlet on St. John of Rochester (Paulest Press), 32 pps.
Eyedropper syringe off Vicks Vatronol. A rusty penny. Eraser. 2 prs.
brn. socks—2 odd ones—empty match cover—an address written
on curious white paper with stiff glaze on other side rectangular—
and last a cartoon from a newspaper, wet, of a guy behind
counter—butcher? A low counter—and another person on other
side, beard, striped-crosswise shirt, patched bum coat, bum derby,
scraggly hair, black face, black rotten eyes, long cock nose, "I'd like
to open a charge account." It's Joe's Bar written in reverse on the
window. The bum is shaking, 4 patches on coat.

* * *

Dream September 14, 1954—in apartment, asleep, too long, into
the day, apartment with Louis—he's out—can't tell what I'm sup-
posed to do—can't remember in time—can't tell the time—I
have to piss—I get up out of bed—wearing child's soft clothes,
white top & sleeping pants—disheveled—I go to the closet & piss
in the can—I empty the can in the receptacle—a receptacle—
under the bed—a can?—I empty it by mistake in the top drawer—
it spreads—I go back around the bed & empty it in the waste
basket can—I see all the piss I've emptied spreading in stain on
the rug thru the wastecan bottom of welded tin—
    Where am I supposed to be? School—what class—too late,
I've missed the 9AM, the 11AM gym classes—Van Doren's* class?
Is it too late—1PM class, first of the afternoon, I haven't even been
to the morning classes, always miss them—how can I ever expect
to get thru school,—understand the curricula?—The afternoon
classes are my intellectual specialty & I can't even get to them
organized—I feel defeated and depressed—in comes the land-

---

* Mark Van Doren, English instructor at Columbia during A.G.'s
matriculation.

lady, a dyke (as at the present Marconi Hotel in S.F.) to clean, with a friend—She doesn't care that I'm there but tries to run me around—First the business of the piss rug which she refuses to leave alone—takes to the closet—opens it "Ah? I forgot this closet is used for cans (vegetable & groceries), but it's not got shelves," or it hasn't a dumbwaiter in it (or escalator to the dump)—She hangs rug on rack near sink—I rinse it out and hang it on faucet— she is annoyed—but o.k.

\* \* \*

Down in Tommy's [bar] tonite meeting Neal on street just leaving my house—We argue about Cayce, he's sweeter tonite— "Your Karma is criticism but (turning to me & talking close to my face after eye glance, into my ear) thru early homosexuality you've learned not to criticize, learned from it—in previous life- times you were undoubtedly worse than this lifetime as an intel- lectual critical character"—and become now therefore not a critic but a poet.

Neal wandering thru S.F. North Beach talking about cunt carrying in his head now the miracle of the idea of reincarnation and eternal Karmaic law.

No writing no reading for several weeks due to job and girl & North Beach Rounds—N.B.R. kept down reasonably. Evenings exhausted asleep—valuable time wasted—socks to be washed. Ovid stands on my dresser unopened. Catullus is a dream—I am a busy dream—busy dreaming—the use of the dash a new factor (noted in Keats too)

Jack shd dig Keats.

The doctor at S.F. Southern Pacific: "He has done me no ill but confirmed thy Glory."

The Medical Dental Bldg. outside window standing speaking to no one in its 1930 Modern Isolation beside the homely old paramecium bldg of the Drake hotel but outside of the window blocks away on the Gothamesque Midtown Ninny Murray Hill horizon skyline full mooned, stolid there with a few futuristic television light windows curved in the spaceship side of the build- ing up in the bleak air above the city not far enough out to be eternal but sorrowful & sad in its unhappy selfhood of curved white brick blocking my vision of the sky.*

\* \* \*

## With Neal†

     . . . speeding up‡
  "Bloody Bayshore,"
     the ribbon of death,
  Tossing beer cans
     out of the window
  Beating on the dashboard
     smoking tea
  radio blaring among the cars.

\* \* \*

He was then (N.) seeking something in sex—now had it all—some broken vision—the end of his cunt, as he explained of LuAnne§ in 1952 N.Y.C. visit—No further to go, the rest emptier since not signifying the end he was seeking—Repetitions of pornography now—repetitions of the dirty dick—with the consciousness of the totally developed cock—no cunt in mind?—acting without desire?—objectless lust?—a kind of masturbation.

Since earlier lust had been the means to speak for the eternal, for liberation. . . .
Now knowing what he could from a thousand cunts, no road up further—out in every direction.

\* \* \*

---

\* Model for "Moloch" section of *Howl.* —A.G., October 4, 1982. See also pp. 61–63.
 † See entry for September 26, 1955, pp. 195–96.
 ‡ Ellipsis periods appear in the journal entry.
 § Luanne Henderson, prototype for Marylou in Kerouac's *On The Road.*

## In Vesuvio's Waiting for Sheila

Here at last a moment
in foreign Frisco
Where I am thoroughly
beautiful
Dark suit—dark eyes
no glasses,
money in my wallet—
Checkbook abreast—
Toward an evening
of fucking and jazz
She knows
and I convinced
of my powers—already familiar,
—listening to the vague
conversation of amateur
concepts on my right
with dark delight
anticipating leaning on the bar.

\* \* \*

Catulli Carmina—Vox records Carl Orff
Ma Rainey—Travellin Blues

\* \* \*

## Imitation of Pound-Cavalcanti

| | |
|---|---|
| Under the smoking tank | a |
| a gentleman sang | b |
| "My body's burnt & lank | a |
| my pecker's a pang— | b |
| Goodby old gang | a |
| of mine, my heart is rank, | a |
| Radios, go hang, | b |
| we saw the world, we drank." | a |

\* \* \*

Depression now (Oct 12) realizing after moving into this great Nob Hill Apt with Sheila that I "don't love her" as "she loves me" thus starving & killing her heart for my "casual" pleasure. "Fathers & teachers,"\* etc.

\* \* \*

(Living in Apartment on Nob Hill)

On Peyote:† San Francisco October 17–18 Saturday Nite 1:15 —Apartment window wide open looking across downtown, the aspect of a ferocious building‡ reared in that center city looming up in the cloudy wisp fog floating across the flat blue sky, sliding across the horizon—

Uprising in the timeless city gloom, Dark Tower over ruddy building, suddenly a vision the Death Head—The building an evil monster—A tower in Hell—("Those poor lost souls making it up in the tower")—Two eyes blast light far apart, brick glass illuminated from within—too corny for a painter to make, the surrealistic reality, that would be too corny—no—deep gong religious.

Impassive robot (antennalike structures) of Sir Francis Drake Hotel.

And quite vegetable that monster too—it may be coming to eat me someday—

*That* was what was familiar all along.

It's got a crown—

Smoke curling up from it—working rooted in the basement.

Snub nosed monster—the hideous Gorgonian aspect— . . .

Description of the tower of Baal or Azriel? Of Lucifer. "The Tower of Lucifer."

---

\* Dostoyevsky: Speech by Father Zosima, *The Brothers Karamazov.*

† Taken together with Sheila Williams and Neal Cassady.

‡ The Sir Francis Drake Hotel, inspiration for *Howl,* Part II ("Moloch").

The star goes out at one AM—the monster appears most grim staring into the sky small noselite—with snout nearly darkened. Someone up late in the tower.

With Fog rolling by down from Twin Peaks & South San Fran to the bridge and embarcadero edge of the cock peninsula in the bottom of the vale of the town are ranged skyline peyotl buildings:
I came to the window and glanced out into the night space at the unreal city below in which I inhabit a building—
as walking street today I noticed the battlement uprearing facade appearance of the ranges of blocks of houses with fantastic graeco-medieval ornamentation juttings and false stone wood pillar and arches porches & crossbow tower'd bedrooms—
Came to the window to stare at the thousand eyed buildings in the smoke filled stone vale crowded with monstrous edifices

shouldering each other rocking stolid on the streets, red lights below and haze purple sky light above as in Rembrandt* it was brown—

and fixed eye & noticed the vegetable horror of the Sir Francis Drake Hotel—had waited long for this perception having spent four hours total over a week looking out the window at the wrong building waiting for something to happen—nothing had but that I'd noticed how modern and large and isolate the Sutter St. Medical building stood in my way, too large for the more homely old Drake and downtown other SP and Insurance edifices making a N.Y. Gotham midtown Murray Hill unreal Wall Street miniature panorama toward Bridge—another coast's apple for the eye—

Found suddenly the gothic eyes of the skull tower glaring out bleak blind blank smoking above in stillness in the atmosphere of the real primeval city world, down grown out of earth—with horrible cross check Dollar sign skull protrusion of lipless jailbarred inhuman long-tooth spectral deathhead brick columns making abstract teeth. This phantom building robot was smoking in inaction as if it had been stuck there in eternity a Golem waiting for the Rabbi of electricity to pull the switch for it to topple forward into the city destroying—Meanwhile serving as an evil tower of thought, glaring profound and open above the streets (into my window)—"for every eye to see"† that could wake from the daily dream to register its central presence in the atmosphere of night.

On top a Star of David in great blue silly neon that goes off at 1 AM leaving the impression of the continually Death-in-Life robot Zombie presence of the Drake (mad crows tear down the bldgs.) fixed for the night to wait sleepless and unseeing while physicists tinker in its bowels toward the day of resurrection.

---

* Possibly Rembrandt's *The Polish Rider.*

† An apocalyptic farm kid, tall lanky Southerner picked up on Times Square 1950–51? & brought to the apartment of Carl Solomon [1923–1993; dedicatee of *Howl*] in Chelsea, said in bed that his preacher had warned that the Apocalypse would come in this End of Days, & that the Second Coming of Christ would be seen on television—that's why TV was invented, "For every eye shall see" (it says in the Bible?). —A.G., June 25, 1991

\* \* \*

—A random comment: madness is a disease you contract from not properly washing after handling human shit. A new physical psychology of the dread disease. Madness! Madness! Oh how often I hear that word in my brain as I behold the human state a mortal. What god of madness rules the heavens? What hierarchy of the mind? What man? Some secret man is god! hidden in India or Idaho.

Tropic or pole hides the Messiah. He comes with lightning flash or stone or ice—primeval hairy being, provincial mystic of the world—to feed her hungry loin, dumb matter, and incarnate paradise.

Ah have I not written of the cunt of the matter?

\* \* \*

The walk home from Sheila's hospital*—where she talked wildly with glittering vague child eyes about her nurse, her intern—

Down Sutter St. to run onto Jackson's Nook at Buchanan, and the Sukiyaki joints—re-finding Bop City I'd once passed with Al Hinkle—and down Sutter again in the steep midtown trafficky hotel-shop window nite. The Full Gospel preacher with his cadences strangled for speech, then up the Drake to see the Starlite Room I been staring at from outside down below on street—Inside full of carpet & cocktail tables & bars. The French restaurant, Alouette—Sensation of belonging to the upper middle class on Sutter St. How pleasant & true to turn up the hill so near Drake-Sutter-Park-light—Trolley to Pine St. home alone.

Al Sublette shot: "I'm going to make it with the lunch-bucket," and crying in bed. Cosmo with a bloody nose—"Was she any good"—(man)—? Bang! a punch in the nose. Cosmo on his ass—

Cosmo shot: "But the man's *only* a genius"—with a hand

---

* After appendicitis? —A.G., May 22, 1992

whispering to his mouth, and the hoarse *down* carney conman hipshaken innuendo.

Cosmo disappears into the sidewalk with his Egyptian black hair, his long prying nose, his beady Assyrian eyes, his unclean muscles, and his imaginary deck of Tarot cards and Jewish sentimental love verse of Broadway and the Black Cat Place Vesuvio's Mikes 12 Adler, residence—visiting friend of various other characters, El Hotel Macaroni—his crying nose in the macaroni. And his footpowder.

A short on DuPeru: on DuPeru's shorts. Does DuPeru wear shorts. Sometimes not. Today he stole my J. & J. Baby Oil, smearing it in the bathroom oily on his redded face. And when he was gone, a whole pot of sour Chinese broccoli (which I had been saving for him) disappeared from view, almost as Cosmo.

In the bathroom searching his skin for microscopic erosions—a Huncke* with an income. At my house no less. When will I never learn? What? Once more dear shadows your inhabitants become more enduring than the world, more interesting than the sidewalks.

* * *

A man covered with oil shouting instructions, white eyes rolling in black promethean frenzy, the "Nigger of oil," under the thundering derrick with infinite desert about: the blowing well.

## Nov. 9

Silence in the house—end of another affair. Sheila goes to bed silent. I in a half-dream writing at the table.

---

* Herbert Huncke, subterranean connection, storyteller, addict, hustler, and later author (*Guilty of Everything*, Paragon House, 1990), was an early influence on Burroughs, Ginsberg, Kerouac.

## Nov. 13—Sat.

## To ——: Haec certe deserta

How many nights struggling
          with that body—
Comparing that stranger to Juventius—
          another Allen and
                    another love—
Until the candle
          ran colorless in the cup—
          Looking in a book
          upon another love
I, another poet in the future world
          —you dead
these thousand years—and I
writing in another book
          about that passion,
                    and sit here
in the old kitchen regarding an image
buried in the heart
          —a poem to that body on a page,
this is how Allen shall love
          you in a later year.

* * *

## Malest Cornifici—Paradigm

[First drafts, including scansion paradigms and the six lines that
follow, of "Malest Cornifici Tuo Catullo," CP 123.]

I'm sick old Kerouac, hallowèd Allen
is sick in eternity—laboring lonesome
and worse worse follows by the days and hours
You're angry at me. For all of my lovers?
But I need a little sweet conversation
Sad as the tears of Sebastian Sampas.

Write to Freer Gallery for photos of (Yangtze) River Landscape
attributed to Chü-Jon, hand scroll.

\* \* \*

# From L.A.\*

Pale and drunk I stood on the corner memorizing the cars speeding down Vine Street. "He shuffled unsteadily North toward the Garden of Allah, etc."

I ate & drank & stared until my shit was black & I vomited blood on Vine St. & wandered sick & lonely past Sunset to sit down in gold brick Pantages Theater and see the last comedy by wasted Laurel & Hardy still fat to watch them destroy the world before they die† and came out in a prophetic rage against Hollywood and went to my aunt's house vomiting on the way to recover my heart.

Then flying home to Peter

Until what hour when the lights burst about me and the illumination is granted and I cease talking to myself and hear the beautiful uncanny silence that hush of eternity land—the choking and vomit of this aeroplane, which is tears let loose—& I cry accepted into divinity.

\* \* \*

She's really an entity beyond herself as I am not the Allen of mirrors but the objective bleak dispassionate entity of these or other notes.

\* \* \*

New season 1403 Gough St. Robert La Vigne Peter Orlovsky, Sutter & Polk, "Polk Gulch" as painter Knute Stiles called it—the dark halls of the Wentley (Hotel), rumors of the old age & demise of the Ghost House—La Vigne's Fauve painting of Peter—

---

\* Returning from brother's New York wedding.

† Their last movie featured an atom bomb on a South Pacific utopian island. A French-Italian coproduction, *Atoll K* (1952) was released in the U.S. as *Robinson Crusoe-Land,* later renamed *Utopia,* the title under which Ginsberg recalls seeing it.

DuPeru's residence & expulsion—Leaving Sheila—"Is this the face that launched a thousand ships?"
Sketching in actuality

Illustration of Gough Street room. In journal page, unreduced, title of manuscript atop dresser, right, is visible: *Visions of Neal* (Kerouac's *Visions of Cody*).

* * *

The long talk in decayed kitchen of 1403 Gough, Robert & I facing it, none unangry, Peter concluding "You guys are nothing but a pain in the ass."

[Rough excerpts noted on first reading Jack Kerouac's *San Francisco Blues* typescript scroll; A.G.'s comments in parentheses:]

1  I see the backs
   of old men rolling
   slowly into black
   Stores.

—Talking to secret
companions with long hair—

2 3rd St. Market/To Lease. (Poem)

3 The rooftop of the
tenement
on 3'd & Harrison
has Belfast painted
black on yellow
on the side—
etc.

4 ah
little girls.

8 The long fat yellow
Eternity cream
of the Third St Bus
roof swimming like
a monsyllablic
Amer-Masosaur

11 Character in plaid
Workcoat & glasses
carrying lunch
Stalking & bouncing
Slowly to his job.

12 . . . to buy bananas
for her love night

13 (—Junk)
. . . to step on it & get some bread
For Poppa's got to sleep tonight
And the Chinaman's on his bed
"No hunger & no wittles
Neither dearie"
Said the Crone
to Edwin Drood.

14 "When
dearie
The pennies in the

palm multiply
as you watch."
(O.K. they'll be an
answer forthcoming)

15  Then I'll go lay my crown
    Body on the heads of 3 men
    Hurrying & laughing
    in the wrong direction,
            my Idol.

16  Sex is an automaton
    sounding like a machine
    thru the stopped up keyhole—
    young men go fastern
    old men. . . .
    . . . young men breathe inwardly.

    There was a sound of slapping
    when the Angel stole come
    and the Angel that had lost
    Lay back satisfied.

17  Hungry addled redface

18  Angrily I must insist
    for a round of crimes
    is Lucifer the Fraud.

20  Rhetorical Third Street
    Grasping at racket
    Groans & stinky
    I've no time
    To daily hassle
    In your heart's house,
    It's too gray
    I'm too cold—
    I wanta go to Golden,
    That's my home.
    I came a wearyin
    From Eastern hills;
    Yonder Nabathaque recessit

The eastward to Aurora rolls,
Somewhere West of Idalia
or East of Russet Falls,
. . .
Clack of the wheel's
my freight train blues.

23  Third Street I seed
And knowd
And under ramps I writ

28  Swing yr umbrella
at the sidewalk
As you pass
or tap a boy on
the shoulder
Saying "I say
where is Threadneedle
Street."

(Later, Sadder—)

32  San Francisco is too old
her chimneys lean
And look sooty
after all this time
of waiting for something
to happen
Betwixt hill & house,
Heart & heaven

34  (—Tired Dawn, Series)
Your corners open out
San Francisco
To arc racks
of the Seals
Lost in vapors
Cold & bleak.

35  I also have loud poems
    Broken plastic coverlets
    Flapping in the rain
    to cover newspapers
    All printed up
    and plain.

\* \* \*

Jan 1, 1955

First 1955 journal entry.

# Jan. 1, 1955

The first time in life I feel evil: conscious loss of innocence, betrayal of Robert—I feel as if I blundered unthinkingly—seen thru his eyes, and Sheila's eyes (unfeeling lout she called me)— shame for situation & complicity shared with Peter—tho I supposed to know better—I not fitted to "teach" him now thru having compromised myself by allowing he & I to screw—Enticing him before Robert had done with the season, too early painfully betraying Robert, without slowly seriously enough accustoming myself to know Peter, lengthy sweet honorable courtship, under Robert's eyes as he departs, so that when we do make love, it is only after knowledge and long longing & real love of each other—this was, Robert was right, too fast, accompanied by guilt & Robt.'s repudiation, over anxiously blindly my grabbing him, fucking (and in *Front* of Robt.) so that we two are set adrift prematurely hardly knowing if we do know or like each other, both doubting, he my motives, I his (was he being specially insensitive and recriminating to Robt?)—each of us not really knowing what we want from each other—so serious a coupling with so serious Robt. an antecedent & so bitter for all the break from Robt.—so that he now hates me—egocentric, crafty, sly—I blundered here not knowing really from the beginning seriousness & sweetness of Robert's intentions—How badly I showed myself.

Therefore project to suffer to repair by seriously beginning chastely to explore issue with Peter & getting to know him— realized New Year's Eve I hardly do know him, just my idea of him from a few pictures of Robt., few conversations, and his apparently harsh behavior toward Robert, as harsh as my own. How much of old innocent intensity can I communicate?

The two of us doomed then as in Conrad, James, to be thrown together lost without the expected possible Rose & find each other grating—a horrible prospect. Slowdown of realization of how right Robert was, I see too late. For if by example of this I teach Peter ingratitude or impatience with Robert what may I myself who am so cheap expect of him in the end?

I was deceived in early enthusiasm for Sheila. I assumed blindly because Peter was a boy I would not lose flair for him but it is possible.

The whole thing hanging a weight over my conscience now for the first time a real knowledge.

I looked in the mirror in room.

## Jan. 2, 1955

Love anguishes & lethargies again—waiting for Peter woke at 10:00 Sunday, went out, wondered if he received my message where I was from Natalie,* bought breakfast groceries at Supermarket, went toward 1403 Gough wondering whether to go in or not, decided to, under excuse of getting bowl & a spoon, entered famous nostalgia hall frightened, peeked in studio, hairy evil Robert asleep on couch, I started, walked past, Mike asleep in my old bare room on pallet, Peter's door closed, Natalie asleep, went trembling in kitchen, put on hot water to have tea breakfast excuse, opened Peter's door, he asleep, got scared Robert was staring would find me sneaking around house, meanwhile suffering near headache from cold & nose blowing & half deaf, gathered utensils back in kitchen, then went into Peter's room, he asleep, shook him, calling name low to wake him, he looks at me, wakes, smiles, I say "You know where I am now? Across from Foster's [Cafeteria]— Natalie knows did she tell you?"—"No"—"At the Young Hotel?"—"I know"—I get up & start to go, he rises on elbow as I leave room, says "like a dream." I say "Remember"—leave, turn off gas under the tea, sneak out back door. Back to my room, lie down, lethargic, still sick—why doesn't he get up & follow me— worries & tests of love—should I lie dreaming & expect him? I sleep, sun crosses heaven, room is hot, I sweating, afternoon, still he hasn't come—I sit up looking out window down on Polk & Sutter Foster's corner as if I might see him crossing street, entering Foster's looking for me. When will he come? Does he want to see me? Why am I waiting monomaniacally? Continue life as if nothing will happen. Too much hope & too much hangup will hex him for me. Mustn't frighten him off with too much love—and fantasies all yesterday & last night of his arrival, and deeper consciousness of

---

* Natalie Jackson (prototype for Rosie in Kerouac's *The Dharma Bums*) was Neal Cassady's lover at the time.

how sweet life will be, how much I can love. Hangup on love. Wish he would come & put an end to it. Has he mistreated Robert? Will I get same treatment as Robert? Exciting prospect of all this ending happily for a change. —Anxiety torment myself for pleasure of his relief arrival.

Better not to wait by the minute for a lover who will come maybe tomorrow.

4:30—He's coming—I say aloud—having watched a black dwarf cross the street, turn from window disgusted with myself for waiting by the minute looking out at Foster's—and seeing the mustached pity cripple that Mike introduced me to walking under the window—telepathic moment of faith—how cd. he not come soon, knowing I wait?

6:00—My misery continuing past anguish point into realistic nowhere drag depression—Ah recording angel. And now why not—took more aspirin, slept till dark, still no lover, sweating, hot lemonade, wow. I done what I could. Results blank. And Sheila also waiting for me at Pine? I prefer to wait here in eventual hope. And tomorrow? Will he even come tomorrow? Must I go seek him out again? Does he understand why I'm waiting? Is this a screwy test? 6:20 down to Foster's. Patience. Intuition of 4:30 not prevailed. Sit & read. Wasting time as before in this love-void. How can I work when etc? Kerouac writes well.

7:30—Read Herb Gold's *Man who was not with it*. I hated Gold.

That should possess my soul now—longing for a boy love, tenderness from Peter—a superficial ambition.

Much misery. Looked in mirror yesterday, New Year's Day, saw familiar Allen Dream face—real in the mirror, I'm real, the suffering is real, the lover is real, the happiness is real.

Meanwhile thrown into doubt by Peter's slowness.

8:40—Had gone out to Foster's no one there, grabbed bus to Sheila. She maybe waiting for me as I for him—she not home, heaters going full blast—left a note—back to Foster's by 8:00 (from 7:30)—There was (oh happy sight) Natalie & Robert, sat down, Robert face still clouded as was mine—I was afraid to ask after Peter—drank tea, then left, said I was going home. Watched out the window muttering to myself, then they left after half an hour—I saw them, he bent over her arm, cross street—I thought, huge eternal Foster's this is the scene where I'll outstare time again—then left off watch, lay back under covers (another aspirin) to read—Propertius—Woman down below well-dressed lower middle class with sailor's voice & housewife's form cursing "You shitass I don't care" staggering across alley with Foster's redglare neon in background—I watched awhile, thought to go down but no, no hope he'll be there for sure, better lay back & sleep or read—Sheila smart not to sit waiting for me, smarter in love than I. And am I even in love or just obsessed with image of possibilities?

9:00—The only thing that calmed my mind all day finally, becoming at least partially absorbed in Pound's Propertius just now (till the quarreling of drunken cabdrivers drew my attention out the window).

10:00—Knock on door—who?—Peter DuPeru—conversation—his problems with a mad hotelkeeper, & trying to cash bank checks for $5.00. We go down to Foster's, I eat chili & french fries, then in walks Peter & Robert, "Fancy meeting you here," I say stupidly. Peter too asks Peter DuPeru how he is, who gets up & goes and Robt. & Peter sit at table near window—I get up to get tea, sit down, Peter waves at me while Robt.'s head's bowed—waves me away? yes, I motion "Go?" showing myself to door by hand gesture, he nods, "Get out," so I hastily pour tea & scram. Suddenly uplifted by his smile & directness, get out—enough for the day. I go home close light & watch them,* Robert gesturing, lighting cigarettes, talking, for an hour, only occasionally glimpse Peter when his head is bowed forward to look at book being passed across table by Robert. 11 oclock, they get up out door, stop by red light, Peter looking down to Robert saying something to cap conversation, then run together across street & disappear. I've had it for the night.

## Monday Eve

Sheila here at 7:00—laughing at me in my lovesick bed—went up to Gough to watch on Peter for me, must have spoken to him. He came in, knocked, later, I was asleep, sweating clothed—

---

* I lived on 2nd floor in hotel across the street, facing plate-glass window of Foster's Cafeteria. —A.G., October 4, 1982

sat on bed, held hand for a moment, we looked, sadly, talked, he absent, not happy, sad, I quiet and too lovesick, not alive—"I missed you—" and no answer. And I guess it's all over. Stayed awhile, he so ill at ease, we both were, I'd hoped for his embrace, more there, I hadn't the initiative nor he the feeling. He looked at my books, smiled when I said anything lively, we talked about Robert—who Peter said he was still warring with, who would again speak to me soon. Said he would come tomorrow to take my books to Library. Aloof—yet sweet, but when he left I had pang, know or guess there is no more hope. Adios boy-love. Never seem to work out. Wonder if ever make it so? Seems spiritually hexed. What foundation in mutual desire? Where find boy to match me? A long prospect—dim years, not to be—would love but can't find boy love me still, cannot woman. How many times the heart not make it come?

Hope springs eternal: next time see him must be alive—not plague air with insatiable sadness of handsome lacklove. See how he reacts to that.

Major mistake—to fall into passive melancholy & sit by waiting for god of love to lap me up—action needed, Goethean action—

So called up Peter Martin*—

Not relieved (as Sheila will tell me) to be out of it—but I'm tired of the pain of all this subjectivity, horseshit—sudden Euphoria—hope it keeps up till I see Peter next & rubs off— obviously success is what is attractive, not misery need. I rode to Peter's promise on confidence, lacked that tonite, or as Sheila said, "This too good to be true" attitude perhaps the most fatal & obnoxious to a shy lover who wants vigor & maturity & fucking. Notice self pity, already noticeable an hour later in previous page.

## Tuesday Nite Jan. 4

Back home from work at 3:00—slept, Peter came about 7:00 after dark, no money, I had let landlady in downstairs, then she he, and some conversation about library (he was to return my books) but he had no money, wanted to study—I again more alive, less

---

* With Lawrence Ferlinghetti, cofounder City Lights Books.

plaguey than night before—no attempts to grab hands—Sheila then came in interrupting, & chattered on, everything lucid I was expounding (Spengler at this point) turning to curious Sheila— vague excitements of mind wonder, contradictions, another ego in the room beside mine—was he bored?—till I wished she'd let me do the talking here—but I kept resolving this sort of thing was inevitable anyway—then Peter out to get $ from Robert, then Sheila telling me she'd spent 3 hrs. bullshitting him about Proust & Balzac reading yesterday before he'd seen me, and afterward said "You seem sad—did Allen make you sad?" and he sd. yes to her, which I'd meant to do. Then I resolved to stay night here, though with money might have gone to 755 Pine, but this way Peter returned alone later, another moment with him alone— I'm getting screwy with this plot now—Robert according to Sheila is coming off it, talks of me & Religion (his lack) praisingly—but I'll hardly know what to say to him now—he's perhaps ruined everything, with his hatred; at any rate Peter certainly sick of the father-son role, which in some ways suited me fine, would have been basis on which to begin a more delicious freedom, not a hassle like this. Sick of others' ideas of what my ideas are, particularly Sheila's interpretations of them—her (all our) talent is empathy not criticism. I'm getting testy all this mixup. So they left together, I waved from the window—I wish she'd lay off him, she has only her idea of what goes—As she had said, "I got to him yesterday before you did—3 hours" and I imagine what flat miasma of "making it" in life she reduced matters to. When she left she left after having chided me "All shd. cool it—leave Peter alone for awhile," her prescription. She sensed I was upset by her & wd. rather see Peter alone later tonite, I think—looked face-fallen a moment as left, unhappy. Kept asking *what* I wanted of Peter—problem now beginning to turn on Peter's need for solitary strength outside of teacher routine, she knows of that. New delicate problems to think through but now seems for what I need to strike thru to a solid core of reality here, an identity, a conception of things, need to follow my inner impulses—present some kind of spiritual idea or excellence to Peter which being an aspect of Love will draw us together in a sacred union—alternative the slipshod drag of daily roommate habits, drunkeness, conversation. Well this line of thought unfinished in my mind. Questions of realism, wish this prose were prose not bullshit. Too much. Stop.

I'm in love, that matters for moment. Do I have a lover?

Sheila "Peter for Peter—whoever can do him most good."

Peter (some time ago) "I buy you since you're verbal, Robt. isn't."

Adding up to a what kind of motive on his part—one that will cool on approach of queer intensity?

Oh the same old hassles—Might have had a decent chance with this kind of setup if Robert had not so aggravated & burlesqued & flipped on same *level* of need as mine—approaches to emotion will meet now with withdrawal rather than sympathy. And I can't give real driving intelligence or creative sense unless integrated in sacramental sexual sympathy. Cannot talk of this to Peter or anyone for being ill defined & indefinite in meaning but unless I can give and take soul I can't discuss soul or anything worth talking about. Off on this tangent again. Not unsimilar to Burroughs or to Ginsberg in San Jose—hung up.

Why is any hangup but this emotionally starved, to me—I only get my kicks thru this peculiar love, wanting finally to be screwed in the ass, where it winds up. "All goes down the same hole in the end"—as I said yrs. ago to Hal, who commented "You're the dirtiest person I've ever seen," laughing in awe?

What matters really I suppose not the bullshit of psychology or estimations of progress toward reality but the active impulses of screwing & spiritual kicks which leave their real vibrations in time or memory. I should make it on my own level as far as possible with gusto—no one has my peculiar kicks, nor except Neal & Jack my appetite for humanistic suffering & coming continually thru life—what must I settle for? But it's a question of being in Love. This all I have to teach Peter.

## January 5

Home, sick again after big empty crowded night—Peter & Robt. came by at 7 last nite, bringing $5 check for my poverty-sickness, Peter in room "Bob's outside"—and turned to go, I called, I caught sight of Robt. profile out open door. Later that nite I went down to cafeteria—(Sheila still around)—and sat, Robt.

after a while uprose—Sheila, Robt., Natalie (& some other?) there—"I don't like this company"—and left—but earlier Sheila here drunk, lay in bed even screwed her asswise at her bidding, she sudden got up after a blank on my part: "How do you picture me?"—and sat in clothes again, Paul Bradley Wentley musician came up, cashed check (I'd been out in rain trying, vainly) and earlier had said to Peter, "come back tomorrow nite with more money, Son" (for Sheila's rent) —Well so I walk out of Foster's and pass Sheila & Bob embracing in Wentley doorway, smile, she calls me, I lean head on Bob's shoulder but feel cold, then leave. Later she & Bob come up and after a while we sight Neal's car pulling up (after trip with Natalie to San Jose) in front of Foster's—it's 4 AM—Robt. goes down to get them, returns half hr later (they've eaten)—we all lie around, Sheila undressed, Bob dressed embracing, Natalie & Neal on chair, me in bed sick, watching Neal. Conversation with Neal about getting old, etc. (Must begin continuous notes on meetings with him.) I maudlin, love Neal, he's happy.

Today Robt. comes by at 1 to borrow dime, I haven't got, returns at 3 with Peter, now reconciliation begun, but both of us embarrassed, Peter silent but answering questions—objective talk about Mexico City University. He (Peter) leaves early on some pretext, undoubtedly I thought can't stand the freeze still in progress. Robt and I fall silent, he leaves finally, bumping head against doorpost. Seems reconciled. Asked him how Peter was treating him now—"I'd rather not discuss it"—so we went on to aimless talk about Mexico, when he was moving, etc. Both will move to Wentley across street tomorrow.

Meanwhile my phantasies run looser & I masturbate today the kick being possibility of definition of roles again between Peter & self—that is, according to Sheila, P. told B. he was going to move in with me (what inanity of gossip I am getting into in this—black ink). I lie in bed all day imagining the arrangements, beds, household, gaining control of my will again with a concrete idea of amatory procedure—we buy each other, leave it at that—I approach it—What I buy in you is a body, flesh, which I haven't had, boy friend—as in the example of man being made of joined split roots you showed from Chinese early in yr. room—but my lack heretofore being the experience of sex to exhaustion with man—

and thus I am to be given your body for my satiety that is what I want—you at most times to take sexual initiative, make me, bring me out—having as I perceive from yr. dream early (holding my waist) greater freedom or less anxiety as of yore, for if I am ever to escape bondage to body to go to Tibet & be pure monk it will not be until I have satisfied my sexual imagination with you or another. So yr value lies in being capable of desiring me and yr capacity to imagine the spiritual reflection & purpose of the aspiritual sexual path I chose, & sympathy & compassion for whatever hangup of suffering I encounter on the way thru you a road—you my holy road—so I don't care who else you screw, make it with girls only to be sure to keep compassion for me, answer call when I break down to need of love moment—initiate my liberation and sexual revelation of self, for as I know I want to be tied to bed & screwed, whipped, want to wrestle & blow and come in unison, sexual ecstasy as I thot yet have & must before I give up on that. This opportunity following an experience of woman with Sheila—as if foreordained for my deliverance from boylove virginity ghost which haunts me still in 28th year.

In return for which (will return to what I want again undoubtedly) I give whatever I have in my being completely to yr. disposal, all explanations and heart cares. My role as teacher already well defined but also promise to deliver with two special talents—my creative sense of literary craft kicks, and my insight into mystical Sanctity union with God. Ambitious program—I call on Neal or Kerouac to affirm my power.

Which amounts to exchange of souls & bodies—but a *serious* exchange of talents & purposes—joyful bargain happy job for me.

The fact that after all this time I've never had a body for a lover in intimate capacity, never having one who I loved as a bodysoul who was interested in keeping me happy.*

Thus yr. job to extend & satisfy my erotic imagination, teach me emotional lovemaking kicks, in this sense, what I *need* most, is a love teacher, someone who I can follow & obey—this most excites my flesh, my masochism reversal of roles here as I cease in bed &

---

* Above notes (beginning with paragraph commencing "Meanwhile my phantasies . . .") are the substance of the vow referred to in "The Green Automobile," CP 85—A.G., August 8, 1994.

emotion to be teacher but to be pupil, dependent, subservient, obedient to yr. will in this magical neurotic process. So in this you be master in bed and I be master in book, relationship takes balance, gives everyone their kicks. That in this last paragraph I begin to give myself a hardon is sign I am giving a truth.

The most important price of introspection—if can only rid self-conscious—is what exactly do I envisage of the cock—what bed rituals—only myself screaming with love in the end. Some masochistic Fuck Me feeling. And the alternative "You like my cock don't you," with pleadings and groans, sighs, and tears of submission. This has been the main hidden motivation of my life for years and the prospect of it accomplished sensuously enacted, wow?! Changed from solitude of high school sexual standstill.

The immense satisfaction I take in this liaison with Peter as once and for all attaining a fulfillment without which life loses formal significance—no future possible till that's done. That life should at last begin; after all these years.

Peter I feel as if I'm in heaven. If this works out I could end notebooks here and go on to impersonal existence.

I am on the verge of a great discovery. And the poems to write.

\* \* \*

Still to write—a sketch of eternal scene at Foster's corner.

\* \* \*

[Another draft of "Malest Cornifici Tuo Catullo," CP 123:]

... It's hard to $\left\{\begin{array}{l}\text{live on earth} \\ \text{eat shit,}\end{array}\right\}$ without having visions ...

\* \* \*

Jan. 5, 10–11 o'clock—Foster's—Sitting at tea, Peter enters alone, comes to my table, we talk for an hour—He begun to dislike Robert. Story of his last T—"stupidity" & violent rejection of Robt. He talks to no one at school I tell him story of Columbia. "Sixty girls turn heads when he walks by"—I say. I tell him I'm

keeping journal—he can't think or write about scene situation he
says. Earlier talk about my relation to Sheila—how she was good
for me. Robert enters, sits at other table. I depart. I asked Peter
about apartment—"Do you still buy apt project?"—"A little
later on."*

owed Peter—
      $10
        5
       45
      +5
    ̄ ̄ ̄ ̄
     $65
    +30 work
    ̄ ̄ ̄ ̄
     $95

\* \* \*

## Sat.

Rereading these notes (after dream of shit, conversations
with Sheila & Peter), knowing that they will be read—certainly a
mistake to allow anyone to read journal, since no matter how
honest I am dishonest and looking thru another's eyes I see the
dishonesty, rereading thru Peter's eyes as he will I see how little I
appear to see of him, his sensitivities, his thoughts, his own thinks
& awareness of self scene—hardly attempted to go into this
except purely in relation to myself—he'll be offended with me
seeing the self-hood of the notes—can only plead they are par-
tial, let us say 1/100th of the actual thoughts—have thought thru
his mind at length—know my awareness is narrow, need another
to know that—well this is special pleading. Mistake is self-
consciousness—I use these for drawing poems from, not for
exhibiting self to self. I reveal self to self accidentally, primarily I
should draw physical descriptions. Can't write everything for lack
of time-energy (which Jack has). Never here possibly reach out-
side of myself but only concern with immediate illusions. For that

---

\* We'd planned to look for an apartment & move in together.
—A.G., October 5, 1982

reason only person I showed journals to was Kerouac, who understood & forgave me & whose word of annoyance was word of love, he knew the illusions.

\* \* \*

Here's account of Fri. eve: Peter in at evening early, got groceries had supper, we talked, no anxiety on either side, I told him I told Robt. & Sheila we wd not live together—after that both of us started on Kafka Reflections on Sin & Hope #45—"The more horses you harness to the job, the faster the thing goes—that is to say, not tearing the block out of its base, which is impossible, but tearing the straps to shreds, and as a result the weightless merry journey." Discussion of the nature of the block—mine being sanctity, his 95% of thought in neurasthenic preoccupation with meaning so unable to read beyond 2nd word of Bible—on to discussion of Illumination and his surprising inevitable description of his own illuminative nature—moments of walks, an example of trees bowing in acceptance of the moment, unmistakable signs of his natural vision—I was surprised—makes understanding between us now inevitable, according to nature. He left & returned—I said "please"—after midnight, we slept together, chaste lovemaking no come, wrapped round each other, lay in bed half the morning and talked naked caressing & looking out the window. Then up to Chinatown for meal, more conversation about cocks souls, beginning an exchange. Perhaps we *will* be happy together. I'm ready.

Went to office & picked up Bill's letters—ms. first chapter of Tangiers novel.*

\* \* \*

From Kafka's *Letter to Father*—Reasons for not marrying—problem of his children, sins of fathers visited on sons, etc.—"All the same I must say that I should find such a mute, glum, dry, doomed son unbearable. I dare say, if there were no other possibility, I should flee from him, emigrate. . . ."

---

* William S. Burroughs' *Naked Lunch.*

* * *

I wonder what Peter feels—I don't know, he never expresses it, though there is a lot of sex and affection in his body. I don't know how to act. His affections seem stable but his attitudes transient. Cannot ask him yet, too early, though I am afraid of hearing something less moving than what I feel. If there's any real love it will come of itself. I imagine now it is animal affection satisfaction. I'm beginning to feel absolute lovethrob heartpangs toward a being which as yet I don't fully perceive, it's still mysterious.

This being a love journal. Handwriting with black ink bad. Still sick, Sat. nite, slight headache, ache in left side of face, stomach upset (Chink food). Have lain in bed 1½ weeks so far, no relief. Ambiguity of Peter. I thought the cold & strain-dull ache above eyes [was caused by] repression of tears of relief, joy disappointment, relief & joy. Wish for a moment between us when I could weep unguardedly the relief. Can't yet, he won't like me that way now.

I am ready. Prayers the last few nights.

The terror of the day or week when he will begin to draw away, the struggle to alter love—and escape suffering absolutely necessary—*no more suffering.* I am ready.

Ready for love and ready not to suffer. ("Love that rarest of realities.")

Pain the last night still lying with Peter all night, pain *as if* too much joy, unaccustomed excess of pleasure on the verge of spiritual ecstasy not yet passing into it, so a tension of unrelieved feelings, anxiety as to whether it will last, a transient week, a transient night (He said, "We have time")—but so much imagination beforehand being bodiless & perfect can only surpass physical reality—except for thrills Peter adds out of his own creative mind—no the imperfection of life's not it, it's the slow impossible struggle to realize highest ecstasies of the imagination made flesh—I think in terms of ecstasies yet in time maybe we find something outside us (in flesh) higher or more permanent than imagination? But sublimity originates in the fantastic, (reality begins in dreams) (reality begins with a dream)—yet Peter surpassed fantasy when he offered to teach me the body. And came to stay over—I'd given up hope. What weirdness.

A truth—we both doubt each other—And yet I don't doubt

he's sublime enough not to doubt me—on that basis we both can make each other. I don't doubt I'm sublime enough not to doubt him. Well enough of this.

\* \* \*

## Sat. Nite

Woke at 9 and Peter said he'd be back after school studies, he's not here yet, light in his room,\* I hesitated braving the hostilities of the Wentley, but went up anyway, wanted to see him, trusted him, hoped he wanted to see me, would be pleased at my visiting him—he showed gladness when I came in, shook my hand, bowed me in, formally, we talked about his writing & read a few poems by Williams & Eliot to exemplify Imagism, fitting in with his native talent of Lucienesque "tortured introspection" notes—he withdrew as I talked, I saw change, as I became more euphoric and definite he become more ashamed—tentative—must do all talking now softly with reassurances in bed?—only intimate place for trust. Project: For me to make complete soul confession risking all for him to see how he is not worthless, it is a humility, but it doesn't really matter, mean anything except I *feel* worthless, not I am worthless, 's but a stage of the soul, good for soul, not to shame self, but glory in nakedness of humility, besides which he is not really worthless, and the thousand other lovely details of mind and love and creatitude that are really so great, including worthlessness (who cares?) and was just on verge of trying to fall on mental knees to give him my halo and beg him for his, laugh together, Dostoyevsky, Kerouac, sneaking together down some side street out of the back exit of the Wentley—when against my premonition we went to Foster's, Robert was there—we both clammed up, I froze, couldn't speak much, Peter depressed & unhappy with self, Robert I fantasized triumphant in revenge—I felt guilty causing Peter weakness when I'd rather he knew how great I know he is— we all sat at table, Peter gone for our coffee—Robert & I discussed project of painting of Peter I'd suggested—another tragic stage of action, Robt's consciousness, a new non-idealized purified by time

---

\* Orlovsky had taken a room by himself at the Hotel Wentley.

barer and bleaker & truer disillusioned sweet or maniacal portrait
of his god of Love—which he now offered to do if I paid $ for it, a
bitter gesture; I'll accept, he needs money & maybe needs to do
the painting, psychologically, and I was trapped into it, misunder-
standing his proposal of $ (I thought he originally wanted to sell
me Foster's pix), and it may be honorable to accede to his chal-
lenge, since challenge it was, and he would take it as sign of
contempt & disregard for his art if I refused, though I don't have
the $. And this last not having the dough may finally be the answer
if I think it over. Anyway I was hoping to slip Peter my key & leave &
see him later tonite another sweet night one, so few, but he left, left
me no sign—so I left, with window shade down in my room writ-
ing. Perhaps he'll call me at window, I am waiting—he perhaps
suffering. He is glad to be alone & rid of me for a while in solitude
to recover his worth. Sick of me seeing me with Robert, thinking of
me as Robert after the weakness of his voice as we walked toward
Foster's. It is perversely exciting to see him weak and feel
dominance—temptation for me to avoid the same weak voice, in
myself. Only safety with him lies clearly in our both having strength
to give and take freely out of choice and love when we are in
*balance,* spiritual health.

Is our relationship dependent on one or the other being
unbalanced—. Or do we like each other enough personally to
make it in talk and bed, whatever the differences of information or
inhibition? Natural balance between us as sexual lovers and as
vision-interested godsouls is already in cards.

What a sweet night we had last night and we were such equal
angels.

I am alone tonight. I wish he knew. Patience. Is he alone
tonight, lonely? Patience Peter, patience Allen. I am beginning to
have faith to wish he knew what I was thinking & wish I knew what
he's thinking now—almost to point where we are perhaps on
verge of beginning to think alike, complementarily. I am willing
to let myself get swept up & lost in the infatuate theories of
youthtime platonic love again—as his reference to Shelley's love
in letter Robt. showed. But all this love talk will kill everything. I
must shut up.

Fear—that tonight will begin a reversal of everything into
the direction of solitude & chaos. I wish he would reassure, prom-

ise, tell me—but can't ask until we are so close it is no longer
necessary for me to fear returning to the void alone. Can't *ask* for
love until it's no longer necessary. Can only give and be patient
and pray. Does he know I'm trying to do this? Is he interested if I
am? And if he is not, how to have strength to give and not be
tormented continually by cravings till I turn masochistic and mad
and abase myself before him & be rejected—only again here I pass
with self pity & must be a Buddhist patiently accepting life's offer-
ings as they appear and gladly bidding adios as they disappear into
the Polk Gulch of the world.

"Sudden decision to trust Peter"—get up & go to him now.

Peter Orlovsky taken in front of giant visage portrait
of himself by La Vigne. Probably Hotel Wentley.
Photo: Allen Ginsberg

## Sunday Morn

I left note—"I want to be with you"—he not home, his lite not on, I went to sleep after reading an hour, Kafka.

Woke up this morning in San Francisco in the rain a long way from home—a long way thru time—on hellish Sutter & Polk city corner—neons in the day, I was sick, outside my raindropped window, gray sky, huge USED CARS written on buildingside (hovering like a ship in rain) ahead, sound of car tires rising behind me thru window. Nostalgia—foreign city, my parents, life my solitariness—Who can I call on here?—afraid to go across street to see Peter, and Neal is a blank far away down in San Jose. (Tho perhaps he is just up the block.)

Dreamt: I was arrested for crossing street wrong, or vagrancy, taken down to waterfront line up station, waited around powerless, we were led loosely all over, I suddenly realize after long time I shd. call lawyer before I am booked or formally arrested, go to phone, stepping out of group being taken to booking H.Q., and lose them, then see I am free, can disappear, start to do so, need to get down a fire escape stairway on one side perpendicular ladder from grill platforms in police station, on the other are ropes—fire escape bars—V shaped, two sides— what's plumber's name for that kind of bar?—detective recognizes me, I still go thru with it, he's explaining to someone else (a fat boy, I think T. S. Eliot) who chooses hard way sliding down bar, dirtying & perhaps burning hand—Then I recognize Paul R—— with the detective, he's home visiting, we talk, they're reclining on bench, the cop is his uncle, has him grasped with hand under the ass by crotch, palm flat, from behind, Paul leaning back, tanned, smiling as ever—I don't remember passing of eyes or words directly between us—he shows me pictures—of his brother's marriage—of several people in a loft singing, around them the white windows of the choir loft—windows which form the loft walls, inscribed with Hebrew characters

It is at any rate a marriage, his or brother's or mutual friend—I am by the way impressed by the magical cabalistic black on white pure Matisse-like beauty in fact unexpected splendor of the synagogue loft as seen from that angle—

Woke wondering what happened to Allen—how Paul's life

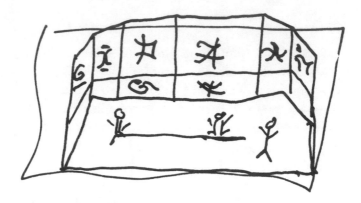

and mine are different, he now a doctor in Paterson with his thin wife—and a baby?—Though I've had more loves than he and travel—how empty my life—Though since waking despite nostalgia I see for first time the inevitability and O.K. my own—I've only missed remaining on childhood streets familiar there, grown up and married—for I had read K.'s journals last night—it's raining now, this dream of Paul, and I woke. It's my poem.

Failure—my relationship with Peter so flimsy, no trust—we were afraid to be together last night, we were not together for whatever hellish Polk-Sutter Reason—my ability to be calm, to bounce in conversation with him, not to press, crave, demand—or would serious need such as this morning's draw him nearer? But the fact of its temporary nature, he's going sooner or later, to women, school, other life, I go on in same road away from home— yet do find temporary peace in him—while Paul R—— wakes in bed at home, his mortal clock set to manly love for the rest of his days.

I want to cross street to Peter this rainy morning—where has he disappeared to?—Was he ever near me? Even in the long nite together? Will my knock on his door be met by absent glance? He wavers and at heart's absent except for moments. "Good morning. Do you want to be alone?" I'd have to ask.

Dream the other night—With Sheila at her parents'— they're Italian I don't speak Italian, they put us up in Mexico concrete courtyard tenement full of laundry they occupy we're visiting, they give us niche to sleep in—Sheila starts later pushing things in my anus, I realize it's shit from the cesspool, I reach back and stick hand up golden empty hole & begin pulling it out in annoyance—her mother's redbrick, her father's brown, I begin spitting it up out of my throat & mouth, rolling it off my tongue into the pool, taste it, its brownshit taste—"Put anything up my ass you want," I say, laughing, "just don't shove shit up it"—

## Important Dream

—Then we are on boat riding past lites of George's Point or Bklyn and I have to uncap triangle pin from chain around stanchion to let ship leave to gain my free passage alone, I do it, fumbling, not sure it's done right, it isn't—the concrete block barge dock is pulled out (me in it) like elastic band to hit ship— but doesn't hit ship nor do I move so I guess I done it right— Brooklyn lites across waters, we are going to Europe together, she and I.

—This dream the night I slept with her here (Fern Hotel Rm. 14 overlooking Sutter Polk cor.) after Peter seemed to have regretted project of apt. together—and I dwelt on what it wd be like to try again on rebound with Sheila.

What's missing in these pages is exhaustive faithful reproduction of *scene* and characters and speeches—the psychological introspective ramblings are already burdensome and in short time will seem absurd and tiresome.

* * *

## Sunday Nite

Spent afternoon at office, Al Hinkle & Peter over room earlier, Peter to breakfast, Hinkle entered, I gave him "news from N.Y.C.," we talked about Sheila. Peter left, I was to see him at 6— and so arrived there—a few minutes beforehand, he preparing to leave, I stood in doorway watching silently, he surprised to see me so, we went, in same rain as morning, ate at Mex. rest. then a pizza. He suggested Blum's for malted and I simpered, "To Blum's on a date," which he shook his head at—then he went home, I asked him if he wanted to come over for the night, he laughed, I felt a change come already—I can hardly keep track—but remember I have been at his door now for 2 days, a bad thing, he wants to be alone.

He's tired of me—what is he thinking? Now must wait. Next move his.

Same misery, I too unstable to give and take, need steady

love-growth upward, he is very changeable, I pick up sensations of differences in him day to day unspoken—reveal no pattern to me except inevitable sense of transience.

When saw him at noon, he'd been in North Beach all last night, didn't find my note, was asleep when I came—met Cosmo & sat there—I look out, his light's not on, he's out again elsewhere—developing a plot elsewhere—which he didn't speak of, that perhaps the reason for my uneasy sensation, mystery of his purposes, in any case a restless man, going otherwhere, where he's presently at.

Lying in dark turning over in my mind ways to escape this love fever by alterations of my attitude—play it straight with Peter, strictly spontaneous game, no attachment

—sudden jump in relief to desire to be rid of him and Robert, and Sheila, go into hiding

—Woops, Neal enters wants to borrow $, I give him $5 to break, Natalie & Bob waiting in Foster's—

go into hiding—

Suddenly in my room an organ sound, penetrating the whole neighborhood, "Let my people go," exit of the spirit from the Body—organsound invading the

—Neal returns gives me 1.27 his change, rubs my head, "Next time I'll spend more time with you"—sweet gesture I sit here filled with self-pity—he sees, or there is something soft about me—I sensed it, this morning's solitude of the furnished room still in the air

invading the neighborhood with its organ echo of eternal beckoning thru the shades of space "In exitu aegipto Israel," sinister in Polk Gulch neon rain—

As I would go escape the shades of space, my mind turning momentarily to Time's inevitable negation of lust and activity—

The poem being: an outline of temporal hassles and one's selfhood, an imaginative flight from selfhood hassle to Nothingness, and (in the structure) a return to the selfhood to work it out by revising one's picture of self and problem. But what possibility, revision after revision, of reaching the terminus of selfhood—

They are leaving Foster's for a ride to Nemmie, Natalie's friend, Neal running back to R.R. & wd. return Mon nite or Tues nite to give me my four bucks.

I fantasized writing Peter a note such as his letter to

Robert—"I thought when we first met we wanted the same thing from each other but now I see I was mistaken and there is little you need of me so the unbalance will cause me misery to continue to court you and I am incapable of remaining aloof while my heart is at your feet so must go and hide myself from all that's happened. I think this is like all that will happen to me if I seek love as I am and see no way of change except escape from involvement such as this into a limited circle of thought which will be pure and if I can make it so will deliver me to another realm of mystical hope."

But these notes, written with Peter as reader in mind—which corrupts them—are not the whole story—the anger that is in me—and I can't even escape in notebooks.

Sun nite—End of the week, last touches of sickness, last hot milk, woke at midnight, his lights are on across the street, rain, rain, neons—Peter doesn't care much as I care—that must be clear—if he don't come down and yell at my window in the rain he has no notion of my heart toward his—I wish he had—I must see that clear, the mystery in the bleak objectivity of midnight wake-up for hot milk is what he *does* want, what he does feel—I feel so removed, all this secret madness scrawled now thru 20 pages to the end of the weird loveweek. Hopeless. Blank. Prayer.

I ought to move next week begin independent life, not hang around here to be near him & watch windows like this, running into horror of Robert over and over, all lacerations—Peter will come if he wants, either way, I can't hang on like this, too night-marish. Not afraid to face life alone—since I am alone.

A glass of cold water. To come to some sweet hard truth. Fiametta—story of lack of relation between Fiametta's preoccupation and her lover's actual conduct—whose fault? Mad Fiametta or her indifferent cocksman?

"Self pity is bad, friend," said she Marianne Moore to me."* Be sure henceforth no writing and no heartthrobs stem from that.

And why shd. I be so wrought up over that furry brown animal, that ill formed inarticulate kid? But I have lowered myself beneath him and ask him to step back & forth on my carpetsoul on his way in and out of the mystical dead self-pity temple I've made of myself.

---

* In letter re *Empty Mirror.* —A.G., June 26, 1991

Henceforth:
NO
SELF-
PITY!!

(in childish big print)

Next pages should be <u>clean</u>.

No writing and no heartthrob stem from that.

And why shd. I be so wrought up over that furry brown animal, that ill formed inarticulate kid? But I have lowered myself beneath him and ask him to step back & forth on my carpetsoul on his way in and out of the mystical dead self-pity temple I've made of myself.

Henceforth:

NO

SELF-

PITY"!!

(in childish big print)

Next pages should be clean.

# Jan. 10

Mon morn—waking up—a dream—gray sky, a day as in child-
hood, cold in room, having to go to school, grind, ruminations—
the picture of S.F. Columbus Exposition Roman temple 1898–1902
on my wall, furnished room hangover—I'd left it up for a moment
(like Himalays in N.Y.C. last) when I'd look at it and see something
strange and I just did, like the organ sound yesterday the temple
looks like a Spenglerian Greek-Roman old dead world's uncon-
scious picture structure of Divinity, God, the Great Being—here in
the photo it's the luminous rounded massive weight, braincase, the
white pillars of the universe capped by a white dome, a ceiling
where the mind is, from where I lie in bed can't distinguish clearly
the pillars only the general looming-up rounded-at-top form—
furthermore reflected, tho half hid in sycamores, doubled in the
lake below, the illusion, as to which is the immaterial archetype,
which the world. . . .

At work—My counsel seems clear this morning in the
office—gain vigor thru activity let Peter be attracted to that
rather than me-self Allen. Inactivity self pity. I have been ill this
week.

Mon eve—While walking on Market Street realized I was
beginning actually to concretize my struggle with myself for the
first time (walking across Market Street having bought a 3-way plug
on the way to the stationer's) this sickly brooding over love &
wanting to be loved—at last in my life actively taking a stand
against my own feelings—a paradise lost—

His light is on across the street. My shade is down. The signal.
He doesn't recognize the moment.

—a stand against my own feelings—to the extent that a new
life-conception dawned on me to be explored—the fact that I have
held on to self pity so long as a primary source of emotion in love, I
hardly know what would replace it in my feelings if it went—feared
that I'd fall into an objective painful tedium.

Project, it occurred to me, to extirpate self pity replacing it
with objective judgment, or objective (non-attached) giving—
elimination of self.

It seems my self pity (as I see it in this situation with Peter) is
tied up with my love emotions (masochistic anal eroticism and its
reverse)—

Self pity feelings so tied up with love feelings that when I try to get rid of the first I wonder how you begin to approach another person on the second—and what is love?—Self pity so bound up with the sense of Allen who loves Peter, and so gratified when Peter seems to love Allen—how can Allen *otherwise* love Peter—When I thrill and gaze in his eyes (after all the *final* sensation, lovemaking acceptance together) is that self pity gratified? But when the gaze is withdrawn I feel tearful in-sorrow incomprehension, & self pity begins to work—"How can he not gaze at me when my eyes are yearning toward him?" or "How can he see my window and stay up there behind his shades?" Self pity is most apparent to me when I feel slighted or rejected. (It is perhaps not in question when I feel accepted. That may be explored another time—at the moment I feel rejected.) And must I go back further and examine the validity of my feelings of acceptance and rejection? Hell this is work for analysis—at Langley Porter Hospital, the time seems to be ripe. "I am ready."

Sense of relief despite imprecision, that I have made a major discovery in self relating to what I've been warned of before and never picked up on and accepted. Perhaps because the acceptance now as painful as continuing the misjudgment.

When will I seek pain of knowledge? As Lucien has done with his "tortured introspective" genius, of yesteryear? Peter has perhaps the talent, which causes his blankness toward me.

\* \* \*

Down to Foster's at 8 o'clock—Peter's light out, I thought, since he can't come here nor I there, meet there perhaps, but not Peter. Sat & drank tea using up tomorrow's carfare, read Kafka, and then later fairy I recognize from Wentley came in, we nodded, I motioned him to table, he went to other to join friend (I hadn't previous noticed)—and he said to me, to acknowledge the recognition, "How are you Neal?" in loud voice; I said, fine—he suddenly shuddered, "I mean Allen, not Neal." I nodded with smile & turned my head down to book, embarrassed.

\* \* \*

Reread all before to Jan 1, and went thru crossing out repetition & unnecessary words and irrelevant theorizing, make it more speedy, a little less closed in. Has structure. First, self deceptions, then inability to grasp Peter's attitude, inability to see my own weakness, slow sight of that with clarification of sexual needs. Can't see whole thing yet.

Going up to Peter to borrow 26¢. Robert yesterday came by my room at night, knocked, I said come in, he did, wildly looked around for Peter, surprised he not there, wanted to borrow $1.00—left message thus—I said "I don't think I'll see him tonight."

\* \* \*

The proof—I felt alive, had written to father enclosing (postdated) check, took care of month old business—bounded into Peter's room, received his handclasp, we laughed, I felt my own vigor, saw its effect, he was more open, we went down for tea. He has a cold beginning, now Robert joined us—dyed hair red—looks better—we were almost natural at the table—some constraint, discussing the painting I am to buy (of Peter naked)—$40 down on Friday, I left first.

Tues.—woke this morning back to normal, forgetting dreams, euphoria gone, but no depression, off to work, no time.

\* \* \*

## Thursday Jan. 13, 1955

Not having written anything for 2 days—for some reason started out with idea of noting every movement of the heart, each time I saw Peter, what happened on each occasion, at least mentioning it for memory—can I remember accurately sequence since Tuesday's note—Tuesday night sat with Robert in Foster's, tea, in came Peter, I suggested cooking supper together, went out and got my can peas & potato powder, returned and we three (after Robt. sd. am I invited?) walked to grocer & bakery up

Polk—returned & all sat in different corners Robert's room, mostly silent—Robt. & I discussed his picture, I still carrying on as if I were going to come up with 150—afraid to back down?— this deception—and then after supper (hamburg, peas, pot. little plates) each eating in different corner of room, Sheila came in with Michael her son, and sat and talked desultory, I trying to be lively, Sheila later going over bending over Robt. at desk—Peter left, I left soon, feeling 1) See Peter 2) Abandon Sheila 3) Give Robert chance to be alone with her—and headed to staircase (great grim brown center old fashioned Pierre ambiguous hotel staircase as in S.F.) wavering to go up to Peter's room or not, Robert speeds out of door going? to the landlady, with eye on me, I backtrack to go downstairs, but his door now open, I go back have a moment's talk with Sheila (she explains, intelligence, curious paper tacked on Bob's white room pure walls left over from smallboned sickly looking nice artist Ernie who lived there before monkish intense lone hairless). Paper with sign—

—the mystery of the relationships—she figures out (memory of previous conversation) 182 as Al Hinkle's weight, 91 as hers, A & P = A + P Allen + Peter (and [&] = +) and below, later, Peter interprets this as integers from Natalie's dream (what dream?)— Robert returns to room—he's always glowering now—his hair, newly red, he turns white under his flesh when glowering—I went up to Peter's room—(Sheila and I laughing at the suspicions & comedy, like a Marx bros picture but I'm too tired, but I laughed for her)—we talked about? but what night was this?

Then Peter came back—Sheila leaving—I thought perhaps thrown out—yelled at?—I decided to go down & see her home or take care, was she upset, suddenly leaving, I leave Peter, meet her & Robt. going down together, we all descend (I wanting to go back up really) in silence, and I leave for home, he to take her to bus, we part on corner, Sheila saying goodnight. Peter (as per agreement?) comes by. We go to North Beach, meet Cosmo in my old paper-littered room at Monkey Block—Cosmo's phrase of "immediate karma shot"—his stolen clarinet stolen from him in a week—We walk with him to The Place, there's Robt. Duncan who eyes me we eye & talk warmly—Peter & I make date to see his play* next Thursday—Peter & I talk beginning then, walk home, after 3 beers or 2—slightly high, I telling him now, explaining, we talk about "bounce" his word, coincidence after these journal notes, more discussion of visions, Kafka, Peter, conversation continues walking up Sutter Hill, about my feeling superficial feeding him information sophistication; walking down Sutter Hill about his soul, holy maybe, I had thoughts it was, then to home, confessions of mine— self-pity on my mind, after decisions, and retrospections, I finally come out and say what I feel now about Robert, don't want to see him, don't like him or to be with him. I accusing Peter of being spiteful to Robert, echoing what Sheila said. Finally how Robert was ruining Peter for me, no boy now, also said should make girls, gave straight thought there, said it once for all, at least that off my conscience, all these superficial guilts, and then—sweet moments, I saw he was going to leave, in my haste not to hold him showed him out, abrupt, actually unhappy, but after confusion at door—every time he opens up there's a moment of bumbling both of us hitting on chairs, turning around helplessly, meaningless jokes—preparing, winking, realizing—Once before up in his room (before he came over here?). Once that nite—so he returned, sat on bed—I had told how Neal rubbed back of my head, Peter caught it, rubbed my head, arm on my knee, said he couldn't stay, closeness not yet, thru more experience, wall of last

---

* Robert Duncan's *Faust Foutu* was presented at the Six Gallery, with the author taking the title role. See A.G.'s comment, p. 105.

weeks, I said I was afraid he'd go away, he said he would not, I was happy—"I can wait happily"—now happy-trance, love-calmed, he left, turned in sleep in pleasure. (and made window signals sign language)

Next night? When was it? Saw Peter in his room, late, he came over—oh DuPeru here, Sheila here, Natalie—I explained about picture to Sheila—getting tight on $—letter from Burroughs also asking for $—Sheila annoyed at me (actually all along building up fear of downstairs Chinese sign language neighbors knocking for noise)—Saw her to bus & ate off her, she gave me $1.00—made lunch date, see her but wd. rather not—indifferent I feel blank after excitement with her, I led her astray, getting a $75 Apt together—afraid she see how vicious I am—and today (receiving letter from Langley Porter Hospital) thought—had not realized before—how much production I put on with her, deceiving into love thinking I really felt energy for her—when only wanted fuck for my own sake, now she's used, worse, she lets self be used unconsciously by me to kill off Robert—Robert's paranoia real—back anyway to Peter's room late, leaving DuPeru here, no—we got to eat, buy can of fish, return to DuPeru—leave him (I sign him anyway—eat in Peter's room, late 1:30—Robert knocks, sees me, blanches again—he looks at those moments white—as also must remember seeing him with Peter recently in Foster's undersea light inside pure Times Sq. Pokerino soul illumination, I see his face, lined as Peter said—saw what Peter signified—soul emerged on Robert's face, in pathos, suffer twisted soul in toothless red skin thin face wide forehead, eyes hurt, skin angry, conscious, blanched, to speak, sometimes dropping words like grapes, aware, mouthing loathing in self, saw him a flash moment he was truly alive, few are, deep emotional sensations, my enemy. Me strange. Thus he whitened doubletook wrath at door, came for Dexedrine, I have some, I went out with him, down to my alley, upstair, silent, he following—I decide—nothing to speak, will not extend self, let him—waiting for me & Peter to show signs of bondage before rejecting him?—I look at him in hall (in dark) turn to look—open room

—Peter DuPeru, kneeling by my bed in the light, white

furniture room, round little heater turned on him, two books, Hopkins & Zukofsky's *A Test of Poetry* turned open on the bed, eyes closed? Down on knees I glimpse flesh bare midriff, his belt off, loose, his pants open, he—I turned to Robert—can you wait outside the door a moment (Peter remains kneeling, nervous side sly glance as usual, continues reading)—I speed in the room—in W. C. Fields exasperated voice low stage whisper— "Pull up yer pants hurry I got company"—toward the Chinese box of drugs, Dexedrine—Peter remains kneeling, I am so speedy, grabbed bottle avert eyes, return to door, Robert standing there (not as before to be hid when he came with Peter a week ago to give me $5 in the shadow away from door not to see, but now in front of door confused, tentative)—what does my keeping him out mean, he cranes his neck when I open door, bring bottle, half close it behind me—my god Peter's still kneeling there all this time calm as daisy—Robert glimpses Peter DuPeru—I shake out pills—just one—Robt. thumbs in pocket—no change "I forgot my money, left it in room, how much—pay you for these"—I smile, feeling strange, at him, gleam in eye—"No need" small mock lordly gesture, he murmurs, goes away, I re-enter room— replace pillbottle, say I'll be right back in he's not changed, only his belt is tighter, fly is buttoned—I am confused—was I mistaken? Could I have been? It seemed so clear, that flash of backbone?—I wash hands, laugh, prance around room, confess, ask him—he digs the humor of it, no he wasn't, loosed his belt, getting heat—probably not even unbuttoned, I am amazed. He hangs on and talks while I go to bed—finally leaves—about 2:00—told me about Green Shelf, and Cosmo and his mixup at court, analyst (going to private Doc & Mt. Zion Hospital at once, confusing both, self) tells me to look up beautiful youth poet named Barker around—I tell him I'm too busy (will dig Barker)—sleep without writing, remember also Peter Orlovsky's description of his family—children born green & blue, his brothers both at once, mad, the Negro—name?—forcing him and older brother to blow & lick asshole he'd just shat from, stand under tree & be pissed on—no wonder he was angry w. Robert—No wonder—I remember my childhood vision of same trauma,* will tell him. Home tonite 6 o'clock—off to Rexroth at 8—Peter's room dark.

1AM—Night, all 14 of my windowshades down in my room overlooking the neon sign. Putt-putt of a motorcycle, rumble of trucks under the green light, whine of cars horizontal far away dreamed of my love—Sat here listening thought I heard his voice at the window below—I just came home from surrealist movies & Barbecue & delivering Jack to Rexroth (Visions & Blues)† (Blues Visions) raucous voice "hey" strangled a block away. "I'll sell ye some hamburger Jack—or it might be meatball in the pan—yah I et some swet potato pie on mighty Fillmore—I want a three cent stamp—Eoo, Father!" Real car honking & hishing and rumbling and hawking up oil on the street—I'd smell petroleum if I had my nose to the curb, dog shit & gas cans in the drain. Not raining tonite as before, hi on Tangiers candy—

His window however not alight, he sleeping I suppose—the first day we have not seen each other in a week or more?—Seems like forever—Time has slowed down to focus—how happy I'll be when we're free—I wonder if there will be a change for the closer, even then—impatience, yet time goes in its own secret childlike clocklike slowness and the hands move together slow—my mind is the second hand turning around the 12 corners of time and Peter is the hand that sets the hour ringing and I wake. I'll lay for all the sweetness I can bear. How sweet the limits of sweetness? What tears, what vows, entreaties under the table, kissings in the alleys, music roaring in the halls—solid eternity in our ear, fugues, bop—

---

* See "A Poem on America," CP 64: Age ten used to frequent "the bathing pool hidden/behind the silk factory/fed by its drainage pipes" above Mill Street near the Passaic Falls downtown Paterson. Once I saw an older boy brutalizing a thin young kid turned blue from cold fear trembling in fright—the bully insisting the kid kneel down before him, both naked, backing him down a concrete walkway to the end of the dam, an unfenced spillway walled by red brick factory sides dropping thirty feet into dank rocky water. The blue boy screamed, I was confused and silent watching with others across the ten-foot waterway, erotically aroused and frightened. I visited the spillway in 1950 with W. C. Williams. —A.G., June 1, 1986

† *Visions of Cody* (then, in manuscript, *Visions of Neal*), *MacDougal Street Blues.*

I left Peter alone one nite.
Goodnight.

* * *

# Fri. Jan 14

[Revision of "Malest Cornifici Tuo Catullo," CP 123]
Night—saw Peter earlier, he going down to North Beach to see if he could make out—I advise it myself but wanting to be close feel bad.

I thought, going to library, he'll (ought) find a girl, have an affair—Can't be two affairs of depth—I'm confusing, want to see him O.K. but still crave him—and I guess he must not have resolved or conceived the impossibility of a real closeness—I'm a burden to him—with me—unless he really wants me, I don't know—think not, basically. I'm a hassle, since his nature will give its real sympathies to a girl, I'll be lacklove unhappy. Well-a-day!
[Notes for "Song," CP 111–12:]


                —must rest in the arms of love
                                at last
            must rest
                    in the arms of love—


And, gave Robt $40 & terminated $150 bargain, can't afford, he gave no trouble we almost liked each other a flash.

Sheila here and gone early too, no role, no interest.

Peter's window dark.
Sequence to inscribe
Saturday: at 3 to see Peter—Chinese downtown, return for ticket, walk & drink Howard & 3rd, meet Robt, return drunk, meet with Neal & Natalie, sleeping, Robert's knocking, Sun morning, shopping, conversation w. Robert, painting me, last look at 1403 Gough Street, late conversation with Peter, sit for Robt.

* * *

—take his cock inside my mouth

* * *

## Tues. Jan. 18

No writing—sequence—Mon. return from work, Robert's room supper (clam chowder) & further conversation, Robert reconciled, Sheila, Natalie arrive we drink Bourbon, Robert tries paintings of me, I go up to see Peter, invite him to sit for Robert, and finally

hair plastered & w. smile he enters the slightly festive drink atmosphere, tickles Sheila & Robert (the painting of shoes on wall), they embrace under shoes at end of couch, Sheila & I playing, reconciliations, Sheila's anger at Peter, Robert drawing,

Tuesday, return from work, another sitting for watercolor— then down in Foster's Bob made a series of fine drawings—His Nibbs (as Alex comments) Peter ill, goes up to room early tho in good mood. The constructions of Foster's (a grand painting) idea flowering finally, everyone caught on—I secretly believing it was my idea naturally—schizoid belief in Ginsberg—Robert now his Nibbs, Peter worried about his own solidity?—Sheila now nostalgizing after me, Natalie getting shrewd axe toward Neal (w. Sheila's counsel—Sheila suspects all men) me alone in room again, waiting communion with Peter his shades drawn, my signal on,* tho expecting Sheila—"Wish I were Peter," she said—Oh! and if I wished I were Neal?

Yellow paper office note on apathy.

Long weekend letter to Kerouac on "X"—mystic element. To write Bill yet.

---

* A drawn shade? —A.G., May 30, 1986

## Wed. Nite

after office, supper & sitting for La Vigne, magical intelligence in watercolor portrait, he approaching the end, drawing & painting much, all fine, first of Neal, Sheila down, me down, first Cosmo, Foster's drawings still in fire.

Peter retired, ill, all day, as yesterday, La Vigne bothered, he hasn't come to sit for painting. I go up finally to see him, he quiet, still, I realize open, sit on bed, hold him, be still, we talk, he makes me comfortable, close on bed, we smiling talking, but I worried about Robt—go down for T & lemon, stupidly (guilty) explain situation to Robt rather than deceive, later suspecting that I said too much about Peter not wanting him wanting me, Robert depressed, comes up with me, I give up, retire finally leave them together, tipping Peter off about window. I wait he not come, now both his shades drawn. He making it now with Robt? I thought he wanted to see me, we understood each other realistically finally, I understood his conflict about Robt—but security of this understanding always fades, leaving me struck by Cupid's bow in middle liver.

Read thru Anacreon tonite first time

* * *

## Thurs. Nite Jan. 20?

Dissatisfaction, hatred of Robert, Peter too questionable—sitting for portraits with Robert—Natalie & I bop—Robert angry at violation—"A studio is a place of contemplation and study"—and Sheila in & out of my bed recently—don't trust me—and went to see Robert Duncan's play, he took off his shirt declaiming "This is my body" before the audience—Rexroth said to me "You're nervous"—and lethargy-ennui of seeing Robert La Vigne too—finally close to tears a few times, irritations, boredom, impatience, dismay—sitting in Foster's Sheila hyper, "I dig you the most—only man around," Natalie cool, intelligent, warm—Neal in and out half the time I miss him, our conversation: he saw Robert's drawings, appreciated them, the lines, and said he felt out of touch with all this creative kick—I can't write it out , and

and and

Robert La Vigne in front of one portion of
his *Foster's Cafeteria*, 1958. Photo: Ken
McLaughlin (*San Francisco Chronicle*)

Peter after I left table Foster's came to my room—at last, first
time—his light now (Fri nite) is out—had (Thurs) left his shade
down—saw mine down, called at my window, I put on pants,
barefoot, went down—he called me outside & pointed to building
"When I came up alley I had feeling white square building was
bulging & falling down this way          —I nodded

hardly appreciating verbally, and the anguish & tears I felt at
Foster's table were gone, and I felt nothing, no relief at all, as I'd
fantasized in bed I'd cry if he came—yet when he did I had no
feeling—happiness yes but not ecstasy—more relief than
happiness—as if when he comes reality returns—but soon re-

placed by the mystery of his presence—why come? answer to my weakness? I asked him, several times, to lie down, put head in his lap when he sat, we read Anacreon—He saw the spirit & clarity— but then he asked its relation to imagism (which I'd expounded a week ago)—surprised me—I half-related them—artificial mental conversation, I wanted heart to heart—lay in his lap, no heart there, kissed & touched hi, cold—he was, I was—he touches me, to soothe me not feel me—absent—he lay down at my bidding I felt better. We talked of his soul—I joked he was mysterious, what did he thinkfeel—what does he feel toward me?—so I reentered this worry openly asked him, asked him if I was burdensome as Robert—bad approach Ginsberg you know it but will you get lost?—in fact expressed hatred impatience with Robert—

(Fri—I feel as if I cd. kill Robert now) If he were gone though would I be happy—will things change? And Peter said, things will change—ambiguously. I said I was sick depressed finally—what am I suffering from—and he answered "We are all suffering the same, Natalie, Robert, Sheila, myself, you"—He touched me gently, my thighs, cock, caressed—still absent— though I felt gentle thrills of ecstasy in my corpse—and he got up, to leave. I criticized Robert, he stayed—finally came out said I disliked Robert & felt drained of blood—he recounted an outrage I forget—all, too.

We agree perhaps (I don't even know) in being sick of Robert

Robert meanwhile leveling off & painting & drawing fine beauty.

I am writing Friday Nite—Windowshade down. 12:00 Midnight.

Tomorrow I move to Wentley to leave this cold room, too expensive—should sketch nite Foster's.

No energy for the details of Foster's sign tho the scene has potentials for spontaneous concentration. Low greek Wentley white Foster's zooming sign leaning to street with zoombar neon below and puppet paperseller below in hat with box stand, cars slowing to stop, one behind cab, another with white miniature road lines & redlite taillight, electric light upstanding near me my level and another in distance arm up wires crisscrossed bullet like front of auto stopt for paper—green light now, the cars move across Sutter toward Civic Center—Across street lower facade with bar bell curves greek style & seafood dock sign, pinpoint neon of Jewelers moving at left in lit window, & someone—No it is a machine—turning endlessly under the phospho bar bluelite on its velvet case—Fire stanchion on corner waiting for unseen fires, the whole street tinted pink asphalt—the cabs zoom by below me—in distance red series of lites on radioplane tower down the street Polkways the late deli grocer, green by the redlights' cross-street of lesser importance—Sound of low voices perhaps under me in restaurant—Crying man walks in black coat by artist Jewish fish-peddler painting store—Burning tiger eye of my little electric heater glowing at me reflected in window with my form and small glimmers of room interior sink around mirror behind my hand, a furniture halo—Cab swiftly speeding turn of corner, whoosh of tires—Snappy gesture of paperseller as he slomps paper out from underarm with one gesture and neat outstretched fingers bending it to a fold extended to customer, a pinky balanced to start dime receiving gesture—the serious bus pulling up waiting for light change, crossing & sneezing its doors backass open—white pants & black shirt moving incognito upstreet—the sign display food & prices in window, all the low aura of the plateglass.

Ah Peter you're out to escape my suffocation—
people's insides I know—
or not—this O.K. but enuf. Must do more.


## The Wentley Hotel—Sun. Nite

Out to Gerd Stern's*—Driven by Neal, Natalie—26hrs there, hi, "Boo-Bam" drums, cool nowhere—then they Neal Natalie & *Peter* came out to get me—drive back, to my room, hi, much tea, from Stern, I left all mss.† there feeling helpless to combat or talk to too cool [souls]—Peter & I out to North Beach, meet with boy Natalie suspected was FBI—intrigue, he asks me if I

---

* Stern was then in public relations, later founded USCO artists collective, active in film and mixed media presentations.

† Kerouac's *Visions of Neal [Cody]*, Cassady's "Joan Anderson Letter," and Ginsberg's *Empty Mirror*.

talked to Knute Stiles*; then walking met Keilty† who showed us Knute's painting—& Ed Woods at the Place, whom Peter didn't like—echoes of Marker & Mexico—Back home walking talking over our funny relationship, to his room, bed, cock, talk, joke.

* * *

## Feb. 3—My pen gave out

Tonite, moved, now at 1010 Montgomery St—Still waiting for Peter,‡ it's absurd. This week Sheila. Well I wonder how long he'll keep me waiting or what he'll do.

* * *

## Peter Orlovsky Takes a Nap

Books fall out of his hands weary of his penetration. Clothes refuse to hide his beautiful body any longer. The pure couch of the afternoon slides under his back. The weary radio indifferently repeats her lullaby into his charming ear. The Muses hush their shrieking. Notebooks close themselves bewildered by the angels of this thought. Poems retreat to the original book of mystery.

---

* Stiles (1923–) also ran The Place, a Grant Avenue bar frequented by poets of the midfifties San Francisco Renaissance.

† James Keilty, poet; participant in the presentation of Robert Duncan's *Faust Foutu* at The Six Gallery, January 1955.

‡ Soon Orlovsky would move in with him. Shortly thereafter, in Foster's Cafeteria late one night, the two poets would take a vow of romantic commitment to each other, in some ways similar to that taken at a rainy Oklahoma crossroads in 1947 by Ginsberg and Cassady (see "The Green Automobile," CP 85). At Foster's, Ginsberg has recalled, "we looked in each other's eyes and there was a kind of celestial cold fire that crept over us and blazed up and illuminated the entire cafeteria and made it an eternal place." (See *Gay Sunshine Interview*, ed. Allen Young [Bolinas, Cal.: Grey Fox Press, 1974], pp. 23–25.) The two would remain together, except for Peter's summer trip East to bring back his younger brother Lafcadio, until Ginsberg moved to Berkeley for graduate school in September 1955. Peter and Lafcadio remained at Montgomery Street until moving into a Turner Terrace apartment on San Francisco's Potrero Hill in February 1956.

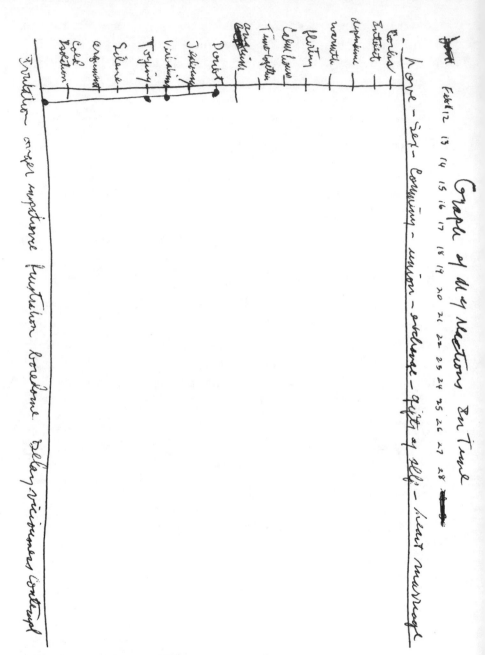

Mood chart, February 1955

Peter Orlovsky, 1010 Montgomery.
Photo: Allen Ginsberg

\* \* \*

Feb. 11, 1955—With Peter Orlovsky at 1010 Montgomery St. Chart
to keep track of moods—

## Feb. 25.

> "This love ending
> in some confusion
> already familiar
> his old conclusion" (in a dream)

He put me down! (1 week or more ago)
The heat seldom lights up my breast with pain.

Waking every morning objective calm desire to go to his bed
(in room down hall) but he will not have me do so.

P. dreamt of murdering my feelings. The same conclusion I
reached. I had been ready.

Standing on ferry returning from Oakland last Sunday. View
of the high iron gate supported in the darkness & mist of space
(Oakland Bay Bridge). Walk on Embarcadero.

Afternoon with Gene Pippin\* on Hills of Berkeley, Peter

---

\* Friend from Columbia mid-forties. —A.G., June 4, 1986

sitting on grass. Clear blue sky, view of Bay and S.F. calm University below.

Pippin & I share sympathies, tho his memory of the Columbia manslaughter is only of its enormity, not the real people he knew, or heard of.

## Dream Feb. 26? 1955

On road hiking, conversation, Eugene is there, he asks me what I been, who been laying, he suspects, has read Jack's letter. I tell him, lying.

Can't write dreams. Can't write. Can't write poetry. Can't write prose

My main worry is that I am no good poet. Too superficial.

I sit here dazed unable to write the dream too far away.

A hitchiking bench—I tell Eugene I am doing nothing—still see Sheila lie about X—Peter queerness—I go preparing for trip—then with Natalie—in the madhouse where I've stored my valuable childhood treasures—Natalie comes in with gang of girls to get one of her old clothes treasures—The caretaker an old grey sordid shoddy man & the caretakeress, he's gone his wife is there, no one's there—Natalie & her gang come in. Too much consciousness of Peter reading this—Natalie tells me "Don't tell them I was here—I mean, can I come in & you overshadow & guide me so they won't be aware I was around"—iron bedstead racks above us—in a room as at Washington Saint Elizabeth Hospital.*

I go looking in the old chests & open closet—a set of closed shelves, below them a set of open shelves stuck to poles upholding closed shelves, lower storage space covered with cloth—hanging for protection—

Bottom shelves, there are blankets & spreads—I realize I had enough stored for the apartment. I recognize my mother's old childhood chests and shelves of material, bedspreads, then I look in closet, next on left, locked, I unlock, it's got little notebooks (2 black small looseleaf) and also the big colored first journal— seems double-size this one, with mottled color—and pictures

---

* Where Ginsberg had attempted to visit Ezra Pound in 1953.

inside—speckled one I recognize, small colorful speckled page (like Mexican notebooks)—all my *old* journals—and then

Wife, sordid, small, thin, smell of Greystone* in her, takes me downstairs, creaky moat stairway to basement to see Ezra Pound—I would have asked, wanted to go, not having asked tho she takes me to Pound's bearpit cell—I go down moatlatch stair to Pound and in dream see

"Though he was armmmm he continued to practice his art with perseverance & creating many new areas of expression translated the great magnificent job of the odes of Confucius with patience and thru all shone spirit of cheerfulness despite the circumstances of his working & limited access to libraries of Europe America."

Woke up thinking of Shi Jing and Achilles Fang.[†] My prose now collected is it any kind of collection, with my letters? And to write dreams down—

\* \* \*

## Sakyamuni, Liang Kai[‡]

faltering out of cave into bushes by stream, everything (created by an intelligence) inanimate about him except (his own) intelligence (spark aware)

I've never been across the nation on foot or humble car only thru magical transport.

The angels in heaven will make it, gossiping about each other's auras, if we don't down here.

\* \* \*

A few short words of wisdom—
Change, Allen
the lesson is clear
Time & Eternity etc.

---

* One of the hospitals in which Naomi Ginsberg was confined: see, for example, *Howl* I ("Pilgrim State's Rockland's and Greystone's foetid halls") as well as *Kaddish* II.

† Harvard Sinologist who corresponded w/Pound during translation of *Odes*. —A.G., June 26, 1991

‡ See "Sakyamuni Coming Out from the Mountain," CP 90–91.

Liang K´ai, *Buddha Leaving the Mountains.* Tokyo,
Shima Eiichi Collection after *The Great Painters of
China,* Phaidon Press Ltd.

Anger at Doctor Philip Hicks for weeks. Anger at Peter. Anger at boss, Market Research Job. Depression. Speculation. Desolate loves.

Dream of yelling at the angry face "Quack"—who? "You're nothing better than a rotten quack, a stupid dentist of the mind. Peddling plastic transparent bridges. A quack! You hear me? Quack! foul sullen fool, bad face & mind."

I thought he despises me as an armored mental mocker, mass of shifting shadows for feelings, deliberate desperate abstract talk—

Projecting my evil feelings toward myself on others, having therefore feeling of injury despising them for not being "approving, supportive" in relationship, therefore unsatisfied in mind— angry. But expression of Anger barred by not realizing anger is anger at fake quack doctorseye sweet Allen.

I am a madman angry at self—2 selfs.

\* \* \*

My personal life's collapsed
    I've got nothing to boast about
    to anyone—not myself,
       nor friends,
       nor accomplishment
on machine or film or shipboard
          Treaty—
alone in San Fran—enough
I'll be my own subject matter,
   all I know . . .
I can't stand living thru the empty days
straining nerves against the robot logic of machines
in the visionary office on Montgomery or Wall.
Cold walls of Montgomery Street
         The Racks! the dreadful
Racks! with their toothpowder and
        women's Hair preparations
Category on category of perfumed commodities

> for the foul guilty bodies of
>    the stinking workers' wives.*

Only the effort to refine a hard bit of this reality—conserve a moment's intact sensation—and rescue it from chance for the heart or intelligence—goes on, as worth while.

God damn the false optimists of my generation. . . .

\* \* \*

"The rain falling like piss in hell."

\* \* \*

## The Dangerous Garden of Robert La Vigne†

> First! the Flower Inside, burst out
>    larger than life, and jacking
> itself up over our drunken heads on
>    the beanstalk of the imagination:
> then Narcissus making it with itself
>    in its blue platonic pool:
> and Butterfly, escaped into the dangerous
>    garden, watching us with nervous
> eye as he goes to it in his Lily ball:
>    he's worried, and with good reason:
> there's Young Geranium with his pastel brain
>    and droopy green nose beneath:
> and the sturdy Virgin Flower of the North
>    with his bright little balls:
> O but Natasha! with her redhead armpits in
>    her ears, and great dollop
> yellow tongue given forward to an
>    orange hairy suck herself:
> and the Breathing Flower's delicate case

---

\* Ginsberg was assigned to research sales of toiletry commodities on front counter racks of supermarket chains in sixteen cities and to correlate statistics with advertising campaigns.

† "The Dangerous Garden," which hung at The Place, was a show of drawings of imaginary flowers by Robert La Vigne.

about which nothing may
be whispered, since the slightest breath
    might disturb her balance:
and Two Wild Yellow Flowers who will
        renounce their tigerish trade
and submit to taming and domestication
        by some kind hand for only $35:
possibly lower their pride for a sensitive gardener:
        and the Cross-eyed Gaga,
with its watchface of twentyeight petals
        (two each for every hour of
Time and four extra for Apocalypse)
            motioning toward the Eternity
deep behind its two round blue eyes:
        and the Blue Flowers Trying
Not To Forget but merely succeeding
        in being very pretty:
and the Flower Knowing Itself By Moonlight,
        lifting its hands in dedication
one moment before the exquisite act—
        notice the little Peter—:
and the weak-wristed Dream Flower's
        redfaced swish, deploring th'
ugliness of his own fantastick Panicles:
        and the Daisies with inflamed
eyes waving so excited and hairy up
        the bedclothes—and him with
his big yellow egg head sniffing
        somebody's green foot—
Help! they're stealing my petals!—Take
        your stem out of my ear!
—I can't I've got a Thistle in my eye!—
        : and last the Farewell Flag,
the flower wrapped on Time's victorious
        arrow flying toward (either
the Wilde Romantics or) Robert La Vigne himself
        who planted that blossom in front
of his lone head and glorified his hand.

* * *

Neal still jumps to the same genius as used to send his flivver scattering down Bayshore out of sight along the magic hiway.

                              * * *

—But we get only Fragments. Where do they go?
—Are you taking this down? How does it go?—

                              * * *

"If all our fragments are associations write them down."
—Ginsberg, transcribed by Orlovsky
"These fragments I have shored against my ruins." —T. S. Eliot
"Those images that yet
Fresh images beget." —Yeats

                              * * *

The Tin Angel,* trumpets splashing in my eyes.

    Peter noting the characteristics of Turk Murphy—singing with his hands in fists.

    Peter: "The Egyptian square of swordsmen & dancers & wailing singers in the Court—and the Tin Angel dance band.

    "This is so Arabian looking—The only difference being it's in the kinds of noise in the cold silvery wet metal and at the piano—sounds off differently from the harp.

    "Imagine buying drinks for the crowd.

    "The Egyptians have turned Indian & the Indians have turned into Irish."

                              * * *

## The Ring (For N.C.)

             Being in your debt for love
                 Why should I not redeem
             the ring you left last September
                     at Ace Loan, on 6th Street?
             The karma gem you left in Pawn
                             —before
                 the ticket you gave me
                     runs out.

---

    * Club on S.F. Embarcadero where Turk Murphy jazz band played.
—A.G., June 24, 1991

* * *

Imagine looking back
at the mandolin cluttered window
relieved on my finger
your singular ring again
can return it to you—
                Think you almost lost it
Time past, 6 months is up—
Soul's like ring
        buried in pawn
We can redeem
        as we desire
        as we do
unhappy Neal
        half forgotten
here's your ring
        unhappy Neal
I love your
unhappy ring.
        I love you
            here's your unhappy
            soul ring

* * *

If you don't jot it down on the instant it disappears.

* * *

Weekend Natalie the Pink girl all pink—as Robt's picture—
Robert came in visiting Fri nite, so he's to stay for Supper. Sat
morn Neal & Natalie. Then Sheila with Sister, Cosmo & DuPeru
for $ for trailer to move. Then up to 755 Pine* to move my stuff [to
1010 Montgomery], with Peter O. & Murf, Sublette's friend girl, w.
huge trunk compartment car. Then Cosmo over sitting reading
paper in Peter's room. Then Neal & Natalie arrive for nites. Then
DuPeru met on street carrying clothes to live at our house for next
days. Refused. Then he left his clothes with us.

_____

* I.e., Ginsberg's belongings left at Sheila Williams' after moving out.

Peter DuPeru, Neal Cassady, Natalie Jackson above
Broadway tunnel, San Francisco. Photo: Allen
Ginsberg

—Natalie & Neal in my bed, Dinah Washington on
records—she staying over, delaying her departure to N.Y.C. on
Neal's trainticket—he gets up, dragged, weekend over, 4 speeding
tix, no $, she to N.Y. tomorrow, to leave her clothes here overnight
with her body, though I warned & objected at first but gave in and
invited her to stay anyway after taking a walk with Al Hinkle &
Sheila who also came by (Sheila to bring blankets)—& during day
making me even more leery of the sordid scene paranoia—&
Peter O in room since Sat nite in a depression—gloom—
withdrawal, so I don't speak to him except for money or
necessaries—Natalie being shunted out.

Neal rising (with his 3'd hardball new arrival rupture?) to go
get Natalie's clothes from car. They have no $ and will probably
have to get it from me by post check—? Just can't say goodbye.

How alike are Natalie & DuPeru—and the germane genuine problems of the beat & damned.

Refusing my help to her. Sheila looked well bounced back from exile in San Jose.

"All the brake fluid's been drained out of the brakes—I got no brakes."

The weight of intangible intractable situations—Natalie, Sheila, Peter—no end in sight maintaining relations as envisaged and guessed at in recent actions—only the silence speak for the lonely future.

To the Sutras then.

* * *

To say now what I might say in Death (speak after)*
Miscellaneous notes around March 10, 1955. 1010 Montgomery St.:
>   How blank I come to this
>           hypocathexis
>   with P with N with J
>       with A.G. himself

* * *

>       A lady crying in the street
>       Breaks open the curtains of grief
>       The buildings part and show
>               The small majesty of the universe
>               of human pain

* * *

## Natalie's Dream (Dragon of Destiny)

Albatross T [marijuana]—W/Neal car riding out country road, past city signs, past housing project. Knock on the door of safe apartment, the FBI. Escape, riding off into the nite with the pack of T., hopeless, restless, helpless.

---

* See *Howl*, I, third line from last (CP 131).

## Notes at Work

*I*

Were it for money? I'd take
Jobs and be taught.
or Love? Mistress is a pain.
I would take thought
          but thought's a thing in vain.


*II*

Thinking all day at the office
Who love me? No bed to feel hurt in—
                    after all these low acts on Gough St.
My money gone
          hung up on a boy
                    Too precipitate to pay attention.
Sometimes he puts on with me, his impulse
          to go thru with it.
                         good boy
(Where does he get the energy?)
          But not much heart for me—
                    or is it me, an
                    artificial tenderness
Look in the office
                    bathroom mirror
—moment of secrecy—
                    Wow! sucker.


*III*

Farewell loves!
     phantom bodies
                    and desires
fantastic physical
          images
                    Neal's naked breast
and Jack's black loins

        Chad's pale false torso,
Joe Army's guarded eyes
             and Peter's arms.


## IV

at 2:50 PM March 10 1955
    reached point in time where life was no longer
suffering but to live was a pleasure.
    Out of the office window,
        poring thru sunshine and several hours of
        spring sickness
  —nostalgia ripening into languor—
Clatter of new building construction
    in afternoon's summerlike
        eternity, a motor.
    I may get a raise
        body for love
    Summer sunshine
        white buildings outside Montgomery Street
    Work up to schedule
        poem ready to revise
  rooted summer world
        Nostalgia for Paterson
  Ice cream,
        Timeless.


## V

A day when the strangled "God" cry
lunges out of the yelling construction worker's throat
in midafternoon, appeal floating up thru the clear blue sky.


## VI

Downstairs the lady at
desk in small advt.
agency reading a book on TV commercial writing

## VII

Imagining sun upon sun evil brilliance of H Bomb whitening my face ghostly thunder in my ears, up in blue sky naked flagpoles atop the arched windows of the Bank, Corinthian supports, buttresses, columns and fortress walls walks and bridges, etruscan fretwork, Mayan corbels, up in the washed out mind of civilization architected in one mess top Greek temple skyscraper, a robot fortress gothic mass—the appearance of Holy Anger from the bournes of the holy Unconscious—we knew all along it would come, the apocalypse is here, cracked pavements, no wheat, no eat.

Sent from Asia! We sent our white brilliance there—the same god appearing all over—we realize only seeing it, the Terror's holy, partook of naked energy, new appearance of Spirit, to change the balance of Being—Creator spirit manifest out of his transhuman depth, sudden transcendent blast of power among the storms of Time.

Up there among the skyscrapers.

\* \* \*

Bloody Bayshore—"The ribbon of Death": Airdomes.

## Mar. 21

Malignant tumor in Neal's left testicle? a cosmic manifestation "we beat apart in 6 decades" (Candide)—Now, start balding, gimpy leg, & missing thumb, one ball less? Battling the radiation of time, against the stream, eaten slowly away . . . Blind heart by 35.

## Mar. 23

Saw Dick Davalos* tonite in movie *East of Eden*—gargoyle beauty in puppet heat smashing World War I training window leaning out.

---

* Richard Davalos was the second lead in *East of Eden* (1954), which starred James Dean.

". . . To eat the ashes of the Dead"
                    "The ashes?"
Ashes, ashes, dust and Ashes
                    for my Mind
Ashes, powder, dryness desert
                    for my mouth,
Death and sand oozing in my eyes


                    \* \* \*


The Balzacian appearance, going out with Sheila baldly appearing at The Place to back up her prestige in the desert colony of North Beach.


## Mar. 31

Tiring of the Journal—no writing in it—promotes slop—an egocentric method.

Life's quiet finally, no love, another plane, after-hours from the office, struggle completed (high tonite on terpinhydrate of codeine), music, rugs, a lousy room and evening robes in which to read, a typewriter.

Lately in revising I've noticed a tendency—revising year pile of notes—to adjust the notes to small groups of lines as in 3-line stanza, begun however before reading the Williams late forms—the division being by active words, number of active words in phrase.

"the sad heart of August dies"

the nouns & verbs have a single weight, the adjectives usually less unless strong words or long ones. Count mainly by eye. But requirement of regularity of some lines is a clarity I find apparent lately, so that the notes don't present themselves totally amorphous.

The lines are not yet free enough—for this reason the concentration process is useful again in order to get a sense of measuring small lines—with later possibility, the expansion to a large form with lines distributed over the page

but equal, each parallel indentation equal or equivalent

So that the structure has a structure at least as an excuse for its form—

following, as we might guess, the given possibilities of lengths of speech mind-think lines—there will probably be a select number to recognize & distinguish, the double:

"here's your Ring
unhappy Neal"

and the triplet

"fantastic physical
images
Neal's naked breast"

\* \* \*

... the original idea of self perfection and introspection I developed a decade no more ago was at the time just a figment of my imagination, nothing has resulted but more and more trappedness over the years, I only realized it recently, but that has been the burden of my dreams for perhaps years and years, the fact that I have been left out, behind, lost in school of life and that my own defiant individual measures of study do not suffice to make up for the long painful eager studies of the kids once beside me, as when even in grammar school—I have thought of this several times recently—I slept or forgot or simply didn't go to arithmetic class— what did actually happen? at any rate one fine day as in the literary reference my teacher sent a note home to the folks, my mother, inquiring what the hell was wrong with me and it was found that somehow or other I hadn't done my homework for 2 months and consequently knew nothing about arithmetic—but I don't remember this, that's unimaginable, not that nowadays I didn't take a same course with chemistry in college, as a result bringing on no end of trouble and getting in similar situation, however the point is that I have no recollection of the actual event in grammar school and the whole scandal broke about my ears: but one thing was certain, that I had fallen behind sufficiently not to know what was going on in class nor even to know what was happening at home with me that I should get this note saying that the apocalypse had broken loose and that harsh reality was intruding on my what must have been a very heavy daydream.

\* \* \*

Dream April 14—Back from (last week Pt. Lobos, this week Tamal-
pais, Stinson Beach)—
    In movie world
    Day after day to cheap restaurants on irish-frisco sidestreets,
booths sawdust & bargain bones
    One day went with black clothes & white collar to the expen-
sive place where I paid & came in the dining room, inquiring of the
waiter "Do you have rare roast beef?" carrying with me what I'd
already ordered on the waiting line, their 59¢ special brown meat
bone in my hands, sucking it, embarrassed.
    Earlier on the beach watching the ships in the low tide, Israel
slave ships, communist folk captains, off Ireland coast—I saw two
ships captained by brothers swayed by the animal tide, their prows
slowly rear up like animals under the waves' force web—and
noiselessly crash into the other—and the captains embrace weep-
ing over the tragedy I saw it all—How ships of such great dimen-
sion clang together rearing up like animals in the tide force—I see
this, Trilling didn't ever see this—I can describe this, I saw the
captains weep in arms, saw the ship in near distance once in a
lifetime crash—
    Then to the Irish wives' house, where I ate a red cake, they
were baking more, I asked what it was—"Worm cakes"—made of
worms, ground up—like a finer hash or a tin of minced ham or
ham spread—I emptied it out of my mouth, disgust, "They're still
bits of motion in it, they're bits of live matter, pinoles not baked to
death, they wiggle in the cake & mouth"—She was moulding the
cake in small glasses (like the small glass at 1010) & putting them
on oven for a minute, food for the Irish captains cooked by 2 dark
haired wives.
    Then a review of a book of poetry—"He knows what to do
and how to do it; we may miss the swing of a final matter—but
there's no mistaking the easy charm of social mature success:
    We know the thing,
    We know the tune
    We still can sing
    We do the trick"

a review in *Hudson Review* etc. or *Perspective* signed by (non-poet) initial S. I. Hu, glib awkward comments hitting the imaginary sincere reaction of the lonely Chinese poetry-interested mind from point of view of modern eccentric insistence on social excellence.


"Great Art learned in desolation:—"
—An were it possible to eliminate myself completely as the subject matter what I write of
        Programme—
                1 year more (1955 to Jan 56) presenting notes
                    in a ruled form of some kind, rhythmical.
                1 year thereafter writing from the margin,
                    starting each line thereat and concerned
                    not with looks of symmetry but pure con-
                    tent & imaginary visualities etc as far as
                    surface.
                1 year thereafter writing out "musical"
                    lines—that is sound effects. And several
                    years to integrate the various steps.
A project as well to examine the kinds of poetry, that is artificial constructions, that color speech—not just descriptions of things their singularities but the metaphors that you use.

* * *


## April 20, 1955

                To pit my thought
                        against the grave

* * *


The green ale bottle and unopened can left
        on the fireplace from last nite's wish-to-be-drunk.
    Not writing enough what can I say—rapid exchange of events, jobloss, Peterloss—isolation, no one I love/loves me no contact, the isolation—facing loss of Jack K. & Bill B. as previous

loss of contact with Joe Army—the myths held for a decade to fill time. These are not enough substance to live off seven decades. Repelled by Naomi to Father Louis for love as later to comfort support & protection of male. No male longer on horizon for such protection, I not being a young boy who needs outside strength, thus complete isolation, there not being any other habit knowledge of exchange.

Peter I can't talk to when I need comfort, he repelled by my need as I was repelled by Burroughs' attachment to me for support.

Faint sickening headache pain heart near nausea, thus from uneasy presence of isolation knowledge.

Leaning over the book, left hand limp on edge of desk, right hand active, head bowed. Uncomfortable desk! Familiar goods of life—my bathrobe, mere matter, my rugs & my notebook and pictures of B. & L. that limit my mind to its obsessions. How tired L. looks drunk in the picture.

* * *

I've just had a long interesting dream, I'm going to write it down—

*I*

We go thru rope & white wood stanchion gate climb on coast guard cutter crossing bay—Peter Gene & I and Louis? "Is this the boat" I say—"Sure come on we're all marines" (or Coast Guard) jon liberty" says Peter as we pass the guard captain— we're in in civilian clothes except for me. Pile on the cutter—it immediately starts moving thru the water—very narrow very long no rails, only a center piece sticking up for me to hang on to, I move on it and clutch—made of rotten, thick tropic matter—the ship sways to & fro no stability I am uneasy & upset but we make it, the ship moves thru the water across S.F. Bay—

## II

We're waiting on the edge of the stream, on the corner, at the gutter, Gene & I, for Louis, I've just arrived there, in that direction (of home?) and what will I do when I see Louis, I'll slope down, swoon headfirst in the air (water) and ascend to kneel in mockery at his cock, imitation of blowing—there's Louis—I swoon up, down in the water and come up toward his middle, and he is naked, his reply is to hold out his unhard long fleshy cock and balls to me as in Tamayo,* he swooning back, folds of skin swooning up at me to my face as he steps back into path of boat-car slushing thru water—almost gets hurt—Gene & I under a telephone pole—then P. comes up—and Gene introduces him, and Louis asks about car—Gene tells Peter to get the papers (Peter acting humble). I want Peter to make believe it's my car, Gene the lawyer "Get Louis the papers"
—"Yes Lord" instead of "Yes Louis" says Peter, going away to the hut to get the papers—back to the hut-like carlot in S.F. ABC—

\* \* \*

Masturbation also an art in desolation learned
Legs straight out, cock vertical one tired right hand passing up & down clenched over the cock tube.
Or with thighs drawn up, dreaming of an entering protuberance up the asshole to the center of the bowel, pushing hard dream weights in the center bowel.
Lying with head down pushed into pillow behind raised up in air shameful attempt offered pumping down the cock to the bed, back arched up to give room
Straddling edge of bed, or chair pushing up to buttocks, cock out halfway high, a nervous kick—raising legs up off floor slightly to come straining.
All accompanied by dirty dreams.

\* \* \*

W. C. Wms. Collected Prose—*Selected Essays,* "Prologue to *Kora in Hell,*" p. 11 [New York: New Directions, 1954]—

---

* Ruffino Tamayo, twentieth-century Mexican painter.

"The true value is that peculiarity which gives an object a character by itself. The associational or sentimental value is the false. Its imposition is due to lack of imagination. . . . The attention has been held too rigid on the one plane instead of following a more flexible, jagged resort."
p. 16—

"Although it is a quality of the imagination that it seeks to place together those things which have a common relationship, yet the coining of similes is a pastime of very low order, depending as it does upon a nearly vegetable coincidence. Much more keen is that power which discovers in things those inimitable particles of dissimilarity to all other things which are the peculiar perfections of the thing in question."

This particular inner signpost—the image in question has a thousand parts and in this case it's a direction to the mind— attention to the unique line (as in a Cézanne abstraction or *summary* of the peculiarities of the lines in a scene—the gothic eyes that stare out of the church at Gardanne) which is, it's the thing that sticks out of it most—as under the aspect of eternity, noticing the essential grotesque of each thing under creation.

And the arrangement of these particular eyes.

Dream of Joe Army this week—who I have not seen but thot of in regard to losing job—woke with pleasure—Soon I'll have known him half my life.

## Writing History

The scene: 1010 Montgomery (S.F., Cal.) in bathrobe and with fireplace and Jap tabis, listening to the relationship of themes in Bach partitas, inscribing in notebooks & on mss., slowly, collecting the evidences of sensibility, buildings, leisure and a car, pictures on my wall, one a portrait of self, not self made, portents of the self—

Long nights in Gough Street,
        an opened robe on the low bed,
    and haven nakedness—the red glare
    of Angry skin—neon, mirrors—
        A great window on the scene
    And half drawn shades

in Sadness as a funeral
—A death of love—
The hills of Montgomery Street
Cablecars of California—
Long walks on the
Embarcadero and B Minor Mass
We might have been
holy metaphysicians
on the cliffs of Time
—stopped on the Pacific highways:
And years later weathered
faces in the Chinese rain—

\* \* \*

Peter going [to New York to fetch brother Lafcadio]
and Eros brooding in the shadows garden cars beds chambers bars heavy pillow—
and Jonah in Leviathan of Love. Bah! ah! the great gathering, God, the high domed foreheads of the whales together in blue platonic seas
Black armor of hide, and weak eyes! Pulsating in pathos.
—Jetplane ribbons of hard mist spread along the sky, one lone path against the endless parallels over the rooftops, over the hills, the street
—Eros dreams of murder, brooding on the pillow, (take that) (the knives of love) Eros in woman's clothes stockings, lipstick brassiere rayon thighs, garters and black panties, legs spread to receive the cock, opened, the weeping hole, jackknife ecstasy, breast touching breast, voices, come, kisses, the bitter fragrance of thighs, where I lost my thought but did not cry for the endlessness of love.
Ugh! what a picture—I'm such a murderous slave

\* \* \*

S.F. in the Athens-like morning—8AM on Wed. May 11 pale morning moon over Twin Peaks, and two soldierly antennae towers with their spokes holding blocks long wires between them in their teeth in a yellow sunrise haze in the cool air, long shadows in the pissing park yellow light, a few old lover ladies, up with their shaggy

Marybelles, big friendly god dog muzzling & bouncing on the grass, and a fat man running down the greensward toward the unemployment office, whirling his arms in the air—the long fart sound of busses ppppphhhhht—bright trees & white hills & glittering windows. The red & purple lobster of Market St. stretched to the yellow horizon.

## May 29

Today a holiday. I don't know which. A dream and its associated fragments. Last night I dreamed—I am up, it is morning retracing my steps in the mind, several thoughts several discoveries. The symbolic connections between things. The dream unravels each night the whole story, the whole history, everything that has happened connected up, relived, thru the dream, the Dream which is consistent night to night, picked up again from the same fragments—Therein is the whole history—lived in the eyes, we must remember thru the very eyes of the dream, the eyeball happenings which contain every movement and history—America is New: all other races in history have grown in time on the same home soil, and like me create a future beyond the present thru the archeological recollection of their history—So that China might know who she is only by remembering thru her poetry what happened in her ancient past—by reconstruction of the "dream state" of pre-history—But here in America we are gathered independent of one soil's history and begin anew with the dreamlike arrival of strangers gathering and propagating on a continent newly created and historically empty (for them) at their arrival. No Fall to disorganize us therefore also no symbolic trauma no nightmare no tragedy no wisdom.*

The dream of last night recalled still only in fragments but those connected, and those fragments also connected with archetypal fragments of other previous nights' dreams.

A class in which through good fortune and also by virtue of previous connection I am seated next to Auden, and students around me are aware of my position, though Auden acts casual.

---

* Actually, non-recollection of 1492's Fall. —A.G., June 25, 1991

A young teacher who is my instructor or advisor with whom I vie, in his relation, I take on a journey. The phys-ed or minor class which I attend to check on, at the hour when (2:45) they are putting on a program. "Do I belong here?" I ask and he says yes. But over the radio is a class with a program interlocuted by WC Williams and I realize I am to be on that program, I say so to the teacher I'm with in the Yucatán classroom—so he accepts my excuse, has to, tho grudgingly.

I return to class or school thru the Yucatán peninsula which has no open roads but I can walk or jeep it thru having been familiar with territory (in dreams?)—Texas, a trip there.

The dream is fragmentary tho I woke with a sense of remembering it in context of other earlier School Dreams, anxiety of being due at several minor classes, technically needed for graduation credit, but not having attended them, and therefore behind in attendance, un-marked in, lack of identity there, and the worry about future, will I graduate? What classes? and how have I missed them? Missed them thru trip to Texas & tho now have Texas experience don't know what classes.

Earlier dream of wandering thru eternity spaces of top floor of Paterson Central High School classrooms (where Louis taught) without walls & with precipitous openings to the wind. The school dream images disorientation in learning lessons of life and graduating to maturity, feeling out of it, out of the school organization, unable to make up for classes I missed & therefore unable to graduate. An ancient dream. Tonight's seemed to go back over my school history, connect with past dreams of same, somehow connect with other dream events, climbing & descending the great Tower or lost in the basement, or travelling in South America plateaus, going to England w. Arthur Lazarus.*

My headache has lasted 3 days & only floats gently, almost, as I use my brain, fear that eyeball recollection jiggling will recall the headache which is perhaps *memory*, not a thing, a memory being a pain & thing.

Dream May 31—In bed amour with John R.† making love to

---

* A roommate of Ginsberg's at Columbia, freshman year 1943–1944.
† John Allen Ryan, painter and poet; founding member, Six Gallery.

him, kissing his body, fondling his pants, he has small tho adequate
genitalia, receded, like Kingsland's, the heat is half strong, there is
a lack, but I persist, and there's inner warmth tho lacking passion-
ate come urge.

* * *

Hearing Bach Chaconne (Partita #2) again today the bril-
liance of the music inspired a mystical sense of the physical pene-
tration of music around my eyes in the room. Mystical physical
music. Sitting on brown rug, staring around, the strings thinner
and thicker zooming about my ears, wires wires arranging them-
selves, crisscrossing and at last merging horizontally in unison.

Just quiet life. I come here in quiet time and meditate what
to do with the rest of our lives. I walk thru the street with a
headache thinking that. I am 29 tomorrow June 2.*
June 2—"I fill'd with woes the passing Wind"—†

Poem of Imagination symbolized thru the withdrawal of the
Angel (of imagination) and a harsh and bleak image Eunuch of
the waste.

> Waking in the morning light
> I had an angel for a friend
> Noontime wearied him with me
> Midnight came to an end
> Harsh and bleak he was a fiend
> Harsh and bleak
> Eunuch unique.

* * *

Young—all the bloom of youth upon them.

* * *

Sex House—Love in the White House

---

* Birthday actually June 3.
† Blake, "The Crystal Cabinet."

\* \* \*

Anapest, says WC Williams, characteristic of American idiom.

\* \* \*

The Green Auto should end on a note of realism, withdrawal from imagination.

## Blessed be the Muses [*CP 125*]

> for their descent,
> dancing round my desk,
> crowning my balding head
> with Laurel.

[First draft of "Dream Record: June 8, 1955," CP 124:]
1010 Montgomery Street, San Francisco

    I dreamed this during a drunken night in my house when I brought home John R. and we lay peacefully at a late hour in each other's arms asleep: I was visiting [St. Louis, a new city] big city, and there saw Joan Burroughs who has been dead now five years— she sat in a chair in a garden with the smile on her face: restored to its former beauty, the sweetness of intelligence which I eternalized in my imagination, that had been lost thru years of Tequila in Mexico City, for Tequila had ruined her face & beauty before the bullet in her brow. And we spoke of her old lover boy John Kingsland, and Burroughs lately in Africa, her children I have not seen with grandparents scattered, in Syracuse, of Kerouac writing sunk in woe & loneliness from Rocky Mount, myself in San Francisco living a different life with new loves, and Joe Army whose mute smile and guarded eyes in photo look down on me as I write this at my desk in the sunny afternoon. Then I realized that this was a dream: and said, "Joan," as she smiled and talked again as would a traveller resting on return, waiting to hear what life he's missed at home—"Do the dead have memory, still love their mortal acquaintances, & do they still remember us," but she faded before there was a reply and in the place where her ghost was I saw her small rain-stained tombstone, scarred, engraved with a Mexican epitaph in an unknown cemetery under a gnarled branch in the unkempt grass garden—a foreign cemetery unvisited.

Following this I realized that since I had leisure in the city I was visiting I should go seek out & pay visit to her grave—and another mission?

Earlier than this I dreamed of my mother, and the previous night resolv'd to write to her.

Another dream, before this, last week, was of sleeping with R. and that he had a thin body, and small loins: our intercourse was tender and weak as we neither knew what to do, but loved each other, not knowing how to express it with our bodies.

After waking went to School of Fine Arts and sat reading Plato in the sunlight of the garden—much like that of the dream. Impression also in the dream, that my feeling of her shadowing me supernaturally in the night streets of Mexico City had been a ghostly intuition.

Aesthetic experience of the sublime: an experience of Time (its reality and unreality juxtaposed) (& the telescoping of Time): "Where the building used to be is now a parking lot." Dawn in San Francisco this morning.

Cézanne's juxtaposed planes: the foreground and also the image of the town painted in same tones (colors) despite distance between them, placed on the same plane, separated by the infinity ellipsis of the cold receding tone blue plains (meadow) [or pond] between them.

The central image in the canvas (at the center) of the faraway city, painted flat; like the foreground of *The Bathers*—

The poem as an equation (a machine), reproducing in verbal images the visual & other images of the dream of Joan—reproducing the elements which juxtaposed gave me the awe & terror & knowledge in the dream—Successfully such an ideal poem could reproduce that "petite sensation" in the reader.

The Art is now given me to recreate after the 1948 Vision of Eternity (slowly substantiated) and finally after long years of thot to communicate it. Thru the science of the poem—this is the key:

What is needed in a poem is a structure (magical, miracles in the head) of clear rational actualities put next to one another to suggest (in the eclipse of Time between the images) Eternity. The "intervals." The *gap* of time. Joan's live body—Joan's tombstone.

Setting up two (images) points (with a gap) separate in time and showing the distance between them:

## Examples

### 1

> The host with someone indistinct
> Converses at the door apart,
> The nightingales are singing near
> The Convent of the Sacred Heart,
>
> And sang within the bloody wood
> When Agamemnon cried aloud . . .

T. S. Eliot, "Sweeney Among the Nightingales"

### 2

> The slant moon on the slanting hill
> Once moved us toward presentiments
> Of what the dead keep, living still,
> And such assessments of the soul
>
> As, perched in the crematory lobby,
> The insistent clock commented on . . .

Hart Crane, "Praise for an Urn"

### 3

Lesser Keats—To Fanny Brawne (on his hand)

> . . . if it were cold
> And in the icy silence of the tomb . . .
> —see here it is—
> I hold it towards you.

and greater Keats

> I saw their starv'd lips in the gloom,
> With horrid warning gaped wide,
> And I awoke, and found me here,
> On the cold hill's side.*

Also "Perhaps the self-same song that found a path / Through the sad heart of Ruth"†—then examine "Ode to a Nightingale" thus.

Actually attaining an inner secret Time shock, the result of telescoping time by setting up two or more image points separated with a wide gap showing distance between them, the jump or interval or ellipsis of consciousness: a sort of mystical eclipse of Time arrived at thru the science of presenting clearly images showing change.

Finally the great final eclipse (of the earth) of Shakespeare:

> . . . the great globe itself,
> Yea, all which it inherit, shall dissolve . . .
> Leave not a rack behind.‡

Key to poetry with a more holy inner structure. The *Cantos* composed of greater ellipses.

Need a significant jump of Change, Time, or experience to reveal as Cézanne says the *Petite Sensation, Pater Omnipotens Aeterna Deus:*§ great gap of change.

Kerouac's walk thru the house backyards in *Sax* does this.

The parallel between Cézanne's theory and poetry theory— to present to the mind's eye two equally strong images without

---

\* "La Belle Dame Sans Merci."
† "Ode to a Nightingale."
‡ *The Tempest,* 4.1.153–56.
§ See *Howl,* I, fifth line from end.

editorial or rhetorical connection—same as without traditional perspective lines, for the effect of the juxtaposition: the resulting pun or ellipsis of Space.

The problem is to learn to speak Cézanne's language of color & space, to see what he is creating, what relationships he is drawing between planes, and how.

## The Red Wheelbarrow

> so much depends
> upon
>
>                                 gap
>
> a red wheelbarrow

No significant relationship (but mysterious tho) is presented here between 2 points or images: just one image presented glistening.

> (inanimate) barrow (gap)
> beside the white chickens

Pound's *In a Station of the Metro*:
> Faces: petals

These are not 2 images showing some great gap of change, merely "vegetable coincidence,"* almost a simile.

I have always unconsciously dug the infinity of the cold blue [pond or] plain/meadow between the bathers & the village in [background of] Cézanne's Bathers.

The ellipses between 2 points in the mind's eye should show the finality of time in no uncertain terms: in Joan poem the sensation leaks through the fuzzy visual points. The clearer & starker & barer, the more "realized" & I suppose equal the visual points, the more sensational the Eclipse.

---

\* See Williams quotation, pp. 130–31.

The dream presented a perfect structure to me by my unconscious—can one be synthesized consciously?

The eclipse of Death's door in "A Wasted Illness."* Hardy's continual practice: "Transcendence rayed the distant urn/where slept the fallen twain." ("The Casterbridge Captains")

The Platonick Society of the Sensation—eternal society

\* \* \*

## A Few Notes on Method

I've already written much on the ellipsis, in letters and conversation, & have given at least one good example of it in the reproduction of a dream, as well as pointing out its classical use in Keats. I had read about it in Pound, forgotten it, and recreated its necessity in my mind in response to need for recrystalizing a specific sensation accurately. Pound has that part of the method in the Cantos. However the Cantos are too literary and [much of] the experience is aesthetic experience of aesthetic experience. He is concerned with generalizations, ethical, esthetic, etc. I am con-

---

\* Illustrative example of eclipse of Death's door in stanzas 3, 7, 8 of Hardy's "A Wasted Illness," *The Complete Poems of Thomas Hardy*, ed. James Gibson (New York: Macmillan, 1972), p. 152:

> "Where lies the end
> To this foul way?" I asked with weakening breath.
> There on ahead I saw a door extend—
>     The door to Death.

> . . . I roam anew,
> Scarce conscious of my late distress. . . . And yet
> Those backward steps to strength I cannot view
>     Without regret.

> For that dire train
> Of waxing shapes and waning, passed before,
> And those grim chambers, must be ranged again
>     To reach that door.

cerned with personal generalizations, or rather concretions of personal experience.

Williams has refined the reproduction of images to a science—that is stripped bare for utility.

We have not yet had a crystalization of real grief in a poem since imagism, nor any of a gamut of human experiences. To say nothing of experiences of the superhuman, which exist as material to be reproduced thru formations & juxtapositions of the images that give rise to them. Do away with symbols and present the facts of the experience. They will speak for themselves whatever they say.

Ellipsis in event gives rise to the grief-realization of time, or the cold shiver of eternity. This concerns the plot of the poem.

Ellipsis in syntax—dropping of articles, connectives, sawdust of the reason—to join images as they are joined in the mind: only thus can two images connect like wires and spark. This the phrasing of the poem.

Phrasing & plot follow the same method, thus.

This gives the ideal poem, the poetry of the writing, not all the writing that goes with a poetic idea.

[I] need to trap sensations and collect the fragments which give rise to them, by any means, reconstructing [sensations] in images.

This means, automatically, narrative of one kind or another, that is, events in time perceived, giving rise to a subjective emotion, illuminating time. A deep look.

Sentimentality & fuzziness of construction will not make us weep at a poem on Hiroshima. Only presentation of the facts, facts juxtaposed, create the significance which is truth & tears. To reach a point of understanding where generalization is not generalization but expression of fact. Till then at least no generalization. The modesty of subjective generalization; the pomposity of objective generalization.

Absolute relativity, that is, life.

* * *

June 10—Natalie's screaming beard spotting wall sex images flashing thru fuck with everybody Dhyana dream, eyelid lowered saw its shade in meditation onehalf hour silence hands on knees knock on door screaming willful woman voice unkempt bed peter coming closer sneeze silence, after sneeze good feeling rest wipe noze depression fatigue all afternoon reading the sutra and sleeping immediately after long immobility eyes closing rocking knees bodies in my bed positions warm backs in my stomach come the disgust at them often the fag who talked too much Ryans ex roommate the trip to T with the young ballet boy who having picked up ignored me ran away my device discovered by grating Alex* myself immobile in depression listening to Robert's mention of incident a surprise nothing secret not my attempt at seduction which got back to him his boy too again the fatigue being thru waste of time watching the sun move across the afternoon sky one half day in which I do nothing weary with the objective art and weary of the solitude I have maneuvered myself into once more while the knockers come and worry me more and I become more aloof to each each being an intruder none being the one I accept as lover who accepts me this is what I want then seeing Sheila married pretty girl I hadnt the energy to keep up with her and one after the other the ugly and tempting boys who pass by questioning my nature and the young fat girls who wish to visit and converse none of them attractive to my heart those attractive the rejectors, they reject me the true beauties, while the ugly need me. I am no closer to the end of the line except death than I was ten years ago and more removed from the innocence that then gave promise of sweetness thru experience now no image presents itself but continuous travel scene to scene each becoming more empty of love than the last or if love more bitter in the issue.

---

* "Mad Alex": a friend of Sheila Williams' who talked obsessively, a stream of apocalyptic puns: "Did you see the starry shower come over City Lights all the wet baby poetry books nine months born underground last year North Beach cellar door womb complex, for cash." —A.G., June 1, 1986

## July 4—Notes from trip to Reno
## with Peter

Old Indian couple by the jukebox in the Wagon Wheel, crowded drunken bums Mexicans Indians

The bus depot "Allnite" cafeteria, oatmeal with Peter, 2 spades w. whitebeard Whitman

In Harold's Club—an Indian woman sitting motionless expressionless—a heavy middleaged dark beauty, with her mother—age 80 in bandanas—only a twitch to her eyes—and a pile of 80 silver dollars at her folded hands under her bosom—leaned back on stool, hands resting on table, then leaning forward with her negligent eye averted, swift gesture picking up her cards.

Plaza Hotel Bar—Bleecker Street type—with narrow moorish entrance arch to small side room, dark and unused, serving only for a few shrouded booths—I entered unexpectedly the tables there & shifting like a sea creature in the darkness an old bum in a pool of saliva.

Pokerino lights, continual clink of coins & clank machinery under submarine pink fluorescent lights and blue air underground on the second floor, July 4 crowds at jackpot machines with drinks & cranks.

July 6—Back from Reno, Virginia City, Carson City, Lake Tahoe—the drunken couple who picked us up. Farewell to Peter on 4th St., Rt. 40 Reno 10 AM July 2.

Now in the house, tedium of the Journey behind me, tedium of the last months of war with Peter gone. War & Love.

War whore.

\* \* \*

Dream several days ago—in London sequel to Trapped in Tea Shop\* & The Cocktail Party—at Eliot's flat in London for a great bohemian party, he's in the bedroom asleep, not in attendance, I don't know anyone but Jack Spicer† (speaking English-Cockney)

---

\* See *Journals Early Fifties Early Sixties* (New York: Grove Press, 1977; 1992), pp. 58–59.

† Spicer (1925–1965) was poet and founding member of the Six Gallery.

who converses with me about London—then Eliot sees me & says "and may I see your work" and I am weeping with loneliness and grief & love unexpressed that chokes my breath, gratitude for his desire to read me.

## July 10, 1955

Portrait of Peter by La Vigne on my wall—

As I sit naked before it staring it seems to move, the golden head—I had been thinking how the picture will remain still unchanged blue and gold & orange thru perhaps centuries while Peter will rot, his colors change & body be withered & dissolved—it seemed in the picture to move—the space behind it shifted, an optical trick—the candor of the eyes remaining the thick brush of light brown hair, the lips still red, childish, receptive, here folded together secretly—eyes staring up openly the face lowered, posing, aware, independent tho still bound to the artist—whose possession the beauty is—but it is the undefinable grace, charm, youthfulness, innocence and complicity with the artist's self that is portrayed—the familiarity before it refuses familiarity any longer, the moment of grace. A certain calculation about the face, watching itself feel loved, beautified—Certainly the beauty there is not abstracted but made to live, it is here alive, what was actually the beauty seen—suggesting the infinite depths of the soul when it was alive and moved in the flesh, disrobed & made itself naked and lay stretched in the bed with open and willing arms—and a softness too to the eyes as if—in the right eye—the left is a round blank staring & judging, the right is the sympathetic boyish—sensual eye of love—golden right cheek rosed—as if sharing the love delight.

A wall, and perhaps a doorknob at the left indicate a future exit off this scene (canvas) out of the holy room—

It stares down on me (as strangely it had on La Vigne) tho Peter is gone to the East, and before that changed his complexion and willingness—remains of a dream, which was real as long as he loved La Vigne & me, now real only in the picture, reminder of our ideal of youth.

Peter, come down and join me in bed, open your arms again, cry "Take me," act like a living soul my equal and not my superior removed in time to another plane of beauty in this picture.

\* \* \*

An old note from 1951–2—With Williams in Paterson:
    In the restaurant—talk about Gertrude Stein interested in an idea as well as rhythm "She had one idea" and repeated that one simple idea to get it across.
    John Herrmann\*—he was always lost.

    Writing as fakery—rhythm the essential, rhythm of individual's feelings & nature.

End—WCW: I'm getting on to 70—almost 2 years, and I don't know it all seems so empty—what's the use.
    me: Are you afraid of death?
    WCW: Yes that's what it amounts to—what's it all for?

\* \* \*

July 1955—At the circus, San Jose—In cadence of Barker "You cannot buy any more General Admission tickets for this afternoon—reserved seats only." I didn't go.
Only the mortal's lost & mortal's all we know
Denver is lonesome for her heroes

    July 19, '55—Conversation in dream with Philip Lamantia?† much parallel to our conversation off Kearny & Market—as to whether because of my eclipse (or renunciation) of illumination I had passed into an illuminated stage. I said "I don't know" meaning yes.

    Reminiscent also my thought that the conception of a "Voice of Rock" of poetry, my preoccupation in 1949, had been embodied finally in the absolute literal voice in the poetry 1955.

---

    \* John Herrmann, American writer and labor organizer, friend of W. C. Williams, author of proletarian novel *What Happens* (1927), then married to writer Josephine Herbst. I'd met him in Mexico City 1951, drinking, with broken leg in cast. —A.G. August 11, 1994
    † Philip Lamantia (1927–), San Francisco Renaissance and Beat poet, associated with Surrealists in N.Y., first published as teenager by André Breton in wartime *VVV*, later by City Lights.

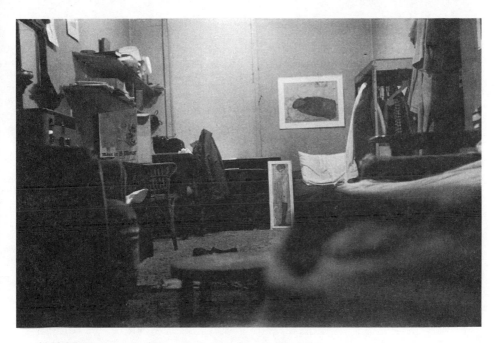

1010 Montgomery Street furnished room facing
street window shade, La Vigne's gesso portrait of
Orlovsky on floor. Part I *Howl* written on desk
typewriter, corner left, same month photo taken.
Photo: Allen Ginsberg

\* \* \*

There's no reason said my grandma that sex should be more
romantic than washing dishes she spoke with a dry voice the
visionary.

> I put it away
> so carefully
> so not to lose it
> that I never
> use it.

July 22—Dream of Joe Army, in an apt. his family's, he's there, they
leave, we greet, wrap arms, touch cheeks, love, nervous, he seems
younger. Softness in my gut & happiness waking.

The fog coming over the miniature Palace of Legion of
Honor lights up the road, the police outside stopping cars to

examine invitations, small crowds outside, a group with leader sightseeing at Hollywood premiere, the fog rolling over the court-yard in the red lights of the sky floating neanderthal over the pillars of the colonnade. Entrance to music, the roomsfull of tuxedoed gentlemen gowned ladies, the skullface baldhead thin man Van Klifens President of U.N., the half handshake "Glad to have you here"—Mr. P. Orlovsky Mr. A. Ginsberg—and then facing the battery of cameramen, the secret service agent requesting our tickets—"This admits only one"—My fright & bafflement, leaving with Peter then—"I think we'll both go."—Back to our black crack-window delivery truck we'd drove up in black ties thru the police cordon—he having no license—and to downtown, the Pal-ace & St. Francis for a looksee, and lost the car, wandering twice, thru bars, thru house, took pictures.

* * *

July 22—The sensation already gone, no further dreams remem-bered, no gaps.

July 28—To Yosemite via Bret Harte & Hangman's Tree Big Oak Flats, Calif.—& Mark Twain's town Jacksonville?—with Peter in "The Hearse"—First sight of the gulf in Space—a great gap of Space—

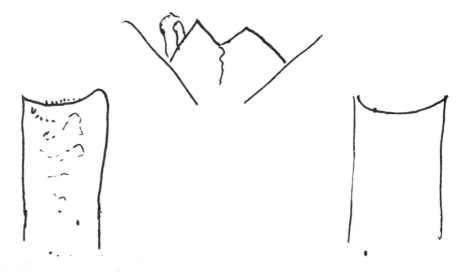

Diagram on left with trees and a man—the relative sublime vast of the cliffs glimmering above—& hi on tea by the river at nite watching the slow descent of fire thru space (the "Firefall") slow because coming from so great height the red ashes fell each for an observably long time at that great upward distance—and the sense of this valley floor being primeval, Eden, Shangri-la, but primeval with giant ferns and tropical valley life surrounded by secret giant cliffs—Peter compared Glacier Point to the stump of the Great Tree of Heaven—inspiring such awe that I could not read Words-worth aloud there ("Ode: Intimations of Immortality")—We climbed up to Half Dome, & descended by night seeing the great standing vast darken'd planes of space overhead, like Jack's celestial machinery (Book of Dreams).

Space is vast & Time's eternal (Eternal Time in vast space).

The lemon was good to taste—its few drops on the peak top, thirsty in sun after upward climb.

The "tropical floor" of the valley with its giant ferns.

July 30—Interesting metrical phrase ending a dream:

A Sudden interruption: Jack black shades

* * *

Several dreams of choking. And another in which I had eaten several cans (whole) could not pass them, and thinking to vomit them out, choked & nauseated, woke me up—my windpipe clogged.

I had been (in truth) collecting too many cheap cans of food against my poverty & sat gloating over my shelf stacked up.

Isolated & preceptorial with all who come in and out—Guy Wernham,* Anne Murphy,† Al Sublette, Neal & Natalie, Dave etc., Cosmo—stiff distant impatient agnostic—I go to sleep or type at desk in their presence.

Met Sheila tonite, with new husband in The Place—they gave details of Alex's sanity trial, weird farce. I envied them together, felt stiff and awkward (like Peter).

---

* Guy Wernham, translator of Lautréamont's *Maldoror* (New Directions), working then as a bartender in North Beach.

† Anne Murphy, a young woman enamored of Neal Cassady.

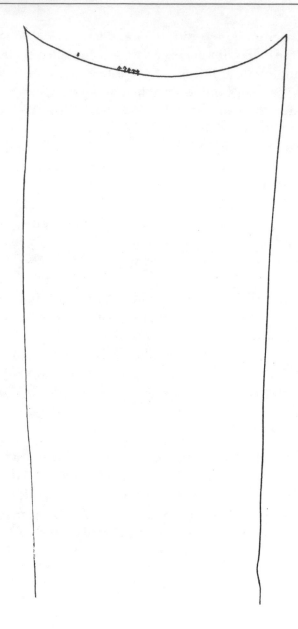

"Diagram on left with trees and a man—the
relative sublime vast of the cliffs glimmering
above. . . ." Yosemite, July 28, 1955.

# Dreams

Of Solomon, Carl—we are walking on the street, in Oakland perhaps, by a telephone pole (my poem) and he grabbed my arm, he's so big, I was frightened a little but angry, I tried to shake him off but he held on, and grabbed my shoulder, I pushed & pulled, he laughs, adamant, I can't get rid of him (he's making a point, & so am I, now refusing to be clutched on to irrationally), he won't let me go.

Of whitehaired collegemate now in San Francisco (I had a crush on & still dig) walking up the street last nite I saw him, and dreamed—? Peter Caswell?*—he is showing his book he's been working on, which is a private secondary school study or narrative or anecdotal "The Egg and I" travel book about the Boston-Cambridge area—I see he has a large olde English type map showing streets & places, and like college text, chapters with sets of discussion questions & test Q. & A.—I think that this is the kind of work he might do—obviously written with curiosity & interest, barren, a weird form, the college text, which no one would use—who would use a text on the Cambridge regions?—Yet set up in the social form of a text, a bastard marginal yet intelligent production—took him ten years—snob appeal of the subject, as he explains it, taken for granted it's an appropriate chic deep subject for study.

\* \* \*

Inspiring—Cocteau's *Film Journal*—energy & ravages of boils and eczema his genius

\* \* \*

# Aug. 6

Cruising Market St.—walking slow, taking it all in, unshaven, always see short fairies rushing quickstop into restaurants as if on a nitely date to meet the cats—Old igloo cat with glasses & camera picking over boy magazines—the beggar legless, Neal's boy—

---

* Acquaintance from Columbia College.

fantasy of handsome blonde youth who eyes me, exchange time & cigarettes—& record this as poem, reverse of reality. Failed. Afflatus yesterday, deenergized today—lost poem.

Cocteau like Pound in dedication, style of essays. Cocteau → Moliere → Voltaire. Cock & Harlequin etc.

Pound & Voltaire.

I am hi

Views of San Francisco—Newly finished Catullus Malest Cornifici—& the night's visit to Neal talking about the imaginary Ubangi girl I was with. Left solitary, happy, sad, worried, mind filled with Whatever & the Art of poetry—

It is all there, in the mind: to record it,
hold the mind in stillness,
                           and then listen,
                                            write,
Wait for a moment for the jazz
                        singing on the radio,
"You got to give up all hope, baby?"
        with saxophones bouncing behind
"A cardtrick of the soul"—Cocteau


I'm sad,
I'm listening
to the blues
phonograph

the pianoman
picks the keys
of the lock
to the door

To the vault
where all that
money's kept
in dollar bills

Blues of Dollars!
Blues of Love!
Blues of barges
Blues of planes

Up in the sky
over skyline
plane flies
with redlight

the long truck
on long road
in desolate
Arizona hill.

# The Shaded Eye of the Police

—A truck, car
the cops stopped
I saluted
and passed

They moved
ahead the car
slowed down
cringing

Inhumanity!
Solitude!
The lousy
Streets of Love.

The "S.F. Bldg." on Telegraph Hill Cliffs overlooks the terraces of Bohemian Broadway & the International settlement, a sentinel over the valley, a two-story tower with rusty concrete bowl on top of its head, one room a dungeon floor, iron balcony, uninhabited, with an accompanying basement oil derrick or goldmine, which can be viewed immediately below the rockwall—as at Paterson, too, of the hill-cliff, where now to its founder-stone is an empty parking lot among the Phinocchio's transvestite club Hotels

& Matador Bar Rooms of Broadway—a gap, a void in the city, bare rock & concrete & old brown useless derrick 20 feet tall what for?—an alley emerging upstairs high on Telegraph Hill walled in with wooden fence leading to a door—locked to the garden— can't get in.

Dream Aug. 21—(after reading *Tears of the Blind Lions*)—Saw Fr. Thomas Merton in the halls, come on a visit to the house, dressed in swinging robes—we talked, he brought a friend, I looked in the bathroom to see friend—a redhead (hipster looking) with small rat red mouth & pale skin, and another cat—He says, "I need to be told how I look," laughing, he's English-like, I say—"Still pimply adolescence not grown old—rather like Hamlet" (he looks awful but I don't want to insult him too much) with his long cassock & I notice big ungainly long legs & wide effeminate ass underneath, and like Auden probably tits on flabby chest and like Hollander long arms, then this head of his which is young English schoolboy big-eared—I say "Tell me once & for all about this divine ecstasy— does it come once or often? How long does it last? Is it long or short? How many times etc." This after I said he was like Hamlet. My feeling a mixture of affection envy & contempt for his body—I thought, with an ass like that no wonder he's a mystic, O well he's no worse than anyone trying to escape not getting laid.

This also after conversation w/Peter in Broadway tunnel explaining prophet-seer Alchemy of Word of Rimbaud.

* * *

Note for Joan Dream: "What consciousness in oblivion?"

* * *

## I dreamt

I was in the show—Pizza Pushers?*—had a free pass, and due to my criticism of it was asked to take seat in front row at table downstairs in orchestra and speak a few words of foolery to the

---

* A show by Jack Goodwin then current at Miss Smith's Tea Room on Grant Avenue, San Francisco. —A.G., October 6, 1982

players as they came down off the stage in their costumes kissing and camping with members of the audience.

I sat there with the gang from North Beach in the auditorium—Civic Center?—in one of the last rows, comparing faces of the old types, like Senators and reconstruction politicians who filled up the seats.

I was alone, perhaps Natalie sat next to me or some young boy—I marvelled that I'd been here that long, ten years, seen all the actors change, seen all the faces—I reviewed them in my mind and they changed before me—Disappear and come to be replaced by the new visages familiar from the pictures in the papers—I saw a vision of the Old Senate—the greedy hunchback from N.J., the scheming dwarf hunchback who got there on patronage; the old fathead curly white-haired florid bald Joe from South, the monkey-face politician from Kansas with striped shirt & galluses—the whole pack of second rate nitwits and now all these new rather respectable solons with sobered faces staring seriously & intelligently at the stage & myself the most brilliant of them elevated by my seniority to a position of elegant freedom, wandering backstage & fore, seated in front, observing & approving, carrying my dark poetic speeches in my pocket & no tie, secret legislator & lover in the audience (& the new faces all familiar in the papers)— "I was here in the days of fat Vandenberg and Borah," I said, "and I have survived them all in my secrecy & sweetness of mind"—

I move forward to a reading table down near the apron of the stage and the play begins—the costumed dancers kick up their heels to music, rapid lines spoken, shuffles & motion onstage changes of scenery, & between acts an old biddy with bright cheeks & alcoholic eyes comes down the side stairs scrambles up the aisle & pats me on the head—I mumble looking into her redhead eye "Yes Mother"—the line I'd invented—it doesn't go over—O well so what—it's not my play, besides it's supposed to have a personal joke significance only I and my intimates can understand.

The play was over, the audience to be fed (or those in the cast to be fed)—before I get down to the steamtable they are closing up, no more food handed out—a big cafeteria under the school in the basement, kind of chromium steamtable 20 feet long (like Calif. School Fine Arts) with long thin Chinamen behind it tending piles of food—Spanish rices, huge ham legs & roast beefs, which they cut in foot-long round inchthick heavy slices, rare—I present my tray, several friends following me, DuPeru?—and am refused service, but say, a white lie, I'm in the play I'm supposed to be fed (I'm hungry I can feel my hollow stomach) the Chinese tall cook looks up pleased, oh yes, sure, Boss—and starts with a huge slab of roast beef on a plate—"What else?"—"Lots," I say, I'll feed my friends, but eat well first, I'll order a huge trayful—I motion, he indicates, we pile up the food—a dish filled with small near-roast potatoes, another dish heaped with Spanish rice—another two potatoes, there's 8 already there, another one potato, salad, rice pudding with raisins, milk, coffee, bread, butter, rolls, french toast, cauliflower, another piece of roast beef. I have them piling up in my tray, I have two trays—I notice DuPeru behind me—While I've been observing the food & Chinamen he's been at my tray— transferring onto his tray—He's following me—he's taken one of the pieces of roast beef—the one the Chinaman had newly carved for me—the brown sheet of beef off the bone—I put it on a plate in his tray, disturbing my spoils, shrivelling my spoils, I say "O no you don't DuPeru my nemesis," he laughs a toothless grin, I grab the plate back & dump the meat on my dish, go on, order another side of macaroni & another potato, move on—Discover he's shrivelled my plate again—I feel hunger in my stomach, grab my tray to try to make off with my plates full to a table, he's following me, the food keeps disappearing off my tray to his plate, arriving there looking all shrivelled & bleak & messy up, he's laughing, he's got me in a dream.

I go out under the dark cellar tunnel & meet—just then— Neal & Natalie, Natalie who's hungry, Neal who's stingy—and like a Magician in the tunnel (Sheila's entrance or Neal's) recount the story of the meat disappearing in a dream to DuPeru's laughing toothless haunting face—I woke & shook him off finally & had to renounce my whole dream tray of food to get rid of his persisting annoying depraved parasitic spectre—the bastard ate me out of a dream banquet with his goddam ghost—Natalie & Neal hardly listen, he gets the point tho, Natalie runs off uphill toward restau-rant shouting you bastards I'm hungry, and Neal turns to me laughing, "Sometimes I feel like acting like Natalie & indulging my wishes, like acting out my hunger, taking my wallet & going in

to Woey Loy Goey's* (now in fact let's do it) restaurant & ordering
up a big plate of Roast Beef"—

And thru all this in the early part of the dream I had seen
Lucien's picture hanging by the door, the stage doors with notices
on it, the bulletin board, by the window cubicle door reaching
downstage to the back of theatre audience where I entered to sit
down in my grand solitude lonely seat amid the Senate—I kept
losing sight of his important picture—Was he there, as Neal?

Finally in my mind I reviewed a manuscript, perhaps the
routines or songs of the play—the last an old burlesque routine of
Frank or Joe Fish, that old comedian—Lyrics strangely written by
that old hoofer with a double clack clack of his palms offside
independent of each stanza, written like a poem on a page:


The example of undeniable reality
        of the Chinese American imagination
enacted down the hill to Embarcadero
        near Chinatown San Francisco

by gangster sinister slanteyed
        restaurant owner one Kong Foo
    or was it Chinese Lee,

by his lamppost leaning in the
        oriental dusk

mustache & hat on head & a weary reefer
        clack clack,
in his pocket,
        Perceiving the western sun
go down on city hills

        an image of 20 years ago
earlier than the depression
        which found its way through
movies & highschools of America


* Inexpensive Chinese restaurant open nearly all night, near City
Lights Bookstore, still in business 1994.

into the clothes and talk
of today's hipness, the present children's generation
which never dreamed of him last nite, Clack Clack.

* * *

# Old note:

**Dawn**

As once by drug cock power
poem or gold
Now naked bare & trembling
into the cold

**Serenade**

What have I got to proffer
to Society but this thistle?
How can it please
myself or another?
What kind of perjury profit
from this meter?
—the human residue of
Supernatural fire

**Buddha song**

I have to go
for golden dough
to ray me
so far,
to go to tea
& lie for dough
Doom to Doom
Doom to Doom.

And I'll be
doomed to doom
and never recover
and never remember
incredible Karma

Doom to Doom
Doom to Doom

And there is
nothing to save
grave after grave
bomb to bomb
but doom to doom . . .

\* \* \*

How to say no in America of stone bombs and libraries full of
          tears?
How to say no in front of the thunderjets on their ramps at
          children's feet?

\* \* \*

I saw the best mind angel-headed hipsters damned.
What consciousness in oblivion, Joan?

\* \* \*

## To Alcatraz

Remembering that in a summer night I stood
          above white roofs in San Francisco
Under white heaven filled with great white clouds
          and yellow splendor of sunset
Enduring the passion of the Christ of Alcatraz
          Enduring the hallucination of
Christ with his arms spread crucifix along the horizon
          and his head haloed by the molten atoms of the orange sun
boiling in the water of the Pacific
          Wracked with the ecstasy of mortal souls of Alcatraz,
and bid him remember in heaven when my soul
          vibrates with his bodily fire
flames up in suffering and explodes in the human inferno.

## Sept. 1, 1955

Last night—with Peter sleeping for last time living together at 1010 Montgomery,* my boxes ready to move today—his brother Lafcadio & he moved into long dark Old Sin room where Neal had lain & smoked, window open in bed all day facing eternity slope curve down plane of earth Telegraph Hill by whose window I'd written in Peter's absence—his brother wandering hall, to bathroom, in and out, tentatively, hand on wood floor, stomping in indecision, washing his hands, bathroom light on, down crack of dark alley hallway, I in bed, shirtless, with underpants, he with a green top shirt he'd worn all day (and at nite on frustrate-date with [Ms.] Phillips†)—green shirt, looking young, sleepy eyes closed, anxiety of being thrown in bed with me, for I & he "doubled up" (as I'd joked about) (warned him I'd try) and Lafcadio still in bathroom—I read Lorca, leaning head on pillow under Japanese wall light—no, Apollinaire—"Zone," halfway, he eyes closed, not reacting, I skipped to

"—One day
One day I said William—"‡


and asked "Sleepy?" but no answer, finally I said "I'll put the light out," and did so, lay back, we on separate pillows, and put my hand on his hand, on his breast, under his folded or clasped hand there, the warmth, a hot nite, one cover & a sheet only, and that (lately) too much, I could feel his heart against mine, toes, comfort, communication, far away down at our feet, yet I had my hand also on his breast, and after a while put my face against his arm and closed my eyes as always in his protection, his bare and healthy young man's arm.

---

* Peter's back room, shared with Lafcadio, was taken over by landlord? —A.G., October 1982

† 3-yr. Harvard-educated symbolic logician pest neurotic. —A.G., October 4, 1982

‡ Likely Ginsberg was reading Apollinaire's "Procession" ["Cortège"], lines 19–21: "One day/One day as I invited my soul/I said to myself William it's time to come" (*Alcools*, trans. Anne Hyde Greet [Berkeley: University of California Press, 1965], p. 67).

Lafcadio came in to sleep & went creaking to bed—Peter turned over toward the outside of his bed, I followed, he had crooked onc knee forward, I put my arm around his waist which in darkness was warm and narrow, no monster, a sensitive thinner boy, and my knee against the inside of his crooked outthrown knee, and with a hard-on grown already, but not always throbbing, slowly over his chest—I felt though he had been quiet and passive in his sleepiness, a miracle of thought between us, I didn't know if it was real or not. That he felt himself then at that moment care for me, a desire to be possessed by me, and we drifted so on the night boat toward sleep, though he breathed, and he coughed, and I touched him on the stomach, which was bare, the green shirt having crept up—we sweating, I felt it along the knees, and felt it too hot for him, thinking in that sweat of heat how sweet it would be to excite more moisture in our skins by the rubber saliva of fucking him in the ass—I took my knee away from him then, and lay back on my back, he had turned too, and so was on his back, and laid my arm on the length of his body, my elbow on his stomach my hand reaching down to his thigh, with my wrist above his pubic bump in the covers, a hard-on—I pressed down to see if it was so, and rubbed my wrist back & forth slowly thru the covers to feel it, it was hard but not completely so, not standing up, I thought it was not meant for me, and soon I turned over, reverse of before, and he followed me & put his loins into my buttock & his knee over my leg so that he could press it in harder and it was then I realized hard enough so that he was taken by desire, he wanted to play at least—Though Lafcadio in the other bed shifted, we were secret & quiet, I could not see his face & soul, what did we desire in the darkness? So I moved my ass aback to him and moved up in bed so that his cock wedged between my buttocks thru the underwear pants I had on, and reached back to his behind & thigh to pull him in, to press harder—and thus we lay for several minutes moving back and forth slowly, infrequently, lazy, trying out the play; as he pushed his cock nearer into my hole till it was straight in me & by pressure I could feel it as a stick in my back—then I reached down & slid my pants down over my curves of buttock, not taking them off, and he reached his hand over me, I had opened up my behind to him, it was bare, the pants below me, and my cock out thru the fly of my pants, he reached & touched & stroked my

cock as he pressed in and on the center of my hole, & pressed—so
that I moved forward on my stomach for him to get in closer with
more longer cock, and reached down to slide his own pants front
down—I felt them soft & silken, and pushed my palm into his
thigh to bring him forward on me, and he had found the hole after
awhile I pushed the head of his cock into outside penumbra circle,
not entirely entered—he stayed there awhile, moving back & forth
not in and not yet out, but I felt so soft that I could take him in then
and asked to have the full force of his body thrust forward to me,
in, and moved more flat on my stomach with my leg up a little, he
threw his knee over my thigh, passed it over, but it was too high, he
drew his leg back & drew away, I thought he had gone too far & was
going to lie back & leave me, I felt down for him, and he pressed
me down again, my back, & moistened his cock with saliva, and lay
on me again arms round me & pulling & rubbing my own pecker
penis & then began in earnest slowly to push in, slowly & deliber-
ately so as not to wake his brother who shifted on his bed, still not
asleep it seemed. I wondered whether this excited Peter & would
excite him into crisis, to make noise of fucking openly, if it were the
naked adolescent incestuous fucking necessitous sensual discov-
ery rawness of his brother's eyes & ears he was excited by—and tho
the bed didn't creak it moved a little so I said in whisper "Quiet"—
& we moved on, he penetrating my asshole & pushing the shaft of
his cock deeper until I could feel his stomach against my back, I
became very excited & pulled up my knee, both knees & pressed
his thigh & back with my right hand, so that he would go into me
altogether to the base & he followed & slid pulling me by the cock
into him, with more violence until I felt him buried in my intestine
altogether, to rest there a second and pull almost all the way out, I
feared he'd fall out, but then he pushed all the way in again &
began riding in & out on me slowly & easily, I felt myself melt
realizing it was here, I felt flesh melt & my asshole soften for him to
slide in and out into, then to give him resistance & hardness
against his sensitive organ I tightened & moved back & forth into
him, erratically synchronizing the beat of our copulating. He
meanwhile excited me by masturbating me, and finally I felt all
power & strength leaving me and relaxed motionless & passive
while he lay astride me & fucked me deep with my asshole wide
open & no pain, a sweet pressure in my bowels and an open

yearning for him—we rode on like this for five or six minutes building and I said "Can you come, will you come"—we were very quiet at it; he whispered "I'll come" and pushed me harder & slackened off while we became self-conscious a minute, then I felt sorry about his brother, then pulled him into me & moved, and then stayed still while he had his pleasure, and he moved slowly & harder in and out till he said "I love you" and began to come, and held his body arched into me, and pulled me to him & said "I want to kiss you" so that I turned my head & twisted my body and "I love you too"—and put my arm under his neck and said "Hold it in me, don't go away" and he said "Yes"—and began to jerk me off, I whispered to him "Yes, yes, Peter, make me come, I love you. I want you to take me, I want you to use me, get everything you can from me, make me give myself to you, I want you to always have me, always keep me, take from me, make me come, faster, harder, oh, I'm coming," and I sighed & closed my eyes & held on to him with arm round his neck & palm at his breast.

We lay so awhile in the dark, & the heat came over us, sweat, and silence & darkness & warmth, I slightly uneasy for fear he would reject me, he had said "I love you" this night our last I realized, as he had never said before, a giving, an admission? a statement of final terms? He needed me? He truly loved me?—I stroked his forehead, wondering & soft, complete, & slowly we parted, I lay facing him, all night we moved one way and another, one time early I separate with only my hand touching him, on the hair, the crown of angels I imagined it in its soft light gold color, brown as I pressed his skull, in life, before death, a moment complete, pathos of my departure tomorrow.

Berkeley and the Bay Area, the Northwest, the Arctic, Mexico, New York

# Introduction

The January 1955 success of Robert Duncan's play *Faust Foutu* at a renovated-garage-become-art-gallery on San Francisco's Fillmore Street had generated the idea of holding a poetry reading there. Michael McClure, asked by painter Wally Hedrick to organize it, instead recruited Ginsberg, who put together the program of poets in consultation with Kenneth Rexroth. On October 7, 1955, Gary Snyder, Philip Whalen, Philip Lamantia, and Allen Ginsberg (with *Howl,* Part I) read at the Six Gallery, for what proved to be one of the best-chronicled nights in American poetry. According to sources as diverse as Richard Eberhart's "West Coast Rhythms" report in the *New York Times,** Jack Kerouac's *Dharma Bums,* Michael McClure's *Scratching the Beat Surface,* and Barry Miles' *Ginsberg: A Biography,* it was around this time that a San Francisco Renaissance and a new American poetry were born. As Ginsberg recalls,

> We were all writing idiomatic verse; everyone was interested in Kerouac, and it was an accumulation of the San Francisco West Coast Bohemian-Anarchist-Modernist tradition, as well as the New York impulse or energy that we brought, and Kerouac's obvious genius which Duncan appreciated and so did Rexroth.

Kerouac was of course the greatest contemporary influence on Ginsberg, but the poet studied past models (Christopher Smart, Blake, William Carlos Williams) as well. Occasional references to Whitman that begin to appear in these journals are evidence of a major reading project. By the fall of 1955, with *Howl,* Part I, essentially complete, Ginsberg was "getting interested in free verse and long-line poetry" and began "ransacking all the literature I could find to correlate with that, including reading Whitman from beginning to end . . . a total turn-on." Its effects may show not only in "Footnote to Howl" but in later writings such as "In the Baggage Room at Greyhound." And the poet proclaims, in the draft of

---

* *Book Review,* September 2, 1956.

"America" in this second section of journals, "I Allen Ginsberg Bard out of New Jersey take up the laurel tree cudgel from Whitman."

Before 1955 was over, Ginsberg had cemented ties with fellow poets Whalen, Snyder and McClure; drafted later parts of *Howl;* written numerous other poems; read, at the invitation of Ruth Witt-Diamant, for the Poetry Center at San Francisco State;* established a visitation relationship with Orlovsky (who remained in San Francisco with his brother Lafcadio); applied for work at sea; and quit graduate school. He recalls: "I didn't have the brains or the mind for that kind of scholarly study; I was reading and studying from the point of view of producing, creating something, rather than writing studies of older texts." Further, he remembers Kerouac's coming by as he was seated under a backyard plum tree trying to read Anglo-Saxon. " 'What're you doin' that fer?' " Jack accosted him. " 'You oughta be studying Sanskrit instead. You ought to be getting some original ancient language instead of the piddling English Department requirements.' "

Before long, Ginsberg would read *Howl* in mimeograph; in August 1956, while at sea, he would receive by mail an early printed City Lights Pocket Poets Series Number Four: *Howl and Other Poems* by Allen Ginsberg, Introduction by William Carlos Williams.

Ginsberg recalls his stay at his Milvia Street, Berkeley, cottage, as idyllically social, from early fall 1955 through just before shipping out late the next spring. Gary Snyder was with him part of the time, as Kerouac had been, before returning East in December 1955. With Ginsberg for a longer spell was Philip Whalen, about whom he remembers:

> He got a job washing test tubes in a chicken experimental laboratory in the agricultural school at Berkeley. . . . They were experimenting with chickens, injecting them with all sorts of hor-

---

* Ginsberg recollects that Witt-Diamant, at the last moment before a scheduled reading, "asked me not to say any of the 'dirty words,' 'cause she was afraid she'd get busted or it would create a scandal for the Poetry Center. It was still that much of a taboo, even in those days . . . a terrible reading [recorded] of *Howl,* in which I'm drunk and I'm censoring it, using the word "Censored" instead of the actual words of the poem." See photo, p. 200.

mones, or whatever. So we had an unending supply of chickens and eggs that he brought home. And food was cheap. . . .

I think I had a crush on Gary, and Philip at that time was half gay. There were times at Milvia Street when me and Peter and Gary and Philip and Jack were all there at once, writing little haiku, and we were studying—Gary had introduced a lot of Zen Buddhist terms and texts and Gary and Philip and Jack were familiar with the Lanakavatara Sutra [which equates nirvana and samsara] and the Surangama Sutra [which explains Ultimate Reality as Absolute Mind] and Blyth's haiku books.


Snyder also introduced Ginsberg to backpacking and camping. When the younger poet decided in January to hitchhike to Seattle, he invited Ginsberg on a journey that was his "first time to sleep in a sleeping bag and get climbing shoes and cork boots and visit giant Salvation Army places." In Portland on the way there, they read at Reed College and Ginsberg sketched the denizens at the rear of a "Skid Road Bar." The sketching is reminiscent of that of Kerouac as found most notably in his posthumous *Visions of Cody;* before his own sketch ends, Ginsberg acknowledges Kerouac's prowess in this mode: "Jack you were deeper than this being more involved, your sketch of the bums eating in the bowery, I give you the Palm & Crown."

An early February 1956 entry during the same trip refers to "tension with Gary—either he or I am doing it?"; a few days later, a short report on how Snyder's "ranger & forester friends" see the Northwest poet proposes, "Sometimes a snotty kid, sometimes a gazing Dharma hero with Aethereal Beard." On return, after embracing Orlovsky in his new Potrero Hill apartment, Ginsberg imagined himself through Peter's eyes as a "neurotic ghost of lacklove & Gary arguments & coldness," and the next night's lovemaking with Peter was interrupted by the reentering Snyder. Later, Ginsberg recorded his shyness at trying to communicate to Gary his new understanding of Paul Klee, reflecting: "I tried talking to Gary but could not get up courage. . . . I have been feeling stiffer and stiffer since he arrived." A season later, on his own at sea, Ginsberg would write: "I loved you & always have, but must I apologize—Gary?"

Settling back into Milvia Street for the spring, he awaited

word on Military Sea Transportation Service work—its pay could help fund a long-intended European trip. In the meantime, he served as baggage handler at San Francisco's Greyhound terminal, late afternoon through early morning.

His continued reading included, as these entries reveal, Williams, Whitman, and Hart Crane. He'd extend his study of Whitman and Crane at sea, but already appreciated the modernist poet for his "grand final rhythm" and "Powerful ear," having "read Atlantis aloud to the voice of Tears." Crane's letters, Ginsberg noted, "show he was simple & straightminded when it came to deal with poetic theory while his friends were incompetents gifted with the gift of Literary Gab."

Among his own new poems at this time is one to friend Herbert Huncke, imprisoned in Sing Sing; a few months later, while at sea, he'd celebrate Huncke in prose: "It was you from Chicago in the middle of America who put us all hip. . . . You who inaugurated the hip revolution . . ." During the period of springtime parties and nakedness chronicled in *The Dharma Bums,* he bade farewell to Gary (departing for Zen studies in Japan) in verse and drafted "In the Baggage Room at Greyhound." The increased number of poems in the fall of 1955 and spring of 1956 suggest that the triumph of *Howl,* as well as his continued reading and solidified relationship with Orlovsky, had an empowering effect.

In early May, Ginsberg began training as a Military Sea Transport Service yeoman–storekeeper, in uniform. He might, he speculated in a letter to his brother, be "bumped by the FBI if they decide I am too sensitive." Soon he'd be working on vessels that went up and down the coast, being fitted to sail to the Arctic Circle, with its antinuclear Distant Early Warning Line installations. Before the longer voyages, there were numerous delays and short trips for supplies, as well as a period in dry dock, which permitted Ginsberg to return home.

Visiting briefly at Milvia Street (he'd given the cottage to Whalen) when his ship returned to harbor, he received a telegram announcing his mother's death. Notes in the weeks preceding suggest that her demise was anticipated: "it's a wonder she has any mind left at all," he observed in May; the earlier "Schumann's Kinderscenen" reviewed maternal memories almost as if she were already dead. A late-April entry recorded a tearful dream encounter with his mother in a Times Square movie theater; its cinema locale would connect with a later note at sea: "My mother Naomi is dead. She used to go to the movies when her mother died in 1920."

The word of her death would be followed by intermittent efforts, over months and years, to focus on it in poetry. His first written response:

Death of Naomi June 9, 1956—
Tenderness & a tomb—the world is a tomb of tenderness.
Life is a short flicker of love.
Went out into the grass knelt down & cried a little—to heaven for her. Otherwise nothing.

Following a meditation on death, he reported, "Where e'er I went I went & said one fucked up Kaddish for her soul."

An entry made within a week or so records a seemingly related strange "room dream,"* in which Charlie Chaplin pantomimes a sunset after a performance of Verdi's *Requiem,* and Allen and Jack and Neal embrace sensually and sexually; in a succeeding dream, less than two weeks later, Naomi appears, pressing close to him with a male organ, half a dozen more genitals on her body like an Ephesian Artemis, and reclaims her space in the family. Except for such intermittent notes in dream record, poem, and fragment, we'd not know that this major event—the loss of his mother—has taken place. They will constitute an elusive path leading to *Kaddish* and related poems.

At sea in early summer, he read the proofs of *Howl and Other Poems* and recorded virtual despair at "the disorganization of it," pronouncing himself "consumed with envy of Jack's holiness & devotion to singleminded expression in writing." At the same time, his continued consideration of Whitman (he'd been reading Gay Wilson Allen's 1955 biography, *The Solitary Singer*) focused on how the earlier poet reconciled his inner self with the vagaries of the world, paralleling Ginsberg's own search for guidance in prayer and dream: studying the Mathew Brady photograph, he wrote of

---

* See note, p. 21.

the "The guarded look in Whitman's eyes . . . certainly a case of self-imposed repression & consciousness . . . all because he had no outside hand or outer validation he was timid to the point of repression." A later entry proposed that "Even the sweet bearded kisses disguise under Christian compassion a more pure animal tenderness . . . holy animal tenderness, mortal tenderness," and depicted Whitman as "an Angel of Transparency—in a world of hooded delight."

Subsequent entries continued to examine the personal-public dilemma, and Whitman's Christlikeness. And as the diarist attempted to probe what motivated himself, he spelled out a yearning for a union of sex and (mystical) spirit, so rich in *Leaves of Grass*, so separate in the apparent life of Whitman. It was a union that was difficult to attain in Ginsberg's own life as well:

> find out what it is I want that I can't get—ideal homosexual union? I think from earliest years—11–14—this has been my deepest almost a mystical longing.
>
> Giving that up, replaced by a purer evanescent mystical longing for one Deity I saw in things once and never again since Harlem?
>
> Both these impulses, the mystical becoming stronger in these years & slowly the queer one becoming nearer & nearer to mystical though as an untranslatable hope.

The numerous stops of the USNS *Sgt. Jack J. Pendleton*, which allowed the crew frequent excursions ashore and permitted Ginsberg a fleeting relationship with a heterosexual companion, came to an end as the ship approached Alaska. Entries of considerable descriptive beauty now record passage through waters near the Bering Strait:

> Many birds flying passage between the continents, the sea choppy tho clear, the air immediately around clear, further away a bleak white haze blinds the sight of the two worlds apart almost touching—the centuries shrouded in white mist. Small flocks of birds crossing low on the water, 5 apiece.

A similar later notation concludes with near nonchalance: "I forgot to say I threw 7¢ into Bering Strait to leave something of me in remembrance of Naomi, so near her Russia." The deliberate recollection of his act on behalf of his mother's memory reminds us that her death was only five weeks distant. A few pages later, he marked his intention to deal with it through poetry:

> Kaddish
> or the Sea Poem
> Irregular Lines
> each perfect.

Reading the Bible—he completed the Old Testament while at sea—Ginsberg dealt with the sexual proscriptions of Leviticus by composing the erotic poem "Many Loves" in biblical style. At the beginning of the second week of August, he received the first edition of *Howl and Other Poems* in the mail, writing that the title poem

> made me ashamed it was so shoddy when I first looked at it—till at the second reading I imagined myself prouder over its unique solitary engine intensity, which almost convinces.

In the meantime, he continued to contemplate a projected union between God, suffering, and love, and recorded that he "sang fragments of Messiah looking at the waters, pieces of Isaiah I read yesterday. Eli Eli Lama sabacthani. Thunder in the mist. Adonoi Elohenu Adonoi Echad. Tears in my eyes." He then connected God, who "dwells in a realm beyond our imagination," with poetry:

> The structures of the imagination are symbols of his actuality.
> Poetry is structure with knowledge of the actuality behind it.

Comments from his reading of Blake's "The Everlasting Gospel" conclude Ginsberg's effort at reconciling God and sexuality and imagination, a project melding his consideration of the careers of Hart Crane and Whitman, the death of his mother, and his months at sea. His MSTS service nearing its end, his next entries, over a month later, are on land (his ship was in dry dock during his final weeks of service). They were made from the same Bay Area social context (gatherings with Corso and Peter and Lafcadio Orlovsky; Kerouac; Michael McClure and Robert Duncan; Ruth Witt-Diamant; Neal Cassady) as detailed by Kerouac in the "Desolation in the World" section of *Desolation Angels.*

Soon, Allen and Gregory hitchhiked to Los Angeles where they'd meet Lafcadio and Peter, who'd taken the bus. From there they'd head for Mexico City, where the foursome would rejoin Kerouac, who'd set out some weeks before them. Ultimately, Ginsberg intended to return to New York, then leave to join Burroughs in Tangier, and thence to Europe.

On the way down the Pacific coast, the two poets had a strange encounter, which Ginsberg has never forgotten. In 1984 he recalled:

> We were trying to go by the coast highway and were going to visit Henry Miller, but we couldn't get a ride. We got stuck in Carmel, a little below Carmel around Monterey. Out there on the coast highway we saw a sign, "Edward Weston." We'd heard of him as a photographer, so we went in and visited him.
>
> And he was this old, old man with Parkinson's disease, in a bathrobe. In a beautiful little separate house studio, aside from his main house, where his younger son lived. So he invited us in, we spent an hour with him, he showed us his old photos, with trembling hands took them out of drawers that were specially built to hold photographs, big enlargements. The one I remember particularly was a photograph of a dead pigeon on a rock at Point Lobos, and photographs of Point Lobos. I hardly knew his name or his history, but it was this amazing old gnome. When we left he waved goodbye from his porch and said, "I was once a young bohemian like you." He was really sweet, 'cause we just knocked out of the blue, and said we were poets, could we visit? And he was alone, this old man, all by himself.

In Los Angeles, Ginsberg and Corso read before an informal audience that included Anaïs Nin. Following the reading of *Howl,* as Ginsberg recollects it, a drunken heckler, seemingly one of a group of Marxists bewildered by the poets' valuing "Beat" poetical insight over political construct, interrupted Corso's reading with:

"What are you guys trying to prove?" When the heckler persisted, Ginsberg answered: "Nakedness." Challenged "Whaddya mean, 'nakedness,' " Ginsberg took off his clothes. "I meant spiritual nakedness," he later explained.

After the reunion with Peter and Lafcadio, the four bused through Mexico, visiting Denise Levertov in Guadalajara and joining Kerouac (who was finishing *Tristessa* and beginning *Desolation Angels*) and Bill Garver* in the capital, where a well-known photo of Ginsberg, Corso, Kerouac, and the two Orlovskys was taken at the Alameda Park fountain. After scarcely a fortnight in Mexico, they headed northward.

New York was only a shared ride away from Mexico City, and everyone but Corso—who flew to Washington, D.C., to join Randall Jarrell—crossed the country in a broken-down car with a "crazy driver," who let them out at the White Horse Tavern on Hudson Street. Shortly, Ginsberg recorded with ironic eye the warm middle-class comforts of his paternal home ("by the dear ruin / of my red rug / and chinese father / Whitehaired furniture / newfangled lamps / expensive television") and dreamed of his early summer companion back in Seattle's skid row—not unlike his recalling his affection for Gary Snyder while at sea. But his Seattle companion, who in the poem is

> the green eyed kid
> dying of love
> and lonely whiskey
> outside in the alley
> where cops walk by
> with strange revolvers
> talking about death

becomes the image of America the poet will take to Europe, by Venice's "stone lions / mosaic palaces / and evil Bellinis."

---

* Former New York City overcoat thief; addict; prototype for Old Bull Gaines in the "Passing Through Mexico" section of Kerouac's *Desolation Angels*.

Ginsberg's winter of 1956–57 was marked by his going to
Naomi's Long Island grave, meeting Peter Orlovsky's family, visit-
ing Carl Solomon at Pilgrim State Hospital, and meeting Salvador
Dalí. It was also the time of his historic last visit—accompanied by
Orlovsky, Corso, and Kerouac—with William Carlos Williams. Wil-
liams, asked for a parting word, gazed out the window toward
Rutherford's Main Street and warned, "There's a lot of bastards
out there."

Allen spent much of the winter calling on editors and pub-
lishers with the manuscripts of nine other poets, as well as his own
City Lights volume. Along with work by Kerouac and Corso, he
contributed *Howl* III and "Fragment 1956" to one of the first
"Mimeograph Revolution" magazines, *Combustion*, edited by Wil-
liams' Toronto correspondent Ray Souster. He saw former Colum-
bia schoolmate Louis Simpson, who with Donald Hall and Robert
Pack was editing an anthology soon to be taken as standard in
many schools and universities. He recalls giving Simpson

> this *great* load of manuscripts of Duncan's, Creeley's, Levertov's,
> mine, Lamantia's, Wieners', Snyder's, Whalen's, Kerouac's, even
> O'Hara's—everything. And he didn't use any of it. . . .

A dozen years following this major omission in the preparation of
the 1957 anthology *New Poets of England and America*, Ginsberg
would tell this editor of Hall's having recently volunteered to him,
vis-à-vis Ginsberg's view of poetry, "You were right."

Characteristically undeterred, Ginsberg tried others:

> I went on this big push and went around all over everywhere I
> could. I think by then *Mademoiselle* had published a picture* of
> me and Jack and Gregory, the famous picture of Jack with a spit
> curl over his forehead with a cross and I was in my merchant
> marine shirt. . . .
>
> So, I went on a kind of campaign trying to introduce all this
> new poetry to these unwilling editors.

---

* The photograph to which Kerouac strongly objects, for *Mademoi-
selle*'s erasure of his crucifix, in his essay "Origins of the Beat Genera-
tion."

Interviewed by the *Village Voice*, Corso, Kerouac, and Ginsberg berated New York's "establishment":

"There is no room for youth and vitality in New York. It is a city full of guilty academicians."* (Corso)

"Too big, too multiple, too jaded." (Kerouac)

"We want everyone to know that we had to leave the Village to find fulfillment and recognition." (Ginsberg)

In the meantime, "Burroughs was still in love with me," Ginsberg recalls, and had been sending the poet, from 1954 on (see, for example, p. 84 of these journals), fragments of *Naked Lunch* routines, which Ginsberg had been compiling in a springboard binder as a manuscript. While in San Francisco, Ginsberg, as West Coast editor for Robert Creeley's *Black Mountain Review*, had offered sections of Burroughs' manuscript to Creeley, who chose the "Interzone" portion for publication in the *Review*'s last issue, number seven. Now, with the spring of 1957 approaching,

> the idea was for Jack and me to go to Tangier, and I was going to pick up with Bill again, who was still sort of desperate in romance with me. That was what the whole *Naked Lunch* correspondence was about—sending me all that magical material, getting more deeply involved with me by mail. Including very sentimental letters, portions of which, alas, he later burned.

At the end of the first week of March 1957, three weeks after Jack Kerouac's departure for Tangier and William Burroughs, Allen Ginsberg and Peter Orlovsky, for the first time in their lives, set sail across the Atlantic for North Africa and Europe. Their passage was covered by a legacy from Naomi; a small National Academy of Arts and Letters grant for Ginsberg, through the efforts of William Carlos Williams; Allen's Sea Transport savings; and Peter's modest monthly disability check from the army. Allen recorded his teary Paterson goodbye with his father, then watched his homeland vanish.

---

* The three quotations appear in Don Balaban's "Witless Madcaps Come Home to Roost," *Village Voice Reader*, ed. Daniel Wolf and Edwin Faushen (New York: Doubleday, 1962), p. 39.

## Back Cottage 1624 Milvia St. Berkeley
## Sept. 2, 1955

Peter Peter go away
I can't love you any more
I would I would but it wouldn't be good
You'd only send me away.

I sang this on the
Berkeley streets tonite.

\* \* \*

First day & nite in Berkeley, wandered afternoon early down-town, bookstores, depressed by all the poetry—Louis Simpson—saw an interlinear Horace ($2.50)—later nite wandering, tea high, saw Gene Pippin again studying in Kips Restaurant, & that name-less character I can't stand—and home midnite to pancakes high & Jupiter Symphony & garden & moonlight & loneliness—The huge horror of Berkeley ahead—could be nice, but ugly forebod-ings all day, job worry & study fears & the million books of scholars unreadable.\*

\* \* \*

Original exploration of the craft alone expresses a poet's individ-ual soul & conscience.

\* \* \*

In reaction to the usual romantic excess he (they) (Trilling) lost sight of the primary good of this here civilization, namely Truth of individual suffering & conscience & creation—not as against the mass, but against false conception of the mass & leaders of the mass which have led the mass to death—for the solitary and haunted individual is now the mass. And who will

---

\* I had matriculated at UC-Berkeley for M.A. study; advisor, Tom Parkinson, poet, anthologist, Yeats scholar, editor of *A Casebook on the Beat* (New York: Crowell, 1961), friend of Rexroth & 1940s S.F. literary anar-chists' circle. —A.G., October 4, 1982

speak for his own wild naked mind will speak for the mass. (And will Trilling speak for his own wild naked mind?) We want to read the individual, not his public thoughts. And Trilling doesn't think the individual is important. Just his Wisdom. As if his Wisdom could be separated from the mistakes juices & privacies of his life. He's rejected himself. We pay politicians to do that to us, we need an affirmation of the individual from artists; especially the screwball.

* * *

Sleepless drifting headache night, left face split at the temple, floor mattress dream:

On railroad train returning in Army to coast from visiting home—around a table with a group of bums—a fire in center, a cafe, in the circle someone else & I passing round a small bottle wine, 2 swigs that's all it holds—the rest are eying it, horseface burnt concentration camp, I hold money in pocket, someone on my right trying to pick my pocket, a railroad jungle cafe bohemia—Who's here, someone with me (Kerouac?) who wants to share their drink—give them of our drink—I uneasy return to my table, the bum next to me's pulled out the handkerchief from my pocket on the bench log where I sat, I stuff it back in, my money's there, my wallet in other pockets—I go to table—One of the group does an imitation of the French, the Social French, a tall mulatto or white Italian (from Sheepshead Bay M.S.T.S. training camp) gets up by microphone, I am in large room at table near front door exit, like Club Room Lesbian Bar somewhere—"L" or The Cage, Monterey—smoke, people, booths (Vesuvio Café–like)—he does imitation of Bad Talking Charlie—hair in circle over his ear—conscious imitation of Bad-Talker, it's the man himself doing an act on himself, pathetic, trustworthy, untrustworthy, I fear him, I keep away as he comes off platform passing near me to the exit, hair foetus-like over eye—

"Yes I'm Bad Talking Charlie
Alright inside
I got bad guts
and hair in my eye

My heart is gold
I steal your money
but if you watch your pocket
I leave you alone

Don't give me up
I'm your only friend
Bad talking Charlie
I'm here with you all

I'm standing before you
tipping my mitt
do the same for me
& don't reject my routine

It's only an act
I don't even get paid
I do it over and over
Watch me bow & exit humble & sad.

You're afraid of me
I'm not afraid of you
If I break your jaw
I come back for love you more

I come back for to see you
Somebody's got to talk to me
Keep watching my performance
I'm almost in tears

Someday, someday, someone
will give me a smoke
and a bottle of wine
around the bum fire

Ah, Charlie ah Charlie
Don't call me Bad-Talking Big boy
I can't help what I say
Watch out when you call me

Smile please smile at me
Mister, don't frown
I'm leaving the stage
Let's hear some applause

So bad Talking Charlie's in town
Come back where he came from
hospital & dream, in the cafe
entertaining you all for free


He passes out of exit next to me I ignore him—


* * *


To explore the Strophe & the Dithyramb?
To write words to Bach's Organ Preludes & Fugues? i.e. poetry
        fitting that long structure
To begin Anew, starting from the concrete blocks of reality
        Berkeley cottage roses etc.
To jump to the next thought, considering,
To form them into another sweeter sentence,
To jump afire into petroleum;
To flame up on the landscape, like an atom bomb;
To jump, to jazz, to kiss, to love everybody come,
To water the flowers, playing the sunlit water each to each, and
        return for godly extra drops,
To listen to music high in the mind, and stop
To pick up and begin again at the Cliffs of Beginningless leaps—
        Horror!
To bow the head like a rabbi in tears, intoning, the sorrowful
        one, Adonoi, Adonoi, where is thy Eden,
To rush with Shelley down East River in the midnite grass, pass
        with Shelley into the grass,
To gasp,
To sit at the desk and meditate, O Imagination thy task is
        endless—
To continue
To equalize the passions, to come to rest
To ride in a long line of horsemen to the Final West,
To watch the sun under the cliffs
To pass on vacation to Yosemite to the sublime to the egotistical
        sublime,
To ask for jobs in the hospital, night clerk in a hotel,

To run down a dark street looking for a ghost, and look at the full
        moon,
To notice light decline in the doors of the ocean,
To sit at the beach intoxicated & cold, in a black sweater,
To begin on a structure that's useless
To sit and worry—
To set loose from the dock,
To drift among asteroids in the cafeteria,
To sink under the ocean and be bumped by whales,
To walk along the roofs with the wings of birds or angels,
To feed vultures with garbage behind the market,
To sit in heaven with binoculars, looking into the shining floor,
To enter the messy submarine,
To walk on the floor of night feeling your way thru the basement
        waiting for meteors—
To paddle with the swan by the river,
To float over cities hungry in love,
To feed the fishes algebra,
To calculate the astronomy of souls,
To capture the roll of earth like a camera in a plane,
To understand higher mathematics or be dumb as a chicken
To go back to the past and connect with the future
To stay in the present, it's all the same,
To end it all to explore the strophe to play a game.

\* \* \*

To continue in rhyme
Time after time,
To ball in the hall,
From one to six,
To play no tricks
From six to seven
Get your kicks
From seven to eight
Deliberate
Eight to Nine
Drink some wine
Nine to ten
Don't tell when

Go back to seven
You'll get even
Ten to eleven
Go to heaven.


7:50 P.M.

\* \* \*


I try to stay at my desk & write but the structure always comes back to the material. I need a structure.

\* \* \*


In the "terrible silence" a child cries "Mommie." Sleepy in the kitchen, put to bed, still broken-voice. Over and over. Shut up. A scream of being hit—another scream louder—silence and a question. "I don't want to go to bed."

\* \* \*


I've loved you for a long time
When we met I was a virgin
I saw you in many beds
and lay on top of you naked
in my dreams

Time passes, I'm alone, I'm thirty.
Childish thoughts—I've had you
in real beds with drunken breath.
I've even heard "I love you."
I can hardly believe it, but
it was worth the trouble.

I see a picture of a skeleton,
in my mind: it will be me,
a square-jawed skull with hollow brow
and long teeth at the end of time.

Nights, days, the years flash
faster behind me, recollection
of your eyes, wonder at your absence.
I wish life had changed for us.

\* \* \*

## Happy Song

My life ill-fits me like a suit
                of somebody else's clothes.
May I change my clothes?
                                May I?
Easy—
        Try another on,
Check grey pants and yellow coat
        and purple porkpie hat
Green sunglasses to protect my chastity
        a thousand dollar diamond at my breast,
and a wallet full of hundred dollar bills.
                                That's my ideal.

\* \* \*

## Dream

    With the Last Tycoon (Burroughs) in a large hotel room—
granting people's wishes in experiments—Ryan (new military ca-
det) is to be brought in. We send the Secty (who's outside the door
of the big furnished room) for chauffeur & limousine to abduct
Ryan from his doorstep—bring him here, white scared & hand-
some. Bill takes out his letter (or journal) & proceeds to open the
box—the box being a fantasy mentioned in the letter-text, or
scaring himself with a suicide bomb in a box. Bill sets fire to the
box as Ryan is brought in—the box blazes, hisses, much noise
streams lights, like a railroad flare—I had been against it—
scared—but Bill insisted, had opened the window & the room was
large, the box just brightened the walls & made noise—Ryan
wandered around intelligent & bewildered—She (a mulatto he
desired) a chic girl from college, came in, also bewildered. I
thought, this will prove scary & excruciating for Ryan, but what
horror & hatred will it be for her! How hateful!

* * *

## Sept. 8, 1955

[Draft of "Transcription of Organ Music":*]

Bach trying to express the straining aching joy of knowledge the
flower in glass peanut bottle formerly in kitchen to
     take a place in the Light . . .
     This place, this house, is where I come in time—Dear Peter
flower thank you for your transmission of the sadness of growth—
     on hearing a piece of music by Bach (Organ Prelude and
Fugue in A Minor . . . (4th side last half)
     The music descends, as does the tall bending stalk of the
heavy blossom, because it has to, to stay alive, to continue to the
last drop of joy.
     Don't sing your sorrows anymore. . . .

     And the creator gave me a shot of his presence to gratify my
desire, so as not to cheat me of my yearning for him.
     Received tonite a letter from my father inquiring my where-
abouts, he's worried about me, did I get accepted in the university?
So he can send tuition.

     All sadness, all pain, in its agency & event (knives & love) is a
remote function—the knives & bad love affairs—a remote func-
tion of our separation from Him . . . the working out of things in
harmony to the basic soul of the flower breast.

* * *

## M. Genet:

     I omit all, but allow me to express my esteem of your angeli-
cal rhetoric. All Reality & Allegory is garbled. Myth is satisfied; the
Muses weep. Will you perish a saint; or have you already perished,
in which case let me address you as one of our illustrious Great
Dead! I hear little word of you; some old books in English to be

---

* First complete draft, including fragments unpublished, CP 140–41.

found in San Francisco & New York—some people around; who might have left one of your books in Halls of English or Times Square: York Avenue's East river, where I rushed mad with Shelley in the grass—an inspiration in the night—your book, later. What Eternity beckons? What man walks underground, in what room or cell? What streets do you walk today? What music listen to? & what tears weep? Who do you love now, Old Father Motherfucker are you in Death? I am listening to Bach organ music in my Cell chained with flowers: I live in a place called Berkeley, campustown, west coast, tragedy & isolation. Memorize poetry. Well this is idle. I shd bring it to a close, but have not included any central image or explanation of my purpose—not that I know myself—a black typewriter Time and a few days leisure.

\* \* \*

I suppose I'll wake up to find myself famous. I usually do.

\* \* \*

## Sept. 13 Nite Dream

—up on the roof, a desert, the tops of the houses we've climbed (myself Rexroth & various students) examining the pyramid-like frames of sand—We cross a gulf, from back to front visual field in dream, the house top looks like roofless triangular frame from old boarding house—examine the window frame, the triangular slope of peaked roof from its inverted V top, and even open a door—It leads downstairs, under the sand to the building (like 416 E. 34 St. Paterson)—not bare, remnants of furniture & old letters like an attic, intriguing, I want to go down—Rexroth says "No, I been down there already" boasting & closing the door—& opening the wall closet door next to it, showing against the wallframe & wire, the wall construction of plaster & wire mesh stapled in with their boards long crisscross—a large brown wrapping paper, something sent to me by Karl Shapiro, perhaps a picture or book (and I had sent to him, to begin with, so he could send me the object) and it contains stamps, postmarked, return address & my address, with a description of me so that it would reach me, like me of the extended joke letters I send Jack

envelopes—a description crazy poetic & flattering—"Allen Gins-
berg 26 handsome sweet saint queerboy writes poetry ex-Columbia
travelling lost & amazed"—& more, "you can find him unique in
his corner of the world"—and Rexroth sniffs at it, I hope he reads
it, he apparently has, no comment—

"Who kept thinking about marching & skulls all afternoon in the
          long high school class"—

Whitman when you got off the bus in your heavenly pants—

Jack—Peter is sure sweet
A—Oh, an angel
J—They were sitting there quietly
A—Angels doing their homework.

                    *  *  *

## Haiku

Thinking about ellipsis,
look in the mirror.

                    *  *  *

Money talks—the endlesss blab of dollar bills in the Key System*—
          The 2 businessmen drunk exchanging confidences—
          "Force him, of course!"

## Naked Lunch

          Gimme a brilliant sandwich,
          a bowl of sun soup,
          a plate of pure meat,
          a heap of metaphysical rice,
          Infinite tea, two foot bananas
          skin cookies, soul ice cream

---

  * Bay Area Transport trolley across Oakland Bay Bridge.

Timeless vegetables, moon stringbeans,
starry beets, albino crabs,
ancient fish, hairy salad,
human kasha, boys' okra,
girls' brussel sprouts,
Worms' apricots, caterpillars' lettuce
Flies' cabbage, centipedes' shrimp,
Ocean's vegetables, ants' tomatoes,
mountain's veal, lake's pork,
River's beef, cities' bacon,
cottage cheese,
taxicab's cauliflower,
ladies' soup, gentlemen's beans,
park's cream, seas' milk,
sky's potroast, horizon's fish
Jewish saliva lungs
Christian bacon intestines
Mohammedan coffee
Buddhist consomme
Hindoo bananas
Zoroastrian jelly
Chinese cheese
English assholes
Equadorian balls
Argentine breasts
Colombian buttocks.

## Dreams

1. The witch who robbed Neal's car, I insist & get it on baggage check.
2. Kerouac Mass before Institute Academy.
3. Boy Savage with spike-comb in breast-head brow fucking me, blood brother initiation indifferent sex masculine

\* \* \*

The nights pass, no one visits, I don't hear a sound
I'm hungry in this lonely house in the ground.

* * *

The New Orleans jazz band—promise of good times to come—
        Allen Joyce,
Rejoyce—we'll sweeten in arms & love with all breasts & hearts &
        cocks & fingers
Maybe, someday, baby, no more blues for me for you let's make it
        in Love, Sweet
I feel lonely like always I am Relieve me of my feeling for a day, I'll
        do you the same
O why won't you—shivering I went home cold in 2 shirts & green
        $2 corduroy jacket & Levis tonite
Music Masturbate tears love Eternity Allen soul ah!

* * *

A lover to come out of my imagination and end this yap about
        solitude.
Don't know who you'll look like, who'll next you be, why you came
        for me,
but have straight eyes, a good strong cock, a well built torso, thighs
        and breasts of a man,
larger than me, the face of an angel, a mind full of memories of the
        streets of heaven.

* * *

    Days pre-6 Gallery with Jack Kerouac & Neal:
    —Neal of Jack "Fret not other's sensibilities"
    —Allen re Peter—Not to forget me I was the angel arch-
priest
        friend & strictest master of Eternity you ever knew

    —"For the beauty of a huge scene in the bed"—J.K.
    —So that they could all go laughing to the cab.

## Ether Notes

With Jack at Jordan Belson's* the Nite we saw *Limelight*.
    "Life reduced to the film" as Jordan said to Jack.
    There's a certain line between Beer & Whiskey.


## Have You? (a song)†


The blues dropped in when I threw you out,
I used to dance and sing and shout—
But now—I'm lonely upside down over you
            (I'm his regular right hand feller)

        Joan's Bones
        Eddie's lonely strut
                or perhaps Eddie's drizzle street.


        A dirty spade song.
    Some people's got good hearts,
                Pick it up over here.
o thou—a plain downhome dirty blues.
                32,000,000 ain't enuf for me.
                Ease thy diamond hand.


## Aether

To remember the tearful nausea
Of the ether awakening in the hospital
—out how long?


-----

* Jordan Belson: independent filmmaker, noted for his Vortex Concerts in planetariums and animated films such as *Allures* and *Samadhi*.
    † These lines, through "chhchtt! khhcht!" on the next page, are probably by Jack Kerouac. —A.G., October 5, 1982

The aperture of another Rigamarole the Blanter
ancestances pancer
Write your name down.
                    Gather ye ether
        While ye may

I tickle Tom's ear
Allen howling Aili Aili
    Outside the door.

Red stream hanging
Little ole red string hanging here
        It's very pretty
                and a little small
chhchtt! khhcht!

                        *  *  *

## A Dream

                Walking with my father
                        down the cobble streets
                                of Frisco Chinatown
                We accosted a Chinese
                        Idiot youth
                With a black and white skeletal stare.

                                "Who is he" my father
                                        asked.
                                "What's he doing here?
                                        So you see him often?
                                        Is he an idiot?
                                        A mongolian?"
                                "No, a Chinese orphan."

                        Joseph     Joseph     Joseph!
                                said the boy
                                        advancing
                        Joseph     Joseph     Joseph!

## Crossing Bay Bridge

                    in the here and now of Fifties.
        o young man
                with beard seersucker
                        & dirty pants
                                & tokay hangover,
        dainty clarity of eye.
        He sees the huge blue sky
        nigh above the bridge
        roilmoil clouds, islands
                    spread around him
        Low mountains of Marin
                    County across the bay
        Treasure Island and streaks of
                    ripple on the water of the
                        Bay as in a Baby pond,
        clear air & atmosphere
                    & fine clockworks of
                    the ships.

                        * * *

## Carl Solomon

They have poured shit on you
They have poured shit all over your Tonsured Beedle.
They have poured liquid shit in your belly button.
They have greased your brown cock with shit.
They have put shit on your eyebrows two little dungballs one
        apiece,
And shit on your back, and shit on your teeth, and shit all over your
        cheeks,
They have dropped their shit over your horizon
They have built a wall of shit and surrounded you with it.
They have invented a nation of shit & called it Rockland,
They have stuffed your asshole with that shit

                        * * *

The Cancerous Capitalistic despotism of Tobacco.

* * *

## Conversation 3rd St Bar to The Place: Fragmentary Poetic Phrases by J.K.

O Ajax Cleansers tires
The dividing line—

     Une occasion—
     My mother, living with me today, was Helen of Troy then, in
fact I became enamored of her—you know—I never married, I
lived with mother
     I spent the war years knitting wigs & sweaters & woolen
diaphragms—

     I told you it already you don't remember.
     I never seen you so young in all my born days.

O Sherman Tanks of Mexico
Your troubled sages shifting together
        on uneasy feet.
It's got to be intelligible!
I'm too young to die.
Ma Rainey kissing together under the bar
and all the poor old Peter
            Abelards.
     They castrated him—
     They cut his balls
        in iv'ry halls
    And her belly was found
        nevermore.

Exploding pianos & lions & tigers
        under the bus
I never got drunk in Topeka

What about them exploding pisspots?
What about all them busted toilets?
What about all them dirty douche bags?

O what of the Allenslisic Burroughsian Queen?
  Vomiting on Kansas floors

Take a shrimp boat to Mérida
To look for Mayan Lore—

Déjà Vu—
The Milpitas* Iliad
    Mrs. Calabash
    Hector's fingernail's leaking.
What bleeding fingers do you have
            Mrs. Calabash?
                    Goodnite Mrs. Dedalus.
Goodnite Mr. Connection
            & Drop dead
Hellon wheels:
    Milpitas O'Neil.

Stumbling in the Aisles of Kansas

Coxophone.

I've never seen such imaginary beauty
    riding out of eyes—Allen
He was made out of blue license plates
    and white wine. —Jack

* * *

(Note to Howl)

And the Future:
    Let there be Communist Revolutions

* * *

Get rid of ourselves, of Angelism of balls, of charms & chests, of crazy loves, of alcohol's vegetables, of all superior thoughts. All other transformations, trees and Dangers, golden autos & gold halos, nirmana-hatta, get rid of, including the highways, & the cars and pens & notebooks, rid of the railroads.
    Aposiopesis . . . a break in syntax.

---

* Milpitas: a town in the Bay Area, Southern Pacific railroad stop.

* * *

## September 26, 1955

With Neal past white floating domes of Airport with weird airplane wing folded back big bug low in the air—up Bayshore highway, rising on the crest in and out of lanes, narrowly missing blind spot filled with cars—clang, clang, up down of gong on engine unseen—I sit 3rd & Townsend—we talked about self-forgiveness, he urged me on in the car, singing to the radio "nigger jazz hymns"—as we rode in over the crest of the overpass viaduct and saw the city he pointed out the long brilliant skyline and shouted with the radio da de dee da da ded de dum dum dum doom doom ("O the Monkey wrapped his tail around the Flag-pole . . .") with the brass band of the Marine Hymn rising raining out of the radio box, instead of bop—saluting the city he got so high & excited to ecstasy till reaching the end of the freeway on 6th St. he was jumping & screaming & shouting.

Last nite my vision in his bed at Los Gatos* of a novel of him now. Neal of the Railroad—The whole scene from Los Gatos to the Place.

The screaming power in the iron casement inside the Diesel Locomotive in darkness we rode on, Jack drunk & singing blues, I respectful & Neal worried about the Head Conductor Bureaucrat of the tracks in private car behind. (we took a trip together to Los Gatos for weekend)

And now the 3rd St. Railroad Bridge—which lifts to admit ships—bird soaring in sky above (dove) flagpoles empty next door on the roof, bonk of horn below, big fat white ass mammy sitting on newspaper truck-stands like Mexico scattered before S.P. station, PARKING, FLAMINGO, big heavy weighted machinery overhead, like the vast invisible machinery of the skies, but here in small a huge mortal load of iron & concrete structural steelwork raising its raw head over the road bevisored & ribboned of steel with rubber carwheels zzinging along underneath on the pave it's made of, it

---

* Not long after Ginsberg left San Jose for San Francisco, the Cassadys moved to Los Gatos.

too with flagpoles and lights about, where a man can stand on platform at the peaktop above only he'd be dumped with the whole works when it bows and bends down low like a giant to lick its own steel cunt and rear its fantastic spiderweb bridgework engineering ass up to heaven humble, toot, to let the ships pass thru the lock it hovers over day & night (invisible) except for lone red & blue & green lights scattered over it like stars on its ashen sides— huge creaking ponderous weight suspension bridge you could jump over with a gigantic pogo stick it's no George Washington, Zip, bam, roar, crash around my heart and ears, a jet bursting thru the sky over the S.P. Station—Fatass eats her lunch, sadly, bent over the waxpaper examining pork Mowls and logmeat from supermarkets in Alabama receding into the night—On this side the bridge reveals, oom, vast laborious concrete piling hung overhead in the air, pull a chain and it slowly lowers its weights, creak, slow, descending within touching distance of the ground this side of the bridge—speedier, and the rearing engine of the air also raises up to the howl and clang of bells & locomotives, cars all stopped for five minutes zoom another jet repassing—an infinity, heximetrical forms riveted together 50 years ago before the quake (or after)— Cabbie in blue fat coat & flower red soup tie, hands folded behind back, waiting, saying Cab, not as loud as a jet—

To pick up on the bridge later again.

* * *

## [Excised from "Sather Gate Illumination" (CP 142–45):]

Standing still and quiet at North Gate, the hump of the rise from street to grassy campus, a vast grey army tree at the end of the lane, against the sky, I stood still, quiet, alone, a thousand voices around me, girls in sweaters and boys in yellow hair, calling to each other, walking, waving, singing communications, the mist in the air, smog, sky, fog, the brilliant sun hidden in the back behind the buildings radiating golden in the dark air, tremendous silence all about except for myriad human cries, voices as of birds chirping in the stillness.

Buddha's reply to the question, What happens to a gift rejected? (After a screaming old woman insulted him)—"The gift returns to the giver." Jack quotes this often.

So Jack's several accusations of "lechery" at me.

So Mrs. Robinson's final excuse when firing me from busboy job at Kips Restaurant, Berkeley—"The work is too much for you." It was too much for her, that's why she thought to say that to me, to change the situation.

Know people in reality (as in Harlem vision) by what they actually say, exhibit, of their inner thoughts. Love thots or Greed thots.

When I lay in bed hurt for Peter thinking I was growing old, impotent, loveless, unfriendly, my grief was at his not loving me. My grief was at not loving myself. . . .

\* \* \*

Kerouac you & I and the jazz musicians sat late into the nite, while my eyes were droopy tired out of beer, waiting for the last session to sing out in final blowjob of the bandsmen's joy.

\* \* \*

—The droppings of the mind on the page (Jack's poetry)— cummings is artificial.

\* \* \*

Li Po said
I'm going to the moon
for a cup of sake*

\* \* \*

# Berkeley & University store

The always-promised department store mystery interior behind Santa Claus or the Zoo of Toy Animals, the unseen dreamlife, hints of which are given by the Show, the window display, the man in a white beard—Where did he come from, what friend will he have tonite.

---

* Guihuajiu, "moon liquor." —A.G., June 27, 1991

\* \* \*

My mind is crazed by homosexuality

\* \* \*

## 10 Minute Sonnet

The cunts of wheelbarrows & the cocks of cars
Fuck in the starry nite; Embarcadero,
I'm working on the S.P. shifting bars
of gold & lead & iron, Jailhouse Joe
he works beside me, & I work by Mars,
the fattened trucksman with his tattered No.
Mailbags, Xmas, Frisco, whores of Port
Time's truck rides down the hiway to the hill
over the road home, over my nose a wart,
Joe's in Carolina, Tangiers in Bill,
Lucien's in N.Y., Neal's stopped short
I'm all alone on the dock I made my will,
all things tend to this moment, shadow,
and the rest, the past, this is my mad meadow.

\* \* \*

Death will confer immortality on me, when what I say seems
true. Now I'm too personal, fit only for an unliving being, with no
relationships, in the grave.

\* \* \*

The stars are Green.

In Foster's (with La Vigne)—Gimme a bowl of sun (soup) &
a napkin.

\* \* \*

Third St. Movie—huge tearful faces, Indians & Negroes,
Chinamen walking before the screen.

* * *

Take another sweeter
Sadder chorus
Jazzman
Blow your bop to the
new hip moon,
unhappy,
Blast the firmament
with soul to the
bottom of God.

* * *

The Eureka house—Neal's musician buddies blowed, the nite out with Ruth Witt-Diamant, Peter, Jack, Louise Bogan.

When we are dead, what will remain of us—all the loves & bodies, night & car rides thru the rainy streets and tossing passionate beds (heads?)

Nothing, baby, body, we'll be gone, others will be fucking, but the whole earth will be shoveled over into corruption till it's incorruptible & void.

Therefore I've written these lines to communicate eternal meetings in time. Passionless, it should last.

* * *

## Dream Mon. Nov. 21, '55 Afternoon

Waked remembering long dark road, lady & young kids running across, tangled shadows in front of the car lights, a bump, the children ran on, I rush forward & stop them, we go back & look at one of their number glimpsed lying under the car, they pick her up, I am 20 feet away, lift her young boy's body up, lift up a baby, farther, I step back & gasp, looking up, a huge scene above, the vast railroad world Trestle Machinery in the air above, Holland Dutch windmill Teahouse V shape upside down a thousand feet above in the gloom by the moon, I draw back, dig the height and the baby

Reading for San Francisco State Poetry Center, November 20, 1955. Phil Whalen extreme right with cigarette; painter Ronnie Bladen next to Helen Adam, dark-haired with eyes closed. "A small school-sponsored affair, not one of our wilder nites," A. G. once wrote on back of this photo.

lifted up sacramentally, & gasp exclamation of roar & wild scenery stage of the image.

Then falling back to sleep, dreamt of an apartment I had, a huge cottage with a long rugged entranceway glass enclosed, pillows along the corridor to the room, we're out in Berkeley, we meet 2 young girls, they take us to their apt, up on street of Haste— business street, 2nd fl. over a garage, small room, a man sitting on bed playing flute reading Dostoyevsky, introduce us, he's a new scene Hipster, they know of me, I'm famous, another man comes in bald, thin, bent, Gary's father, the broken wit of the scene, a half hunchback, mechanic, Chess, reads love Sagas & Sutras, lays the girls, digs us, and we all go off to my house, there a boy appears, dressed in rags, another of their bunch, I sit on pillow in hall watching him thru glass loiter at my door, his pants, his crotch,

# POETRY CENTER

San Francisco State College

19th and Holloway

San Francisco, California

### KEEP THESE DATES OPEN FOR POETRY

#### 1955-56 SEASON

OCTOBER 30 . . . . . . . *GARY SNYDER*
NOVEMBER 4 . . . . . . . *LOUISE BOGAN*
NOVEMBER 20 . . . . . . *ALLEN GINSBERG*
DECEMBER 4 . . . . . . . *PHILIP WHALEN*
DECEMBER 11 . . . . .*KENNETH ROXROTH*
JANUARY 8 . . . . . . . . *JACK GILBERT*
JANUARY 22 . . . . . . . *POETRY CENTER
WORKSHOP POETS*
FEBRUARY 12 . . . . . . *SELDON RODMAN*
FEBRUARY 24 . . . . . *MALCOLM COWLEY*
MARCH 11 . . . . . . . *MICHAEL McCLURE*
MARCH 25 . . . . . . . . *JAMES HARMON*
APRIL 3 . . . . . . . *RICHARD EBERHART*
APRIL 15 . . . . . . . *CHEN SHIH-HSIANG*

## *WATCH FOR ANNOUNCEMENTS*

Support the *Poetry Center Program* to bring distinguished poets of our day to the West Coast; to encourage young poets by providing a sympathetic and informed audience. Membership includes free admission to all *Poetry Center* events.

Associate Membership . . . . . .    $5.00 a year
Sponsoring Fellow . . . . . . . . . .    $25.00
Life Member . . . . . . . . . . . .    $50.00
Patron . . . . . . . . . . . . . . .    $100.00

Make checks payable to *POETRY CENTER
San Francisco State College*

ragged, razor holes, plucked cloth full of moth breaks & holes, DuPeru like, then Neal comes up, brings him in, looks, asks, Can the upstairs porch people see in here (landlady rumors?). I say look & see, *No,* so he settled his suitcase down in the hall, says, I'll stay here, I'll live here then, in and out, just to change clothes roll tea & ball, go to work & Los Gatos, and also the young fellow, he'll settle with us—and I realize with joy a new hip younger generation

of real interesting deadbeat bum secret conspirers in mechanic
Bobbysox attire has appeared before us.

* * *

Lying there on the pallet
with my hard-on out
            of my underwear
rubbing fast with my hand
        and finger clenched
imagine sexual phantoms
        of Peter, of other days, other bodies
in the sun ray misty dust mote shaft
            into the empty room thru the window.

* * *

[Fragment parallel to "The Names," CP 176–79:]

Many a soul has founded a tomb in the wilderness,
many a soul gone riding outward in the rain,
many a soul in jail and prison or asylum,
many a soul gone singing in the sea

* * *

Metrical Paradigm for unfinished section of Howl, a reverse
fugue, Diminution of Bass & augmentation of response:*

Under the archways under the Eiffel Tower electricity bulbs
            beyond Kodaks and Dakotas
Their wisdom is ended

Under the triphammer of the stars congealing in misery
Their wisdom is ended with bloody fingers

Under the negative constructions & psychoanalytic couches
They lie down & expire out of their vacant ears delighted

---

* A reverse interchange (last line) litany also intended as part of a
later section of *Howl.* —A.G., Oct. 5, 1982

* * *

[Entry of uncertain date made after an argument with Kerouac:]

"Then go—why don't you go then," I said, with black Lucifer in my eye riding across the dusky room to him on the bed.

And he rose slowly saying, "Yes it is a good idea," muttered for me to hear, "It's a good idea," he muttered again—

And thinking once more, I desired to undo his going, after a moment, I said,

"Jack don't go."

But he went.

So I waited a moment, and thinking still he might be hiding under the stairs I went down creaking barefoot to the rural street & found him gone, shouting "Jack!" to each direction—

And now pack a back he's riding the range & railroad to the desert to beweep himself.

* * *

## Inside the Stands, Tanforan Racetrack Dec. 1955

The ramp slope precipice (down which a Spanish beauty suddenly appears, black haired), leading up to the overlook precipice cliff of the world with a low concrete corbeled roof straight across, a slot to the sky, 30 feet forward from where Neal Peter & I sit, Neal in middle, saying, everybody here has got his own idea about what's happening so you don't pay no attention to them, except a few people you notice or know—

But I notice the lineup as in the great ramp to heaven, the lineup of worried faces, humans, with hats & raincoats folding papers, the slot into the sky with them all silhouetted, staring down on the great racetrack of illusion.

* * *

Holy! Holy! Holy! Holy! Holy! Holy! Holy!
Holy! Holy! Holy! Holy! Holy! Holy! Holy!
The world is holy, the soul is holy
The skin is holy, the nose is holy
the hand is holy! The eyeball holy!
The nose & cock & ass & asshole holy!

Holy! Holy! Holy! Holy! Holy! Holy! Holy!
Holy! Holy! Holy! Holy! Holy! Holy! Holy!
The world is holy! the soul is holy!
The skin is holy! the nose is holy
the hand is holy! The eyeball holy!
The nose + Cock + ass + asshole holy!

Everything is holy everybody's holy everyone's an angel
Everywhere is heaven Everyplace a paradise
Every every is a seraph every Everyness is god.

The pig is holy as the Seraphim ( is holy)
The bum is holy as you my soul are holy.
the notebook is holy the poem is holy
the voice is holy the audience is holy the typewriter
                                    is holy
        —— First Version in Bus up & along St.
to 1010 Montgomery to see peter.  Dec '55?

Journal entry, "Footnote to *Howl*." Comment
by Ginsberg at bottom was added later. See
drafts in *Howl: Original Draft Facsimile*,
pp. 97–107.

Everything is holy everybody's holy everyone's an Angel
Everywhere is heaven Everyplace is paradise
Every every is a seraph every Everyness is god.

The pig is holy as the Seraphim (is holy)
The bum is holy as you my soul are holy.
The notebook is holy the poem is holy
the voice is holy the audience is holy the Typewriter is holy


First Version [of "Footnote to *Howl*" CP 134] in Bus up
Kearny St. to 1010 Montgomery to see Peter. Dec. '55?

\* \* \*

Morning—the steel grey sky—must
        sleep—rust & sleep in my heart—
        eyes aching ready to weep—waiting
        for a bus to look for a job—Xmas
There be poems, there be lovers, there be
        conversations all day, there be
        meetings and gatherings—I'm alone
        looking for a job.
Stock Boy, Mail Handler—Real Iron Co.
        closed at 7:30 AM—Fat He in
        gabardine jacket 50 opens his
        dingy office—
O mister you've been working too long—
        your wife is rubbing her eyes in
        the dawn as you put on your pants
        by the TV set. The bus.
Coffee and Danish while the sun rises over
        S.P. terminal and illuminates the
        spiderweb R.R. bridgework against
        the dingy clouds—
Chinaman lights cigarette butt black
        where ash was—
The Dumps—the chill—my sneakers and
        leather jacket (dirty suede)—
Small handwriting in the notebook—an eternal

round, looking for a job, if not this,
what, the void?
Anxiety of poverty—pressing need—I have to
get some paycheck love meat soon
or worry more.

\* \* \*

Francis Dark & Marilyn Blonde

\* \* \*

## Dream (at Al Sublette's House)

Coming down street, on way to city, no money, Berkeley, Dwight Way at nite, I enter small grocery, see pastry, talk to girl, ask prices, has she more? And her mother an old nasty thin woman comes by joining us, shows where pastry is, it's four interesting kinds, one a chewy good sweet turnover, one Eclair, one a bright ladyfinger bun, one a sweet large Danish-French exotic, I am hungry & entranced, I buy one, the girl who looks interested at me talks to her mother, her mother goes back behind store, they know me, poet, she offers me an extra sweet, I say yes, and ask for more in fact, free, and begin assignating with her, if she likes me, I will lay her, I'm getting hot, and she says here's something interesting—a note her mother brings from the back of the store to the lower partition meat counter. The paper, as I look at it, is a shortened version of a letter of mine, or a Journal, saying "Be, it's all die, I help kill them all—am guilty and Al Sublette thinks I'm OK but secretly I betray; so was Natalie killed, I never gave them money, I'm superior."—I say, where did you get this, it's unjust, that's not the context, it's a literal misreading of my kind of text—She shows me a whole sheaf of same, quotes, letters, reports—A whole detective system—I'm being screwed out of my pastry—I object to it, looking obviously worse than newspaper misrepresentations—and

in the same room, now a living room, seated around, Berkeley cats, Norma's paranoic set of middlebrows—conversing and taunting me, I deny it, Browman says, "Oh it's true you're in it too, don't you exchange final shots with Alex all the time?" And I

get angry. I have a stick, a cane of some kind, I attack him if he dares
to speak again, I wave it in front of him (I see myself exchanging
final fluff-off shots with Alex)—and I leave the room, angry, de-
fending myself, my honor, my image, but angry enough to think
they're all crazy trying to involve me in mad plot. I am actually
angry enough to throw them all over and their stupid evil opinion.

Dream began with Connie Sublette in the other room saying
something to Al, to make him shut up (6410 Filbert St.)

> Sitting on the bench
> Waiting for the 10:37,
> It's now 10:22

New Jazz is balls & soul.
Jazz has a soul. The Soul of Jazz.

And those poets who came thru Louise Bogan's Eyes, who
had fantastic secret connections with the jazz musicians based on a
weekend of private hungering balls together.

Intelligent sentience dawns on the mind and turns tele-
phones into strange animals.

* * *

**[Draft of "America," CP 146–48:]**

America I've given you all and now I'm nothing—
Amcrica when will we end the war?
America when will you be angelic?
America when will you take off your clothes and be human?
America when will you give me back my mother?
America when will you give me back my love?
America when will you look at yourself through the grave?
America when will you be worthy of your million Christs?
America what's wrong? Why are your libraries full of tears?
America when will you send your eggs to India?
America when will you stop destroying human souls? Your soul my
        soul?
America when will you send me a lover?
I Allen Ginsberg Bard out of New Jersey take up the laurel tree
        cudgel from Whitman

* * *

Already Time for your Elegy, dear Natalie?
Already time for the angelic shock?
Already your blood meaningless,
        and your truthful eyes
        troubling me too late?
Should I have invited you to Berkeley?
Given you money? or more love?
        or a rest home in my crazy lovely garden?
In the car over for Thanksgiving
        you gave me a look so tearful
            I knew it was death
            or thought so
            and it passed my mind
            not my time yet
            I ignored you.
I closed my light lay back
        & try to pray for you.
Take refuge in my prayer.
        Take refuge in Pater Omnipotens Aeterne Deus
            Take refuge in Love (which is God)
                Self Love—
Oh, Natalie, where is refuge?
Take refuge in Death.
        Finally it is death I wish
—not the horror of blood bedabbled knees
        and ankles on a pavement
        or a throat cut by electric bulbs—
Dark death, Soft Death
        Black eternal grave
                and rest.

* * *

**Haiku composed in the backyard cottage at 1624
Milvia Street, Berkeley 1955, while reading
R. H. Blyth's 4 volumes *Haiku:***


Drinking my tea
Without sugar—
    No difference.


\* \* \*


The sparrow shits
    upside down
—ah! my brains & eggs!


\* \* \*


Mayan head in a
Pacific driftwood bole
—Someday I'll live in N.Y.


\* \* \*


Looking over my shoulder
my behind was covered
with cherry blossoms.


\* \* \*


Winter Haiku
I didn't know the names
of the flowers—now
my garden is gone.


\* \* \*


I slapped the mosquito
and missed.
What made me do that?

* * *

Reading haiku
I am unhappy,
longing for the Nameless.

* * *

A frog floating
in the drugstore jar:
summer rain on grey pavements.
                                    (after Shiki)

* * *

On the porch
in my shorts;
auto lights in the rain.

* * *

Another year
has past—the world
is no different.

* * *

The first thing I looked for
in my old garden was
The Cherry Tree.

* * *

My old desk:
the first thing I looked for
in my house.

* * *

My early journal:
the first thing I found
in my old desk.

* * *

My mother's ghost:
the first thing I found
in the living room.

* * *

I quit shaving
but the eyes that glanced at me
remained in the mirror.

* * *

The madman
emerges from the movies:
the street at lunchtime.

* * *

Cities of boys
are in their graves,
and in this town . . .*

* * *

Lying on my side
in the void:
The breath in my nose.

* * *

On the fifteenth floor
the dog chews a bone—
Screech of taxicabs.

* * *

A hardon in New York,
a boy
in San Francisco.

---

* Ellipsis periods appear in the journal entry.

\* \* \*

The moon over the roof,
worms in the garden.
I rent this house.

\* \* \*

1.) All conversation—"I need a spoon to eat soup"—is bridg-
ing Ellipse, all my talk is haiku.
2.) The Western image (metaphor the apt relation of
dissimilars—Aristotle) is compressed haiku.
3.) Study of primary forms of ellipse, naked haiku, useful for
advancement of practice of western metaphor
—"hydrogen jukebox."
but not superior form
really, just the essentials &
bones.
4.) Haiku = objective images written down outside mind the
result is inevitable mind sensation of relations. Never try
to write of relations themselves, just the images which are
all that can be written down on the subject (conversation
w/DuPeru).

\* \* \*

My God!
Uncle Harry, what happened
to you—are you really gone
already past the deathbed to the grave,
disappeared into B'nai Israel Cemetery
with the rest of the ancestors we knew
and watched go by, and ate our Seder
Suppers over again every year at your house?
I didn't think of it happening to you,
you didn't either, I guess, nor think
of the last long painful bitterness of cancer,
visible flesh wasting away in a bed,
final bitterness of what must have been
your hopeless knowledge at the last,
the vision of life as a dream more dreamlike
for its finale hours, all time a dream,

all Newark a dream, the family, Buba & Clara a dream
—myself perhaps receded even in your thoughts
as dreamy as the rest—vast horrible New York
Petroleum and English Anguish Ham* a dream,
All time a dream, the gape of black eternity
more real than these fleet visionary years—
we're all caught in this closing withering
mental flower, trapped by our imagination
—still since we didn't know each other much
inside, preoccupied with appearance,
Salute, Uncle, for your descent to knowledge
and your final suffering, a Hebrew prayer at last,
I'll be your nephew, you my uncle, in your
imagination, my imagination, and the grave.

## April–May SF 1955

H. Hesse—Siddhartha
D. H. Lawrence—Selected poems (Rexroth ed.)
Corbière translations C. F. MacIntyre
Randall Jarrell—Selected Poems
Graves & Riding—Survey of Modern Poetry
Collected poetry—Laura Riding
Edw. Dahlberg—Do These Bones Live? (23 pages)
W. C. Williams—Selected Essays
K. Rexroth—Signature of All Things, In What Hour, Phoenix &
            Tortoise
Ezra Pound—Classic Anthology Defined by Confucius
Eliot—all poems reread (aloud)
Zukofsky—*Anew,* and *A Test of Poetry*
Nahm—Selections from Early Greek Philosophy—Heraclitus
W. H. Auden—Shield of Achilles
Godolphin Mod Lib Treas Latin poets
Hadas          "      "      "    Greek poets
Anacreon (19th cent Locke ed. interlinear)
Sappho (Pauper Press ed. various translations)
Pound—Collected Criticism 1954 ed.
Pound—Kulchur

---

* Uncle Harry Meltzer's last job was selling English Ham.

## July 1955

Chas. Reznikoff—Poems (early)
Buddha—Diamond Sutra, beginning of Surangama Sutra, in
           Goddard, *Buddhist Bible*
Collected Poems—Laura Riding (most of)
Brave New World—Huxley
Shakespeare—A Winter's Tale
J. M. Keynes—Two Memoirs (Lawrence & Dr. Melchior)
           (plus some of essays)
The Vestal Lady on Brattle St.—Corso, Gregory
10 Centuries of Spanish poetry—Turnbull (Unamuno & St.
           John Cross)
Cocaine—Pettigrilli (couldn't finish)
Faulkner—A Fable
Pound—Translations
Vollard—Cézanne
Art of Indian Asia—Bollingen Vol. 2 (plates)
Eberhart—Undercliff (parts)
Auden—Shield of Achilles (reread)
Jarrell—Collected Poems
Keats—Reviewed Odes & Sonnets, etc., late poems

## Aug.

Old Testament Begun First time thru since High School—
           Genesis
Mark Schorer—The Shores of Light??* A novel anyway very
           poor
Josephine Miles—Lines at Intersection, Local Measures, Diction
           Book
Genet—2 plays *Haute surveillance* & *Les bonnes*
Cocteau—The Typewriter; Diary of Film (Beauty & Beast)
Paul Klee—On Modern Art; and Gideon Wellick volume
Wallace Stevens—later poems in Collected Poems
e. e. cummings—later poems in Collected Poems
Cocteau—Call to Order

---

* Likely, Schorer's *The Wars of Love.*

Genet—Letter to Lenore Fini & *Le Condamné à mort* & *Chant d'amour*

Genet—Gutter in the Sky (Miracle of Rose, Leva Phila tr.) (reread Frechtman tr.?)

Céline—Guignol's Band, finished

Dudley Fitts—Anthology of Latin American Poetry

New Directions 1940—Surrealist Anthology

Guillaume Apollinaire—Some of N.D. Selected Writing

Lorca—Various translations & originals (Spanish)—N. Dir. vol. also

Wallace Fowlie—Mid-century French poetry

A Mirror for French Poetry (read book read already in N.Y.)

Gogo Lamantia—various writings

Gary Snyder & Mike McClure—S.F. poets various MSS (also Robt Howard, Dave Toplis, etc.)

Horace—Interlinear tr. of complete Horace begun

## Dec.

Various books on Zen, Blyth's 4 vols. Haiku (in & out), Senryu, Sutras, etc.

Whitman Complete, Modern Library Edition

Cendrars, Blaise (a bit in Fr.)

Artaud—Pour en finir avec le jugement de dieu (Guy Werhnam tr. in MS)

## January 1956 1624 Milvia Street, Berkeley

Jan 1—that was end
of Record
here
look elsewhere
look
love
elsewhere.
Oh goodby half familiar
drunk
sweet red book
O me.

\* \* \*

Peter DuPeru on a singlebed striped pallet on the floor mattress, leaning on a big crazyquilt pillow, mind in his hand, musing & scratching his neck over Blyth's *Haiku*, sniffing—"The thing is, if I go to the Y tonite, you wouldn't want to . . ."—sniff, nose, O, outbreathed laugh.

\* \* \*

## Vision of Eternity

A great undulating moiling black infinite massive ocean at nite from which a great undulating huge throat shrieks like an elephant or whale a hideous-eyed howl of pain. As elephant scream in the movies. With science fiction cave-of-brain roofless cavern sea darkness bubbling with plastic-oil-protoplasm.

\* \* \*

## Structure: Howl

In strophic movement—alternation of rise, with blue fall, to rise higher again, stay on same peak & rise even higher—final— series on peak.

\* \* \*

## Waking on my Pallet

Opening my eyes
The spatter of 27 raindrops
Big black Bird swoops by the windowpane
First morning sight
eyes opened Jan 11, 1956


## Hymn to Marijuana


If it wasn't for you, Mr. Marijuana, noblest of intoxicants, we'd all
        be lying in a drunken bloodynose stupor in a gutter
we'd be exploding into cancer under the archway of the Triboro
        Bridge, our right forefingers stained with cunt and nicotine
never would've heard great waves of eternity flowing through the
        basses of Bach

# Jan–Feb Hitchhike trip 1956 with
# Gary Snyder to Seattle

Seated along the back wall of Erickson's Portland Skid Road bar (the Valhalla Hotel across the street)—here under electrocution-neon white light, beside me old wimple with a brown hat finishes his white cigarette wet tip & shifts his feet, stretched out with black leather laces tied, on the linoleum white splotched floor squares—the float of chewing tobacco in my nostrils and a man standing over me perhaps observing—Old Gold pack at me knee, folded under my right knee where I watch the inner pale of the wall uncomforting my back so to begin. A Domino. D'a match buddy—and he on my left reading the *Reader's Digest*, "I'm Glad I'm an Army Wife" first article reaches forward to the strange "LLF" cigarette paper folder—puff—on the floor, crinkles & rubs it in forefingers & now it's back on the floor next to a shining godlike cellophane cigarette wrapper & a scattering of flat roll your own roaches. Everything's on the floor including me so I begin as long as attention lasts on the floor. Now next to me Buster Brown the Mustache from Mexico with his brown overseer's hat & about a foot of lite-brown slacks rolled up above his squared workshoes, leather heavy boots, & coat hanging over the side of the yellow chair with chrome-sided backrests, I mean, they lean back, hats on, reading the Daily Socialist Oregonian, with middleaged glasses, with their coats on, and the coats hang over flapping to the flo'! or wander over to the staunch round tables & pick up a spare sheet of newspaper to examine, negroes, standing or gazing above it cig in mouth—ah, the cigarettes—looking into the middle distance haze between horizon of upstairs lights & the floor's brown haze. Who's next to me, relinquishing the *Reader's Digest* sits now with his thumbs pressed to the brow, now hands folded in prayer meditation and boredom gazing ahead chair legs & table legs and Oregons of Boots down the aisle to the thicket at the bar. The clock says quarter to 3, hands spread wide to the ends of Time. Now he's straightening out the aluminum foil smooth, & now tossing it to join LLF & instructions & wooden matches littering the floor. My footsole's here too. Now his head's bent on his arms. Now as I put out my butt he says "Let's see you there—" I flub it out unknowingly but aptly catch the spark & hand it on, he picks it up &

puffs toward heaven till it's lit again. With thumb and forefinger stuck in his mouth as to whistle, he puckers & smokes.

Up six feet & 8 feet forward the huger and more prosperous flare of a wooden match under a cap beside a mackinaw lights up a straight cigarette.

Around the wall: old blackeye reads his handsome face in a pocket-book of lore and blood, crosslegged, injun style with red shirt. Joe comes out of the bathroom door & rubs his jaw emerges into the world again. Sniffs & rubs his nose into his cigarette hand—and lurches back into the book. A voice announcing "dimes & energy," hawk tones like Reno gambler, from the bar. All mixtup. What do I know about these people anyway— Nothing but I too am against the wall in jeans & heavy hoofy shoes. Next him an indian old man, face square light skin, attentively observing outward, black coat folded over back of chair he straddles, Railroad pants wanders thru & cowboy hat on him. Smoker next to me in excellent brown shoes, picks back of zinc cigarette paper, *ɑɑɑɑɑɑɑɑ* puts down oval circles, name "PAT" & what looks like a hung genitalia—& scratches and obliterates the balls. Leaves it between his feet. Instructions for rolling LLF are on the floor too, yellow sheetlets, and a fly has joined me & explores my genie bluegreen knee. Welcome little thoughtless fly and your brother on my right knee but why mine? Now the hats are in semicircle on table—brown feet in black socks laid at rest, leaner-&-sleeper whose face is hid on table wood. One head bowed next to another with black locks, prayers around circular table, one with black navy beanie (watchcap) leaning in green mackinaw, eyes shut the senior rabbi of the table, & grey-black banded hair & straight firm feet, hand on cheeks, he sleeps. Old Hollow Throat wanders in the scene above the sleepers in his army coat lite brown & skinny blue sweater—his humped back, worn out over how many logs or libraries? Battered thorny hat he has, hook nose. Jeremiah or an Isaac. With his thinner & older friend, leaning together to talk & with a "hit git that of me" smile—the two old wizen-cheeked warlocks, one glum, go to the bathroom. My boy at the left wears striped coat blue & chino pants & hat with sweatband soiled. They got no money. Got no matches, no, nor cigarettes, nor nothing to do but sit & wait for snowy time to melt. Red Mackinaw headgear, brown busted gambler cowboy hats, little brown caps. "You gonna work?" "Aehheh guess I could right now." Green Fly get off my hand. Black suspenders on a big belly against the wall. There's Joe Jackson of the big nose poopy-doll pathos expression squatting away there—An indian (aforementioned hat) bumming a chaw—"You got any money to buy any more?"—woven colored neckerchiefs & hankies & Bohemian primitive shirts all wrapped & jolly joking round his neck, then huge sheet of black rubber pants draped down to his toes, overcoat too. Poopydoll holds his mouth with his hand & stares about, now picks his cheek. Also a liberal anthropologist Francis Lawyer—"I ain't gonta gamble anymore, fuckit," with hornrims over his mackinaw on Mexican dream-bellbottom trousers clanging along floor. Lower jaw with dismayed atombombed a-lout-born-expression in chair, great blue innocent sexless eyes staring out, picking his belly-button under the mackinaw I might have known, the glasses fall over his nose he's unhappy, staring at me now he sees me the bitch—but I might have known that Cézanne's card player'd be here too, he even brought his umbrelly and his brown hat brim all pulled down like a Burgomeister Beer Crown, a crown pushed up to form a perfect dome, a characteristically silly high Dutch crown and striped barber-shirt, tho he's dignified & small, in a suit, pants fall straight down to above the ankles, no further baggy knees, using napkins for kerchief, lips folded under his toothless mouthy falsies, giving him a sharp & bored professional waiter look, who knows his dry mouth, beerless, "I saw their teeth flash like the mouths of minstrels while they ate."—J.K. But it's his round hat & humor, ah, he's found at last a seat, a very dignified man, really Otto Kruger,* silverhaired, smiling, he arranges his coat—a drama—he's been waiting to get a seat at one of the tables, rushes to it, smiling, folds his coat sits down & leans back, smiles in all directions, rocks on his thin ankles, big flat feet, & overlooks the comfortable table. Before him snoozes the black cap, oops, here comes Manager with big cornific brooms to sweep the floors, Jack you were deeper than this being more involved, your sketch of the bums eating in the bowery, I give you the Palm & Crown. Why do I always yell at you? I'm no saint but that drama of Otto Kruger

---

* Suave Wall Street–lawyerly character actor, 1930s Hollywood.

rushing for his comfort seat I did see. Imagine them all rushing together to the seat in the bathroom, the lonely empty seat, the hole in the void. Here's a real old foxy gramp with crooked nose, he has a red-knit Goopy hat on his white hairs, not old in vain at all, best hat I seen in Portland & I spent hours from the Mission Salvage to the Ladies Cunt & Junior League today—Above me a white cross & a bandage patch above one eye. And a nice young executive out of the Army with pale glasses & manager with broom approaching dangerously close—Here comes the man with a giant heavy staff, thin & crooked legged & stumbling, shambling, trying to get away from the manager with the broom, running to the other wall. And Otto Kruger with his immense mind and hat grabbing his chair—rushing to the edge of the great pile of papers being godswept into the backroom garbage can—Ah I've found— See it—the matches in the pile of trash, and with what benevolence Kruger leans back on the wall and watches the trash being piled for oblivion—"There's a match"—"There's a map, who wants to go someplace" says proprietor with beat face unfolding the dirty map to reveal its tatters—Kruger still ironic sleeps against the wall. The iron grill is closed against the trash cans which stand like soldiers waiting oblivion next to the broom and black mouthed shovel leaned against the basement door.

* * *

## Seattle Feb. 2, 1956

Unfinished Notes Seattle [Draft of "Afternoon Seattle," CP 150:]

### Walk in Seattle Afternoon

Busride along cliff hillstreet looking down out window flat shine sea below, waterfront, where we are, photo allover view in Real Estate window—

round corner under the el, Aorta Mfg. Co. 3rd floor redbrick bldg., and on Jessup St. the Wobblie Hall, the mandala of Labor, one Big Union, "We eat for you."

—Old men bleareyed & cardplaying behind counter and round table with surreal posters. Pamphlets. Soldiers of discontent—talk about the young fellers cant see ahead and we have nothing to offer

Paris Rexroth Ashley, fruit, Whitman, he cried tears in Communist champagne glass.

I left with Snyder & his little red beard & bristling buddha mind walked crying across the street to Soc. St. Vince de Paul for old clothing

walked down to Russo's bar—beer 10¢ & smelly good food, Skid Road, the original

(ah, in Paterson the 2nd floor upstairs communist hall, bricks and garbanzos meetings too, atheist)

then drinking a beer cube, and walked up 2nd past the Green Parrot Theatre, markee blinking 4pm with little running perfect lights of '20s, to Farmers Market, a lb. of indian smoked salmon, wandering thru the dream market, labyrinth reached for blocks perched on the docks

and downstairs alleys crisscrossed with fat bacon & overcoats & Greek Theatres

3rd beer, in bar, now,

and down trestle wood stairway under the city a huge labyrinth for peyotl bums down to the waterfront, the ships,

ferryboat coming faraway in mist from Bremerton Island dreamlike small on the waters of Holland to me

and walked down road together silent & wondering, love, anger,

and entered my head the seagull, a shriek, the Sentinels

standing over the harborside by the rusted poles crisscrossed iron work, I saw it then, the decadence of the cities, the rotten rocks dripping down under the (wharves) walls . . .

\* \* \*

Go shrieking laughing & chattering into the dust

Moloch's on Fire—the sex thief runs out the door

High Mountain Hymn

Mount Baker (Shuksan) firmament walls of snow
Impassive giant of ice & rock
Silent motionless being with eternal thoughts.

\* \* \*

## Feb. 2 Seattle 1956

Once again a second time with you Hart Crane.\* This time I understand, your visions were solid, your sex was real. It breaks up out of Atlantis and is completely expressed. And the suffering struggle to believe your own senses despite the fear you were mad & sordid?

Allen Tate that Catholic iron head thin bleak nasty fool? Weak sisters Malcolm Cowley & John Peale Bishop at the time.

Go be a saint Hart Crane suck all the cock you want. . . . As for the god of the Bridge he was listening & weeping when you cried out "Unspeakable Thou Bridge to Thee, O Love" and when you asked "Thy pardon for this history" the pardon was granted with ten thousand more sunrises over your grave in the Caribbean and the sunrise of the natural holy

waters of my tears tonite, thought over your book.

"Forgive me! Forgive me!" that was your cry—But "a tear is an intellectual thing." Everybody gave you good advice instead.

\* \* \*

## Feb. 2, 1956

**Tears**

I'm crying all the time now . . . [First draft of "Tears," CP 151]

\* \* \*

## Dream

Apprenticed to the Northwestern steamfitter behind his jacket desk in the Dickens sidestreet of Portsmouth. Wandering down the street asking for work; went in to see Mr. Lou Scrooge Keeper of Books—behind slot-bellied windows in a small office. Grew with the business, expansions to China & Northwest trade,

---

\* A.G. had just read Philip Horton's biography, *Hart Crane: The Life of an American Poet* (New York: W. W. Norton, 1937), with its accounts of Crane's poetic genius by his friends.

then out on new route by highway and boat—The kindly old man having built up the business, left it in your hands—with instructions, a plan to carry on through the New Route—But there was trouble, pirates or Mysterium at the other side of the mountains—So I go forth on a single definite exploring trip—and with me the policeman pal Buddy Buddy who's to look after me up there—but then is the mystery—who's the betrayer, or secret Con Man of Dreams down the Highway?—Was it the old Man who died, creator of Samsara?—or the Buddy?

Then in a market buying with little money, breakfast food for the boys home (Peter & Lafcadio)—I go to get milk, cereal, then think of eggs, bacon, love, staples, life—

Woke up wondering who was who in the dream—tension with Gary—either he or I am doing it?

\* \* \*

Demonic Mills          (Satanic Mills)
Demonic Industries          Blake
Bellingham.          Moloch.

\* \* \*

Feb 5, 56. Richard Meigs Bellingham Wash: Long walk to Emerson on way to Sumas on way to Canada on Nooksack Valley plain—where I heard the telegraph wires sing under the cloudy dusty sky against mountains, walked on following the flat road past fields where farmers worked, off distance, shovelling fermented pea-smelling pea silage over fields & an old man hacking at brush with an ax, & 6 guys on a R.R. baby car riding along chugging, later at crossing where they broke down, I saw them jacking up the car, I walked past, they receded still fixing baby car—Emerson where I shat, wrote postcards & said excuse me—Walked back (6 miles?)—& stood still on highway in the fields, a cow came across pasture visiting me at the fence, we stared at each other, I talked to her awhile, beautiful white fur and calm living cow eyes blank eyeballs rolled back in ecstasy of dangled udders caught in fruit machine—

Today in Bellingham talking with Gary's ranger & forester

friends, they see him as a little golden Dharma hero of Northwest Bull Durham woods—the agile mind outwitting theirs, the admissions of tobacco chawing humanistic fear ("danged if I want to lose my balls on that mountain") and "Danged if that city slicker weren't afraid to lose *his* balls on that mountain." Sometimes a snotty kid, sometimes a gazing Dharma hero with Aethereal Beard.

Walking down backstreet Dock area sundown back of broke city hall, Salvation Army, rummage sale, swop shops, waterfront cafe, the Shroudy Stranger's hairy boylike rendezvous, like Paterson where he runs down the tincan rubber embankment covered with hay & wilted horse grass to the tackle-field horrors below, happily, a bodhisattva-angel-saint of yore, whirling his rags about him as he gazes at the stars (he knows their names) and runs on the planet from city to city contacting angels of all descriptions in all walks of life.

In Seattle, I saw his grey weatherbeaten interior dark–dusty shack under bridge, with houseboats all about & as in Kerouac's Dr. Sax in Bklyn. cartoon* Dr. Sax climbs out of a rotten sunken Barge & climbs up a telephone pole & peers about listening to the wires hum. He's looking for an Angel, free blood, in all the City.

* * *

## Dreaming of Neal in the Cabin in the Northwest

He is lying on the bed naked, and I'm washing him, I go back & forth from a sink at other side of the stove for cups of frothy warm soap water, bring them back & lave his breasts & armpits & thighs & balls, turn him over, his inner back & buttocks & sides white by his arms; he reclines and waits for me to serve and worship him. He is a fight manager, talking about the problem of intelligence & direction of the fighter (make him meeker & more

---

* As on back of inside front page of Kerouac's *Heaven,* ed. Don Allen (San Francisco: Grey Fox Press, 1977).

humane & a better boxer—I suggest Love such as I give Neal, Neal do the same to his iron boxer).

Tchaikovsky is here, full of strained nerves & hystcrics & hands to the brow in despair—has something to do with dream—

Have not masturbated since leaving San Francisco, seems like a month, & this the first love dream since, occurred as Alarm bell woke me from it in cabin under Mt. Baker on farm plain, rose made fire clenched teeth ruminating & illuminated by familiar love theme. Fondness.

\* \* \*

## Vancouver, B.C.—Pacific Stage Terminal Waiting Bench

A veritable London, an oriental London, first the crazy wool sweaters with collars everyone wears—2 Sikhs, Punjabis of yore, black rainsoaked turbans wound round araby bearded brown heads, wrinkles & mackinaws' plaid collars & scarves, wrapped. And the ladies' charm drapes, sweaters, everyone wearing beat clothes, perspiration in the fog, all very British the young ugly clarks stomping by in the fog, speeding round traffic corners with yellow rain capes on their bicycles, Scotch MacAccents, plaid caps in Hastings St.–Bowery, cheap meals & meat, a lovely woven red black green & violet mainly violet crocheted sweater on my bench neighbor—Assyrians with canes & big black snow-shoes—gents with umbrellas—everybody short like yr uncle & myopic eye-glasses blinking & blinking about thru the foggy streets.

\* \* \*

On the Ferry—it floats sinking across foggy strait—evanescent city in rain & fog I walk around deck alone w. cigarette—It's totally silent on water but for throbbing of boat (English Channel passengers waiting floating on white void having family chatting tea party)—cry of seagull like a high cat, & lone toot of howl boat horn. Whether it be the great sick Turbaned bums of Vancouver on Hastings Street with enormous cotton bellies, in underwear, pushing out like mountains—

or Indian-wool sweatered Indians wandering the rainy street,
or me—the Sikhs coughing, hollow wheezes—

* * *

## To Peter Orlovsky

[Written on bus returning to Bellingham from Vancouver]

This being a month since I've seen you
beginning a trip, tho I'll be back for a while
I can already feel the future, my travels,
& our separation.

I loved you by the love that's in the trees,
       as gull cries over a boat, as
       dog to dog,
you who are you, and all you are
       and your nose—
good enough for me
But whether future ages find it so
or carping men right now,
I'll care, but never know,
So having little time to speak the
       truth
My life being mine, my life,
Love being love, unpunishable & austere,
and if not holy in itself
fuck holiness, I'll make my own sweet
       holy
and give you the halo of it now,
       once & for all.
Peter, what did you care for me for?
Why did we come & live together, sleep & eat
Together half a year?
I see the night outside
       my bus window,
          riding home
—years of gaiety to come:
            goodby.

\* \* \*

Returned Feb. 16 1956
    The house wrecked by DuPeru.
    Vesuvio's bar—Trent, Bad talking Charlie,
        gravel voice kid
run down to bus—get on, Neal on seat, talk with him about Sri
Aurobindo*—wait at R.R. station for him to go to work, masturba-
tion talk, he putting on work pants, holey dungarees, pathos of bus
meeting like Jack's in boxcar—miss bus to Peter's, walk & wander-
ing thru 22nd St & 3rd up Sierra hill to Peter's new apartment,
fence, night back of Potrero hill, Kafka welfare project homes,
can't find his # on door, finally do, house dark, knock, wake him
up, he comes to door in sleep shirt & shorts to his crotch & bare
legs like a dancer or Knight of projects, he hugs me, says "Allen,"
welcomes, I am taken in his openness, I am awkward, like a
"ghost" he later says, neurotic ghost of lacklove & Gary arguments
& coldness—look over his house, I work next day, sleep there that
night again, go walking that next eve & ride to North Beach, see La
Vigne, borrow $2 from 2 different people, return sleep together &
then move to different beds, begs, Lafcadio welcoming me hospi-
tably, then hitch to Berkeley, Peter goes to Napa for his girl, Sheila,
Whalen & Gary here, we drink, Peter returns we wander to Oak-
land & hear Jazz rock & roll, return, sit talk sleep, he reads me
Miller, then once in bed, Gary Phil & Girl N—— come in, singing,
I sit up & so does Peter, I take off covers, during songs slowly drift
off Peter's Covers, clothing, he rises, drinks, dances naked out
of bathroom, I disrobe & dance Indian dance while Gary plays
naked, expressive wild rhythmical jumpings till my heart beats &
breath exhausted, & dance with N—— naked, Gary takes her
home, Peter & I go to bed naked, my head against his shoulder,
"Are you hot?" he asks, masturbating himself, my hand on his
stomach hair, "Yes, let me blow you," I go down on him, we play
that way, I take it in all the way, drunken, to my back of throat, "Are
you swallowing it?" Yes, I say, watch:—take it down again, sucking

---

*Famous XX century yogi theosophist, ex-revolutionary, who
founded utopian Auroville, India. —A.G., October 4, 1982.

wildly & sweetly solid in my back of throat, reaching around to his buttocks & thighs, "Get the vaseline"—I haven't any—oh yes, the olive oil, I jump out to kitchen & get olive oil, come back blow him & then grease his cock & he turns me on my side facing out, & sticks it in me, easy, I am open, finally gets it all in deep all the way, satisfying to my belly, I begin shoving in and out, then I try to get on my stomach but he holds me there, I bend forward, he says ah that feels good and fucks away I am overjoyed turn on my belly, he's got me, & drives rubbery down, & builds up, not coming, Gary enters the door. Peter does not stop but stays with me fucking, but after Gary asks for his sleeping bag (we are on it) I give it to him from head top of bed Peter turns me over his cock slipped out uncome & grabs my cock to make me come, my back to him holds me around chest right hand & left hand moves round my belly & up to my cock head I grab his hand to make him go faster I say ah that's it, go on, he sez "Now you've got it," till I come (Gary

Lafcadio Orlovsky, Peter Orlovsky, kitchen ("Peter's new apartment") 5 Turner Terrace, San Francisco. Photo: Allen Ginsberg

listening silent) & we sleep naked in each other's arms. Wake up in morning with Parkinson* bringing money.

## Greyhound Terminal Unloading

Feb '56 Grey rain tracks of bicycles in concrete bus parking field, the blue & white longies busses lined up diagonal from their human feeding troughs the loaders standing hand-a-pocket humming looking at the white bleary sky: Crystal Palace market above the Hotel Whitcomb above that a radio-sending Antenna rising up over the low roof into the white blank of heaven. Hotel Alex on sidestreet facing the back Bleak platforms. Korens Distribu Co a broken sign, fumes of exhaust smoke, one or another of the buses blowing its nose, hum & roar of them waiting.

John Ryan—a beauty, who looks like Stephen Crane's tragic portrait, with droop sinister gambler's mustache & thin body & secret cool love of God, pure sentimentalist—let him throw his feet at beauty without critic qualm & lose his soul in drunk revelry & delight in his own being. Your own joy—be it cocks or little girls of fresh new crazy paintings in the social school—remembering the solitude is eternal, therefore giving the body & all there is of the soul loses nothing—no pride—only warmth of continuous lovers, intimacy & cleaning rooms, new beer, new projects, understandings, rapports—secret to give & become radiant again thru acceptation of souls & continued open-ness & humble idiotic indefatigable oft rewarded Chaplin Search.

\* \* \*

Salmon Fishing—Seattle Canneries, or Alaska Fisherman's Union.

---

* Ginsberg's faculty advisor at UC-Berkeley; see note p. 178.

* * *

## Berkeley March 2, 1956 Dream

Hitchhiking to Central Long Island starting from Rosebud in Connecticut, trying to get perhaps to Pilgrim State or Rockland.

Once I get there, for a visit, I find Louis is there also, I am glad to see him & look with curiosity on his address book, which has a space above each address for pictures, line drawings of a situation with each person listed in the book—it's a big book I notice, not too dogeared, with black leather binding—I wonder how he carries it, in what pocket, he opens his jacket & puts it in the old brown inner suit breast pocket I remember so well, the classic poppa-poet-teacher's breast pocket. I've always been fascinated by his heavy breast pocket.

I wander around the villages, like Yosemite, where we live, in and out of Seattle Barge Lake Washington dark road & Yosemite lampless camps—finally visit some big heavy fellow Laird Cregar* intelligent with whom I talk—"The trouble is you have no single specialty you could teach—for instance you know some Chinese & like it, the Chinese poets, like Rexroth, but you don't speak or study it—English the same, what period do you know well?—So even if you could get a teaching job, what would you teach?"—I am abashed & depressed—it's all perfectly true. I wander back toward the cabin where I know Whalen is—I don't want to just wind up like him washing test tubes for part time work, but I am in his position—no other job can I do—Going to school to study again means the same hassle with tough subjects like Anglo-Saxon & Chemistry, I am depressed & frightened by the prospect.

Louis says, stay overnight, Uncle Abe is coming tomorrow, but I think of the complicated road I have to go home on, thru Long Island, the ferry, up to Connecticut, and think of asking will they drive me? But no it's hundreds of miles out of the way—and I've got to be back in the morning to answer the phone if my

---

* Hollywood actor, a "heavy."

substitute job at Greyhound calls me in—I woke up chilled by my scholastic inadequacy & looked at Pound's collected *Literary Essays* which tho hung up on I never finished reading.

\* \* \*

## Gary Present, Milvia St.

Tonight reading Klee (Architecture: yellow stepped cubes) I doped out the building blocks in their magical optical dimensions, but did not see the picture clearly. Then I unfocussed my eyes at the center and it all sprang to life, flying buttresses, Mayan stonework, archetype space.

All along I have been seeing the pictures as two-dimensional and never seeing dimension in space, never seen them recede like simple constructions going in, which they are.

The shock brought me to my senses. I don't know what I'm talking about, I theorized about the Klees for years and pored over them straining & trying to piece them together with a vague idea of what I might ultimately discover but I never actually saw that it was right there in front of me in every picture, not just scientific successes on his part.

I'm still not in my right senses and confused. I have never seen a Braque or Picasso in that case, much less a Cézanne, who I've been looking at for years. All along I thought I was making advances into their minds which few others dug. Now it appears everybody sees what I don't see.

I don't know how many levels this works out on, life, personal relations. I tried talking to Gary but could not get up courage to speak directly. The shattering of the image of myself that I have built up and has been making me nervous like an egoistic 20 year old ever since he's been here—

I thought that he saw me as a divinely endowed innocent-wise saintly type and conducted my conversations on that level, all my humor being a reflection of that, but I have been feeling stiffer & stiffer since he arrived till tonight when I felt myself open for a moment as a result of seeing 3 dimensions of Klee.

I had a sudden feeling then that I was completely mad.

The parallel of this minor satori to the great vision of Harlem in which I suddenly saw depth in everything.* And feeling that I was unique and chosen.

All my humility reflects this a form of pride.

My thought processes—simply stop thinking. Thinking gets me nowhere.

The black window, tree outside of it, myself now dead at typewriter the red camelia on the crotch of the tree sticking up, Gary with cute truman capote hair & fuzzbeard reading Stendhal like a Stendhal, pallets on either side.

The need to communicate, warmth, I would like to get up from here and wake the dead. As if there were a great gulf between us in understanding, my mute ignorance, whatever—tho there's nothing to understand—I would like to kiss him. That seems verboten, tho the verboten exists in my mental world & rational judgment not in unexpressed world of—no, not in equally speculative world of action. So the kiss doesn't exist any more than the taboo. So why worry.

How neatly in stepped cubes the books are arranged on the right of the typewriter, like little boxes the little dears, in fact the Klee box is uplifted leaning on its side supported by a useless green small journal book supported in turn by William Blake & the Angels.

A used sheet of carbon paper on the other side.

Hiroshige: the rain also falls at different depth, each straight line.

Mar 5—
—Dream of flying—into the wrong part of a machine, to escape, I was trapped by old caretaker—

Eternity is the same world you see in a dream when flying—except that I have it in waking states (To Dr. Hicks) (never spoken)

* * *

---

* Auditory illumination, transcendental vision, which came upon re-reading William Blake's "Ah! Sun-flower!" in 1948. Ginsberg has described it in numerous places, perhaps most notably in his *Paris Review* interview, *Writers at Work*; ed. George Plimpton; Third Series (Viking: 1967), pp. 301–311.

Gary Snyder in his backyard cabin. We'd recently
met, he showed me his binder full of poems, they
looked influenced by W. C. Williams just like mine,
Berkeley 1955. Photo: Allen Ginsberg

Who lived, without toilets electricity or heat or water & even
gas with none of the modern conveniences in fact, writing poem by
the blue rose light on top of the leaky gas stove

oh that the dam electricity will go on again—writing in the
dark I can't keep track of the sequence of my thought

Who lived in Paterson doctors of the semen of the Passaic,
the misty voice of the falls—who sharpened the grey rocks, sharp-
ened & wore down the granite of his skull—tho gaunt and even
womanly of mind & face, cheek, nose & eyeglasss—and weak
chin, poor feller, and turned into whitehaired trembley saints of
death in their late and seventieth summer—ah will I die early?—
and he used to like the youth Keats—& old bard Whitman of
same state,

Williams did you ever visit Whitman's house in Camden?—I
will do that when I come back to Jersey, return to the East.

## Personal Father

(Chinese written at) 1776

Allee same,
    Chinaman stop shuddering—
What goes next?

                                O Page?

S
T
R
A
I
G
H
T
(starlight
too)
down
the
center.

a                                               ball
to                    the             left
right                then          to
   and         uʍop ǝpısdn     inside

out
splash all over the rocks

Saxifrage
was his flower*

and the blue light of the stove
Down!

\* \* \*

___
  \* "that splits the rocks": William Carlos Williams, "A Sort of Song."
—A.G., June 25, 1991

Always through spiring Cordage!* Hart Crane in his letters reveals that he did understand his "sensation" and went out to reduce it to words if possible—very like Cézanne. Combinations of words & a grand final rhythm. Powerful ear. I have a powerful ear and appreciate his achievement & have read Atlantis aloud to the voice of Tears. I sat over it in a rooming house in Seattle weeping, surrounded by a decayed mess of babies, family, friends travel new cities, release of soul—His attempt to release his soul into his work—Letters also show he was simple & straightminded when it came to deal with poetic theory while his friends were incompetents gifted with the gift of Literary Gab—Cowley, Winters, Tate, Bishop (Wilson too) talking about theories & nonsensical frightened standards of composition. What is experiment but an experiment into the unknown depths of emotion—all released on his page—How he had seen God—The shining bridge of absolute abstract Love, Word Made Flesh, all that & Heaven too.

His compassionate vision of Poe. Poe also a Rimbaud. Seer—cracked seer of early night—but in the subway, Poe's face & skull in the subway.

What other poet has known Times Square but Whitman?

Also I must write a poem on time's square.

Blue light of the stove, dark moment of depression & misery, my spirit is low, my head is high, my house is warm, but my lights are out, and nose infected, right knee bugged with year old strain feet blistered, bad shoes, cold or flu, bronchial, smoke too much, no money much, neither singing nor silent—continuing with the transcription. So far this year we have seen lights & sunflowers & Rocklands & Molochs, and whose?

What if my father heard that I committed suicide in my cottage in Berkeley. But as ah what dark-mystery-drama therein went untold? What if I now left in flame & ruin to the depths of Hell? or wrote a last abandoned & despairing cry of death notes as the windows were sealed, the door stuffed with white rags & newspapers (tornup sheets)

---

* From the sixth line of the tenth stanza, "Atlantis" section, Part VIII of The Bridge.

* * *

or the room hung with flowers & grass on the floor instead of a shag rug?

Charming romantic vision—my (joke) windows don't ever close—ah the chill air leaks thru all nite, they're broken

By the blue rose of the stove I sat imagining suicide & scrawled large in my journal, drew pictures of my mind, on T—old tired story ever fresh when the heart is not old or the T lemonade

The light's been out for 2 hours—and no one's fixed it yet— I shall have to wait for the morrow.

* * *

To continue————
Lying in bed fixing my mind on nothing—suddenly the lights went on, the one in the bathroom, the one in the kitchenette the one on the ceiling & the one above the desk—the Telephone leaped into being, typewriter glared there bleak, white stove shone brightly in the kitchen nook.

Noon. It's noon the birds are outside. Blue lights play over the trees. An inhuman pallor shines & ripples over the grass, an uncanny artificial light, as if the sun had burned out and the ecstatic filament fused and popped in the shelves of sky. Strangers walk about on the grass, appearances from nowhere, disappearing in a mild wave of blue vibrations, Rocks tumbled into Atlantis.

Of course, Crane *was* speaking of Plato's Atlantis—Crane a Platonist—a distinguished Platonist.

There is no god and we do not have to be passing thru to god in order to receive approval and compassion from fellow humans—the light is our own, the light exists for everyone, the light of human mercy.

* * *

Mar 17 '56

Today is the springtime
The marvelous lonely
bird outside

reminding me of my drunkeness
last night

—Orlovsky who will be a great
stranger & traveller.

—I had lost my poetry mind for several weeks working in the
Greyhound terminal under the stairs in the basement.

\* \* \*

Prisoner of Moloch!
        Cold Concrete & steel.

    Metrical paradigm for extension of a cadence latent at one
point in Moloch Chorus—(propulsion from "frightened me out
of my natural ecstasy"):
            Moloch who burns down the love of the world in the
fear of the self that cries in abandon exists in despair. [Decameter]

\* \* \*

My apologies are here for all
the pretty girls,
I got a later greater redder rose
for them in store.

\* \* \*

# In Berkeley Cottage

    The instant of dawn—dawn's here, dear one—at desk in
early grey light looking out window, the red geraniums still up-
standing among fronds, green protuberances, wavy newborn
green shoot-boughs, small brown branches, a garden of grass, a
brown still house, brown trees across the road, the sky beyond
white.
    The early wind moves and shimmers in the little tree leaves
six feet from my head. The iris has grown over the windowsill. The
light green spring leaves reflect the pale blue dawn sky. Brown dry
tangles of vines still hang on the porch post from last year.
    Whalen moves around the kitchen, rising early for work—
"Oh, stringbeans"—"Neal Cassady, boy railroadman"—

sleeps wrapped in blankets on the bed, red necked, no sleep for 48 hours (met me in iron hellish midnight Greyhound downtown off all-nite-wakened Market St. in S.F.)

Came home we disrobed lay down in pallet on floor for satisfying taste of cock down throat first when wake lying down, then late mutually waked at 6 AM for more easy love job thrills, ingression of cock to back of throat and hard sucking till he came.

—Later note—succession of 4 (orgasms) that nite first time so ever. Woke that morn with Whalen to celebrate the time by writing note before it vanished.

\* \* \*

Dream: "Shorn of buds and leaves the branch sticks out over the city."

Bob Donlin, Neal Cassady, Peter Orlovsky, Robert La Vigne, Larry Ferlinghetti, in front of City Lights Bookstore, March 1956. Photo: Allen Ginsberg

Ginsberg, La Vigne, unidentified woman, backyard,
Milvia Street cottage, afternoon of March 18, 1956,
before "Celebrated Good Time Poetry Night," in
Berkeley, an encore of the Six Gallery reading the
preceding October. Photo: Harry Redl

\* \* \*

ZZZip of Jet, seems everytime I sit down to write one of them
things passes over me with noise

Joe's story that rainy nite in Frisco—handsome Joe, the crazy
black haired athlete from L.A.:

Walked across the Golden Gate back and forth, the Bridge
screaming moaning in the Tempest—God's hand rocking the
great He bridge that had taken 12 lives—put his hands on the
cables & felt the vibrations shake his body.

## Rhythm*

Down to the dorms down to the barns
Down to the beans down to the bones
down to the bonds down to the dreams
Down to the brains down to the booms
Down to the bones banes dorms beans bonds.
Down to the barns beans dimes bones booms.

## Poem

Soon it'll be goodbye
To all those cocks
and arms and impossible positions
—I can't find a lover
who fits in bed, for a man—
too many cocks, too much sucking and assholes.
How can we lie together arm in arm and
            stare in each other's eyes?
How can breast and belly touch and cling
            together warm from thigh to neck?
—an impotent position, tough white tender
arms around the breast, clasped in back,
his arm around my neck
            Palms in my hair, kissing,
That's all you can do,
            exchanging angelic confidences,
But then comes the matter of coming, the
            action,
The cock sperm shoot, the rubbing and fucking,
in the hand in the mouth in behind, between
            legs, & that's all,
but you can't come at once, someone's got to be
            queer,
Someone's got to give up his come, material
            queen of the night,

---

* Or, "Down to the Damned Blind Dream Bombs' Booms." Choriambic foot (-uu-) plus dispondee last two lines. —A.G. & G.B., October 4, 1982

How selfless can you get—That's only
            what's wrong with men—
who gets it, who takes & the pressures &
            unhappiness thereof
Who'll be king, who'll be cock president
            and pimp, motorcyclist and aviator
            hero, who wears the dungarees,
who eats it, and who lays back and is eaten
—Except 69 that memorable lovers rapport—
both arms wrapped around both bellies,
            both eyes
closed in the pubic hair, both mouths filled
both cocks stuck in each other sucking
Together, welded a final kiss, a lasting kiss,
            a sweet kiss where it hurts, the nausea,
The distraction of moving your buttocks & belly
to get some heat going out,
forget to do your proper share of the sucking
            (get your proper shame)
Till one gives up and abandons himself to the
            blowjob
either giving or taking
                        and the gaiety
and the guilty one lays back & abandons himself
            to his cock being blowed,
"or worshipped" as Huncke said,
pushing forward, grabbing hair & pushing
            the question head down on the balls
—strange positions to be in, cold & selfless
            staring down
from a pillow with energy rage & tenderness
            distance, grabbing a
handful of head and grinding and pulling it
            in and out of your vitals, moving
            it round your organ, under
            your control, cover,
Till you lunge and shove it in all
            the way down to the glottal female
            neck hole inside dark
& come—
            and the bittersweet taste

of the male glue
                    emotional,
Shudder & come with a groan or sigh
It's over,
              and maybe you're next.

## To Huncke in Sing Sing*

Shine Herbert in your prison cell,
Eternity's behind bars with you in the Shadows.
Compassion is sweet, punishment is bitter,
and there's no true judgement but compassion.
Sing Sing Herbie Singsing in Prison—
Here in California in a Jewish Viennese
              musician's living room
Listening to Mozart on the couch
              —all Europe in the brown
              Cellos and Pianos
              and Children in the chairs—
I a stranger here, need compassion too, tho out
              of jail—
and were I there what sweeter meed or music could
              there be
than a note from you giving soul stamp of
              Approval—

There's a machine that judged you, courts
              judges lawyers police yourself,
But what have I to do with that?
I'm not the law I'm Allen—
they gave you bars I give you life—
the bars will be open in 20 years
and rust in a hundred
but the work of my hand
remains when prisons fall
because it is the hand of compassion.

* * *

* Later integrated with "The Names," Paris, Spring 1958 (CP 176–79), a draft of which appears on pp. 441–44

## Schumann's Kinderscenen

My Mother
. . . speak of the cause of All
            childhood passing
            Naomi withering
Age, it's the flower of immortality lost
We see we're dying
            Childhood already in memory,
the room about me, bleak,
only the music immortal.

Our souls die—hasn't childhood already
            died?
The soul's as long as time and gets shorter as
            we grow old,
I have 20 years more, am already past middle,
Seen what there is to be seen, had it already,
future same as past—unimaginable
but a vanishing thing
& regret lost lawschools, loves,
            Naomi & myself.
And with Poem to Naomi goes all
            farewells
to her myself childhood
            life itself
            Farewells—
—in the phonograph, in the air,
            my warm heart, in my eyes,
            Tears
Farewell
      Sweet
            Dream
Farewell
      Sweet
            Memory
Farewell
      Sweet
            Mother

Haledon's empty pond where I played
      I'll see it no more,
the old house on Graham Avenue I cried to leave,
      The cats I cried to die,
Childhood, dresses I put on
      in front of a mirror
Dreams of a magic spell,
White haired playmate, Norman,
(Shade I encounter in other boys)
the tree in the empty lot, grass meadow
a secret pathway thru the woods
I'll walk no more,

—until I heard the gentle voice of
      god in the piano
A child hand infinitely tender
all the sadness I heard was love,
What I took to be grief, such innocence,
What unhappiness such unhappiness
            Unknown
a secret,
      Till I heard
      and tears fell out of
            my eyes
                again.
The child was happiness
the god was happiness
      the grief a dream

—I'm back dreaming
         Trying to devise—
Let's listen to the music again
Sudden faith refreshed
      me in misery, god speaks,
when I get tender & sad enough,
      I see the joy beneath it all,
the joy beneath God.

* * *

Plato Shakespeare Michaelangelo and
    Ginsberg all Loved boys.
Plato Shakespeare Michaelangelo and Whitman
    Michaelangelo Michaelangelo.

\* \* \*

Humiliate me!
    Let me lick your ass
      Fuck me
Let me suck your cock
    humiliate me
Please,
    Ah
      I'm coming.

\* \* \*

*Neal*    Waist 31–32
    Length 31–32
    Sleeves Medium

\* \* \*

Work Resume as per M.S.T.S. Application:\*
Towne-Oller Advt. Co.    —June 54–June 55
City Lites    —June 53–May 54 1.00
Levy (Uncle's pharmacy    —May 52–Apr 53 2.00
    in Riverside, Calif.)
National Opinion Research Center Dec 50–Mar 52 1.25

\* \* \*

March 1956
*Copied Down From Greyhound John*
Sex perversion destroys soul/reason
The man without reason is like a

---

\* Some dates faked for Military Sea Transportation Service application. —A.G., October 5, 1982

Woman without beauty
The personality is destructive
To truth that is beauty
As the lie is ugly
But in the end
All mistakes will
be corrected with
The truth that is
Knowledge that comes
From god to destroy
the lies of my mother
                    The *Devil*


\* \* \*


Cheap fare to Europe—to Gibraltar

| | | | |
|---|---|---|---|
| Independence Constitution Tourist Fare— | | | $205 |
| 8 day Italian Saturnia, Valencia | " | " | $175 |
| Lauro Lines—Mar. 27— | " | " | $180 |
| Home Lines—"Homeland"—Mar. 27 | " | " | $180 |


\* \* \*


# April '56

### Dream 4-3-56

In school blue skies balconies the Casbah below Eastside park modern school building top floor Central High School grand ruinary wander corridor beginning from basement of freaks and late arrivals ending on top floor with building cracked open and walls out to reveal panorama of city below—

Entering class A (as we did Pearl Harbor Day looking out the window expecting Jap planes)—Whistle roar of jets now over head at writing instantaneously—

Schoolteacher a pretty frail girl. Everything happened, how to give up everything to recollection of dream?

I am in the dark. The rest of the class follows. We go out the building into the Casbah corridors of the streets. The radio. The war has begun? or is this an air raid attack for real? Grand announcements of hiding and retreat. The whole class makes its way thru the street—towards the Walls section. Passing thru Casbah alleys, lit by bright sunlight, toward the upper part of the city, over the walls of the upper roofs in the bright sunlight we fear & expect to hear the Atomic planes emerge—Passing the bright daylight alley, a child still plays ball on the cobblestone, small girl in white print-red dress 6 years old playing in bright solitude. We head toward my apartment—There are several of us saints who live there, several girls from India—Here are the glass & iron-grill doors of my room facing the park below & industrial landscape, and sea beyond—nothing has happened yet, apocalypse not yet begun—One of the dark skinned girls speaks to 3 bums in Vancouver rain-soaked black turbans & underwear at the door, hanging around, noplace to go in the raid—I ignore them but she goes right up & talks to them in Indian inviting them to come in with us—I see she is holy, and not afraid of the bums and feels a human kin with them—One thin high glossy-cheek sick bum looks meek & intelligent & grateful for her words & follows us in, as do the rest—I recognize the signs of meekness & holiness about them & learn a lesson from her—I ask her, noticing thru her accent she is speaking comprehensible English—"Yes I speak English not very well however," in a thick Indian accent but quite real English. We are all in our room. I feel safe with all these helpful saints.

On the way there I had noticed people taking cover, moving out of their rat's nests—up on the Corner the one-room adobe house, the curtains are down you can see in its yellow walls, the gypsy family that occupied it has disappeared with the curtains—A good place to live too, very cheap I think of looking it up later as cubby hole residence—all over people are disappearing from their houses in face of the raid for now for once for real.

* * *

**Spontaneous Alphabestiary**

A is for Asshole

B is for Breast

C is for Cunt

D is for Dick

E is for Eye

F is for Fuck

G is for God

H is for Hot

I is for I

J is for Jack

K is for Cock

L is for Love

M is for Meat

N is for Nose

O is for Mouth

P is for Prick

Q is for Queer

R is for Rare

S is for Shit

T is for Marijuana

U is for You

V is for Crotch

W is for Wow

X is for Sex

Y is for because

Z is for Zebra

God! how great to be great like
Hart Crane! To realize in one
life all the longing for real glory.
Riding in F train smiling at
myself image in the window at
nite. I am the greatest poet in
America I know it and others do
too—let Jack be greater. I have
my own glorious glory tonite.

Greyhound:
    What it is, is Ignorance
in the dark—the little
dark beautiful Chinaman
21, staring up at the great round
policeman's face
in Greyhound 1 AM 4-4-56
thinks the Policeman is God.

That lonely man struggling on the cross—made too much of
him & shamed him out of his real skin—a loss—he wasn't god not
what is thought—he was what he said he was, he was you (me,
us)—He was only just like a man, imagine your feelings on the
cross—can't—he went thru it.

O Square Russia!
The emotional liberty of Europe
—& Rexroth's face reflecting human tired bliss . . .*

---

* Draft of "Scribble," CP 152. The first two lines do not appear in the
printed version.

* * *

Spade, the baggage buster, unloader of the oily black concrete gates of the Greyhound Station, at Midnight, entering the barn door to the yellow light inside

drest in antique blue & black, night shuddering thru the whole scene, sky skin and concrete, all black on blue—drest in blue, holding aloft an iron crook, shepherding along his hand truck full of bags (of dirty black wool) full of handbags & valises & trunks, with the care of the Lord's anointed, a Shepherd, his back erect, his belly pressed against the rails of the hand truck a figure all dressed in overalls & cap of blue, one swatch of clothes rivering down him from head to foot, black foot drag, pumping along thru the iron gates— down the incline from the dark outside into the fluorescent—

Joe Army sweetest Angel of the East

### 4-4-56 Dream

Dr. Williams—at a party—he arrives, we go to the window to look out, he takes me around, his arm around my chest we lie down to look out window—and I still can't figure him out—he launches into an explanation of the key poets, rapidly so I can't follow or remember—"Then Herbert, who was the last to finesse & split up the image into particles, after all that is relative." I say "Stop, wait," laughing, "what *are* you talking about"—he looks displeased & annoyed. "I'm just too dumb, I can't think, it's got to be spelled out real slow like."

Is he Burroughs?

* * *

### Dream

I am selecting packages for Greyhound bus shipment in the baggage room, *Santa Rosa* I remember on the labels, confused as to which is which.

* * *

### Notes

Walking up the Potrero hill against moving scenery of industrial landscape last night, thought of Whitman's line ". . . is enough to stagger sextillions of infidels"*—and looked at the telephone pole, hoping to be staggered, and was by the uprearing brown raw wooden tree raised instantaneously by outside intelligence to stand there propped up dumb holding up the wires—then eyed the grass alongside the street, each particular blade under the half moon on the glimmering whale-like hill starting staring sticking up suspended & balanced in undersea-like life, whole fields of blades each alone spurting up balanced into the air, pushed or pulled but suspended up in an inch of air, above them the delicate ferny pubic green bushes exploded out, with brittle stalks 3 feet high further up—trudging thru the center, my eye took in the whole sweep of street, as I walked up hill thru a sea of ferns & grass, as in the "muscular bearded grass of the oceanic prairie"—Walking then thru the bushes started up the hill, caught familiar glimpse of American Can Co. on 3rd St. Below, sweep and panorama of South San Francisco, the bay, lights across bay on the hills, Berkeley & Oakland & Bridge, and the floating saucer domes of the two gas tanks on the water's edge, huge in the night & black below with the round edges & tops painted silver, one floating portable station flying saucer each, hovering in the clouds suspended by the industrial imagination, I crossed around & up hill to modern housing project—the guests staggering upsprouting, the housing project "grooking" placed there also by "hand a hand no more,"† stolid waiting for occupants to emerge—Moving around aware of death preparing for my departure building my fortune for eternity—a handful of writing, a shell of poems.‡

---

* "Song of Myself," 31, line 7: "And a mouse is miracle enough to stagger sextillions of infidels."

† A phrase somewhere in Kerouac's prose, "writ by hand a hand no more." —A.G., December 31, 1986

‡ "Build thee more stately mansions, O my soul" —Oliver Wendell Holmes, "The Chambered Nautilus"

# All the Grace All the Love

I wrote so that
      in some lone midnight
on a farm
      in Kansas City
furnished room
      streets outside, autos
under an electric bulb
      on varnished brown wood table
when some wild boy
      with beautiful eyes
reads my page
      and sees me clearly,
sees my automobile
      moving in the sky
he'll recognize himself
      in the wild beauty
of his close cropped hair
      hard forearm
and knuckle with a bruise

                * * *

While I was alive
I knew that others would come

While I was alive
I wrote as if I would dic

While I was alive
I saw the permanent moon

While I was alive
I saw the transience of buildings

While I was alive
I trembled with ecstasy

While I was alive
I brooded in solitude, too

While I was alive
I left you a message.

While I was alive
I transmitted electricity

While I was alive
I kissed the one flower

While I was alive
Everything became quiet

\* \* \*

## Prophetic Numbers

1. Dumb creature remember my shout of Being.
2. Those lips in Kansas City I thought were meant for me.
3. I had lips in Kansas and Texas, all were sweet.
4. Oblivion has no lips and cocks, there's nobody to fuck.
5. Knife fights and insults are wearisome in eternity.
6. The electric chair is responsible for many holy visions.
7. Keep yourself open for the next Shrouded Stranger.
8. Whoever has intensity of eye or heart, say hello.
9. Don't reject the struggling friend who drops his pants.
10. Advertising and ship building are mechanical tasks.
11. The human body and soul never work for a living. It may be hard to get money, but bliss is easy.
12. Bliss has nothing to do with Bullfights or Courage. Responsibility is charming but love is holy. Success is meet if you're happy, but fuck the world.
13. Never criticize, what's unhappy is only illusion—
14. You think you are tough and can accept the problem of evil—
15. Intellectual bullshit compared to your better moments.
16. Your best moments were those animistic mystic experiences.
17. Regard them as illusions, self created heavens,
    All is illusion heaven or hell, but who wants to be the Devil?

\* \* \*

# Berkeley April 26, '56 Dream

. . . In the Times Square movie house, there's Naomi, I sit next to her, suddenly recognize her, she me, I say "Are you Naomi" she looks at me suspiciously, I say "It's me, Allen" & break down crying, on her shoulder, leaning over seat on her breast, weeping.

\* \* \*

*Theater & Its Double*—Antonin Artaud
M. C. Richards Translation
"our nervous system after a certain period absorbs the vibrations of the subtlest music and in a sense is modified by it in a lasting way."
Example of ignuschizoid perception.

\* \* \*

Boat, roll Gary over the Pacific
halfway round the ancient world
to legendary Asia, marketplace
& cows: Boat take Gary faraway
from me and my machinery city;
a little death, boat, let it be,
a little more death in life for me,
a little image of the great voyage
for Gary; transworld, transcendent,
—trans time, trans love, trans cocks
& earth for ever; inch another year;
foot another decade, more or less,
oceans, poems cities; mile a lifetime,
Pacific span and all eternity
unremembering beyond, little boat.

\* \* \*

The imagination—it represents a futile gesture in the U.S.A.
—And yet the heart lives on it.

\* \* \*

[Draft of "In the Baggage Room at Greyhound," CP 153–54:]

*I*

In the depths of the Greyhound Terminal
I saw millions of the poor rushing around
        from city to city to see their loved ones.
Loves, marriages, negroes, weeping relatives,
        farewells, the poverty of their lives, irritable
        baggage clerks;
I sat on a baggage truck waiting for the
        Los Angeles Valley Express to depart
        looking at the sky

A truck full of baggage piled
together, aluminum packages of blood, cardboard
boxes with names & waybills fixed thereon
        10677431
Numbers. Tragedy reduced to numbers.

The pay is in numbers
        and the numbers don't meet
The need is for higher
        numbers.

Infinitely higher numbers
        with Dollar Signs prefixed
This is for the poor shepherds.
    I am a communist.
Abolish property.

                    * * *


Ray—who had a nervous breakdown
Jimmy Roe—sexy kid who wore cowboy
        tight dungarees silk shirts
        and once appeared in a black
        hat threatening to wear his boots.
Joe, I called him Joey—"You gotta
        be there, give me the precise
        reading"—short dark intense
        efficient Latin.
Lindsay—fat heavy sausage spade

who was in Liverpool 1918
and helped me oft to push my
    trucks.
Fat fairy baby—who whistled &
        shrieked & camped completely
        innocent.
Mr. Gragg—who smil'd & smil'd &
        committed suicide by
        reading an imaginary New Yorker

\* \* \*

& when the moon came over the Greyhound
        roof
I saw an old man thru the window of
        the Hotel Alex
Bald, walking between his icebox & his
        table

\* \* \*

## My Schedule at Greyhound

4:45    Sacto express Shorts Bull Semen
5:30    Coast Local papers Salinas Gilroy
6:00    Valley Express Scenicruiser Modesto Fresno Bakersfield
6:55    Calistoga Blood to Napa
7:00    Sacto Exp Papers
7:45    Valley Express Thurs    108 & 98
8:15    Santa Rosa, San Rafael
9:30    Sacto, Exp #368
9:50    St. Louis–Salt Lake Reno Elko Wells
10:15   San Jose
11:45   Santa Rosa Sebastopol San Rafael Sunday only
12:10   Salt Lake. 2 Sections papers
1:00    Portland Pacific thru Redding Front Short Rear

\* \* \*

Begin begin and bring back poetry upon the fucking stage with the
        first words
See, dear audience, the miracle we can do
and raise ourselves off our seats into the sight of the grave
or the sight of crazy love; or the sublime great groan of
        Divinity we hear in the sea, city, machine, subway
Poem: a romance, a tragedy, a comedy
and a long line of flowery rhetoric to appease the iron ear.

It creaks! the god damned language creaks in its own rhythm
The great American Creak's begun to move

* * *

"Walt Whitman in Camden" is subject—and the scene?
        A parlor for this play—a coy parlor, with curtains and lace, a
ship in a bottle, a pair of canes, some frayed tho' once elegant
white gloves stained with yellow genital butterflies
        Horace Traubel in the kitchen, making a cheese sandwich
while the old man suns himself by the faded window and the sun
burns in the Jersey sky, over Delaware River—Talking about In-
dians
        "Now them Delawares. There was a crazy drunk named Half
Moon Face that came around back in the 'fifties. High on peyote
all the time—and gave me lectures on the moon. He saw it all the
time even when it was not shining."

        "How's the river look tonite?"

        "I can't even get up to leave the room & go to the bathroom
without thinking of my good grey ass gone rotten. As for the river
my dear, she's still there."

* * *

                coming in the brown door
                    —a crack in it—
                in a flash of eyelids
                    buttocks fucking

a big vanilla envelope
full of blood words
from Tangiers—
"My ath is thore"

\* \* \*

The space on which
the building stood is now
a black parking lot.

\* \* \*

# Hymn to Homosexuality

Have I not seen the fairies in red fronted bars
staggering, American youths bedressed in Halloween satin and
become imaginary women
Screaming *Cunt* into the night air—
have I not seen, become myself of them, the same,
the squeak, shriek
shudder out of
a dream
in lipstick, dresses and brassieres
singing

\* \* \*

# May 1956

The U.S. Federal Govt is a big daisy.

My mother it's a wonder she has any mind left at all—she's
had it shocked by insulin, electrocuted, blown to bits, drugged,
cut, analyzed—

The filth what they print in the newspapers isn't true.
Overlooking the world from the height of platonic Ever rest.
Oakland Naval Supply Center—amid the grey vast doors of
the warehouses—
How sweet the flower will look in 20 years.

* * *

Shipyard #3—Richmond a vast desolate place, square miles of empty building, noise as of faraway trains, as on a desert, or on a mountain a few springlike bird chirps in the 5 o'clock shadow, warbling from the hills—on top of which Richmond petroleum tanks are mushrooms—an American flag flying in the silence above the gate, a negro in uniform stares at fingerprinted photographed FBI passes & Identity Cards—Low modern building, rural Pentagon—the abandoned Administration Bldg. has a pile of chairs and splintered slot machines blocking the glass entrance facade. The Janitor even is gone. California sun going down over it all, a blue sky & peacefulness.

Meanwhile at the Dock of the Shipyard the P-2-Walker, P-2 being a huge ship, like an ocean liner, full of holes, full of bottomless holes, where once the gamblers soldiered together coming to & fro from Korea—now also abandoned, with a skeleton crew racing madly & dispiritedly up & down the passageways working vainly to keep the mountain, the mammoth, the Iron leviathan from falling into rust and dismantlement in the long year since she was tied up there inactivated out of permanent service—in hope or fear of another war, kept alive—and tied up next to her an even more absurd LST,* with a big cave in the middle for cargo, where I work.

The great spread of the plant, a fire station, huge motionless cranes poised in the air over the ships & buildings silent so that the clink of a tin can echoes more loud than all the barndoors of the ships of battle. And the song of the train faraway—

* * *

## Sextillions of Infidels Staggering Home from Work

I look up at the telephone pole hoping to be staggered, and am!—the uprearing brown raw wooden tree stands there instantaneously propped up dumb holding wires of high intelligence.

---

* LST: Landing Ship Tank. Intermediary ship-to-shore amphibious warfare vessel for delivering tanks and other large vehicles.

A sea of fern and grass—each particular blade starting up
suspended and balanced under the half-moon on the glimmering
whale-like hill

—scattered delicate green bushes explode out three feet
high. Ah! I caught God again!

The American Can Company below, Oakland lights across
the Bay Bridge

—floating silver domes of gastanks hovering in the clouds
over a shipyard

—and my apartment* in the housing project resting solid on
industrial imagination's hill.

* * *

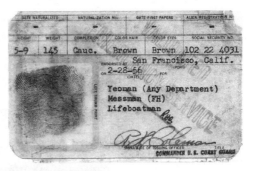

Documents pertaining to Ginsberg's work at sea.

---

* That is, Peter Orlovsky's Turner Terrace apartment, Potrero Hill,
San Francisco.

I sang a song with Allen on my breast. Eat rosses Allen cried at me—Bending over I snaped off his cock—& held it tall & straight for all the life around me to see—I threw it into the sky, it became a satalite all of its own, for all the world to see—the stars blinked at each other with knowing eye—wile an old lady prayed for our salvation in a christain church.

June 1956—P. Orlovsky

\* \* \*

Death of Naomi June 9, 1956—
　　Tenderness & a tomb—the world is a tomb of tenderness. Life is a short flicker of love.
　　Went out into the grass knelt down & cried a little—to heaven for her. Otherwise nothing.

\* \* \*

Everything changes toward death. My mother. Myself. The asphalt pavement of the dock I am sitting on. The chair I am sitting on is labeled consigned for scrap. Along the dock, blue water, blue sky. USNS Kern sits on water, being changed for Arctic trip. Iron bulkheads disappearing and replaced by different walls. Then later mothballs. Then rust. Then salvage. Whole navies float across the waters. To disappear. A man walks along the dock in grimy clothes, head bent down, carrying dead lunch.
　　The pavement boils in the sun. The dock is already old and battered. My childhood is gone with my mother. My memory becomes less clear. My body will go. There is no me left. Naomi is memory. Naomi is a memory. My 30 years is a memory to me. Memory will be nothing. Memory changes toward death. Toward death, memory changes. Memories. Memory. Mors. M. . . . .*

\* \* \*

Where e'er I went I went & said one fucked up Kaddish for her soul.

---

\* Ellipsis periods appear in the journal entry.

# U.S.N.S. Jack J. Pendleton June 15, Pt. Malote, Calif.

Leaving S.F.: Boom ropes clacking like a clock, late afternoon, the Pendleton creaking thru the water, the bay, shadow flying across the deck, S. Francisco emerging at the prow, a lone green earthen isle set in the bay eroded & left there unused an antenna atop it, and another on the rock below its skirt—silent, red buoys on the grey water, chug of a tug, crisscross of ropes around the mast, sadness at heart, the calm blaat of voices over the bridge, voices amidships.

—Stand on the fantail deck by an empty flagpole leaning against an iron rail shouting my poetry to the roaring sea.

*    *    *

This is the speech of stones.
This is the speech of the lady getting a nail out of her shoe.
This is the speech of the Doctor of the Mills.
This is the speech of the lights across the bay.

*    *    *

# First Trip to Seattle on Pendleton

To Wobbly hall, lurched & upset spittoon on floor, which old dodderer had just filled, and then I gave them fifty cents for what? "The lights," he asked? A wave of the hand toward all the brown walls—

Out to the shoeshine stand by the brown wood entrance to the Turkish Bath on Yessler Way—Laughing with sadness all WC Fields with big noses, pain in the forehead, they stumbled along the street above my head as I walked up the steps from the sucker shoeshine parlor where the spade (in striped pants with ragged cuffs & no press) talked to my shoes, telling me where the queer bars were in answer to my question, where—"Well some of 'em hangs out here & comes in but I don't know you understand I just works here I sees them all sorts come here I don't care you know everybody to them own kind of kicks, you got your pleasure I got mine." He was a soul, with secret honesty afraid to level completely—he didn't really care "I mean I go to those places (The Mocambo & Square Dollar) and have a good time I mean I have a better time than sometimes if I go out with some fat girl & she give me a bad time & take all my money away."

I floated out in the street laughing at all the faces the suffering seemed so transitory the hopelessness so eternal to them, the fixed masks of dreamlike incoherence, each with his private big-nosed woe & suffering beatness for lack of a quarter and locked up cock in the bloody bank.

Down into the subterranean poolhall, up on the street and out, sudden reverberation of bass drum & congregation across street the Salvation Army preaching, first the old man, I approached & listened leaning against the corner building directly in front of curb, below on street the band and invisible altar the old man yelling, "You bums you're not saved I was like you but Jesus in his sweet love taught me I was worthy to be saved & now I'm standing here telling you that if Jesus saved me he can save you but unless you accept Jesus you're doomed to be what you see you are but if you confess your misery to Jesus he will not reject you—"

"You're Goddamn right!" sang the laughing drunken harlequin bum on my left. "Your absolutely right that's true, that's really true, I couldn't agree with you more."

"And he who is the lamb will wash your sins with his own blood and you who stand on this corner in misery will join the company of saints."

"That's the living truth," sang the bum again, reeling around the sidewalk.

A spirit entered the air, I stared around the whole company of assembled bums listening with interest—the hush the jealous speech of the neat homely blank eyed evangelist, the drunken careless agreement & enthusiasm of middleaged portly young listeners foremost—

Sudden hand of cop who glided in on the sidewalk seized the bum & violently hustled him off to opposite corner, joined by other cop & squadcar at police phone—

My transport of happiness floating down street faced with incoherent suffering red faces to the announcements of Salvation Army—Suddenly the white amoebic hemophiliac dread horror light of the preying police vans come up to take away the now silent

& humbled bum of St. Drunken Francis who looked from across the street browbeated & woebegone & resigned to being not sassy to his policeman captors—with evil white light the hearse paddy-wagon approached driven by devils with badges & clubs while the speaker announced the compassion & mercy of Christ continuing his mechanical rant uninterrupted without batting eyelash or moving head aside as if the diabolic proceedings were either beneath contempt or ordained by Christ to occur as temptation for other obscurer reasons—in any case not lifting a finger to stop the police—and all the audience attention was now directed away from the speech to the small faraway dumbshow scene across the street where the bum was hustled into the deathly white truck & a black policeman jumped into the darkness with him & the door slammed behind.

Later I picked up with young college Berkeley fellow and a white-frisco-sailor-cap negro named Tom with whom I wandered drinking in Jackson area—drugstore—he stayed at Hotel on Yessler Square—

That same night drunk I left him & looking for souls entered the Square Dollar bar & saw tough kid Tom Tagalong for the first time over a beer spilled table bloodshot eye with an absolutely drunk old man in wool shirt from woods & later the cripple whom Tagalong as Prince abased himself to kissing & necking with openly as sign of regard & compassion, with all the fairies about— Like a Neal to Jim Holmes the hunchback in Denver.

Then our arguments and I bought beer & he spilled it on me & I spilled mine on him & then emptied glass over my head—and he asked me how much money you got—you want to spend the night with me & we'll be lovers?—I saying I have check for $15.00 and thinking I'd be well rid of the money, he replying with painful sweet drunk look in his eye "That's too much. I ain't worth it—$5 is enough." Then in the bathroom re-recognitions but he got involved in conversation with negroes who later turn out to be in for a fight—and conversation with old Hemingway who glares at him lovingly calls him Muscles looks on him as bad great son, speaks, tries to speak, of his own pride of youth, cannot for every time he does Tagalong grabs him by the arm, grips him in contest of will, the old man protests against the toughness of the contest shakes head masochistic sadly & hopeless I shout "Mercy," spill beer on Tagalong he gazes at me angrily then curiously and asks

for more beer I buy more & spill it and buy more, waiter running
back and forth all the bums drinking—Queen waiter eyeing me &
camping waitressy courteous, Tom goes to the head again, bar
closing, waiters gang up on him drag him out, shirt torn, on his ass
to the door, tossed out, lands sitting on sidewalk I sidle over so do
the colored queers in for the kill—Suddenly black eyed heavy
unshaved young truckdriver walks by door—"Montana," they
shout, Tom staggers to his feet—where should I go—what should I
do now—it's up to you Montana he says Tender younger
brother—Go home—and so Tom grabs beer rough & courteous
from arms of imploring negro (like 45th St. Huncke friend, Jake
Spencer), who gives him the offering unwilling but happy in the
noticing & pain thrill, I cut in to join Tom & Montana who motions
me away, Tom recognizes me drunk introduces Montana frowns I
say he no trust me & gaze at Montana so into an alley Montana
dark opens beer I talk of heaven Tom with imaginary knife rips
open my stomach, I suddenly bridle rush out alley screaming
"That's not how it is in heaven—there aren't any knives in
heaven"—Police walk down street stop me search alley grab all of
us, send me in direction of ship, Tom to his Travellers hotel, end.

\* \* \*

June 17—Beaver Point, Oregon, went into town with Mike the
pockfaced masochistic electrician & the Birmingham Fireman.
Drinking, pool, Fireman's story, bumming after ships in Depres-
sion. Ride home with Cops, sitting on pursey old Purser's lap, him
fingering my dungarees.

\* \* \*

Dream: Saw Marlon Brando at last we talked about Kerouac,
    "He never even got in touch with me," says Brando, "Why?"
    "Well here you are now."
    "I mean you guys never even sent me a postcard what was
happening to you, so how was I supposed to know."
    "Here, now I am, here's the copy"—Peter's proof sheets
of Howl—I hand them, preserved under glassine plastic clear
binders.

\* \* \*

Dream of extremely polite & courteous meeting with St.-Jean Perse over MS of Howl.

\* \* \*

You who were poor and walked thru revolving doors onward in another man's overcoat—True Democrat.

It was you from Chicago in the middle of America who put us all hip.

It was you who handed down the Laws of Perception to a million jiving juveniles not yet born, still in the realms of black eternity, while you talked in Bickford's with heavy-lidded junk-sick eye & dreaming of that darkness then.

You who inaugurated the hip revolution in Pokerino, "Beat Beatitude."

When Huncke said, "I've got my hip boots on," and strode thru Harlem, I saw his hair flash by the movies and his hip walk fade into eternity, the pavements. A poem with direct personal crying to him.

I'll be there in Harlem when you pick up your next joint.

Huncke! Huncke! forgive me! I didn't know what I was doing.

Let Huncke be Huncke himself and not be changed by Van Doren's Mental image gaze.

Familiar brokendown Ivy League balding types in their twenties—seen in employment offices—for whom the social process has broken down & they wander smiling and sweating from cubicle to cubicle trying to find out if anybody else is scared too.

\* \* \*

Dream: In large house, many rooms. Subway station in background.

Charlie Chaplin there, with Jewish botanist friend, or symphony conductor, at performance of Verdi's Requiem.

"How come you know Chaplin so well?" we ask him—I and reporters & hangers on. "Oh we just met a long time ago—and we're old friends—we didn't know each other by reputation—I never heard of him or he of me—we talked & believed the same things." (After reading Farrell's *The Martyr.*) The friend looked like Moses, or Zukofsky—bearded, need shave, blue face, sickly, Jewish.

Charlie Chaplin got up on a table, on the boat, on a hatch, and as the sun went down yellow in the evening, took the sun with gentle pathetic gestures, plucking it apart in the air in pantomime, breaking off the pieces, enfolding it, and laying it away with infinite tenderness into an imaginary box at his feet, saying eternal farewell to the eternal symbol of life. "In the elegant melancholy of twilight."

Given a chance he was going to get up on a podium & take Verdi's requiem, his favorite sentimental piece of music, apart too. Give a public pantomime performance of the whole requiem.

Much as I like it, I heard the movement of the orchestra & the sawing of oboes & wondered what does he see in it, sitting there in the audience like everyone else, with the orchestra going thru section after section—Now a small theme, he's hearing it too like me, what can he make of that—it's just music. Maybe the *Tuba Mirum,* but all thru the whole piece?

Neal, entering—I had moved from room to room in the house, hidden in one lower cheap front furnished room downstairs & gone back to the old big one where Jack lived to get my mail— Neal came in bounding, naked, kissed Jack full on the mouth, a long sweet embrace, I rushed up—joining their party, kissed Neal on his behind and tore off handful of meat I had bought from the market, & wrapped it around his cock while I knelt & kissed him—realizing he might think it weird but would appreciate also the beauty, of the dead meat, it's all one and the same, flesh of mortality, we're clutching & kissing & wrapping around ourselves.

At this the USNS Sgt. Jack J. Pendleton—I was asleep on an upper bunk—boomed its horn, & moved down the Columbia River from Beaver Point to Seattle. Carrying on its decks some landing barges for Alaska—In my dream it meant 5:30, time for the performance to begin of the requiem. —Neal incident took place in a large house I knew of old.

June 19. Seattle. Letter to Gary—Visit Laura Uronowitz, and girl friend & Jack Gilbert & Jean (Blonde) & Jo (Bump on Forehead) McClaine* at University, drive home losing way—I goofed.

Entering Puget Sound. The white range of Olympic Mts.

---

* Uronowitz, Gilbert, and McClaine were poets who'd lived in San Francisco mid-'50s.

flickering in distance beyond shoreline shelf of Olympic penin-
sula. Gulls cry, heated conversations on the Masts, sudden shriek
and all vanishes to the rear of the ship, water down below, rising &
rolling backward all 11 gulls at once. The Silver Gulls at Golden
Gate.

1 Love's Labour's Lost—Pride: Intellectual, & Lover's approach
   type. Resolved in patience & humility by temporary loss of
   love's labor. The fantastic Spaniard of pride too.

2 Comedy of Errors—Jealousy: creation & doubles—reducing
   scene to one man's affairs by substitution of stronger soul in
   one man's body carrying on same affairs to show in relief the
   transparency of actions & relations.

3 Two Gentlemen of Verona
   Love & Infatuation: first real sin, proteus changeability—
   Valentine's fidelity. First stroke of forgiveness & mercy on
   Valentine's part, & Theory of Mercy expounded in outlaws
   Band's state pardon.

\* \* \*

# June 20, 1956

The misty vast nebulous clouds on the thin blue distant hills
over the Columbia River, never-to-be knowable but by a cloud
geometer & expert sailor who can name their general types—but
the individual clouds so wondrous never familiar, not even seen
again.

Two high cliffs aside the big flat brown river, covered with
needle point grey spars, toothpicks of hairy giants.

Fishermen in boats whose noises rebound on the broad
water pull in their nets.

Chinese cooks lean over the nearest rail

I write a sentence on the palm of my hand in the sunset,
standing on the prow with the rail up to my breast or chin.

The boat the Pendleton floats on upstream silent as a canoe
and thin as a boy from where I stand.

The lovely sailor waist stripped paints red lead orange on
iron castle wall in the sunset with color reflected all over his body
in unreal flash of red light as I pass the gangway.

Shelley the red haired storekeeper preparing a game of monopoly in the officers' mess room.

The best lemon meringue pie ever et, tasted—

My mother Naomi is dead. She used to go to the movies when her mother died in 1920.

The misty red furbelow castle of the clouds singing furbelow furbelow in the vast grey twilight of the world.

My back is sore, heart empty.

Write a hymn to courage, the next step—imagining with Bill a suicidal wild Amazon trek where he'd be sure to get in trouble— yet if I don't give up my fear of Death & Dishonor and accept fortune as it comes I'll never meet glorious fortune. My heart's empty, I must continue writing.

Earlier today in Bunk I thought how earlier years had brought on wave after wave of major poem—*Death in Violence, Denver Doldrums*—the sad horns of the world wind over the mountains of the radio in the mess room—*Green Auto, Siesta in Xbalba, Howl.*

"My youth is ending, all my youth
& Death & Beauty cry like horns & motors
of a ship afar, half heard, an echo in the sea beneath."

\* \* \*

June 20–21—Back to Beaver Point, return to Seattle.

Woke up 4 AM in Straits of Juan de Fuca with dream of Naomi—pressure & horror woke me up—

In a motel or familiar visiting quarters, ran into her, settled down for the night—She undressed and I saw she had a large dull fleshly cock and a cluster of 6 genitals attached to her body by a piece of wen-like flesh tube. We lay side by side, I turned my back to her, horrified & silent, to sleep it off, she pressed up close to me, the mutant sex apparatus bunched up at my back, I moved, reached hand back, felt it was there, woke. Didn't write dream down immediately but fell asleep. Dreamed it was in 288 Graham Ave. house,

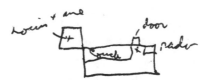

in the living room talking to Louis, told him my dream, horrified, he shrugged it off, I said "She's a mutant"—remembering from earlier dream the look of her face, extremely high dome hair, like a stovepipe curved or bowler hat shape, with french-block oily glistening shock of hair all over her, neatly and artificially arranged, black, as on a window dressing dummy, & blank black eyes & pallid skin, as if a robot or a mutant—the peculiar look on the face I ascribed in dream to the lobotomy. So Louis shrugged while I pleaded, "She's a mutant," afraid, and then I went into the living room—she was *there*! Where did you come from? How long have you been here? I asked, afraid she had heard my complaint conversation—She smiled evilly & busied herself with preparations for bed?—"I've been here all along, it's my home, isn't it? I wrote my name on the pillow here, right here (pointing to the pillow overhanging the edge of the couch), I wrote my name in the pillow so I wouldn't be forgotten or get lost."

* * *

# Psalm III [*First draft of poem, CP 155:*]

To God: To illuminate all men.

Begin with the beggars on Skid Road and show them real holiness.

Let Occidental & Washington* be transformed into a higher place; the plaza of eternity, with dripping buildings rotting thereon.

Let the soul be the only thing stable there, let it shine forth eternal.

Illuminate the workers, let the welders in shipyards see the brilliance of their torches. Let their sweat & scraped fingers bleed forth thy glory.

Let the rich man in automobile passing the hitchhiker be illuminated thru his windshield—Let the mountains bleat like lambs to his astonished eye.

Let the mercy of the flower's direction beckon him in the eye.

Let the sun shine directly with no name but holy Adonai.

Illuminate me that I may write more correctly.

Illuminate the rich at banquet tables. Let the waiters be angels, serving their rich portions.

---

* Occidental Street, corner of Washington Street, Seattle.

Let the headwaiters be archangels and the cook be god—as all men.

Let the automobile salesmen be appalled at the holiness of their machines.

Let the crane operator lift up his arm for joy.

Let fairies drink in the bars and seek love, their sadness is holy. They seek love.

Let the sailors in the streets stop still and gaze at the multitudes transported.

Let all at once be riven with a blast of light. Let Jesus crash thru time. Let Buddha be apparent. Let radiance inhabit the buildings. Let elevators creak & speak, ascending & descending in awe.

Let the crooked flower bespeak its purpose in straightness—to seek the light.

Let crookedness & straightness bespeak the light.

Let these psalms bespeak the light.

Let all things bespeak their Maker. The cornice stone bespeaks the architect's hand. The sky bespeaks the creator. The Created bespeaks the Creator. The uncreated bespeaks the Created. Death bespeaks love, the Created.

Let the bright room bespeak the dark room.

Let the river be a blast of light.

I feed on thy name like a cockroach on a crumb—but this cockroach is holy.

\* \* \*

## July 5, 1956

### S.S. Pendleton, deep dream—aboard ship

Working on the Tally Cards for the national machine, under duress, in Moscow for a visit, I have chance to sneak away and see the country—as in a science fiction dream—I'm in Moscow—I've been filing on cards the names of the streets of Russia—Carl Tilley is my superior he is also a spy—Red the Storekeeper and I wandered off but could not find our way to the old man at the end of the grey street up the balconies—down the raceway of downtown cars—

The question is, what are the points of interest to visit, where are the Franciscan Skid Rows of Moscow—how do we get there? This is all a deep political secret & mystery—I am willing to go anywhere & break all the rules to see—I ask Tilley, who is evasive, but indicates that all the information is down there recorded on my tally cards. I am elated by having the information. Woke up realizing it is my first nostalgic dream of Russia & have Uncle Max ahead in Riverside to ask for info on who of family is still alive, where to go and what to see there—and also what streets, what places are the secret living places of the artists and the Damned & the queers & the poor.

Woke up at 11:15 PM after dropping off to sleep in Bunk at 7:30 & unconscious all that time while ship fell asleep, alone I went wandering corridors.

Bothered by my isolation sterility and vanity—brought to head reading St. Francis' life, I realized I had no longer the drive to truth that would flip me out toward my ideal of god, but because of doubt am living no kind of singleminded life. Returning to S.F. I saw how grasping to maintain intimacy with Peter was leading me to bank on his love & feeling of care I believe in from him, unwilling to go all out, but I'm hung up on sex, so not wholeheartedly absorbed. Other than that I wander between worlds of Burroughs and Poetry and S.F. Peter's interlude I cherish as an eternal fact—as my mother's death—There are no eternal facts unless they are lifetime—and even lifetime facts, I see thru St. Francis, are not enough to ground the soul in—In any case trying straining to make a lifetime fact & truth of Peter is not enough.

So I tend to cling to older attachments as ideals including the ground of revelation & divinity which is another part time commitment.

Reading my poetry over for proof for book I see the disorganization of it, its form—part I of *Howl*—and how that is not even eternally perfect & lifetime fact.

I'm consumed with envy of Jack's holiness & devotion to singleminded expression in writing.

I myself write nothing and am sick of fragment sketching. The poems I build out of them are fragmentary, slight.

\* \* \*

July 9—Read about the Sahara all Friday evening, in my bunk, got up at Midnight and went out, it having occurred to me to pray— after reading last week St. Francis & this week of DeFoucould of the Hoggars*—picked my way in near absolute darkness along the forward hatches among ropes & rails to the prow where I climbed & stood looking awhile at light off California coast— missed Los Angeles and didn't know where the lights were, no map. The stars were very bright and Milky way last night as the night before stretched directly across the heavens from Bow to starboard like a long infinite blanket of thin cloud. The water moved continually as if alive. Staring out into the Pacific darkness I saw a huge hump of darkness sitting in the water I didn't recognize—the dim horizon line broken by it as if a huge whale dead black beast were sitting humping with its bulk the middle of the water. I looked at it & tried to pick out its nature in light of flash from the south that came periodically but finally turned away the hump still mysterious.

On my knees I prayed for a sign of further enlightenment— that my mind was still more confused—I didn't know what I was doing any more—suffering acceptable if accompanied by some sign of the direction I was to go—thru asceticism, or thru family world, either one meaningless in regard to the goal of Vision. No sign of course. I was unable to get with it, in the mood, & my voice sounded silly & unacceptable. But my prayer came from near the center of my heart for I am confused.

Walking back I saw the hump had moved it was a cloud.

* * *

Whitman first noticed the ants in America—then Kerouac.†

Whitman's insane biographers quibble about his love of men.

Calamus—Whitman's sublime nakedness.

---

* Biography of Catholic N. Afric colonist "saint." —A.G., October 4, 1982

† "America is a permissible dream,/Providing you remember ants/ Have Americas...": Kerouac, "51st Chorus," *Mexico City Blues* (New York: Grove Press, 1959).

\* \* \*

The guarded look in Whitman's eyes—as in the Brady photo—certainly a case of self-imposed repression & consciousness—the honesty of the poems in talking about queerness fits in—fear perhaps, but loveless-ness, fear of response, or no response. See G. W. Allen's Biography, his journal notes & p. 421 to p. 424 *Solitary Singer.*\* Parting with Peter Doyle—thot Doyle didn't love him, and surprised to find that he really did. But all because he had no outside hand or outer validation he was timid to the point of repression. Therefore the seriousness of his statement of love plight as eternal—as in early story of *Dai & Eris*—"their own unreturned & unhallowed passion."

It's a big jump to outline sketch of a superb calm character years later (1870)—"his emotions etc. are complete in himself irrespective (indifferent) of whether his love, friendship, etc. are returned or not."

He may have had some small love life but this is the main fate & I think the last word on Whitman's love life in general.

The poetry attempts to express & *validate* or see as real his own feelings which are genuine, the struggle to find a way to feel as he actually felt in conflict with what he thot was possible on earth with society & people & boys—

Walt Whitman finally in the old pale white haired evanescent pictures still clinging to the reality of his emotions unexpressed except in consciousness & writing & thus drifting into infinity of thought.

The remarkable thing here is the clarity—the complete & open revelation in his writing & biography—of a soul. You see his inside & deepest thots & worries & the ground of his sense of mortality, his sensible deeps.

The simple Transference of sexual love to spiritual & the teaching of boys & the healing of sick—all unexpressed amor. Even the sweet bearded kisses disguise under Christian compas-

\* Gay Wilson Allen, *The Solitary Singer: A Critical Biography of Walt Whitman* (New York: Macmillan, 1955).

sion a more pure animal tenderness—more pure that is, direct and holy animal tenderness, mortal tenderness. "Animal raw mortal sexual tenderness" is what Whitman felt, which he thought unexpressible in rawest form—uninhibited unlimited lovers contact.

His feelings were very real and there seemed no possibility of expression.

He indicates something a little beyond homosexuality, too, beyond what homosexuals know or talk about as queerness, freedom to suck cocks, develop passionate attachments—an underlying base tenderness that life itself is made up of. Nearer to Socrates & the greeks, tho they had their own social style. Near David & Jonathan of the Bible? Something beyond the forms of love, something beyond homosexuality or heterosexuality which are after all only expressions of something, mere forms for the great beast to copulate with itself in order to realize itself in order to exist in order that is to love.

"My cock is your Satori" means that if love is true its truth must be appreciated despite its external forms.

I loved you & always have, but must I apologize—Gary?

The light in my eyes—is it my fantasy? I think it is god, but who is my fantasy?

In this world Whitman is an Angel of Transparency—in a world of hooded delight.

At the end he seeks to transform himself into pure feeling & beneficent ecstasy. No more conflict with acting out his erotic impulses, pure transference to the non-sexual & hypocritic-saintly "Self-Discipline." A kind of Christ for that, his knowledge being near perfect—the only flaw being he didn't even know he could get away with being queer too—a robust possibility he envisioned for ideal Whitman in writings & glimpsed perhaps on occasions with responsive types like Peter Doyle.

The deep sadness & resignation & compliance both to his Nature, and outer necessity, even Death, a boon finally, to end the love struggle. To end the struggle, since love itself is existence, to end his existence peacefully, since he could hardly love.

No direct outlet & response for his love, man to man.

\* \* \*

## July 9, 1956

Other night on the bow under the stars, on knees, asking for Crucifixion as St. Francis to feel suffering of Christ in order to feel love—wondering what Christ was—resolving to have no more to do with Peter as it is only futile anyway as any other sexual joy I might seek now, except thru generalized love; I had not yet read Whitman's case in the book, seeing he did the same & his head was replaced by a statue.*

With Peter a futile desire as it is unreturned in kind—his love is equal to mine but what do I want other? his sexual nature not matched to mine. At 30th birthday find out what it is I want that I can't get—ideal homosexual union? I think from earliest years—11–14—this has been my deepest almost a mystical longing.

Giving that up, replaced by a purer evanescent mystical longing for the Deity I saw in things once & never again since Harlem?

Both these impulses, the mystical becoming stronger in these years & slowly the queer one becoming nearer & nearer to mystical though as an untranslatable hope.

So on the bow, at night, tonight, under the full flash of stars, the milky way streaming dimly across the black sky, standing up above the prow, looking into the black water 20 feet below and the vague solid evanescent darkish reaches of water beyond, rolls of the ship, turning the horizon lifting & falling it, wind whirling past me in my ears & sleeves lifting the cap off my head making me uneasy.

"Let the spirit of the Lord go forth on the water.

"Let the spirit of the Lord go forth on the stars.

"Let the spirit of the Lord go forth on the ships."

and suddenly a creak behind me, I thought it was black spies in the machinery & shrouds, a figure of a climbing man on the gun turret, only a large pulley hook—Staring fixed & blank at the anchor windlass, watching the flat water behind the rails & midship rise and fall, and the motion of the ship, suddenly realized as small and powerful iron machine with garish dim face before me, lifting me up and down slowly like cosmic elevators on the vast black reach of the sea.

---

* *"A casser une statue on risque d'en devenir une."*—Cocteau, *The Blood of a Poet.* —A.G. May 26, 1993

A resolve to trust faith, trust the waters, am I ready tho for death? as the shapes of my mind before scared me with dread as often—will get used to these trips at night to pray on the bow. A repose to come, carelessness over the water, trust & roll of the sea.

Deeper into death, & life more solid—as I saw the pure white shape of bearded Whitman tonight looking at 5 in the afternoon into the yellow mist toward land, he on his deathbed fifty years ago in Camden across the nation. Crost time & crost space, I imagined him die in the mist; real as my mother was.

* * *

## Psalm

Real as my mother was: Lord life is fading.
The sea surrounds me dark as night.
I have too much peace. Food & money come easily, with a little discomfort.
Manna I lack and wait for it hungry with fat belly and decaying flesh. Hair's out.
My teeth don't hurt but someday they will.
Walking on the ship I am safe unless the ship goes down.
Illumine me up again.

Unsatisfied longing for the nameless follows me around. Already I'm in love with a deck sailor & afraid to talk to him.
I am not unhappy or happy just complaining as usual.
Where's my regular naked imagination?
Endless hope for Satori. Endless hope for Divine You.
Too many eyes in my mind watch me and I want to sleep, & Be shut up.

* * *

"What part of San Anselmo do you live in?"

"Oh I live down there by the Miracle Mile past that Carver's Drive-In—by the Methodist Church. . . .

"How bout that motel there over by the hotel? Nothin but subdivisions out there—knock a hill down & set up in the mud-flats. I hear they're going to put some big dam up there just got in Congress. Jeez I better get goin." Officers' conversation.

\* \* \*

St. Elizabeth of Hungary hiding Jesus in her bedroom.

Princess Liliuokalani visiting Molokai leper island reduced to tears.

St. Peter of Long Island, St. Lucien of St. Louis. St. Neal of Denver St. Jack of Lowell St. Bill of Tangiers St. Allen of Paterson.

\* \* \*

Irenic—"promoting peace; peaceful; pacific"

Prescind—"to detach, abstract, or isolate"

Consubstantiation—"the doctrine that the substance of the bread and wine of the Eucharist exists, after consecration, side by side with the substance of the body and blood of Christ but is not changed into it"

July 10, 1956—

Big leaved rainy trees in the depths of the beautiful empty corner lot in Tacoma overlooking the square Haarlem sunken basin harbor where my ship floats—Far away is the huge monster Mt. Rainier amid the smoke of the factories, so huge it seems floating in the sky, the base hidden in iron smoke coal & mist & grey dim landfall dusk. The sides stretched out, curve down & disappear into the cloudy land, so that the base looks bigger than the Mt. is high under cloud—a black spot on top centers all this snowy massiveness.

\* \* \*

## At the Movies

People are tired of listening to dead
poetry—reduce them to ecstasy.
Nothing will save us,
nothing will save us
from the grave.

Children invented
spiritual sexual dances
in the aisles of the Paramount
Theater when Benny Goodman
opened on Broadway.

> The feeling of death, of things
>                 gone by—
> infinite shiny joyous delicacy
>                 of Lionel Hampton with his eye
>                 open & tongue poised in his
>                         teeth
>                                 hammering the vibraphone.

* * *

All the Phony that the Lamb has to put up with.

* * *

On prow of ship—stars, roaring water, we all die, a kind of instantaneous universal joy of the Creation, and everything in the ocean moves.

But because of Pride drest in dungarees and the inevitable brown Army shirt I sit in Bar in Seattle with Davalos–Dean Moriarty–Tagalong drinking, near drunk, but in my eye in the Bar Mirror sudden alooking I saw myself not young and in my prime longhaired but thin-faced dark browed swart & thirsty silly old kid—eyeglasses set upon my skull screwy squinting at myself cross-eyed.

"Blind as the heavens which these words inspire."

* * *

## On the Bridge in Tacoma

Why was I created? To be a saint? And all this created? For me to look into? The empty corridor of the building leads to the elevator shaft, the blind up on the first floor office window with an empty chair for me to see.

Melancholy railroad cars pass under the bridge lurching and clanking slowly.

Smokestacks twin at night down in the factory by the Puyallup River, white fumes slowly curl upward to a single star off across the basin—red glare as in Hell lighting up all the smoke stretched flat slowly collecting around the distant Breughel Iron Pot of the iron factory burner with small watertowers in the distance silhouetted standing up over industrial roofs, noise of cars clanking clocking the adjustments of a bridge overhead, ticking of some time machine in a lighted warehouse below, and irregular clank of iron bars shifted and smashed together under the telephone pole electric wire, red lite on the tracks a block away below me, as I stand on the Bridge inscribing step of footsteps in the pavement, chain of yellow highway lights and haze settling down on bright lamps stretched across the small valley enclosed by low hills & cliffs of buildings set back from highway all around a 90° bend of head to the left to the Iron Pot—and a ship anchored waits across the narrow dock water, a few great signs beyond in the night, one green a mile away on a roof reflected in the water, another on the dock street below, a green neon fish with red fisherman's justice scales saying Mairish Fish & Oyster Co. Rails gleam starry electric bulbs high over road ("gleam of stars on rails")—White ramp slow down from this bridge, extra concrete poles I know not wherefore, hish faraway of steam unloaded from a locomotive ass, small bright firefly carlight passing slow silently half-mile away across another bridge decorated with red light, darkness all around, iron rollers in the basement rolling on concrete, and then I noticed a narrow hole in the arcs and abutments of passageways up from the bridge toward downtown Mainstreet Pacific Ave, a row of flue & flashy bar and hotel marquee signs, chirp of bird on the wire or cricket and Toot Toot of train, the double throated Claxon friendly, bare, red silhouette of the smokestacks with their incessant steamy head in the mystical deepening haze lying blanket low above industrial valley roofs thru which all the lights burn unreflectingly, three ahead lined up on the hill—a bridge?—and to the right—the bridge is shaking throbbing—a riot of mercury vapor highway lights—one deep pink hotel window lower story all lit up, huge, and a car moving toward the bridge at left hand below———

Mt. Rainier sits on a promontory with outcropping sheaves and upjutting shouts of rock—down below the white foamy nebulous cloudy bright abyss which is the world, filled up with rolling snowy impenetrable mist. Straight above rivers of snow, rocks of snow, works of snow up to the dull vast peak of Rainier.

* * *

## July 21, 1956

List what I dreamed in my bunk on the ship after reading the Lifes of Sir François Villon and Saint Francis of Assisi, two days out in the drear waste, on a dull grey rainy day on the Pacific, my heart empty and having wandered many hours from table to bunk to book, to sleep to dream, and lay considering a Book of Dreams, Prophecies—at mid day in the afternoon this dreamed I awoke and wrote at the sound of the ship's bell at 2:30:

Returning from a voyage to the mountains of solitude I came back to camp where my brother lay asleep in his cabin, passed by the porch to the drugstore, old Emil familiar shook milkshakes & took the mail, he told me the postman was here with my letters & bade me with a wave of his finger see to the slot in the door of the cabin.

Entering I passed my brother on the porch and looked to the next cabin where surprise my father and new wife stepmother Edith lay sleeping. I couldn't see except heard the radio portable wireless, and scrambled on the floor for the mail, a few letters maybe bills maybe from afar a Burroughs or Peter, returning hearing the music out the door—the music strong and clear a holy symphony I thot in my dream was the Jupiter or Mozart or late Haydn or Beethoven.

Dom Dom Dom Dom Dom
                        Daaaa!
de de
Dom Dom Dom Dom
                        Daaa!
De De
Dom Dom    Dom Dom        Dom        DA!
            De            de
        Do
                Dom.
(Repeat)

and I left the family stirring in bed to the tune of the loud music which I turned higher in joyous volume on the radio and sang myself in clear voice, tuned in solitude to harmony with the music, in my head, sang aloud—

Out on the porch I met the Lady Clare Bright, young nun whom I had not met but knew, and saluted her with that song, and the elder nun or prioress who hearing my clear heart ring forth to Jupiter approved and nodded and welcomed me.

—They sat in deck chairs and I went around to the back of the chair to talk to Clare, when she put her foot, besandaled in leather, a broad foot, straight down by mistake into a full shit bowl toilet seat whereat I without warning flushed the toilet telling her to pull her foot out, and as the toilet flushed & cleard, the water still running violently, told her to plunge her foot in again, which she did right graciously, cleaning it off completely, whereat we joyed together further.

\* \* \*

Woke and remembered the death of my mother a late dream of converse with my father, the advancing years of my grand-mother, the refuge which is the Love of God, and my need for a virgin of great holiness to espouse and shrive my soul of its past sins & miseries. Only she or such as she would have the clarity & grace to love such a queer as I and sharpen my senses to women. So my brother picked a mild holy religious maid. So the older roués of Henry James, a girl from a convent—so I saw a usefulness of the old dog marrying a pure maid. I am so tainted by corruption only an innocent girl could be undisturbed and forgive. This is the sexy project.

In extremity, tho suffering lead to compassion, the first thought I have, as on Mount Rainier exhausted in the bleak white endless weariness of the snow field, is of the impersonal death & pain against which we are pitted. Hence "For the Love of God, will you get me out of this." Only the Love of god, something above & outside the field of fleshly limitation & pain, could have that excess of mild 'during charity, which is not human, at the bottom of suffering is suffering so far as I saw.

Tho I pray for suffering, when I suffer I see nothing but suffering & no merciful release natural to it.

Returning from wounded in the rosy courts of Skid Row by that knight of the gracious heart Sir Thomas Tagalong of the cock with the large eye.

\* \* \*

Looking from the prow, three ships ahead of us wallow northward in the grey green gulf around.

A sensation watching the light go down northward, toward sunset, seeing the full moon in zagged parts behind bits of cloud, and puffs of cloud overhead, the sky a bowl of cloud except this area of the sea whereover float rags and strips & ribbons of mist, piled up in great harmonic billows near the earth, running parallel to each other grey near transparent with a blue cerulean light of the sky beyond them and a few higher more sharply defined white fleefs of cloud (at the azimuth of the eye) behind them between me and the cloud, all transported in slow motion south. All earth transported in motion, the sea, the clouds, the ship my eye.

The sensation similar to the great banks of clouds seen faraway on the Columbia, and years ago ah! years ago at Last! seen faraway on the sky bowl massy on the water to Dakar 1947. Nearly ten years since I been on the ocean.

The movie today, Mitzi Gaynor, couldn't sit near Chuck the handsome sailor and so left to look at the ocean.

The sensation of vast transport of the clouds, sensation of the North, sensation of vasty power moving over the horizon in the clouds, sensation of unknowing purpose (intelligence sans self-awareness moving itself around).

As a man seeing the clouds it's his own mighty soul he sees or not, sees nothing of himself all the unknown outside eternal clouds & miles deep ocean & the ships ahead small merciful rowboats over the deep.

On the steel hard Moloch ships all's work & craft & hammers & sweat but on the prow the ships are small diminutive & minute on the ocean, each a speck afloat out there.

Flash Fantasy—Coming back from the Head piss in underwear (red top teashirt especially my motto these days) past saloon, saw cardgame I sit down all winning hands 5 aces continuously yes I'm always lucky at cards I say that's why I never play. They astound at my saintly behavior with all these magic gifts. Into my room realize I've just had a typical fast fantasy.

## Sunday July 22

Clear day, haven't been out much yet, clouds faraway, sky bright. Woke at 8, ate breakfast, came back bunk restless bored & sleepy, slept, worried, dreamt . . .

Recalling Ruth Witt-Diamant's house & her daughter-in-law—friendliness & plight. Waking I realized what remarkable lady Witt-Diamant is, how prejudiced & strongminded & how it's necessary to break thru that purposive old woman family insistence on her way of thinking in order to be & express any individual truth to her. Treats me & everyone as if they were charming children & we do not realize she's thereby not taking us seriously when for instance I give advice of sober or crazy kind—as the times I asked her to arrange for reading for Jack.

\* \* \*

All weekend weary, weary, indecisive, abed over what, dunno—the affair with Tagalong—his select moments, he stopped in front of the Double Header to talk to the fairies assembled there—Our final discussion where he finally gave in ("I'd been waiting for a week to talk") & sat down on the fence round the block from Yessler & said "Alright if that's it let's stop here & talk this thru." Then had me explain queerness, then put it down, simply said no to sleeping together tho accepting me. "I mean if you or I are buddies or whatever you call it Love or I say friendship maybe it's the same thing or if you even think of it as an affair though that's not what I mean, there's something that has happened between us that you're not supposed to forget and I don't either but as far as what you want I didn't want to talk about it because it's outside of my business, it's your business, I'm not anyone to tell you your business tho now I see I am, but I'm just not your baby, the right guy for you for that kind of thing and you

had ought to learn to control yourself like for me it's drinking &
for you it's that."

My only feeling after, too bad, as Neal took me on, a certain
abandon I'd hoped for was not there, a conspiracy of secrecy &
love between us.

\* \* \*

July 22, 1956—Up on prow at 8:30—the water deep steel blue, a
few brown birds following ship, sitting on water, flabbing up &
skimming in and out of the geography of waves or floating down
valleys & up crests, sky covered with bowl of blue clouds misty
Northwest whereat we plod toward evening light tho blue grey
behind us, a great white film of blue luminousness deep into space
along the horizon and sky when I lift my head, tho the rain begins
to clog my glasses. Reciting Villon's Ballade *Regrets de la belle Hëaul-
miere*:

> *ce sadinet*
> *Assis sur grosses fermes cuisses*
> *Dedens son joly jardinet?\**

Such a line & the image of young sexual body & concentrate image
of juicy young 15th century cunt rocked my poetry mind head. The
sound, juicy to show Neal, if only he heard French.

\* \* \*

Dream—Entering rock to live—Earthquake slowly breaking
off pieces of mountain, heap of big rock, the part we live on—Gary
knows in Japan—Snow and cold coming, he's ready—So I also
with Arctic clothing—too many people dying—1988 of cold earth-
quakes slowly destroying the rock, the private rock.

---

\* "that jewel/set in large firm thighs/in her pretty little garden?"
See note, p. 286.

7/25/56

### Flash Fantasy

Seeing purser and steward talking, I imagine going off to Seattle bar Drunk Town with them and being Friendly—suddenly in rushes beauty blonde girl "Allen—you in Seattle—why didn't you tell us—" followed by a horde of girls, men, handsome strong men; terrifying Strong rough—a bohemian multitude?—no—better be Rich, dapper, encrusted with tophats canes and black trousers shining—Even the Mayor of Seattle in the Crowd—But I say "I'm with my shipmates" and mysteriously refuse to go unless—as of course they are—all invited to the party at which I am celebrated.

[Addition 1/15/57:]

And of course each shipmate later taken aside and questioned, as by the mayor, confidently—"Do you really ship Allen Ginsberg? What's he like in private—ever hear him say anything—or act funny—I bet he's a regular straightman or walking corpse, hiding his light out at sea there you ought to watch everything he says and does—it's all curious because of his essential character like a money saint."

\* \* \*

I've gone insane with abstraction.

\* \* \*

Whitman—rough bearded
    open carefree american
    character, a rough, one of
    the boys
        wandering on trains thru
    America, working loving
    hours, unabashed
        but with a fear of death
    gnawing at his vitals.

\* \* \*

All hail! All hail heart! All hail home! All hail hallowed
      hallowed heaven!
King! Christ! Angel! Receiver! Savior! Comforter!
All hail high! All hail low! All hail hallelujahlike the Lord!

\* \* \*

Note on John Wall in Seattle:
      All queers are
                  hell bound
      Fun now
                  eternal fire later.

\* \* \*

      "Que'st devenu ce Front poly . . .
      Ces gentes espaules menues
      Ces bras longs et ces mains traictisses
      Petiz tetins, hanchs charnues,
      Eslevées, propres, faictississes
      A tenir amoureuses lises;
      Ces larges rains, ce sadinet
      Assis sur grosses fermes cuisses
      Dedens son joly jardinet?"
                        Villon, *Hëaulmiere**

\* \* \*

   A Bearded Workingman . . . As a rule I don't like young
husbands, too much of the milk of the baby about them . . . Your
sweet rose-petal ass.

------------

   \* Some weeks earlier, Ginsberg, having read a biography of Villon,
sent from the *Pendleton* this lament of the "old whore" to Peter Orlovsky,
with translation and instructions for him to "Read the French aloud,
particularly the next to last line, such lip-smacking cuntlike sounds—
sadinet, assis etc. Real sensual writing." See SHD, pp. 123–24.

\* \* \*

Anonymity is a good thing for poet because he can then see the vast camp of the world.

Save the philosopher from his philosophy prism.

\* \* \*

Tom D'Ambrosia—boy who lived on street North side of Passaic River below Haledon Ave. My dream of industrial corridor bar room shutters by that street. The bank—the bridge—the bottom of the hill.

The Trauma—moving from 7B in School #7 to school #12 full of mad mean dirty negros, nasty crazy negros. And I protested the change. I began failing at school, goofing on Technic, and reading books and withdrawing into dream world thereafter—where was Naomi when I changed?

\* \* \*

"The army is the enemy of love." —Peter O.

\* \* \*

Apocalyptic drumbeat of Moloch.

# July 27, 1956

Passing thru the Bering Strait—out on deck in unnecessary coat, sad, dull day, nothing of the meeting of Asia & America visible, continents shrouded in lighted mist, earlier in the morning waking saw the blue sky, sun brilliant in a lite low mist, ¾ declining moon, and a rainbow with 2 white albatross birds flying cross the bulge of light in the blue air.

Many birds flying passage between the continents, the sea choppy tho clear, the air immediately around clear, further away a bleak white haze blinds the sight of the two worlds apart almost touching—centuries shrouded in white mist. Small flocks of birds crossing low on the water, 5 apiece.

\* \* \*

Mortal aspirations sex poetry Friendship
Farewell realizing all must die.
Looking about the forc'sle Shelley reads in his bunk. His lamp
    shines over his red brow.

Down below my imaginary boyfriend sleeps in iron bunk hanging
                from the ceiling.
I know the Lord Exists and so must take a step of madness out of
                Time.
Get rid of my possessions & make myself naked to the elements.
                Would anything happen?
Deliver myself from arbitrary belief to absolute conviction.
I fall in love they reciprocate every way but sex.
Then possibly the order from above is give up sex.

                            *  *  *

## Bering Strait Blues

Sky illuminated in auroral lead
kiss of dolloping waves on the jackknife prow.
Passing between continents between tears and laughter—
Little birds with white stomachs
cross from invisible Russia to Alaska
Sage Diomedes drest in mist stands
                between the promontories
Vast Siberia I can't see
herds of reindeers moujiks & Russian Esquimaux

Fresh Alaska that I cross the bow to address
Blessings on polar wave's aloneness!

One black bird flapping wings
Crossing over the grainy waters,
3 ships ahead in the mist
                Wavy, greyer than the rain
Ugly, unsettled ships, loughing up & down
                sinking & rising on the waters,
familiar sperm flecked movable sea.
Shapes in shrouds, high breasted bloated
                suffering prideful boats
                            My fingers are cold.

A bird flew over the Forepeak
                o'er my head,
I hallucinated a fly—

Funny gaiety of Joke
To cross the Bering Strait
and see the same grey sea.
Strange how illuminated I am by nothing.

Little geese going across to visit Russia
flap fast over the straits,
No winds so they have to flap away & can't glide far.

Vast areas of cold & water & mist—it takes an iron ship to get
        here
Girded for ices & dead to pain of cold waves & skinless under
            inhuman skies in long bleak latitudes
And suddenly beneath the iron prow, potato peels floated fifty
        feet long
        —into the grey waste.

    White wavecaps rising from the deep broken with heads of
air, sage souls & hoary Karmas merged with the sea rising to the
surface disappear after an instant's look at the blue opaque
hooden drifting numberless roof of cloudy sky.
    Birds whirling their wings like pinwheels taking a lowly curve
over the water.
    An occasional louder crest of personal wave repelled from
prow cold heads of the water
    Colder hands, bare brown, grey olive jacket crude & rough
on my reddish wrists.


## Northward Idea

            Grey Ships
            grey waves
            grey prow
            my hands
            a black bird
            opaque numberless sky
            whitecaps
            continual upward confused
            rolling & chopping of waters
            Instantaneous universal joy of the Creation
            and everything in the ocean moves.

* * *

One fingernail dirty,
and the Bering Sea.

Midnight—
The ships ahead shrouded, sunken, faded into the blue mist like a fuzzy indistinct spectral theatre geography curtain that falls on the sea—how far—a block? A half mile ahead.

The iron on the bow is cold to the side of my hand, no wind and little chill in the grey daylight air.

The ship a theatre surrounded by curtains of impenetrable ghostly air, sky an indistinct solid entity all about, fog now closed in so that only a few hundred yards of greenish water can be seen, the ship throbbing under my foot. Foghorns from afar, the three ghosts' ships—a few white spots here and there on the water in which we roll, and no birds at all in the silent dumb air which hangs in uncanny halflight as of blue dawn, as if the sky were veiled by rising dews of the grey watery lawns of the sea, but thru it filtering the unblinking unseeing dead light—where's the sun, inconsolable?—Neither east nor west, as if lunar light were reflected out of the dull water mirror—an unclear light, hazed with sleepishness of midnight eyes, restless water revealed still moving even at the hour it would be black silent & death unseen—still put to work to ripple roll & fleck upward in answer to waves of same invisible force that diffuses light thru the fog into heaven & on the page, same color as ink of page, light indecipherable blue, with dead grey behind it. Dead light of midnight crossing into the Arctic Circle.

Forgot to say I threw 7¢ into Bering Strait to leave something of me in remembrance of Naomi, so near her Russia.

## 69°.06N × 166°.23W

The Bow rail my scrivening table again and I standing Bartleby in the sunshine—a clear day clouds overhead, high & scattered, long streamers, one milky overhead in midsky long as the world like the belly of a whale streaked from end to end—bright white sun standing high starboard West, there on the horizon lower ruffles and voices of delicate puffball clouds streaking toward the south—the dim promontory of an Alaskan headland above Icy Cape—which I missed seeing earlier this morning Saturday lying abunk reading Ahab Moby Dick to the end.

Ships ahead 3 of them heading Northwest, the narrowest sleekest sharkiest & highest forward, the two others behind, LSMs* flatbottom-sterned crude pancaked high with faraway lifeboats & equipment & men like casbah roofs—the clouds in front of them like a Chinese cut-out on the horizon long & low sending streams of clear finely etched flat white silhouette a hundred miles long, modernistic Jap print or polar abstract noses & fingers to the west, a pretty picture sailing into that cloudstreaked north.

Supreme daylight & spume spit on the waters left by breaking swells, every inch of the water chopt & wrinkled & stamped as if by iron brush of wind which is slight.

\* \* \*

## Sat. July 28, 1956

At last at Icy Cape, Transcribing Xbalba for mimeograph, missed entrance to Cape Bay.

Woke at 8:30 Armada of ghost ships all around silent stretching on horizon & small flat on water (like long matches taken from cardboard holder) in rendezvous in area, & radio antenna on a thin almost invisible spit of land far in fog.

"Rough winds do shake the darling buds of May."

Watched in sleet & rain Chuck & Bo'sun batten down the forepeak hatch first oped for action then closed, weather too rough suddenly, up anchor.

"Cargo ships & tankers"—metre.

\* \* \*

---

\* LSM: Landing Ship Medium. Intermediary ship-to-shore amphibious warfare vessel, smaller than LST.

I emptied my mind of the world, in hope of the Lord,
          my heart empty
But kept some fatness against the day of His Silence
Now Fatness must go and I suffer his Silence.
Better however the bitter-sweet of actual beauty.
—Wretched, that I'm in solitude.

\* \* \*

July 29—Woke morning after light sleep in which I heard the words "You have forsaken your god."

          Kaddish
       or the Sea Poem
     Irregular lines
          each perfect.

     Now all is changed for me
     as all is changed for thee
                    Naomi,
     Worry until the brain broke down—
                    cerebral Hemorrhage
     I hear the heart torn out of the world

\* \* \*

Duties—Finish Books (Reading)
       Transcribe all Notes Complete
       Write Kaddish
       Letters

\* \* \*

Rereading *Siesta in Xbalba*—mimeographed 52 copies on ship—first impression, unbalanced & egoistic; second impression a short poem with mostly logical jumps but no *bottom,* no outbreak of truth in it, no emotional outbreak, no decision, no discovery, just notes thoughts & nostalgias here & there a touch of pity, no crisis, no drama. Never comes to a point—tho that random ordinaryness was mood & purpose of Siesta title but seems shallow while I'm reading the Life of St. Francis.

## Reading List Jan. 1956 to July 1956

All Whitman poetry
Tropic of Cancer—Henry Miller
4 Vols Haiku, R. H. Blyth
Blaise Cendrars—Voyage Transiberian—Translation by Dos
    Passos*
Surrealist poetry in France—Tr. Fr. Carmody & C. F. Mackentyre
Hart Crane—Poetry (reread), Letters, ed. Brom Weber
Robinson Jeffers—Hungerfield & other poems in Mod. Library
    Collection

## June–July 1956

Shakespeare—Love's Labour's Lost, Two Gentlemen of Verona,
    Comedy of Errors, Henry IV part I, Sonnets
Count Orgel—Raymond Radiguet
Sahara—René Léclèr (Hanover House 1954)
Psalms of David
Fr. Timmerman—The Perfect Joy of St. Francis
The Solitary Singer (Biography of W. Whitman)—Gay Wilson
    Allen
7 Men of Spandau—Jack Fishman—(War Criminals)
Theodore Maynard—Saints for Our Times
Henry Miller—Nights of Love & Laughter (Pocket Book Ed.)
René Fulop-Müller—Theresa of Avila, 120p. biography
D. B. Wyndham-Lewis—François Villon
Essays on Theresa Avila & St. John of Cross by Thos. Merton &
    others in Claire Luce's book
Bought Rand McNally Pocket World Atlas for 25¢
Melville, H.—Moby Dick (shorter edition pocket)
Johannes Joergensen—St. Francis of Assisi
Robert Burns—some poems
Old Testament—Finished

---

* Black Sun Press, loaned to A.G. in North Beach, San Francisco, by
Kenneth Patchen.

# August 2, 1956

Dream, Evening 7–7:30–8 o'clock light nite Wainwright Alaska. In which Naomi is adored as an immortal Movie Star of old.

In small-town home, confused, so travelled I know not where home is—on corner near Sentinel Bldg. S.F. with Eugene go into movie to see Naomi as actress—a bad later film, she snake woman hysterical & embarrassing bad overwrought. She is 1930s acting.

Cross square by accident another movie, earlier of her as simple princess shepherd saint of flowers, a movie as Clara Bow *The Hat,* where with peculiar innocent faded-film charm & nostalgia she dances & waltzes & looks girlish & lovely as a flower—alone in a rear seat of the theater, crowded, I overhear familiar relatives talking beside me, I am about to explain proudly that she was my mother, "I am Allen," when suddenly one of the cousins whispers, "Look, the uncle is coming out, the uncles will dance"—and out of the seats file three uncles I stare in wonder at their ritual beauty & pride—they come out into the aisle at the dramatic height of the movie (at a festival or Ball in the movie) as if in an ancestral processional rite and stride three of them together rapidly with steps like a biblical military corn dance hebrew & simple, ten or twelve steps in perfect clockwork order together Russian Kazatskan rhythmical & vigorous & energetically turn about their faces & reverse their bodies' steps & stride back up the aisle, as if wearing long bears' robes dangling down between their legs swaying with their dead march, their eyes lit up with humor and dignity hair standing out of their heads white & yiddish like pawnbrokers transfigured into aspect of patriarch, Uncle Moses, Uncle Abraham, Uncle Max, the thinnest in the middle, short thin Max, who suddenly rhythmically breaks the cadence stands off by himself at the edge of the aisle in skintight acrobat woolen underwear and lifts up his chin proudly, erects & distorts his whole body in pride so that his sharp long pelvis sticks out theatrically & immemorially dancelike pantomime absurd. . . .

Scene shifts to the gilded Roman apartment in N.Y. or Phila. or Cleveland of the proud goy would-be candidate for president dressed in dressing gown with blonde whore snake woman girlfriend as in rotten villain of movie in Capetown S.A. whom Alan

Ladd beats up at beginning, *Hell Below Zero* I saw on ship last nite—
Presidential Slick & with Mustache & girlfriend are cavorting ob-
scene narcissistic around modern couches drunk, cocktails & hors
d'oeuvres & kissing, I interrupt their mad dance & begin getting
sexy toward the slicker, dame disappears into bedroom (rather
like poet–critic Stanley Kunitz & [poet] Carolyn Kizer's house in
Seattle) and I naked get down & entice him to blowjob unwillingly
but it finally appeals to his presidential pride to be knelt before &
blowed & I think I want to on account of perhaps seeing & feeling
his naked cock & balls & soul under the gold bathrobe & presiden-
tial narcissistic mask pride so blow but dislike him but carried
away, transport myself sexually in self-abasement so that his limp
hard-on stiffens & he shoots come in my mouth which rather than
swallowing since I gag at him I raise up my head & spit out slowly all
over his chest & with mouth kisses spread over his upper torso a
whitish gluey mess frothy on his breasts which he doesn't object to
but wants to go into the bathroom & look in the mirror so I carry
him in (he's on my shoulders, standing) but as we get in I feel the
strain, my own balls are weak, sore, I've just come somehow and I
say "Stanley, Stanley" his name urgently, "Get down, get down
now get down now," which he does, thankfully I feel in dream, I
feel as if the balls were breaking thru the lower intestinal wall &
dropping into the testes-sac. And wake with anxiety wondering
who Norman is I mean, Stanley.

I keep, awake, wondering about Norman S—— & his friend
Stanley who were sort of Broadway Sam foolies, wanted to be great
salesmen.

\* \* \*

## August 3, 1956

Slept poorly considering my worth & worth of these journals
which is what I pride myself in and was wretched, praying to St.
Francis lay naked in bunk, gusts of erotic memory Tagalong, por-
trait of Van Gogh on roof of bunk, asked for vision woke after
troubled sleep & remember only snatches of dreams.

A garden old house in Paterson moved back there whole
family except Naomi dead many rooms a long hall and two bed-
rooms down the hall perhaps 72 Haledon or 155 Haledon Ave

(Paterson, NJ), Gene and I in first room, try to move my bed in but doesn't fit with new Naomi-Louis bed carved in half & set down as couches & sofa, in halves, and flower vases & pianos and the old round mahogany table (Which we sold for $20, she was so disappointed in hospital she complained it cost hundreds she'd saved as young girl wife). So I move myself into the second room down the hall, going thru the garden. . . .

I am putting on a show with a child a little girl over a springboard over a stage she is to climb on my outstretched body on the springboard naked & display two signs before and after . . . "I am she who am hopeless & dumb" followed by "I am holy and a little lamb."

## August 4, 1956   Wainwright, Alaska

Clear sky after 7pm—bright sadness yellow sun sinking down to Northwest leaving Gulf of shifting orange-gold shiny dimes on the waters, like paths of moonbeams but tinsel like, X ray sunset lite on the thin horizon half mile away—the two immense gastanks on the slope looking bright & minute, the houses had little squares on the shore, the village clustered on the sharp little cliff, behind the long slope behind the village a few antennae sticking out of earth to signal the invisible airbase hidden there, from view, and the rolling of water, almost flat & glassy all day, in the blue-sky-yellow-etched light giving serenity & peace & sadness to the scene of ships silent at 10pm at night in everliving light waiting for death.

I am always as tonite frustrated in solitude expecting momentarily some divine illumination half grasping it my thoughts turning to verbal deaths & solitudes.

\* \* \*

The Bible—
    Abraham laughing with his face in the dust.
    Jacob—"How dreadful is this place! this is none other
    but the house of God, and this is the gate of Heaven."
                      —Genesis 28:17

* * *

Aug 5—Dreamed—in large, cubicle prison—held prisoner by great dark rough guard—in bed together, finally roll over & go down under covers between his legs to blow, submissive joy, and wake—of Neal.

Waking image recollection of Peter's softness & eyes lying in bed with shirt off demanding I pick crabs out of his golden arm-pit—& anointing him with anti-lice oil (at Turner Terrace in S.F.).

Aug 6—Ice

At noon way off out to sea, I thought a whitecap but was a white piece of ice floating eyelevel so far away and soon after all along the horizon what looked like broken clouds—the clouds are so small far away at the edge of the ocean—but soon saw it was white ice, ramparts of broken-headed eyce, then around 3 it was nearer, great floes coming on us toward shore, so we turned south (upped anchor) and for 3 hours I stood on the bow watching as ice came around us—one small piece like head of a snowman & 2 fat arms sticking out of the water, then big standing reefs with clear water beyond, into which the ship moved, gouged a path & was stuck, backed up, and went around—till at 7 we were all surrounded in an ice lagoon like in the movies—and to the right, out to sea, northward the blobs were solid far as I could look all the way up to the thousand mile pole. We turned in to shore & dodged in and out—great flocks of white snowy seabirds on the ice & resting on the water, thru binoculars glimpsed brown ones like lice moving slow motion in great antlike stream—and still to the right of the edge of the ice floe 20 feet away, one half a mile from the shore, the edge jagged & dirty with crusts of blue & green interior juicy caves & mush of white, broken all along the surface, weather-beaten & pitted & half sunk but solid stretching all the way, landscapes & continents & miniature valleys and minute himalays for ice worms & the lowly eye and imagination of footsteps crunching outward in chilly freezing breeze, everywhere changeable slow float & breakup & still solid sisters & brothers of ice crowding down terminal sheaved & agitated one on another to the edge of the boreal fix-land to melt & begone. And now at 11 pm the sun a streak of bright red along the edge of the ocean under the long hood of cloud going down illuminating nemesis ice still crowding down tropical to die ranged up against the sun-light like armies of snowmen barely visible Alexander Nevsky Polacks of ice, an army lined up & almost invisible except for jutting ax poles & horse-heads & grooks & creaks & poles sticking up all along the faraway horizon moving in for attack, mysterious & silent and I'm going to bed & read the Bible.

Ray the colored waiter & me at the prow all early evening watching the maneuvering thru the close banks & reefs like coral but pushable white & the ship trembled agone, one thru the boom.

\* \* \*

Yeats: "Trembling on the brink of revelation"

On trembling and on tenderness
Carl Solomon had great tenderness, he couldn't let it out (reversed, anger, spite, self justification, rage at being tenderness-wise stymied & frustrated). He too would tremble, inexpressible the urge.

I tremble when Peter makes a tender touch or move to me—"trembling with tenderness" phrase T. S. Eliot.

The tenderness of Revelation?

\* \* \*

You can tell the way the wind blows by the way the waves go

\* \* \*

Leviticus 18:
21 "And thou shalt not let any of thy seed pass through the fire to Moloch, neither shalt thou profane the name of thy God: I am the Lord."
22 "Thou shalt not lie with mankind, as with womankind: it is an abomination."
29 "For whosoever shall commit any of these abominations, even the souls that commit them, shall be cut off from among their people."

\* \* \*

## Many Loves*

[First portion of first draft of "Many Loves," CP 156–58:]

# I

*"Resolved to sing no songs henceforth but those of Manly Attachment"* —
*In the manner of Whitman*

Now I will speak out boldly, nay sing, not argue, dispute or
     justify, dainty,
But preach by example the image of love known between men,
And number my lovers among men, their names and stations,
     carnal days together,
Proving by life what was not known in books, nor morals, nor
     Bibles—

And there was Paul my first friend, but I lusted & dreamed & didn't
     know him because of high school timidity . . .
And there was Eric Law a handsome youth and drunkard angel,
     rich and brilliant and I didn't know him thru timidity
Tho he stript himself naked in his room and sat crosslegged on the
     bed mocking in pride of youth
and smiled & beguiled me: but I wouldn't, out of shame & distrust
—so slept all that night in his chair, and regretted my stiffnecked
     fear
But occasion was gone, he woke in the morning impatient & pissed
     off his hard-on.
Later we knew each other, made it, I his first, and he my first love,
     he lay on my couch, I climbed on him, lay with my cock at
     his back,
and he groaned, and moved with me—I came, he caressed me, we
     were sweet together,
And after that many times in disguise, then no more. But we loved
     each other, so went our ways: he to marriage, I to search
     out other loves—

---

* This excerpt complements published portion. —A.G., July 14, 1992

Met Dom whom I loved a blonde prince of college, athlete with
      starry forehead, an indian head & mind,
piercing eyes & hooked nose, wiry pale body, had known the snows
      of Denver, exhaustion, and bodies of girls in cabins, read
      Nietzsche.
We were acquainted room mates, slept together months, and
      moved close to each other friends on the same mattress
      clasping silent, but never open.
Stripped naked one day he lay on the bed for prosaic massage, face
      down his limbs pale muscular hairless: I felt them, moved
      them,
ran my hand down his back from nape of neck to the bone of his
      ankle,
touched palm to his buttock, and moved it, gripped under arm
      round his biceps, spread out his hands, caressed his
      shoulders, my knuckle went down his backbone, almost
      an hour in his half sleep
turned him over, his arm lay over closed eyes; yellow hair on his
      loins,
put my palms on his muscles on his breasts, lay my hands down his
      abdomen played with light finger on his nipples which
      were red.
And I bent down and put my lips to his breast, and passed over
      down to his belly: and his belly shuddered.
And I saw the beautiful works of the body naked, the man's body,
      his muscles and loins, at ease, in a bed, golden hair on the
      pillow,
the lines of the wall of the stomach, and the lines of the hips to the
      thigh, the hollow of the muscle of the thigh,
and the breastplate of the man who has strength and affections,
      the sensibility of the inside of the thigh
and the slow rising of the cock, its throbbing, the dew of heart on
      its head, pale semen of offering and the nest of yellow
      hair in which man held his beauty.
And I blew him, after long play with my lips to his body, his
      buttocks, his hole and the backs of his ears, the sensitive
      eyelid, fine cheek, and inside hollow of armpit—
in all his beauty I blew him: he rose up with his buttocks & pushed
      up toward me as I knelt, he groaned and said "Make me
      come, Allen, take it in and swallow it"—

and shuddered all over and came, I swallowed his come and tasted
          his manhood & knew him
And blew further, he pushed himself up again, and arched his back
          & lifted his buttocks, straining,
and came; I blew him more, and my head was attached to his body
          and swallowed his cock
and his come flowed into me for an hour; then lay with his eyes
          closed, and rested.
Dom why reject me years thereafter? I was ever your lover, that was
          my great pleasure, remember me then, and bless me
          again
For ecstasy's rare among men; and liberation of ecstasy's a bless-
          ing.
And god'll speak for me and plead my case when we come to him,
          and so will the beautiful angels, such is my hope for
          Mercy.
And I lusted to get my asshole fucked, these are the words of my
          bowels.
To feel the goring of a cock in my belly coming from behind,
humiliation before the pride of man: and ecstasy in the humilia-
          tion:
and adoration of the living body of pride; for the proud cock will
          suffer & perish, shrivelled into dust
And the perishing cock in its pathos I redeem with my honor
and make it eternal with love; and cherish its pride for a year
For the cock that fucks me remembering Change is meek to its
          maker
to take its orgasm in a day, and dig its delight for an hour—
and I'm beholden to it for a lesson of love, a mastery humble and
          soon to perish, I take on the suffering & pleasure,
My manhood and godhead nailed together at the root.

Jack Kerouac who heard my first confession when I was virgin to
          men
groaned & ran down to the village & got drunk; he was on a ship.
Phoned later, in Macdougal's Bar scrivened poems together &
          rewrote Eric's parable
"Human-kindness versus Humankind-ness" on the enamel top of
          the narrow urinal.

## II

Neal Cassady was my animal: he brought me about to my knees and taught me the love of his cock & the secrets of his mind. . . .

* * *

## Aug. 8, 1956

Woke after tangled evening dream—I get sleepy reading & close my eyes around 6:00 & put pillow over my head & succumb to sleep & hope & dream—

but dont remember much except long strange unpleasant pilgrimage—in bus station up north somewhere looking vainly at schedules to return me to home, Paterson, stopping off somewhere on the way for refuge to stay & entering room with mattresses on floor, I go to sleep with woman in mattress farthest from door (young Naomi or Carolyn) and am caught by the leg by baby in first mattress, shitting & vomiting all over me, I lie down with it & my face in its slimy red asshole, it faces round me & gives me instructions for tending its sickness, dwarflike grown-up intelligent even sympathetic baby's face telling me its confidences, red faced sick tho, I listen

* * *

In dreams seems important to remember one after the other each morning's—miss a morning thru inattention or laziness & you begin missing the next whole series of dreams—remember one & the next day's will follow in memory too. Thus I force myself to record these fragments.

## Dream of 8/8/56

On a side road in a village or suburb, old English, Cape Cod, or movies' Chicago.

Taken by police, I was in the house with Neal, and passed out the door unseen, and saw a great crowd of people by the store and detectives guessing which house he was in combing the area and searching alleys with searchlights.

I passed among them terrified and realizing the dread that

Neal would come out unaware and be taken by them so at a crucial moment when they began to suspect his house, I yelled out of the crowd in hysterical voice

"Neal Watchout!"

triumphant over their secrecy, yelled again "Neal Watchout" into the air, hoping he'd hear and escape back way or come out genius and shooting escape front thru the crowd with me.

\* \* \*

Shelley, red head storekeeper, whom I despised—sitting there on bed—as good as me high or low under heaven—all equal in spirit—but that man imagines victories over his nothingness—and prides himself above others—"There is no individual soul" says Whalen in letter today. And I received Howl, which also made me ashamed it was so shoddy when I first looked at it—till at the second reading I imagined myself prouder over its unique solitary engine intensity, which almost convinces.

\* \* \*

## August 10–11–12    Wainwright (Alaska)

Returned here to wait out southerly and now northerly movement of ice floes about 5–10 miles out to sea passing in parade—like army on horizon—bleak dead corpses and castles slowly silently motionlessly passing in review at the edge of the ocean.

\* \* \*

## Sun. Aug. 11 1956

Went to Protestant services held on ship—Micintzky, Bus, Leo, Walter (spade) 1st Off., the Captain, Tilley—hymns, dark short ugly chaplain, sermon on seeing god after sailing thru Pacific and noticing at last that the sunset was not a work of human intelligence.

Back to room, with headache, dreamed with head under

pillow—On a ship, water, night fire, me writing a poem and when I
got to the line
    "Behold a goat cometh with his hair parted
        in the middle and smileth"
Out of the line "Behold a goat cometh and smileth," I got an
aesthetic familiar shock out of a goat with the phrase "hair parted
in the middle" (or whatever) and felt a kind of epileptic pressure
on my body in the dream, and then when I added in the phrase
false tooth (—so that it ran:
    "Behold a goat with false teeth cometh along smiling with
hair parted in the middle"
—I am confused about the sentence—) the pressure increased as
if it were a mystic experience and wave of religious shock ran thru
my outstretched body in bed recognizing the seemingly familiar
crown of creation of poetry thereby exhibited.

    This peculiar pressure-shock I've felt before in dreams—a
feeling as if my body turned solid of lead, or heavy with an invisible
weight on it everywhere against which I struggle to move, as if in
sleep struggling to be conscious and wake struggling against the
spell of sleep.

    The phrase "A goat with false teeth" gave the most aesthetic-
pressure-shock.
    "Baal-Zebub?"
    a Phallic God?

* * *

    What god expects (in falling sleep last nite) I realized was
love. He being pure love so all that is necessary is treat the holy
spirit as one suffering from absence of human response in love.

* * *

## Dream Aug. 16

    Reunion with Jack and Neal at record shop run by Seymour
Wyse—I go in small crowded shop—It's Seymour—he's got dark
skin, negro—like I noticed on the Filipino last nite thinking he
looked like white painter I knew in S.F.—and selfish lips upcurled,
like Jack's friend in N.Y.–S.F. (Henri Cru)—and Neal and Jack

buddy together at the door, set to leave for a while, return later, they're going out but will be back, leaving me to dig the store with Henri Cru—a dark faced Cru—with curled lips—I say, O.K. but please come back, I'll wait here lone and dignified digging store with Henri Cru. Disgruntled.

\* \* \*

## Aug. 20

Sunsets at Point Barrow—its appearance of Moscow, the two Kremlin Towers way off on the landspit. The Indian totem-pole painted-zigzag-red radar tower, rows of boxes on beach, houses, and fields of oil drums.

Sun molten color at ocean edge.

I took a ride on the LCM\*, the larger ships appeared huge hulls like castles on the water. Instead of treading familiar decks, I looked up on moats and castles isolated a mile apart.

On the prow today passing back south by Diomede Island and Bering Strait, still invisible in rainy rolling water, thin drizzle, for half an hour, the waves wilder than usual, orange footed birds suddenly appeared up out of combers at crests rising into the air or dived right down in front of the ship just before prow foam reached it.

I sang fragments of Messiah looking at the waters, pieces of Isaiah I read yesterday. Eli Eli Lama sabacthani. Thunder in the mist. Adonoi Elohenu Adonoi Echad.† Tears in my eyes. The waters are still strange. For a moment they seemed at the mercy of the Lamb. A continual rolling as of a million sheep backs. Birds in and out of great waves, at home. Looking back, the iron ship, welded gun turret raised up its grey (milky) maw immediately before me. I am afraid of the ship, and the ocean shows no mercy. Only my own voice singing pitiful in the wilderness and rain.

---

\* LCM: Landing Craft Mechanized. The smallest of the intermediary ship-to-shore amphibious warfare vessels Ginsberg refers to in these entries.

† The Lord is God; The Lord is One.

* * *

## Dream Aug. 20, 1956

With Carl Solomon, he was on my hands, I had to take care of him—did not know what to do—he wanted to sleep with me—his body sleek and heavy, like whale—in a room in the Wentley. He was extremely fat, from insulin, which is why he had withdrawn so, corpulent. "I do not appear at my best so will not write . . ." as in letter. Anguished, I consented, it being no cost to me, but I was afraid of him.

## Free or Review
## Copies of *Howl*

[Copies were sent to the following persons and places, as well as a gamut of 32 established journals such as *Kenyon Review*. In addition the review list included rarer little magazines as follows: *Coastlines, Mattachine Review, The American Socialist, The New Leader, Liberation, Mad Comics, Poetry London–New York, Nine, Window, Midstream, East & West, Quest, Freedom Press, Climax, Dissent, Masses & Mainstream, Meangin, Merlin, One, Resistance.*]

| | | |
|---|---|---|
| Chaplin | Rexroth | Cummings |
| Garver | Luther Nichols | Patchen |
| Tamayo | Fred. Eckman | C. Bullitt |
| Brando | Lib of Cong | Tour de Feu |
| Helen Eliot | Pound | Seghers |
| Hoodlatch | Creeley | Max J. Herzberg |
| Tom Darst | Bogan | Antonio Sousa Gallery |
| Lucien C. | John Snow | Natalie Barney |
| Louis | Moore, M. | A. & H. De Campos |
| Eugene | Snyder, G. | Chris Logue |
| H. Miller | Jarrell | Nat Hentoff |
| Jeffers | Cassady | Louis Simpson |
| Kingsland | Betty Keck | Dan Hoffman |
| Zukofsky | W. S. Burroughs | Wayne Burns |
| John Holmes | Ansen | Josephine Miles |
| Auden | Peter Russell | Wm. Faulkner |
| Solomon | S. P. Dunn | Parker Tyler |
| Kunitz | Lawrence Lipton | Karena Shields |
| Eliot | Jno. Williams | Lionel Trilling |
| Hollander | J. B. May | Mark Van Doren |
| Dick Howard | W.C.W. | Meyer Schapiro |
| Harvey Breit | Eberhart | |

* * *

## Dream Aug. 21, 1956

The joys of religion. Two sisters, nuns, both weak of faith, and in solitude clinging to each other, persevered waiting for the appointment of the Lord.

But there was no Lord other than this: That the weaker clasped the other in the stadium and the stronger stood first. And a bus full of refugees pulled in from the boats of Europe. The first family came out of the bus and a younger girl who looked like the weaker nun came down from the step of the bus, saw the nun standing there bewildered, in the lobby of the stadium outside the wall of the game, outside the walls of the grave, and rushed up to her weeping fell on her knees clasping her sighing and weary with trouble and gratitude. So the weaker nun's confusion was changed immediately to weeping and compassion, and she held the girl around and comforted her. For she understood her misery in her own heart.

The stronger nun also stood in solitude: and an old woman and a child and a lovely young man all weeping came to her for mercy, out of the bus with their handkerchiefs and valises. Their father had died and their sister; and she was their Sister. So she comforted them, and was not lonely any more.

Then they all got in the bus to go home, the sisters to show the way to the homes; and on the way the bus stopped in a large park or empty lot in the middle of the city, where there was a lot of green grass. And a multitude of refugees stood in there with their handkerchiefs of mourning and desolation, and comforted each other: and brother found brother and sister found sister and child found mother and grandfather found grandson: the bus stopped and they all got out to join the multitude and comfort and be comforted.

He who had no brother found one there. And she who had no mother found a mother there. And a white-haired man preached over them all, like an evangelist in a tent, and bid them comfort each other and comforted himself in them, and they in him.

* * *

There is a living God. Who can understand this? He dwells in a realm beyond our imagination.

The structures of the imagination are symbols of his actuality.

Poetry is structure with knowledge of the actuality behind it.

* * *

# Dream

I open a letter from Burroughs—describing a new project—a cave—the cave of religious mysteries, a tourist attraction in Venice or Rome—gonna make showbiz history and religious history—gotta die holy—anyone enters cave never comes out alive, the final thrill real death leave your possessions at the door with the attendants—(higher turnover in attendants, hard to keep them from rushing screaming into the cave)—Only the gimmick is nobody dies without making it—The Illumination, Ecstasy, See God and Die—only problem get the right drug—or witch doctor. At the entrance—a real innovation—the cave of Heaven, Paradise, Eternal Mystery—make a fortune—benefit humanity—Big signs, tho, for 1920s American tourists—and also is connected with jazz—absolutely no salvation without jazz—the spirit of salvation is Jazz—"No squares allowed" sign—if you ain't hip we don't want your money—keep out if you don't dig that Jive.

I am reading his letter laughing aloud, a sombre letter from Venice wire-transforwarded by Whalen, with another note on envelope marked "Please Return" from Sgt. McKeon or McKay of Berkeley Police saying why haven't you called me or sent the $10.00 on traffic ticket—envelope marked with funny boys' town jokes "From the American Gestapo—Pay or Go to Concentration Camp" type jokes . . . Later I'm writing a poem

> "The lob of the throat
> The lob of the kirtle
> or the proletariat
> grey rain

> still icy pavements
> the lob
> of the speech
> of the kirtle of the throat
> of the proletariat
> in the fog."

Poetry like Williams but with magical vocabulary.

\* \* \*

# Dream 24 Aug., Fri. Eve.

### Gunter-aus-Unterauregehaben in the Beach

Peter and I together at last, he's joined the MSTS and has a ship—Mealtime noon, we all have liberty to go ashore, on the field, like a summer camp by a river, to lunch and snooze. Many a youth and many a maid dancing in the checkered shade. The green grass, lovers lying thereon, sleeping, arms round each other, careless faces in Eden. A stream of companions up from the river by a green road thru the woods. Peter takes me round neck, says he has understood that we are free, and now sure we are together and he loves me, he will take pleasure in sleeping with me, and we go off the ship on the grass. I have been on ship before and know many of the people on beach, I am afraid they will see us if we lie together napping in the grass, so I lead on thru the path to the inner pasture. Sheep may safely graze. Peter wants to lie down with me, put our heads together to kiss. I am still afraid in front of all the people. I lead him or we find ourselves at a picnic table. The big fat Captain Ritsky, Russian, is there with a jolly peasant wench. We sit down at the table, bow our heads, arms round each other's necks and close our eyes, heads on the table, sort of obscured in the crowd. No sooner down than the Captain notices Peter, a lowly messboy, at the table, and says peremptorily "Gunter-aus-Unterauregehaben in de Beach"—"Go you to (your place at) the beach"—meaning back thru the meadow to the ship.

We both get up, I still anxious lest our intimacy be noticed, but no one does, Peter goes back, I tarry to hear what the officers will say, but decide there's no use my waiting I should be with Peter who's had to get back alone. I pass thru a door in the meadow, 2nd officer Austin is there discussing the Captain's irritableness which seems to have upset the picnic—"We're really in trouble now"—Seems that Captain and everybody (as on actual MSTS Pendleton ship) have suddenly become aware of their incompetence and the rust on the ship which is decaying, and are therefore full of authority and edgy. Thus explaining Captain's sudden annoyance at seeing messman at his table.

Captain is like Jehovah, I've been reading Blake's commentary "The Everlasting Gospel"—describing freedom and forgiveness from Sin

> "Thou art a man, God is no more,
> Thine own humanity learn to adore"
> . . . . . . . . . .
> "That they may call a shame & Sin
> Love's temple that God dwelleth in,
> And hide in secret hidden shrine
> The Naked Human form divine,
> And render that a Lawless thing
> On which the Soul Expands its wing."
> . . . . . . . . . .
> Humility is only doubt,
> And does the Sun & Moon blot out,
> Rooting over with thorns & stems
> The buried Soul & all its Gems.
> This Life's [the body's] dim Windows of the Soul
> Distorts the Heavens from Pole to Pole
> And leads you to Believe a Lie
> When you see with, not thro', the Eye*

Meaning, Eden is in Imagination; the body's five senses are expression of the soul, the body does not exist soul does, my love for Peter therefore doesn't sin against my body.

---

\* Ginsberg has transposed the second and third excerpts from Blake.

\* \* \*

[Note: One notebook may be unretrieved, missing, or nonexistent. A gap in notebook entries on the *Pendleton* follows, from late August until Ginsberg's fall discharge. Succeeding entries on land—a few weeks back in the Bay Area, a short trip to Mexico, and a return stay in New York— are infrequent. For further information on this period in Ginsberg's life, readers might consult the "Desolation in the World," "Passing Through Mexico," and "Passing Through New York" sections of Kerouac's *Desolation Angels,* the biographies by Barry Miles (*Ginsberg*) and Michael Schumacher (*Dharma Lion*), and the forthcoming selected letters of Ginsberg, edited by Miles.]

## S.F. Oct. 10

To Neal—I love you—I bring this howl into the middle of the world happily—O Tenderness!—to see you again in the middle of time O Tenderness to recognize you in the midst of time\*

\* \* \*

## The Place Oct. 15, 1956

Facing a heavy negro guardian of the gate with his hair bebopped back (Chicago Box style) DuPeru delicate & embarrassed just slipped in at door, black pants & sweater & white shirted over midriff thin skeleton.

John Chance at first table, silently mumbling to Crumbs a bearded whitecapped Guitar artist, then Mark the 17 yr. old painter, Hube the Cube in beard, Mary Stewart, Peter and Lafcadio sit round on table, Neal next between them.

Paul Osborn sitting with Gui de Angulo, 2 square chicks, Bob Donlon and Peggy the sweet looking French chick who worked with Barrault.

---

\* A draft of the last line of "The Names," CP 179.

* * *

## ALGREINORSO*

(AG) Farewell, Time ashened and reduced in fyres:

(GC) Vaulted, absolute—cindered beyond the sundial of Black
      Sunday;

(AG) But I'd re-body every endless clock of labor

(GC) And break the Southern Cross—the Northern Light—

(AG) If East and Western hand, tho nailed with blood

(GC) Ariseth from the pyre—phoenix-like—in search of Time
      immortal.

(AG) Ah, no! Farewell withal! O Starry Crematory, burn!

(GC) Throw in same such orgiastic splendor as the mystic widow's
      tell-tale!

(AG) True! the spider, blackened and spun out with salten tears

(GC) Withdraws nimble with hoary countenance;

(AG) Yet Angel, like that grieving weeper bears his web of radiance

(GC) aware of mortal prey lashed upon Time's disembowered
      Granite . . .†

(AG) When rock runs honeylike, and web itself's a rose

(GC) Innocence becomes carrion for the spiral continuance.

(AG) Open, Thou incognizable Blind Gate of Death,

(GC) Ring out thy Mental psalm, awaken the reedy Sloth!

(AG) The bells of mind clang up my body's decad

(GC) In ready ritual trumpet blown Herald! Herald!

(AG) O torso'd radiance in whom my flesh ascends:—

(GC) Receiveth!

(AG) Thou, my eternal Soul and Sun above the Waste of Light!

(GC) Receiveth! erase the aggravated air, and praise O Jowls of
      God! Herald! Herald!

(AG) O brilliant Fang! O thou consuming mouth of music!

(GC) Loud bellow, receiveth, thou hair-falling madsaint homaged!

(AG) Break! thou balded skull afire and open thy golden Bone . . .

(GC) Brass throats angelic—sweet angered choraled—Herald!

(AG) How many Heralds must I suffer, ear-aflame, O Horn?

---

* Linked verse poem collaboration by Ginsberg and Corso.

† Ellipsis periods in this poem appear in the journal entry.

(GC) Strike, newly sainted—upward!

(AG) Purest smoke, and spiring essence, and aerial Form

(GC) Fatigued—surge the marble image, the Joy of insensible being!

(AG) But we'll meet, Yes! not Zeus, but God upwheres we wing

(GC) Wherewith twenty wideeyed lambs become certain of terrible yet pious sacrifice!

(AG) And bleating vowels of molten silver chaunt His Hallelujah

(GC) Hallelujah! Hallelujah! Spin, Twist, O Light! Upward!

(AG) Jump me Angels! and archangels hop my Glory!

(GC) Give light to the legion released from nightly Stone

(AG) for I am Multitude, my name is Myriad, my soul is Million!

\* \* \*

## Poem

I have nothing to teach.

One man said to another: bring me
an empty glass. Reply: let me fill it with
wine.

Both were talking about something else
but God knows what.

Cows come into the pasture. Buildings
rise and fall. Men read in the F train.

A horde of Chinamen sweep down thru Korea.

Pop. A rifle shot. A woman falls from a
chair bleeding at the forehead.

Lovers in bed. They feel sweet toward each
other—a hand caresses the (hairy) thigh.

A man turns the page of the newspaper in the
F train.

The sky is brilliant and dark over the bay
at sunset gloomy light.

Gasoline winks its eye.

\* \* \*

Sr. Arturo Huy
Don Urgenio
Colume para entregar a Polo Perez
    Finca San Leandro

* * *

## Hitching on T on Hiway*

Slow strawberries in the field—and Carmel High
School with strawberry flowers.

> Scarred with the faces of a thousand Mexicans.
> Stick out your thumb at the cars whizzing by the
artichokes.
> Roaring by the artichokes a wop veg.—10¢ ea.

"A thousand cars past by and none noticed my cashmere
sweater"

I have my finger to God.

Who named the innumerable streets of Los Angeles?
Who built the thousand Derricks on the hills?

* * *

## Written on L.A. John Wall

> "I would like a well built
> man to shove his big
> fat cock in my ass
> up to the fucking hilt
> and fuck me slow and
> long. After he comes a
> couple of times like that
> I would like to suck
> him all over until he's
> ready to shoot his hot cream
> down my throat."

* * *

The whole earth is a person.

---

* Poem composed on way to Los Angeles and Mexico with Gregory
Corso. Corso's "Poets Hitchhiking on the Highway" (in *Mindfield: New &
Selected Poems* [New York: Thunder's Mouth Press, 1989], p. 60) was
written on the same occasion.

* * *

## Mexico City Notes

Rimbaud's Pad (given by Alphine Michel) 53 rue Lacepede near Place Contrescarpe, Paris.

* * *

At Tibet Restaurant—Plateglass window on Alameda Park, the sky floating by.

* * *

Mota—Tea
Joel White—Rio Poe—the ride home

* * *

The Virgin: black hair over his head curled & spiraled o'er the ear, a lock on his brow curled down to the eye, black eyes with rouge and eyelids extended from the dark 10¢ store, his ears delicate & perfect as his adolescent nose, a black turtleneck sweater, black peg pants & shoes, black silken stockings to his haunches perhaps thin, camping & prancing near Garibaldi near San Juan Latran, to give us directions to the queer bar, and leading by the hand a small boy in baggy pants with round innocent starry eyes (his mother perhaps locked in the embrace of nite), hands holding together to walk the streets, the small one in rough wrinkled shirt dirty grey, his hands in the delicate feminine one of the dark princess, whose waist was a model of beauty, as if kept to a narrow ring by Hangman's knot of Genet.

The younger innocent, holding hands as they strode downstreet, the younger of 11 years, trusting and silent, never said a word, one word, he just stood there in the street gawking & listening whilst the older told us where to go, the cops came on the streetcorner and we eluded them, moving across the street to the bright lit stand, tacos, to not eat but pass by—till they got away from the police and found us, keeping 10 feet delicate distance, as we walked back me & Peter, around the block to the street of the fag bar—where the police car had preceded us, stopping in front

of the yellow light bulb overhanging before the curtained door. So
we stared & waited buying cigarettes, while the two excellent heav-
enly waifs of dirty mcxcity streets came round the corner, withdrew
& stood on the brilliant shining street hiding behind the corner of
the building leaning one head over another to peek up street at
policecar which waited a minute two minutes and set off for
[Avenida de] Brazil. Then they emerged around the block corner
smiling & dancing together pointing to the yellow light, and ran
off the opposite direction, the smaller meanwhile not having said a
word.

* * *

A pond,
   or a Tarn,
one.
—J.K.

* * *

# New York

I thought the moon downtown
was a red light
so stopped the car and stared.


Walking to Naomi's grave
      white clouds
and the sun burning over there

* * *

# Sign in Hicksville, L.I., John

"Are there ever any
colored guys with big
cocks come in here
that would like to
fuck a white ass?"

* * *

Home again
in Paterson
by the dear ruin
of my red rug
and chinese father
Whitehaired furniture
newfangled lamps
expensive television
sofas and pictures
on the walls,
Warm in the living
room I sit and dream
of skid-row Seattle
a wild youth
with green eyes
drunk at a table
kissing a cripple
drunk with crutches
leaning over his face
by a broken chair
and spilled bottles
of rancid beer
in a dark saloon.*


Heart of America
in my imagination
leaving for Europe,
when I return
I'll go back to see
the green eyed kid
dying of love
and lonely whiskey
outside in the alley
where cops walk by

* See p. 263.

with strange revolvers
talking about death.
Heart of America
this is the picture
I carry in head
over the ocean—
To walk in Venice
by stone lions
mosaic palaces
and evil Bellinis
hand on balustrade
stand still dreaming
of a dark saloon
in a crooked alley
on Cincinnati Flats
where a skeleton talks
with halo on head
to a boy in black pants
crouched in a corner
of a black door
talks about cops
and revolvers of Denver;
Cops in Eternity
stolen gold watches
with red city sky
night full of stars
over the buildings
moon in the alley
Bums on the street
stumbling to Portland
dreaming of God.

                *  *  *


Lying asleep in my room
returned home,
dreaming of a boy at a table
in bulb-lit Seattle,
airplane droning outside

the second floor window
Shapes of trees blur
night without eyeglasses—
I'm used to this place

What's next? Being here
is enough—lazy enough
to sleep all morning—
tho I woke to write it down—
imaginary ecstasy
saints under trees backyard
—Another trip, to Europe,
Climb the Eiffel Tower
waiting for poetry—
crash and a burst of light
thunder skeletons and death.

## Dream Paterson Dec. 7, 1956

Sitting by the river the steamboat goes by. A high caravan boat circus stops like a train at the wharf. I get in the front end and walk back.

A huge dirty engineer sits way up high on a ladder in the black front cab with a 20 foot long steering wheel from the floor to his hand.

Chairs piled high with people.

Many small cabs like a huge caterpillar. In the central cabin a great ferris-wheel water paddle moves the boat's circus tent facade.

Negroes, people in black, sitting on each other's laps, freaks, colored midgets, cigars, cardplayers at tables, trapeze artists napping in their seats, spitting politicians, owners in fur coats, mangy horses, jockeys on giants' laps, schoolteachers weeping, the freight of the circus floats by as I walk thru slowly.

A huge gallery filled with black men, singing. A preacher sings like Father Mapple in the darkness. One giant leans down to hand a "Holy Gospel" pamphlet to the preacher. I walk past down the aisle to the swinging door.

Outside, daylight. The caravan rears into view like a sea dragon on the Hudson Channel. I get on my knees and pray for the boat of thieves and freaks. It slowly passes me by. The center round huge cathedral-like facade 50 feet high of wood and cardboard and ancient old style lettering floats past. My chance to pray.

At the end, it passes. I see Uncle Abe [Ginsberg] lounging nearby at a post, observing me and the boat. He's all dressed up.

I don't see his cock like the other night when drunk and stupefied by goof balls Louis and Aunt Anna his wife called the officers and ambulance to take him to the hospital.

\* \* \*

The Sensitive Car

\* \* \*

# Dec. 21, 1956

Strange faces in the subway—the minute I sat down I realized I had power to see them straight in the eye and dig the eternal moment's mask—as they ride by dreaming rocked in the dark with neon on their faces.

The 59th St. stop—recollecting Burroughs and Lucien, Columbus Circle, IRT Station, the dark pavement and endless outpouring of students and ballet dancers and musicians and fairies on this platform, waiting in their youth for life to begin—while I come back here dead (for the fourth time), disconnected.

The new IRT B'way train—brighter and shinier—futuristic 1930s air conditioning aluminum big flowers growing out of the roof—parkay tile floors, glassy lights, shining steel poles to hold on to, even the people seem cleaner and richer—and the seats so nice and soft, red cushions.

A man with a notebook in front of me making notes for an ad. My own rusty (gaudy) book.

Beside me a fat well-dressed little kid bow tie, bright Jewish eyes, ass-length salt and pepper jacket—he don't work on nothing, just lies in bed and eats ham in the morning. And gets up to ride the subway showing off all afternoon, at nite he goes back to supper and eats huge pork chops with lots of greasy potatoes and peas.

Approaching 116 St. Columbia Stop.

* * *

## Carl Solomon—[*in Pilgrim State Hospital*]

"When I was a seaman the world was wonderful and real and externalized as an idea—but

"During the period of our association I was relying on meeting the challenge by relying on internal resources.

"3rd Stage—World Eternalized no longer an idea in short I am no longer illuminated."

"My eye is gone and I can't see anything but my nose. My nose gets in my way." (Holding it while he speaks.)

"A head is to smoke with not to think.

"In order to be socially acceptable it is first necessary to be socially acceptable.

"Tell everybody I am sane.

"I have tried for the last 5 years to make sanctity as uninteresting as possible."

* * *

## Small Satori—N.Y.C. Feb. 1957

Looking out of hotel window
on the gulf of the City
across from monster apartment
    red house
down in a small flat,
    a man in red underwear
    with a white handkerchief
    in his pocket
I saw looking out of his window,
    rising in the morning
Music, and he bounced and beat
    his hands on the windowsill
Music, invisible behind him
    and he danced and stared
    out the bedroom window
transfixed thru glasses, he

                    stared on the city
            unknowing, and I too unknowing
                    stared at the city
            We stared at the gulf of
                    the city at the heaven
                    at the air
            and heaven lightened a minute
                    a flash passed thru me—

                    at *what* were we staring?
            Both staring at the same thing,
                    in the morning, waking
                    in the city

            I in red sweater—he in
                    red pyjamas rubbing his
                    balls
            —a monster flash in the
                    air that we stared
                    into
            flashing on the bricks of
                    the buildings
            flaring on the walls
                    of heaven.

                            *  *  *

## Fighting Society

Noses
Gargoyles
Broken-jawed boxers
Not socially accepted homosexuals
Beethoven Piano Concerto playing forever How can you fight
        society?

Babies
Babycarriages Cribs
Cars, houses, garages
Country estates, huge cranes lifting
Derricks Dirigibles How can you fight society?

Hiways
Millions of miles
Asphalt huge supercarriers across Atlantic
Bombs, armies, airplanes, hydrogen explosions bullets
Teeth blood broken bones arms How can you fight society?

Walt
Whitman
Would've revolved in his polar grave
and clapped his walrus hand in joy
for what I say: fighting American society

My Uncle Leo
Says I am only trying to fight society
How can you fight society? How can you fight the fighting Society
        take on the whole fighting society shooting match?

\* \* \*

## Leaving Paterson—March 7

Louis in the nite under the glow of street globe by the candystore—Crying, & then it was the wrong bus—so more talk—and as I boarded bus, avoiding ticket to stare out of the window at him and wave—he waving and then losing sight of me, turning rapidly O tears of father down the street. Thru Hiway lights so blind reminders of Heaven.

\* \* \*

## Mar. 10, 1957

Parting at shipboard standing high on the ship rail top gallant deck delight in the rain waving farewell to receding smaller-ing pier with black dressed girls Elise\* and Carol and T. S. Eliot-like-umbrella'd Lafcadio taller disappearing into space smallness with apron of water before their stage, & curtains of rain descend-

---

\* Elise Cowen, Ginsberg's friend since 1953, would type most of the *Kaddish* manuscript; she is a major character in Joyce Johnson's *Minor Characters* (Boston: Houghton Mifflin, 1983).

ing, and the back bank box black house wharf pier they sat on waving growing smaller under foot and we ascending the harbor over the sea rising like an airplane past the docks of Brooklyn and black dirty ships' asses stuck out in void green water floating with mercury and condom doom and alas alast the towers of Manhattan spiring & rocking on the Island behind us symmetrical the four stanchions of miniature buildings displayed on the side glued together in the wind, green statue standing & turning in the world as we passed, Isles of Staten & houses ahill, Brooklyn apartments on the banks of Channel Park, Sandy Fort, Coney Island Ferris Wheel and miniature hotel and the grey rainy sea ahead for life.

Morocco, Italy, Paris
Amsterdam, Paris,
London, Paris

# Introduction

Ginsberg and Orlovsky's Moroccan and European trip temporarily strained their relationship.* Nevertheless, it was rich in the variety of experiences it afforded these nearly indigent travellers. For Ginsberg, the extraordinary amount of European art and artifacts they beheld, coupled with his firsthand observations of social and political conditions from North Africa to Paris, greatly enlarged and enriched his perspective.

During much of these sixteen months away from the United States, Allen devoted considerable time and space to the writing and rewriting of poetry, completing substantial new works such as "Poem Rocket," "Death to Van Gogh's Ear!" "The Names," "Europe! Europe!" "The Lion for Real," "At Apollinaire's Grave," and the much-anthologized "To Aunt Rose." He continued intermittent notations on the death of his mother; he wrote a draft, reproduced here, of *Kaddish,* Part IV ("Litany"). Back in New York in the fall of 1958, in a "marathon" weekend of nonstop writing, he'd compose the principal draft for what finally—by October 1960—would become the *Kaddish* we know in print.

The rainy goodbye to friends and Manhattan that ended the preceding section was soon followed by Ginsberg's lyrical anticipation as their Yugoslav freighter, the *Hrvatska,* approached Casablanca:

> Blue sky, bluegreen flat water, slow silent ship whooshing thru mist no land in sight, everyone expectant, anchor chain machinery clanking, rope being hauled, blast of foghorn, passengers on deck.

In the city but three days, Ginsberg entered numerous notes and sketches on Casablanca streets and the Medina, boys, émigrés,

---

* Difficulty arose at the outset between Burroughs and Orlovsky in Tangier. Late in the fall, Peter became anxious about two of his brothers back in the U.S., and left Paris in early 1958. When Ginsberg rejoined him six months later, the two again set up house together.

hash in a teashop; painted vivid capsule portraits of beggars; wrote a poem on a cemetery; and recorded a barber "startled & inspired" by Peter's "crown of bushy golden hair."

As the two poets settled in for a couple of months at Burroughs' Villa Muniria in Tangier (when Kerouac left in early April, they got their own apartment there for twenty dollars a month), Ginsberg devoted major portions of most days to helping Burroughs—now detoxified from heroin, thanks to Dr. Dent in London—compile and edit what would be *Naked Lunch.*

Ginsberg's diary entries continued sporadic, though his attention was focused on present surroundings, as his now classic photographic snapshots of Tangier-scene companions attest (see pp. 356–58). Three weeks passed between notations as he recommenced, "My poor Book, nothing for you yet till this dawn." A vivid transcendent notation of the sunrise over Cape Malabat ("the new sun whirling around still a clear disc of orange in the white sky . . . vast space around echoing with bird cries") ends with a recognition of the "Relief" it offers "from the human, entanglements of Bleak—Peter & Bill." As Ginsberg recalled in 1984, Alan Ansen had arrived,

> And so all of us were typing on *Naked Lunch.* And I was writing and Peter was writing, but Peter and Bill didn't get along. . . . Bill rejected Peter quite a bit, 'cause he saw him as a rival. Although Peter and I tried to take Bill to bed—figured we'd give him all he could get, exhaust him.

Several weeks later, Ginsberg learned by letter from Ferlinghetti that the San Francisco police had arrested him and bookstore manager Shigeyoshi Murao for publishing and selling *Howl.* ("Imagine being arrested for selling poetry!" Shig would write a generation later.) Soon Allen and Peter, bearing knapsacks, ferried across to Algeciras to hitchhike, train, and bus through Spain, en route to Venice. At Madrid's Prado, Breughel's *The Triumph of Death* made a lasting impression: "I suddenly realized that the whole cumulative culture of Europe was ahead of us," Ginsberg has recalled. Venice, where they stayed at Ansen's, inspired a draft of what would become "Man's glory" (CP 260), in part a hymn to religious monuments of Europe, Mexico, and Asia. It was also where, in a "room dream," the poet recognized, belatedly, that his female companion was Naomi.

By day, Ginsberg's and Orlovsky's lives were filled with literary and social contacts among the acquaintances of Alan Ansen. For frequent company they had Caresse Crosby (to whom Allen read *Howl* in Ansen's living room), Mary McCarthy, Nicolas Calas, and, until a slight faux pas, Peggy Guggenheim. One hot afternoon at Ansen's San Sammuele apartment, Orlovsky tossed a towel across the room to Ginsberg, to wipe off sweat; the towel passed near Guggenheim's cocktail. This may have been the reason, Ginsberg recalls, Guggenheim "86'd" Peter from her palazzo and museum. When Allen subsequently received her invitation to a reception for surrealist poet Calas, he declined, since Peter was not invited. Crosby, McCarthy, and others continued seeing Ginsberg and Orlovsky at Ansen's.

Before July was out, Allen and Peter were hitchhiking through other parts of Italy; Ginsberg was visiting religious and artistic centers extensively, as he had in Spain and would do in the Netherlands and Paris. Several extremely long days in Florence included "studies" at the Loggia and Palazzo and the Ponte Vecchio; the Uffizi and Dostoyevsky's house; and the Duomo and the Medici tombs. In Rome, they repeatedly visited the Pantheon and the Colosseum, and went to St. Peter's, Shelley's grave (which Ginsberg kissed, taking a clover), and Keats' grave in the Protestant English Cemetery; the seaside at Ostia; the Palazzo Venezia and the Capitoline Hill; the Forum, which he entered high on marijuana; the Vatican Museum ("Fig leaves on all the statues I got mad"); the Piazza del Popolo and the Spanish Steps, with no money to see the Keats-Shelley room.

Considering their extremely limited means,* the amount of territory Ginsberg and Orlovsky covered is astonishing. At Assisi, as Barry Miles has pointed out in his Ginsberg biography, the very monastery of St. Francis denied them refuge and then asked for financial contributions. The poets slept outside on the grass.

---

* In April, Ginsberg had written Neal Cassady from Tangier, "Bill in debt trying to support us (and beginning to rebel against it)," asking for money. See *As Ever: The Collected Correspondence of Allen Ginsberg & Neal Cassady*, ed. Barry Gifford (Berkeley: Creative Arts, 1977), p. 186.

A major article on the San Francisco Renaissance, its center-piece the *Howl* obscenity trial, was being planned by *Life* magazine, which paid Ginsberg to fly back to Rome for an interview (Peter remained in Venice). After the interview, Ginsberg headed south for the Naples area, visiting W. H. Auden at home on Ischia, before rejoining Peter. He recalls getting into "a big argument" with his elder the first evening at an outdoor café:

> I said there had to be a revolution in poetry, he said "Oh, pshaw, nonsense." I said something like "You old fool, at your age! Discouraging the revolutionary young! That's terrible, not the right spirit for an elder poet. How dare you act like Wordsworth, a spiritual wet blanket?" I was drunk, perhaps we both were, by hindsight.

Heading for Paris at the end of the first week of September, Ginsberg and Orlovsky first took the train to Vienna, where they beheld more Breughels, "sixteen in one room," as Ginsberg recalls. They were barred from the opera house for being tieless, despite their attempt to improvise neckties with their handkerchiefs.

Arriving in Paris, they headed for Gregory's hotel but found him gone and no room available for another month: thus the lines of poetry (see pp. 373–74) written on the bench Allen claimed for the night at the Gare de L'Est. Corso had left a note suggesting that they share his room in Amsterdam for the month and then return to Paris. In ten days of walking about Paris before leaving for Amsterdam, they visited the Louvre several times, as well as the great central abattoir, which inspired a poem, published here for the first time. A wee-hours-to-dawn merger of Ginsbergian gallows humor and precise detail, "Apocalypse of Les Halles" catalogs "Vast barn over the streets / Puddles of mud and blood in the gutter . . . / Carts full of lungs carts full of liver carts full of hearts."

Amsterdam, cheaper than Paris, was home for three weeks. With Corso they stayed on Reinerwinklestraat, a small side street near a canal. They met poet Simon Vinkenoog and the older poet-critic Adrian Mourian. Ginsberg recalls:

Vinkenoog was hospitable, and others were, and took us around to see all the literary people there, and started translating little poems and interviewing us. We made a little money from interviews, or from publishing poems in little magazines, like fifty dollars, which was great. And went to all the museums and saw all the Rembrandts and the Van Goghs, all the Vermeers, and Gregory pointed out Averkamp's tiny ice-skating panoramas.

And they continued writing, singly and collaboratively. Ginsberg's first entry there ("Sitting in the Bar in Amsterdam") records his continuing impecuniary state: "I got no money/ain't even got the blues/all I got is Amsterdam/and a red lite on the table." The much longer, collaborative "Moon Prevention" is a surrealistic response by Corso, Ginsberg, and Orlovsky to the ascent of the first Sputnik on October 4, 1957. It was one day after Judge Clayton Horn in San Francisco, finding literary merit and "redeeming social importance," ruled "Howl and Other Poems" "not obscene."

Returning to Paris in mid-October, the three settled into the same hotel Ginsberg and Orlovsky had visited in search of Corso in September; it was here, at 9 rue Gît-le-Coeur, that Ginsberg stayed until returning to the United States in July 1958. Of his residence, Ginsberg recalls

It was the cheapest hotel around, and you could cook there—there was a little two-burner gas stove, which was rare, one of those little iron ones. . . . Only 30 [dollars] a month, or 35 a month, for a room with a giant bed, half a block from the Seine, right in the Latin Quarter . . . through a short alley to the great big Place St. Michel, and five blocks through the markets on rue St. Jacques to Saint Germain des Prés. And several blocks from George Whitman's bookstore (later renamed Shakespeare & Company), on the Seine, facing Notre Dame from the Left Bank across the Quai.

It was an interesting setup because Peggy Guggenheim's daughter, who did get along with her or didn't get along with her—ambiguous relationship—was off on her own, living with Guy Harloff, a Dutch painter, in one room. Gregory finally got his poetic attic room, and Peter and I had a third floor room facing the street—you could crook your head out the window to see the Seine. Folk guitarists busked in the street—Darryl Adams and Ramblin' Jack Elliot, whom Kerouac and I had known way before, in early fifties, were in town, playing at Place Contrescarpe, I think, where musicians hung out. For guitarists in Europe it was a little historic period, also, an advance of the Guthrie folk craze renaissance in Paris, just as in America.

Ginsberg's first Paris notation as resident begins with the simulation of a phone call and includes a laconic inventory of the three travelers: "Peter needs a shave. I need a bath. Gregory needs a new personality." Our diarist then entered his first notes as a resident seer of sights: after his first visit to Sacre Coeur, we find him in tears on his first visit to Montmartre, "gaslights and Balzac roofs poking out of the murk."

Shortly he was sick in bed a week with the "Asian flu," whose bad cough kept him up at night. A dream record during this period offers another dimension to Ginsberg's expressed sense of inferiority as an artist in comparison to Jack Kerouac and "his immense brown Rembrandt Industry"; the lofting of the second Sputnik on November 3 prompted recollection of Whitman's "fabled damned" warning about the state of his nation's soul, to which Ginsberg added his own observation on spiritual promise and material failure.

In less than a week his mind once again returned to the death of his mother. As he sat in the Café Sélect, he wrote, weeping, a rough draft of what he'd first conceived at sea nearly eighteen months before, his *Kaddish* elegy for Naomi, beginning

> Farewell
> with long black shoe
> Farewell
> smoking corsets & ribs of steel

Soon, he'd devoted the first six pages in a new notebook to an "Elegy for Mama."

Even an extensive notation that starts with the situation at rue Gît-le-Coeur (Corso's future and the impending departure of Peter and Gregory) quickly takes in Naomi's absence:

. . . I have no mother's belly left to crawl back to under the covers she's in the grave, she's a void—a longing for what was once not void but trembling weepy insane flesh.

All of us caught on the hook of the world, grasping in time for love for food for poetry for glory—love's cold poetry of glory.

And the world so small, the passage so fast, the grey rain, the wrinkle around the eye of the grave.

Gregory was soon diverted to Germany for several weeks to assemble, with critic Walter Höllerer, an anthology of "young American poets"—and to sell encyclopedias. Allen and Peter had developed a relationship with two French secretaries, each of them sleeping with both of the girls; one, Françoise, had a crush on Allen. But the poets were, Ginsberg recalls, mostly on their own in Paris, "without too much literary connection."

Earlier in 1957, Orlovsky and Ginsberg had sent Peter's brother Lafcadio to his mother's, and the renewed relationship proved violently dysfunctional. Another of Peter's brothers, Julius, had been in a mental hospital over half a decade in a more or less catatonic state. Twenty-six years later, Ginsberg recalled Peter's waking in bed in Paris one day at the end of November,

. . . weeping, saying "Julius is in the hospital and I can't just leave him there and enjoy myself here, stay around the world enjoying myself. I've been away a year already."

So Peter mid-January went back to New York to get Julius, to visit his brother in Central Islip Hospital and try and work with him and get him out—after six years of his being in there!

In these months, Ginsberg continued active as poet. Pages immediately following are rich with drafts for his own poems, including notation for the first part of "At Apollinaire's Grave." Ginsberg had heard a recording of Apollinaire reading, then sought out his grave at Père Lachaise Cemetery.*

---

* For further information not only on the poem but on the lives of Ginsberg and colleagues at 9 rue Gît-le-Coeur, see the "At the Beat Hotel" chapter in Christopher Sawyer Lauçanno's *The Continual Pilgrimage: American Writers in Paris, 1944–1960* (New York: Grove Press, 1992), pp. 261–287.

Entries for the remaining days of 1957 include exposition of the crucial Blake poem "Ah! Sun-flower," the subject of his 1948 Harlem auditory epiphany. One of Ginsberg's first notations for the new year is on journal keeping itself: "This notebook having become too unspontaneous," he rejects a hardbound one for soft-cover "blue schoolbooks" with "loose poems rather than formal journal—which is now too narrow a habit."

As the year progresses, his entries become almost exclusively poems, and familiar themes continue: the loss of his mother; metaphysics and consciousness; history, race, politics; his emotional and sexual relationship with Peter. The year was scarcely two weeks old before Orlovsky, as prefigured in Ginsberg's late-night entry six weeks earlier, left for the United States.

William S. Burroughs arrived from Tangier the day before Orlovsky departed; the novelist, who'd maintained a regular correspondence with Ginsberg, would also reside at rue Gît-le-Coeur. Returning the day after Peter's departure was Gregory Corso. His Frankfurt connections soon led to a visit from, as Allen recalls, "two leather-jacketed German writers"—Walter Höllerer (then editor of Group 47's *Akzente*) and Günter Grass. They "came to see the Americans":

> He [Grass] was already quite accomplished, but we didn't know that. So we told 'em all about marijuana. . . . Gregory'd somehow made a hit with Höllerer—his poetry was very good, see— anybody in any language could see it, especially if they knew some English. They knew about me, as sort of a powerful poet, but Gregory was the big surprise.

But what sort of literary connections did Ginsberg have with the French? One evening early in 1958, he had dinner with translator Alain Bosquet, who was preparing an anthology of contemporary American verse. Before a month was out, he was working with Bosquet:

> I tried to interest him in the new poetry, and he was just totally uninterested. He didn't pick up on Gregory or Creeley or anybody with open verse form, and they wound up having this anthology of American poetry that was mostly Robert Lowell and

Donald Hall and Louie Simpson and Howard Moss, the standard academics of the time, and so it was a mediocre anthology. I think it led naturally to French disinterest, for the next decade, in postwar American poetry.

And [in preparing Ginsberg's "America," the only poem by a Beat or Black Mountain poet, for this anthology] I caused a very funny *contretemps* in translation. I kept insisting on a literal translation of "putting my queer shoulder to the wheel," and didn't realize until thirty years later that "shoulder to the wheel" is an image in America that doesn't make any sense in French, and the French equivalent is "put our fingers to the dough," "get your hands in the dough." . . . So the last line nobody understood, much less the word *queer*. They didn't have quite that word, either.

In London, meanwhile, Thomas Parkinson, Ginsberg's graduate advisor at UC-Berkeley back in 1955, was producing contemporary poetry readings for the BBC and invited Ginsberg to cross the Channel and record. Leaving his train at Calais before embarking for Dover, Ginsberg noted in his journals: "Gypsy musicians with tambourines & violin in the civilized green carriages." Soon he arrived, for the first time in his life, in the land of one of his greatest poetic influences: "enchanted in England/weeping at the foggy earth of England's Blake."

His recorded reading for the BBC, intended for five minutes, expanded upon immediate request to include both "Howl" and "A Supermarket in California"; several days later, Ginsberg wrote Orlovsky that he

> . . . gave slow sorrowful reading, built up, almost broke down in tears again, dreaming I was talking thru microphone to the Soul in the Fog, read to Blake himself—even Parkinson saw it was great. . . .*

During two and a half weeks in England, he visited the British Museum, Salisbury Cathedral, Stonehenge, and Oxford University, where he gave an intimate reading; his last days before return-

---

* Ginsberg to Orlovsky, February 15, 1958, SHD p. 137.

ing to Paris included two absorbing visual experiences on sunny days. The first was his view from the dome of St. Paul's Cathedral; in journal pages it became poetry, a panoramic celebration of London resurrecting. He integrated his second sunny vision, which occurred as he left Dover to cross the Channel, into another poem, which he drafted upon returning to Paris. It was the first notation for "Europe! Europe!" a state-of-the world short-lined ode that attempted to reconcile the aspirations of the imagination with the world of man.

Except for a second short trip to England in May, Ginsberg would remain in Paris until his July departure. He engaged in much correspondence: in addition to Orlovsky and other personal and literary confidants such as his father, Kerouac, and Lucien Carr, he replied to young poets back in America (LeRoi Jones among them) who were encountering his work for the first time.

Simultaneously, attention given the Beat Generation in print continued to grow, though some of it was lurid or sensationalist. Allen now had Corso's *Gasoline* in hand from City Lights; John Clellon Holmes' impressive article, "The Philosophy of the Beat Generation," appeared in the February *Esquire;* the *Saturday Review*'s "Trade Winds" column recorded the unsuccessful effort of Ginsberg, Corso, and Orlovsky to persuade Brentano's Paris store to accept copies of the celebrated San Francisco poetry issue of *Evergreen Review.* Norman Podhoretz's signal denunciation, "The Know-Nothing Bohemians," had just appeared in the February *Partisan Review;* imitating the latter, a supercilious and insulting unsigned *Time* review of *The Subterraneans* characterized Kerouac as "latrine laureate of Hobohemia." Kenneth Rexroth, ironically, two and a half years after unofficially "sponsoring" the Beats at the Six Gallery and Berkeley readings, published a gratuitously contentious review of *The Subterraneans* in the April *Nation.* LeRoi Jones in New York began publishing *Yugen,* containing contributions from Ginsberg, Corso, Creeley, Charles Olson, and Frank O'Hara. Irving Rosenthal would soon prepare to publish *Naked Lunch* (which Ginsberg had continued to type up, even after an initial rejection in the fall by Maurice Girodias at Olympia Press) serially in the *Chicago Review.* Ginsberg recalls having sent off

a large chunk of *Naked Lunch* to Stephen Spender at *Encounter,* 'cause I'd met Spender a number of times. . . . And Spender rejected it, saying it was only good for psychiatric testimony. And I wrote him back a letter saying "What is this, C.I.A.?" I was already paranoid about the C.I.A. back then!

At the time *Encounter* was [funded by the C.I.A.] and somehow by his *tone* I thought there was sumpin' wrong. 'Cause he's a poet, he should be able to appreciate the *language* if nothing else, if he doesn't like the sex. Spender likes sex anyway, so what's he complaining about? But it was a real put-down. Must've aroused him, 'cause he wrote a really long letter, denouncing it.

For immediate company, Ginsberg of course had Burroughs and, intermittently, Corso; and enjoyed occasional visits with Terry Southern, Mason Hoffenberg, Galway Kinnell, Darryl Adams, and others. In a bar on the Paris street (Place du 18 juin 1940) where three decades later a gallery would exhibit his photographs, he met Richard Wright, whose *Native Son* he'd seen on Broadway in Orson Welles' production, starring Canada Lee. Through Burroughs he met interesting expatriate young men at the Monaco Café; at the Bonaparte, Corso's hangout in Saint-Germain-des-Prés, he met an Arab youth whom he brought home, only to be robbed. Characteristically, Ginsberg instructed the young man to take also several shirts he no longer needed.

Ginsberg recalls a number of artists being around during this period, with Tristan Tzara "sitting at the Café Dôme." But outside of some translation work, Ginsberg's French literary contacts were occasional. He recalls:

France was kind of dead at the time. The great people were the old ones, and there were no young inspired poets that I know of. Henri Michaux recommended Joyce Mansour. I did meet Yves Bonnefoy, but Bonnefoy was more of an aesthetician like Ashbery, or a refined poet, but not a political one or visionary activist. Corso's *copain* Jean-Jacques Lebel and his circle of younger friends were more our style.

So in a way we were sort of on our own in Paris, without too much literary connection. Well, we had the Montparnasse, where I glimpsed Giacometti at a café table, and Saint Germain scene. . . . Very little Montmartre, I was very disappointed—when young I'd thought that's where all the action was, but that had been a half century earlier!—Picasso, Apollinaire, and the

Bateau Lavoir banquet. We visited Utrillo's alleys, but now it was more commercial, like North Beach.

There was Les Halles, where you could stay up all night and eat great onion soup, and the Jewish black market at rue de Rosiers, where American dollars were exchanged at a high rate, that Gregory found fast. And good shopping—we had just enough money*. . . I had just a little bit enough, you know, just about enough, some money from my family occasionally if I needed it. Rent was thirty a month, food was very cheap, we could buy and cook it ourselves.

And nothing to do. No work, not that much mail, so days out on the street, days in the Louvre, days walking around Paris, seeing old French movies at the Cinematheque. But we didn't connect with any young group of energetic brilliant Frenchmen. Two young people we did connect with were Jean-Jacques Lebel and Alain Jouffroi (a poet, later French consul in the Far East). Among the younger ones there didn't seem to be a strong group that we could ally ourselves with, hold readings, so we never did any public readings there in 1958.

Which was just as well, 'cause we had this intense private life. And in a way we were in an enclave of our own 'cause our French wasn't that good. I couldn't read French well enough to read magazines and find out what was going on. Not to read except scan newspapers; I could talk pretty well, but reading was painful. I'm slow—it'd take me half an hour to read a page, really, with a dictionary.

Ginsberg's comparatively reclusive social and literary life was sometimes "socialized" in dreams. At the end of February, he dreamed of being welcomed by a loving T. S. Eliot: he read his English host "Corso Creeley Kerouac" and informed him of "Burroughs Olson Huncke" as a starter; by the dream's end, however, after Eliot tucked him in bed, he pronounced himself "ashamed of myself" and asked, "What's my motive dreaming his / manna? What English Department / would that impress?" He charac-

---

* Early on, a check for $225, considerable money for Ginsberg in those days, arrived from Kerouac as loan repayment. It enabled Allen in turn to repay Burroughs for Tangier money and still have some left over.

terized his nocturnal vision as "overambitious dream of eccentric boy," and revised, "Last nite I dreamed of Allen Ginsberg. / T. S. Eliot would've been ashamed of me."

Notebook poems of external affairs include an extended rant against his homeland for its materialist militarism, ending with a rueful proclamation uniting selfhood and avarice as the cause: "America is fallen, is fallen—ah the horror wreck of all that ego money in its mad black structure toppling into the night." But fall and blame are by no means limited to the United States, for this jeremiad is followed almost immediately by another, nearly as long, focusing on the other protagonists of the Cold War. Mao Tse-tung, Stalin, and Khrushchev are identified as Burroughsian Senders. Refusing to be brainwashed by totalitarians, Ginsberg concluded his poem in a spirit not unlike Corso's "Bomb," which also was composed at rue Gît-le-Coéur: "ah for the bomb!"

By the first of April, Ginsberg had received LeRoi Jones' *Yugen*, with his own contributions. Learning that Carl Solomon was hospitalized again, he wrote Orlovsky of a letter from Solomon's mother: her son was "worried about publicity & thought he would be interviewed on TV or something."* Early in April, Neal Cassady was arrested at home after having given, in February, two joints of marijuana to two plainclothes narcotics agents in thanks for a ride from a party to his job at the Southern Pacific station. (On the Fourth of July, he would begin serving two concurrent sentences of five years to life for his crime.†) Kerouac, back in the States after departing Tangier and visiting France and London, now had more books coming out. He'd ventured public poetry readings in the Village—and was attacked. Dan Wakefield, for example, writing in *The Nation* of January 4, 1958, pronounced after seeing Kerouac at the Village Vanguard:

> Richard Wilbur is 36 years old and Jack Kerouac is 35. The painful difference is that Wilbur is a man and Kerouac a kid.
>     . . . there are born each year a certain number of men and a

---

*April 1, 1958, SHD p. 159.

† See Neal Cassady, *Grace Beats Karma: Letters from Prison 1958–1960* (New York: Blast Books, 1993) and Carolyn Cassady, *Off the Road: My Years with Cassady, Kerouac and Ginsberg* (New York: William Morris, 1990).

certain number of boys ... out of each era in our national
history there come a few poets and a few poor boys who wander
with words. . . .

Ginsberg's perspective was different, of course. A generation
later, he reflected:

His book [*On the Road*] was out, and there were big reviews and a
huge scene for him. But then he was left to hold the bag in New
York for the whole Beat Generation and the San Francisco Ren-
aissance all by himself. He didn't have the mutual support like
you know I had Peter, Peter had me, and Gregory and I were
there together and Burroughs, we were all there together, and
Alan Ansen, and we were a team like Superman and Spider-Man,
and what one person couldn't do the other could do. 'Cause
Burroughs had Harvard and I had Columbia and Peter had the
Army and the madhouse and Gregory had the jails—so we could
cover a lot of territory. Whereas Jack was drinkin', and I think
while we were away [in France] there were a lot of poetry read-
ings starting in New York, and LeRoi Jones met him, Ray
Bremser and Jack Micheline were around, and Howard Hart and
Philip Lamantia were there, but some were not strong poets,
some much inferior to Jack, but Jack went along in the spirit of
poetry, in a funny way—there's famous pictures of him going
wide-armed Christlike up on a ladder reading in some loft. But
drinking. At the Village Vanguard engagement, Elvin Jones had
been playing there then, he heard Jack and appreciated his
language. Jazz musicians appreciated him but he was put down
in the *Village Voice* alas by Nat Hentoff and others, so it was
supposed to be a "disaster," apparently, and he drank too much.
It was an exhibition of new-style poetry reading, and Jack was an
exquisite reader-vocalist as you can hear on contemporaneous
recordings, but the problem was he was doin' it for money, not
much at that, rather than for fun. And he wasn't doing it at home
or in universities, he was doing it in a nightclub, which is a tough
thing, critic-ninnies mocked him for it, it discouraged him.

After visiting the sarcophagus of Eleanor of Aquitaine in the
Louvre, Ginsberg wrote again of Naomi; and an inventory of the
contents of his apartment as well as of the phenomenal universe in
Paris also introduces Naomi, with a portion of a statement from

her last letter, received by Allen after her death, which would be reproduced in *Kaddish*: " 'the key is in/the sunlight.' "

During this time, tension and violence in North Africa mounted, as independence from European hegemony became an increasingly popular cause. "News" of it was reported in the European edition of *Time* magazine, and in a poetic monologue Ginsberg pleaded with Henry Luce ("Take poverty, Henry Luce, follow Christ, abandon the world you created") and called for a reportage "Benevolent, Indifferent, sentient/To both Frenchman & Algerian."

By April's end, Corso and Ginsberg had met the Anglo-Indian poet Dom Moraes, who invited them to England, with a promise of Oxford readings. Before May's first week ended, the two Americans were again in England, for two weeks of meetings with Soho youths; another BBC broadcast; visits with "Apocalyptic" poets George Barker and David Gascoyne; lunches with Dame Edith Sitwell and Cyril Connolly; tea with W. H. Auden.* At a reading in student digs at New College in Oxford, Corso's new, now classic "Bomb" was greeted with a shoe thrown at its author as Ginsberg attempted to explain Corso's imaginative ode to young members of Bertrand Russell's antinuclear group. All the while, Allen and Gregory were borrowing money, waiting for payment for a magazine article.

Ginsberg's journal notations for this fortnight include sound experiments with "metric paradigms" and an exchange of notes with Corso during their Oxford appearance. Among Ginsberg's, in his red-covered breast-pocket spiral notebook, are the lines:

> Let's walk out, get a train & go
> To London right **Now!**

What Allen didn't record in these journals regarding his second trip to England was its reaffirmation of his own (and Corso's)

---

* Upon returning to Paris, Ginsberg wrote Orlovsky, "Auden said at a party I heard he was sorry he really had acted like a shit to me in Italy" (May 30, 1958, SHD p. 170).

poetic worth; its fellowship of generous colleagues, male and female, of poetic sensibilities; and the much more precise sense of recent English literary and social history it afforded him. Since Ginsberg's journal notes were scant, the editor requested a further (1984) account of this period, as follows:

> It was like the leftover heritage of the "Apocalyptic poets": David Gascoyne, and Barker, and Dylan Thomas, who was dead by then, whom we'd known briefly in America. There was the French Pub in Soho, the traditional literary pub, but by then I met hardly anyone there except drunken Irishmen. But we had the luck of meeting an extremely sensitive person central to the whole literary scene—David Archer, Dylan Thomas' first publisher at the legendary small Parton Press. We were literally penniless in the rain on Trafalgar Square, or almost penniless, enough change for a phone call, and we called him up and he got a cab and picked us up and took us to a meal and got us home to a flat at 33 Tregunter Road that pataphysician Simon Watson Taylor shared with bandleader George Melly.
>
> Through David Archer we got connected in with the really serious literary scene. Parton Press had been like San Francisco's rare Auerhaun Press, in a way—the really great poetry of the age, the great marginal poetry. He was an old queen who said he liked to be whipped, candid and trustful, and he was really nice to us, totally appreciative of our poetry. He treated us with respect as if we were literary figures, not just American Boy Scouts! Showed us around London and told us where to go, and introduced us to Cyril Connolly, who took us to lunch upstairs at the Tour Eiffel, a restaurant where literary people had gathered all the way back to T. E. Hulme and Pound, back to 1909. . . . the people we met were not the official literary Angry Young Men, but were literary intelligentsia of a high order, what was left of an older active poetry scene.
>
> Edith Sitwell took me and Gregory to lunch at the Sesame Club, her ladies' club, which was generous. She appreciated the poetry—understood the language. The whole key was the inventiveness of words—putting two words together that were unusual—she could see that in our poetry. And we liked Christopher Smart and Whitman, and few English poets had any strong appreciation of that kind of stuff. And Blake, of course. The English thing was, Blake was still not considered "mature," so to speak, by the wits of Oxford.

Returning to Paris, where riots over Algeria had taken place in his absence, Ginsberg visited the Eiffel Tower where he composed a rough ode. He returned to Père Lachaise, finding Apollinaire's tomb and extending the draft he'd begun in December. Revisions made before "At Apollinaire's Grave" appeared in *Kaddish and Other Poems 1958–1960* (1961) demonstrate his gift for condensation.

As June began, Ginsberg was again short of funds but planned to get back to the United States by midsummer; eventually, a loan came from his father. Continuing to compose poetry, he testified "that I love my mother, and she put me down all thru my childhood, with her paranoia." The later "Poem Written in Green Pen Ink" projects his departure and itemizes things left undone, including two of the unfinished major themes of his poetry ("the elegy of my Mother . . . the Fall of America"). Doubtless with Kerouac's lonely role in mind, he recognized that he "now must go home & face the television mob and radio fireworks announcer." What may have served, in part, as consolation for his doing so is given in the poem's last line: "and lay my head in Peter's arms, and lay my body along his tender thighs."

In early July, a few days after proclaiming to his journal "Only poetry will save America," he depicted himself in the mirrors at Versailles' Hall of Mirrors:

. . . —my face, grimacing behind the heavy glasses taped
because broken—balding—black coat weighted down
with 1924 red Baedeker in left hand, torn pocket, white
lunchbag eggs hamburgers in right.

These last notebook pages may offer a vivid self-portrait of the poet, but they don't depict the comparatively active social life, with several artistic and literary rendezvous, that he enjoyed during his final month in Paris. At Deux Magots, Ginsberg encountered Tristan Tzara; at a party, Marcel Duchamp and Benjamin Peret. He then visited Tzara and Man Ray in their apartments. Important to both Ginsberg and Burroughs was their meeting the wealthy Jacques Stern and their visit to Louis-Ferdinand Céline. Of equal value to Ginsberg, perhaps, was his contact with Jean-Jacques Lebel. Lebel's father, Robert Lebel, was a major art dealer connected with the surrealists and dadaists; through Jean-Jacques, Ginsberg was supposed to meet André Breton. However, circumstances—and Ginsberg's own error, as he recalls it—prevented that meeting from ever taking place:

> Breton sent me a little note in tiny purple ink—a cramped hand—and I couldn't read it. I didn't know who it was from, and I thought it was a crank note. He even made an appointment with me to meet him at a certain café. It was in French, which I could just about barely read, but I couldn't read the name, nearly illegible, so I missed that.

Two nights before departing on the *Liberté* for New York, Ginsberg met Henri Michaux, poet, painter and psychedelic aesthetician. Michaux, living around the corner, responded to a note left by Ginsberg, and surprised the expatriate poet:

> He knocked and came in the room while I taking a peepee in the sink and he was amazed. "These Americans!" He loved Gregory's poetry and quoted, "mad children of soda caps."

But Michaux's contact with the visiting Beats was uncharacteristic of the French literary establishment; outside of a small anthology of Beat poetry that Jean-Jacques Lebel was to bring out in 1961, there was virtually no French interest in their work for another fifteen years. Why? Ginsberg believes:

> Nothing was happening poetically, and they were very conservative, and very proud of themselves, because they have this great literary tradition in France and everything (including much of my own style) came from France. And they *had* had this big deal with Existentialism, which was Sartre and Camus, but it was more rationalistic and novelistic and very little poetry—there was no grand lyricism. And it was a world-class ideological thing, but then the Beat writers were not actually very interested or familiar with the existential philosophy, because it was a very ideologically roundabout way of talking about primordial wisdom and primordial consciousness.
>
> Actually, it turns out that Sartre's novel *Nausée*, which was a major document, was based on a mescaline "horror trip." You know the great visionary experience in his book, a description of

the horrific, writhing snakelike trunks of a tree going into the earth? That was a mescaline experience. Somehow we never connected on that level with Sartre, which probably woulda done him good and done us good, you know, 'cause we were really totally experienced with all that by this time—with grass and peyote—and you know I had that whole thing down, more or less—and Yage, with Bill. But I never did get to meet Sartre.

Ginsberg once spoke of his tendency to bid adieu, almost sacramentally, to a habitation before leaving it. His discovery that Kerouac acted upon the same inclination was key to his recognition of the profound psychic bond between them. In the final entry of this volume, "Last Poem There," Ginsberg says goodbye to his room and its various components: its "can of sugar once a can of peas"; its photo of Roosevelt next to one of Genet; its rose in a beer bottle; and the poet himself, sketched in as realistic a hand as at Versailles' mirrors. But Ginsberg's elegy looks to the future as well as his past, as he contemplates returning to his homeland.

And what did the future bring this diarist? *Journals Mid-Fifties* ends with Ginsberg's departure from Paris. But on his return to the United States, he immediately plunged into New York's artistic and bohemian life and, once again, the complications of love and friendship. He rejoined Peter Orlovsky, who introduced him to LeRoi Jones and his circle of younger poets. With Orlovsky he visited Peter's brother Julius, who'd been "vegetating in the back wards" (another six years would pass before Julius could be released in their care). On his own he experienced "drug transcendencies" through both synthetic psilocybin (mushroom) pills and (with the help of a friendly dentist cousin) "infinite Buddhist laughing gas voids."

In renewed contact with Kerouac, Ginsberg discouraged him from gratifying the market-driven appetites of his agent, urging him instead to bring out his best work chronologically through Grove Press (as it turned out, *Maggie Cassidy* and *Tristessa* were published in cheap Avon editions). On occasion, Allen joined other poets (including Kerouac, Frank O'Hara, LeRoi Jones) and painters (Franz Kline, Willem de Kooning, and Larry Rivers) at the Cedar Tavern. And he managed to visit Kerouac on Long Island, in spite of the basic proscription, on the part of Jack's mother, against

Ginsberg and other close friends.* And at home—an East Second Street apartment he and Peter had moved into in August—in one marathon November weekend of composition, Ginsberg wrote the first drafts of the major sections ("Proem," "Narrative," "Hymmnn") of what would become *Kaddish*. In the fall and winter he was invited for a weekend visit with Norman Mailer; was asked to read at Harvard and Yale; to return to Columbia University not as *enfant terrible* but to declaim his poetry; and to appear in what would become one of the memorable works of American independent cinema, *Pull My Daisy* (1959).

In spite of Ginsberg's individual accomplishments and the increasing publication of works by Kerouac, public reception of the Beat Generation continued mixed. Approximately one year after *Howl* had been declared "not obscene," the chancellor of the University of Chicago forbade the *Chicago Review* to bring out its winter issue featuring Kerouac, Burroughs, and Edward Dahlberg. Only a few months later, in prelude to a vigorous national "anti-smut" campaign, the U.S. Post Office would impose censorship by impounding, then banning from the mails, copies of *Big Table* containing the same material.

* * *

In this book's selections from twelve separate notebooks used over four years, we see Ginsberg growing in confidence and mastery. True, he had nearly as little money at the diaries' end as at

---

* Apparently both of Kerouac's parents, Leo and Gabrielle ("Mémère") distrusted those different from themselves, in general, and Burroughs and Ginsberg in particular. Among Leo's last words to his son were "Beware of the niggers and the Jews"; his very last implored Jack to look after his mother (see Gerald Nicosia, *Memory Babe. A Critical Biography of Jack Kerouac* [New York: Grove Press, 1983], p. 163). In 1958, Mémère, determined to keep "Jackie" from the wicked influences of his friends, intercepted a Paris letter from Allen to Jack and announced a proscription (which would dominate Kerouac's last decade) against his visiting their home.

The ban was evidently seldom resisted by her son. Shortly after Ginsberg left Paris, Burroughs (who at Allen's request was opening Allen's mail, including a letter from Mémère) wrote Ginsberg vis-à-vis their friend and his mother, "She really has him sewed up like an incision." (See William S. Burroughs, *The Letters of William S. Burroughs 1945–1959*, ed. Oliver Harris [New York: Viking Penguin, 1993], pp. 391–392.)

their beginning. But in other ways the differences between the poet in 1954 and 1958 were considerable. Rather than languish for Neal Cassady, from whom complete commitment was out of the question, he had taken with Peter "eternal vows," cementing a tender, passionate, and intimate relationship that would last for decades. Persevering in poetic theorizing and composition, he had excelled in literary creation. Whether traveling abroad or working within a poetic community at home, he demonstrated resourcefulness and an understanding of a public that recognized him. His Arctic trip triggered thoughts of his departed mother and of the nature of suffering; his fifteen months in Europe and Morocco, as well as his first months back in New York, enlarged his perspective and produced early notations for what would become his magnificent elegy, *Kaddish*.

When Ginsberg returned to New York, it was not only to rejoin Peter Orlovsky but to aid Kerouac in dealing with a phenomenon essentially unknown when these journals began: the "Beats" as celebrities. Whereas *Howl* celebrated the "lost battalion" of "unknown buggered and suffering beggars" that peopled Ginsberg's familiar world of the forties and early fifties, his 1958 return to the U.S. revealed young people inspired by his work. Not only had an alternative culture begun to develop, but by the fall of 1958—after *On the Road* had been available for a year—fairly large segments of American society had become familiar with the names Ginsberg and Kerouac and with some of their titles. In the minds of more than a few, the word "beat" was now connected with the word "generation."

## Mar. 12 [*On the Hrvatska*]

Making it with Peter occasionally (once blowing, once jerked off, once blowing again, irregular simple screws nowhere); the sea rising & we rushing outside for the Great Wave which never comes—he boyishly amazed at how big the sea is—and one night sleep apart angry on the ocean.

* * *

## Mar. 14

Today I went up in fur coat in warm weather in nearly full moonlight to escape Peter & the world, & sat & brooded about last night's nothing, fighting impatience & fidgeting in chair till I began noticing the cloud formations on the right far horizon a huge neanderthal man striding forward: a shift of vision and he faded into the flat sky and the massy cloud. I shifted sight mentally and saw him stand forth individual archetypical stature in the sky of huge massive stance in the air over the sea—shifted sight & he became a cloud. As in Klee painting, a shift of an optical view shifts the space relations: so here, clouds stood embodying forth peyote god-like figures in the sky—an ancient indian, a vast dog, the great Wrestler, and a universal head of an angel.

The waves & ship: after rolling around unconscious for four days I began at this meditation time to figure at last the roll of the tide, the pull and rise of the water in advance, high up on the ship, by watching the map of gleaming moonlight checkered & splotched in the crevices of the water rolling and changing around the ship—which rocked & rose and fell forward into the maw of the shining mass of water around, pushed and flattened by the moving water map of force sparkling undulating in the darkness.

After, having at last escaped I lost mostly my mind in immersion in "healing" nature, I came back to cabin happier & at ease.

Long talk with Peter naked after shower, will I still love him if we don't make love—and he blew me and kissed my breasts anew. Then above in top bunk he with enormous straight hardon lay back & I blew in love. Then vaseline acock he mounted me I lay back legs up to ceiling feet spread against pipes for support, he entered & hung on screwed & I jerked off when he drove on in hard and held it there crying "Come on hold it in don't make me stop loving you."

After he told me to write & left me half an orange.

\* \* \*

Peter says let's begin "Let's declare a war of love"—"on whom? the whole world?" "Yes, we only live once."

"Clothes are the only things that stay with us historically"— waking for lunch P. says smiling with wet rumpled sweat of sleep.

& to tell Burroughs "Close yr. mouth you give me a hard on," to stop a "routine."

\* \* \*

4 am Mar. 18, 1957—Last nite on ship, approaching Casablanca, cross-Atlantic dream:

High tension wires, a steel-bar thin newspaper trap stand on which papers are perched. Over the wire bars, photographs are draped to dry: me and Lucien, me & Gregory. Notoriety. I leave them there & depart, Fame.

Much later, alone, I return & see photo of Gregory, cut from 25¢ small photo of me & he, with three bullet holes in face, reproduced as blowups in Paterson Newspaper. It's Gregory, a notice "Wanted after escape from Jail," shot trying to escape in gun battle: Gregory is dead. Corso, under pseudonym alias passport, Cleveland to Europe, Italian gangster refugee desperate last hours. My blood chill, my heart numb, I've killed him indirectly— it's great scandal in papers—and—Apparently *such* a scandal that one copy of that day's Paterson News was ordered here faraway. Whole front page filled with photos from Paterson courtroom, my mother and father, shamed, dressed up, rich, testifying, don't know my whereabouts—She lipsticked and in furs, staring forward side by side with father in smaller front page photo. Chill feeling I am wanted and Gregory dead—misnamed Joseph and shot by F.B.I. in desperate Lower East Side hideout battle.

I look, sometime in same dream, to see what's playing at Five Spot, Jazz Reichian revival hall—See woman dressed like hermaphrodite in dancing fancy dress showing of huge areas of body, Elise, whole front belly down the leg showing thru, Velvet flouncing up street to teaching dancing there—That's what came of the old time Trotskyite girls.

March '57—Approaching Casablanca—Blue sky, bluegreen flat water, slow silent ship whooshing thru mist no land in sight, everyone expectant, anchor chain machinery clanking, rope being hauled, blast of foghorn, passengers on deck. Above the mist in false visions of land, the Scimitar in the sky over N. Africa, a white jet ribbon streaming thru the blue.

"There's pretty pussy in Rabat"

* * *

"Casablanca Fez Marrakech Rabat Agadir Meknès—dead dead dead." —Old arab merchant, myopic, bald head, slippers shipboard.

* * *

Casablanca the long white concrete jetty into green water like 7 Wonders, like pyramids of Egypt—a world of blocks with boys bicycling slowly along the marble-like hulk. The city long and white, too long to see at one glance. Modern bldgs., here and there a church. Smoke and stink of industry, rocks ranged along the harbor waters (thru spyglasses see fezzed stragglers on the R.R. tracks)—straight lines and rectangular large space with clop clop of small boats, noises echoing on the waters.

* * *

## March 19, 1957—Casablanca

Entering Arab quarter—wander thru alleys filled with booths, bicyclists, hooded women—Arab businessman 34 with portfolio asks what we are—walks with us, conversing—to tea shop, mint hot sweet delicious tea, man with long brown T pipe comes by I get a puff get high wander out again—horse and cart take up whole narrow alley (clopping in gay silence) round miniature street corner bend—

\* \* \*

Meet the old Fudd mustache retired Englishman Fred Wilkes with oversize pants folded at fly like Turkish pantaloons & spotted oxford coat, in his groundfloor Tetuan Hotel room painting phony fawns & cosmic Disney sunsets—he talks of his 20,000,000-word book of philosophy "deeper than Plato" (a thousand-page explanation of the universe, including archangels)—Catholic priests and bishops are of course all interested, Wilkes asks for tobacco, been thru Mexico "I lived there of course years—Guadalajara, Laredo, all those towns"—

Eating Napoleon for 10 fr. and 10 fr. oranges, go down the alleys in late afternoon high isolated Peter ahead, to the cemetery with old lady branches & an old gnarled animal sexy green ancient meditation bearded tree fenced around, and small concrete-bordered graveyard filled with little slabs, worn away names, and a house with green flag & door at side (2 mats & bench for prayers, & a niche)—a lamb cropping sparse grass before the green bunker door—a white toilet seat askew among the graves at the foot of the tree—boys with rubber slingshots aiming at birds—Past a barbershop where the Arab barber looks up from his immediate dark pate with round eyes & lifts his finger frenchy into the air startled & inspired as Peter walks by the door his crown of bushy golden hair—and barber says "ah!"

Graffiti:

* * *

Characters of Casablanca—an old jew with red face and swollen legs pale red and sick and skin slightly salted and caking and peeling out of ripe sick leg with pale thin anklets and easy slippers, squinting his swollen face as though blind.

—a woman, small beggar against the wall with white bone buttons at end of fallen off truncated slurp of leg sticking footless & ankle-less out of dress, blue black threads. Tin cup.

—an old man dressed in seedy black burnoose with hood and yarmulke sits 'gainst doorway.

—another holy type beggar running 10 franc pieces thru his fingers with his eyes closed leaning against the sun (by a wall)

* * *

| 17½ | Francs | = a nickel |
|-----|--------|------------|
| 35 | " | = a dime—52½ francs = 15¢ |
| 70 | " | = 20¢ |
| 87½ | " | = 25¢ |

* * *

## March 20 Casablanca

Last nite wandering in Medina again—Old prophetic hooded figures—Jews with black soiled skullcaps and burnoose, the hood of burnoose thrown back over shoulder, a young girl putting groceries in it for carrying safely.

* * *

## Dream

We Now Present a Documentary on Greta Garbo

Camera pans to window of house under bridge. Thru kitchen venetian blinds, gauzy, a figure inside as if seen thru telephoto lenses—She (Greta) dresses in simple house clothes, or red skirt, making meal for guest, dinner, at sink and sideboard. Lens clarifies, she's young and attractive and very straightforward. She seems happy. She talks to herself and laughs and chuckles, lifting her head and laughing to ceiling as she peels an onion.

Camera moves in close-up—clearer and clearer—it is a movie—she talks—"You see I live here all alone and like it. I have friends, but they are my only friends, true friends. I am not unhappy. I have no needs for anything." She makes salad—a big bowl of lettuce, chives, endives, she's coring tomatoes & putting large whole tomatoes in the big bowl, à la natural style. Closeup of big tomatoes unsliced with center chonked out by knife, just top center not all the way thru.

"Man needs very little to live" Greta close-up again, superimposed on a view of bridge under which she lives. Her face and bust in dress get larger & larger & seems to atomize and dissolve into the bridge—with the giant interorganic view of her bust on the screen faded into nature, the bridge in the background.

"There is no use for all the money, all the worry, all the work, all the war. I live very simply alone. All men should forget about their great radio needs"—her form as an immense television image fading into eternity—"Too few of us can see ourselves as things, like this bridge under which my house is sheltered—but in God's eye we are things, with our needs. And things like us have no want of a civilization. We shall survive atomic ruins because man is in mind eternal.

"Too many cars, people, too many unreal movies, too many passions clutter our lives, too much of everything—and we all work for nothing when we assemble and gather it all around us—for what? No need to do anything but just live." She was talking like Gary Snyder. Plea for simpler life, privacy. Ship's bell rings for breakfast and I wait & wake.

Probably influenced by French edition of *Secret Life of Salvador Dalí* with pix.

\* \* \*

Ville Arabe—old Medina [Probably Tangier]
On a corner, two alleys run into a main alley, a little rise in cobblestone narrow street we tarry, high, & black-garbed arab sitting on box against building wall, across alley 6 feet from him, his pastry stand. Flyblown Napoleons and tarts—little isolate stand nobody around, silence, afternoon, a few people passing in either direction, the sad stand of pastry, we spent 10 minutes waiting for friend to come out of hotel door.

Jack Kerouac with Burroughs' cat outside Bill's
ground-floor garden room, Villa Muniria, Tangier,
1957. Kerouac's place upstairs had large windows
with spacious red-tiled veranda overlooking harbor
and Gibraltar distant, rent $40 a month, less. Photo:
Allen Ginsberg

## Tangier: Cape Spartel

Under a short gnarled aged shady tree, like parasol with
Eucalyptus dwarf tree spikes falling above my brow, looking down
past my feet see miniature light green fir trees 3 inches high
transparent—Farther below grey stalks of inchy outworn dwarf
cliff scrub, and all the way down green steeps a cliff overhangs a
shelf that slopes into flat furry-treed farmland, with a few culti-
vated squares way distant on the edge of the sea—and thatch roofs
and fences and a village half mile long down there—past that,
small flat blue ocean so wide and vast I have to lift with my head to
glimpse it all, seen from so great height—and far across in molten
blue light, a haze, and the coast of Spain at the gate of the
Mediterranean—Sat here a month contemplating Europe—with
little ships hugging the Afric shore making way inside an ancient
lake. The Cricket shakes the Rock.

\* \* \*

Soco Chico, Tangier, 1957, Allen Ginsberg in distant
center under awning. Photo: Peter Orlovsky

Blvd. Pasteur Tangier across from Café de Paris—sitting
approached by arab boys for shoeshine lottery newspapers rubber-
squeakers picture scarves leather bags peanuts and Beggars.

## March 29—Tangier

A Dream Remembered Backward
(see Ouspensky*)

*I*

Prefiguration: Early Archaic Dream

*II*

Wedding Night and Clothes

---

* P. D. Ouspensky's novel *The Strange Life of Ivan Osokin*, like *Finnegans
Wake,* begins in one spot of time and returns in an Einsteinian cycle to the
same spot, as does "A Dream Remembered Backward." —A.G., August 4,
1984

Orlovsky, Burroughs, and Paul Lund at Dutch
Tony's Restaurant, Tangier. Photo: Allen Ginsberg

### III
### Naked in Rockefeller Center
### IV
### The Packet of Poems
### V
### The Overflowing Toilet

Written while thousands of cocks were crowing in the walls of
Medina—thousands re-echoing.

### I

Looking for Gene or home beyond upper viaduct 125th
Street Harlem-Bronx—I cross the great park-viaduct but can't find
room or house I'm looking for. Block on block of great apartments

in the negro darkness, a labyrinth, under the city, the Harlem River even, I have to walk thru that great depression to get where I'm going and I get lost in that.

Furthermore—a part of same archaic dream—I also have to cross the enormous dream Hudson, which is as wide as the great lakes by now—huge Yosemite palisades on either side the wall of lighted New York rising a thousand feet in the air broken by stars of the windows, a small ledge of piers at the base of fantastic miles of cliff Manhattan where I can get a foothold if I find the right spot to dock—trying to cross the vast river at night toward dawn, no one around to know the way, I get a rowboat off an ocean liner and try to get ashore alone perhaps—but I have to face the vast silent confusion of the wall of magnified New York—seen perhaps as from bridge of small cargo ship—impossible to enter—

As leaving U.S. on Hrvatska the Yugo ship, standing high on the ship's bow I saw the island's vastness—Brooklyn's shore streets seemed minuscule, small, and confused as boat moved out of the harbor past rows of huge docks and boats, I standing above them waving goodby to Lafcadio Carol and Elise—who stood waving farewell down there below on the dock blocks away back receding into the waterfront immensity, growing smaller as we chugged past further ships. I stood above Brooklyn to wave goodby, in dream stood above Manhattan as we passed it far away.

## II

In a furnished room, as 92nd St. or in the apartment of my fiancée, Gregory's family apartment, probably Gregory's old room—in Brooklyn—I am standing by the low ¾ bed, covered with brown bed cover, some cheap furniture, shaving dresser & high clothes closet.

Some gorilla, bride's older brother perhaps, is giving me my wedding clothes—in any case at least a change of clothing. His friend, my rival, is there—but I have beat them out for hand of the sister—both of them meatballs, that is lowclass need a shave dumb Brooklyn working stiffs and bums. Trying to tell me how to live. They hand me their underwear. Which pair of jockey shorts to use? He points them out for me—"I pissed in this one, John here pissed in the other—take your choice." I don't want either, I want my own tho it's dirty too maybe. And perhaps pants tie shirt and coat shoes for the wedding.

### III

Where can I put these on—and where to go?

I take an elevator up in Rockefeller Center to get to a high floor of polished marble. To see someone . . .* I take elevator down. I am naked. I have to find a place to don my wedding clothes. I press elevator door, hoping to stand behind door, closed. But door is glass. Both sides of the front of elevator right and left of the door are also glass. People can see thru the left or right side. Meanwhile I get my underwear top on & press the ascend button so I can get shirt & pants on rapidly too as I rise.

### IV

On a table in the furnished room—a volume—a large envelope tied with string, containing carbons of early *Empty Mirror* originals plus side poems unworked on and various small poetical Mss. no one's seen. They are being returned from Williams, as well as a packet of letters from him to me, which I loaned him for NYU professor's use.† He's sent all this material back to me finally via my girlfriend.

He says, as for Elise, I think she's a figure of your imagination, I have never located her precisely in any case.

I look in his letters & find he *has*. I shovel thru the sheaf to find the handwritten Winston Hotel letter‡—fortunately, it's there. I'm glad that wild one's in. Also I notice some references to Wm. Pillin and Leslie Wolf Hedley etc. there, and am appalled. He's cut out and pasted the back cover of Hedley book—with reference to publications of West Coast 2nd rate Trotskyite-anarchists, a list of books of same nature—Apparently he's referred to the same list in some letter to me & is reproducing the cover so as to get in big plug for Pillin and others—I am

---

* Ellipsis periods appear in the journal entry.

† John C. Thirwall—I did lend letters to Prof. T. —A.G., August 8, 1984

‡ A letter from William Carlos Williams appreciating *Empty Mirror* poems, written on Hotel Winston stationery (c. 1954).

disheartened—don't want to be associated with Pillin—But it's Williams' responsibility, it's his book nothing I can do about it.

## V

I'm in bed with Louis at 288 Graham or 53 Fair Street or 48 Haledon Avenue—a room with a bed, him alone in it, and a cot for me. I get up with naked Peter and go thru side doors, French typical doors, to get thru to bathroom, as the piece of flesh in the side of my cheek's been bothering me badly for a month now's got so big and fat and thin-necked attached to the cheek tissue I've begun biting it off, though it hurts, and skinning it off propping it up inside my cheek with my inner tongue, and my mouth is full of bits of pink inside-cheek flesh, I am angry, I have to spit it all out somewhere I go to bathroom—out the hall past main living room where there are 2 more cots on one side of which Elise is asleep, white sheets rumpled on the other cot. I remember W.C.W.'s wonder if she did exist. In the bathroom I spit out a great gob of foamy spit mixed with bits of pink tissue-flesh, but miss the toilet— Peter's there, to my embarrassment it hits partly the floor and partly the back of toilet. But my shame confounded and made unnecessary by the final external annoyance—which makes me mad at my father—that the toilet gives a big gulp and enormous water floods down from the ceiling-wall box, but toilet doesn't swallow it all and it floods the floor, pieces of my foamy mouth come and flesh floating at my naked feet on the white tile floor of the bathroom, though I notice a drain-hole for it, & am relieved & point out it to Peter, who's still annoyed with me.

## April 22, 1957—Tangier

My poor Book, nothing for you yet* till this dawn—6 A.M. Woke from a dream:

---

* Ginsberg's diary entries will continue infrequent, sometimes with gaps of several weeks, until he's settled in Paris later in the year. This may be owing—in part, at least—to his typing sections of *Naked Lunch* in Tangier, travel itself, photograph taking, and letter writing. Readers seeking more details on this period of his life are referred to the biographies by Barry Miles ( *Ginsberg*) and Michael Schumacher (*Dharma Lion*) and to the forthcoming edition of Ginsberg's selected letters, edited by Miles.

## A

After a walk in Central Park someone takes me up to an apartment where I go to bed—a big luxurious apartment in large modern building with a big silent door which is open. I go in lie down and sleep.

I am wakened when the girl comes in, a nice looking young brunette—she seems rich—and well mannered & hip in fact tragic silent and moody and doesn't kick me out but asks me who I am what doing there.

In her living room a big party, I sit on floor, basking in her attention—a strange piano with copper large keyboard—the keys are long and curved and oval, and

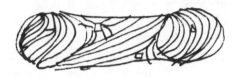

strangely built on new or ancient principle—so that you can play without knowing music (just brush fingers over keys in rectangular straight motion and the formula of curves will supply the harmony)—so I strike several Bachlike chords in succession. My sense of Rhythm makes up for monotony of mechanical harmony—but I don't get far & am interrupted.

We go out, perhaps to part & say goodby—The door is open & she says wait I'll go back & I say no "I'll close it mentally," she laughs how? and I look at the door & concentrate aware of my power—a gamble—and say "perhaps if I look at it sadly enough it will close"—Miracles respect sadness—and slowly the door silently shuts on its hinges by magic a minute later—great feeling of power and understanding in me at the moment & sadness. . . .

Somewhere in the dream I had seen that she had use of only one hand, like Jane Bowles. A young dark brunette girl, with understanding depth & didn't ask much questions & loved me as mysterious.

## B

I ascend to the balcony of the white house, Truman is there, bare to the waist, as well as everyone else of the official family, small

Johnny Roosevelt barefoot and with barechest, wearing only pants. Truman is dipping a big piece of Silver Service into a stone balustrade which has water in it—the tray's been used for night-before party & he's cleaning it of black impurity—strange to see him like Eleanor Roosevelt doing this housework—and I walk around them to the other side of the balcony—See two Britishers, they have gabardine coats & scarves on tho, not undressed for the view—you look out & see all Washington City spread out down there in front—Sir Harold Macmillan the visiting Britisher & his aide—Macmillan horsefaced & longtoothed, they're all talking.

And the pet Rabbit is there—they're talking about it, a special excellent breed, with long human face—a long face, I hold it in arms & look, it's like a baby with the long pendulous Roosevelt Eleanor skull & Roosevelt jaw—so long & thick a jaw that you have to hold it carefully lest it fall apart—so refined it's like a baby has to be taken special care of—They say "Such a remarkable aristocratic breed it's brittle & very intelligent and needs attention, the family project, the Roosevelt pet official Rabbit"—I take it in arms, go around balcony downstairs, thru a kitchen back door where I'm not supposed to be, & back on grounds outside the Castle, White House, I'm hiding on the grounds on my stomach—holding the Rabbit.

A pile of people in a load of hay on the ground—a plane pulls up—it's dawn. It's time, they wake up, the whole hayrick alive with people getting up to visit the White House—also as they point out on the cliff above the grounds, a large antenna & North Polar Guard Service Station Brick Building—I'd never have seen these sights if I hadn't wandered out & around—

Suddenly I notice the Rabbit with long sensitive human jaw of flesh has no right leg, and a hole in the fur where meat, red as liver & not bleeding, can be seen—I am horrified—It turned its neck & snaps & bites at the spot taking a nibble more of its flesh—I am frightened, this is its fatal aristocratic mad proclivity, I try holding the huge delicate head in place, but it has more strength than I thought & snaps back viciously arching its whole body, like steel spring, in my arms to reach the torn leg—I am afraid to hold it bound too stiff and straight in my arms for fear I rupture its neck skin, its power is so great when arching its neck back—I get help, & two of us begin trying to hold it down—it struggles half out of my grip & tears the leg further, a strip of skin hangs down. I am desperate, destroying the Roosevelt-Burroughs Rabbit—but one last hope—if he can get a good grip on paws and neck and head and I can hold back the bottom and we can straighten it out once and for all—but Rabbit wriggles and snaps and bends back—the skin on the breast begins to tear off revealing a strip of intestine and yellow fat, the rabbit is tearing itself to pieces in our hands, we've mismanaged, made a mistake, huge strips of fur being rubbed off, practically skinning the rabbit it's all in tatters with guts & intestine hanging out—I give up dream ends in horror I wake up.

* * *

Then woke up after dream & opening my eyes saw pale orange on the window pane & realized it was dawn—rose up to look out window & saw clear orange sun halfway up across dawn-dark Malabat Cape—stared out window—birds flying in pairs talking thru the air, the long wide beach with a few people walking faraway small on the thin lip edge of water, a crack of little waves all along the beach bringing ocean power sound up to balcony tho the sea looks still & from here the waves look wavelets, slowly, the silent white ship at the jetty—began at dawn to throb its motors, petroleum vats shining aluminum in new sunlight—the new sun whirling around still a clear disc of orange in the white sky, fires in the sun whirling round in the eyeball, sense of Dawn Satori, first dawn I saw here I climbed into my clothes and came out on veranda to write & watch sunrise. Sunrise official flames seacalm birds chirp sight of Spain dawn sparkle new sun fire white sky and old beggar in ragged brown shroud poking with bag and stick in empty lot below. Everywhere as in a room, the vast space around echoing with bird cries.

A bolt of fire in the bay between the sun disc & the shore. See the houses & palmtrees motionless, no breeze.

Small ships black at anchor on the bay. The bay itself like rippled white glass with clear black ship and buoy spot on it.

Relief from the human, entanglements of Bleak—Peter & Bill.

Dawn, birds crying & flying in space at the sight of the faraway sun, birds circling in air, nervous flights like flies in the sunlight—Today, cloudy

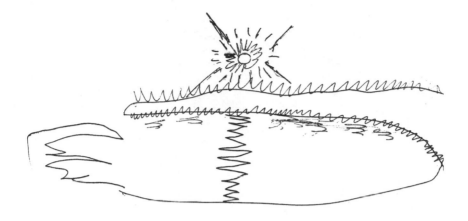

6:20 A M   Mm 11,'57

\* \* \*

## May 23

Till I rid myself of idea of God I will not enter spiritual heaven.

Corso: "Lead us to a paradise far from God."

\* \* \*

June 11—Ferry to Algeciras—There's "the ancient parapets of Europe," Gibraltar looming up out of my dreams.

Guided by dolphins to the continent, big manly porpoises jumping in front of the prow—up out of water a dozen times—and a rainbow in the spume

That woman by the sail—her hair waving on her skull in the breeze

\* \* \*

## Madrid June 17

Lonely, like cadaver must feel after mourners have gone away from funeral left him alone, looking for shadows—

May 11, 1957 - 6 AM Sunrise from Hotel Mammunia, Tangers

\* \* \*

In Barcelona—Death to Van Gogh's Ear!

\* \* \*

## July 14, 1957—Venice—Dream

Hitchhiking via train and road—to California toward beach and sand dunes of Big Sur with Dusty (or some girl)—came near highway to Big Sur—on our way South? So decided we could settle there and make it on the beach in an abandoned family shack. We laid out knapsacks, she had no trouble carrying hers—all of a sudden a car came, going back to town—I said "I'll take it, I can come back in a day you want to come?"—she was indecisive—"I will in any case, you wait I'll be back, sleep softly on the beach"—and sped up to town, to be spied on by neighbors where we'd left—and been forgotten by them already. . . .

I wait upstairs in the huge townhouse attic—while up there wandering around, I hear noise of the family below going about their lives, returning from work & trips to the country—nobody knows I am up there—big dusty sofas and old mahogany side table full of scratchy memories. I cough—and hear someone else wandering in the attic—oh, at last my travel companion—how has she done?—It's a sudden glimpse, now I'm returned to the attic of the huge family house on the beach—I see her—it's Naomi, comes up to me, I say hello feeling great to see her again—she's been wandering around the shore in the attic up to her own business I guess—the recognition, she's in a dress, a woman, and as I encounter her, I wake up.

\* \* \*

## July 15, 1957

In a bed a dream (after Nicolas Calas\*) about Peggy Guggenheim† who has rejected me.

## The Bonfire [*Rescued at the Last Minute*]

What has made me seek the fame of Poetry?
What Shall I do with it?
      Burn it up in a poem.
Here's an invitation to Peggy Guggenheim's
      Palace delivered by a chauffeured gondola
          with shiny stockings and a silver tray
—Into the fire, him and his invitation
      and Peggy Guggenheim & her palace too.

Fame, into the bonfire,
      burn in the poem,
Money also, what shall I do with my millions
      my millions of dollars
      my millions of oversized ten thousand lira notes
      —into the fire
        Burn in the poem
Burn up my life in the poem
      —there in the fire of Truth—
And this poem also,
      into the fire.
          Venice '57

---

\* Nicolas Calas: member of surrealist circle, poet, cultural historian, later taught briefly at Naropa Institute.
† Peggy Guggenheim (1898–1979): art collector–socialite. The faux pas that brought rejection is discussed on p. 331.

Allen Ginsberg on San Sammuele, Venice, visiting
Alan Ansen. Photo: Peter Orlovsky

* * *

Florence—First afternoon Loggia & Palazzo & Ponte Vec-
chio & Church & Giotto Tower & Baptistry
Second day—Uffizi all day. Dostoyevsky's House.
Third—Baptistry Interior San Marco & Academy
Fourth—Big Church [Duomo], Bargello, Medici Tombs,
Massaccio

## Rome—August 1

RR station—out on dark tree'd square—cafés under
arches—the young bearded beggar—walk down street—map with
3-D pix—To the Coliseum—To Pantheon at nite, aweful—feet
hurt—to International House—to St. Peter's facade with saints
dancing on top—Sleep

## 2nd day August 2

To St. Peter's morning (after milk around corner on Tiber)—inside, tomb of Cherubini—walk by Maximus over hill to Protestant cemetery—kissed Shelley's grave goodby & took a clover—wept at Keats—Crawled in Cestus' pyramid*—R.R. to Ostia Antiqua & Clam Spaget—all thru Ostia—the sweet columns—with the professor (argument at lunch)—back drinking at Ostia Lido—train & bus back (& temples & Pyramids & church on way)

## 3rd day   August 3

Walk—to Pantheon, Trevi, Palazzo Venezia, Victor Emmanuel II Monument, then up Michelangelo steps to Capitoline Hill, down into Forum, t high, Pete sleep I walk an hour, then all over again & around Palatine Hill to Coliseum, then up Via Imperial to Forum & then bus to slum by S. Peter, eat & then sit in S.P. & home.

## 4th Day   August 4

Vatican Museum—Last Judgement—Michelangelo's—skin the key to the picture—how he fits into scheme—Angelico dull & Raphael dull—Fig leaves on all the statues I got mad—over to Pinacoteca, hi on T, Fra Angelico boxes colored hit my head as soon as I stepped in room—strange sensation of weird in early paintings (on T)—then lunch at ECA Mensa, over to Botteghe Oscure, then bus to Terme Museum, pictures with same roman ass, grey-lined age, then St. Maria Maggiore, and St. Peter in Vincoli, home to Simpson, then to R.R. Station & Fountain at nite, & home.

## 5th Day   August 5

Bus to Piazza del Popolo, & walk to Spanish Steps, try to see Keats-Shelley Room, no money. Then met Bob from Tangiers, then

---

* See "Adonais," XLIX–L: tomb of Gaius Cestus, built in time of Augustus.

to Palace Barberini, another Angelico & Fra Lippo Lippi—tickets at station & Capitoline Museum charge, no money, later Forum, get high, take pix of ass, sit & walk an hour. Train 2 PM to Assisi great landscape full of castles & cities on hills. At Assisi the Giotto, and tour of old & new churches. Slept on grass in front of church.

## Dawn 6th Day    Assisi August 6

Sunrise, wake, chimes at 5:30, answering back & forth between St. Fr. & St. Chiara. A monk was up w. a mule cart. Cat by road. Church open. Up thru gate to see sunrise. Peter up, morning spent in church, noon arguing Catholicism with Brothers, afternoon long walk up to Hermitage along side of mountain— hung around in Courtyard, tried Francis' bed, returned down got white (carryall) bag and argued more with all 13 monks at nite before bed. Ice cream in Plaza, postcards, slept on grass again.

## 7th Day    August 7

Up at 7:30 wandered Giotto Church (had seen Clare's body) and walked down to Porziuncola—N.Y. Franciscan priest took us all around for 3 hours—then hitchhiked to Perugia—saw Angelico at Pinacoteca and few Perugino pix. I liked, and out on highway at Dusk.

\* \* \*

Rome—Queer places: Flora at 5 o'clock, Brick Top, Giardino
    d'Europa, Via Veneto, Trastevere
Alan Ansen, 3219 della Carrozze (San Sammuele) Venice phone
    81975
Caresse Crosby, Moran and Cie., 14 Place Vendôme Paris
Paris—Monastery L'Eau Vie, Soissy-Sur-Seine—Robt Lax?
Dr. Destouches—Meudon
Hi Hirsch—7170–71, Sarphati Park 84

\* \* \*

Nor Xmas Hymns, nor Figleaf Vatican, nor St. Francis Fartboys of
    Assisi grubbing in a grotto rubbing stone

nor Christ nor crosses nor the Church I will take none, Father, but
  thee.

* * *

## Venice–Rome Flight August 22*

  Rocking back & forth in front right seat of plane purr
growl of tinny motor—sudden lift forward on the flat brown grass
of Lido, & turn, the nose rocking.
  A mile & a half down daytime blue I can see the houses like
little boxes thru the clouds, bright sun shining.
  Gianfillipo Usellini: Il Figlio Prodigo
    Sunset at Herculaneum

* * *

## Ischia

    Volcanic peninsula, jagged into the sea
  Blue sky, pale around the edges sharp clear air flickery blue
      water
  like movie photograph or trout-fishing lake
      Pier sticking out on hundred legs
      4 nuns in a rowboat figures
          of death, dressed up
          thinking judging skulls
      rowed by a vigorous Italian girl
      with long hair & Anna Magnani
          silk dress loose & sloppy
  —into the yellow sunset.
  Poor girl don't be nun.

---

  * *Life* magazine paid to fly Ginsberg to Rome to be interviewed for an
article, "Big Day for Bards at Bay," appearing September 9, 1957.

Allen Ginsberg, Forum, Rome. Photo: Peter
Orlovsky

\* \* \*

## Forum, Rome

Look at all these broken stones,
and by the wall
The rainstained fragment of an ass
a human ass
was here two thousand years ago
—some boy turned round
stuck out his behind
and posed
Michelangelo remembered
when the palaces had fallen—
When the cities are forgotten
there'll be a human ass

\* \* \*

Riding a train in Austria, my soul free—
My blue dungarees faded, my eyes own entire Alps,
Small money in pocket for future, Time not measured by Marks,
look at the fields of sunflowers, the sunflowers look at heaven.
Run bright rivers, green ye fields, shine meadows in the moun-
          tains,
Pass yellow train—international joyride to Vienna,
Love at my side sleeping in a red shirt, pen in hand!
Woe to the fat faced Germans who forget the sufferings of the Jews.

\* \* \*

## Hallucination in Gare de L'Est

Suddenly he turned around and saw
what he had been looking for.

Of course the lightning lasted
only ten seconds—

There against the blind white sky
black branches writhing out of the trunk

automobiles passing, you walking,
lightning resting on the roofs like rain,

& Silence moving down the long wide street
smashes into the RR station like a great black train

\* \* \*

There aren't any more peaches on the tree
only bananas grow there now

I used to like to fuck girls
But only boys kiss my belly spiritually.

God knows between the boys & the Bananas
Maybe I'm a sort of Tropical Monk—

Walking down the street with a bagful of bananas,
I wonder what happened under that tree

* * *

These are the days in Paris—
There's no place to sleep any more

Some sleep in holes in the sidewalk,
the Metro keeps them warm.

A man with a beard has a flat
and a bed and a wife & a cat.

Some rich ladies under mansard roofs
nervously sleep in thirteen beds.

The baker has his bedroom. The landlady
has hers. The tenants have theirs warm.

Auden has 9 rooms on Ischia.
Eliot must have a flat in London.

But where do I sleep?
In a bench on Gare de l'Est

Waking all night
I wrote out these doublets

Six o'clock six o'clock
the RR station gets noisy

Coughers sing in their dreams
hard dreamers grow more weight

Hard benches float down the tracks
RR clanking fills the waiting head

the man on the next bench moves
When I open my eyes he's gone.

* * *

## Apocalypse of Les Halles

Vast barn over the streets
Puddles of mud and blood in the gutter
Red truck heads growl and push asleep

Carts full of lungs carts full of liver carts full of hearts
Carts full of heads
The lungs shaking and quivering
A huge cow's head ogled and nodded at the curb
A cart full of flowers, cortège piled on wooden rollers from the
       basement
A cart full of jaws entering the elevator
Enamel trays tin buckets and stomachs emerging
Hollow bong, an empty cart bellowing against the wall
An old woman stained with blood
Six men standing on the corner shaking hands, blood running
       down white smocks
A man with the head of a skinned pig walks the cobble street
A man with head full of wires appears Plug him in
Slowly judiciously methodically a red corpse on his shoulders he
       marches the slippery aisle
A cart full of hooves
Red tails hang the steaky thighs rap the laborer's back
A grey shirt under his smock sways over dungareed buttocks he
       pushes his meat into the door
Snuffle and grunt of dopey trucks
Rumble of iron wheels against splintered wood, Mud-track of truck
       wheels huge sneakers of Martian athletes laid across the
       road
Corpses identical hanging in hundred perspective under the star-
       ing light bulb
Candelabra of the racks
Legs laid out on the ground like silverware
Heads of sudden menace the herds of trucks the bloody smeared
       apron of a fool
Fat butchers clutching their corpse breasts split down the middle
       with an ax
Ribs and backbones in rows six carts coming at once in different
       directions.
Pushers in hip boots
Elevators full of blood descending
Six wheeled carts rumbling empty over Rimbaud's grave
Sweet lady in an apron what're you doing here
Ten fat men struggling with the ass end of a cow

A ballet dancer pushes an empty cart to midstreet and leaves it
        there with a despairing gesture
Comes back pulling a cart full of cows' heads
Here come the secret prisoners wrapped in brown burlap
Here come the mummies of Egypt for breakfast
Layers of Lard trains full of pigeons
Great bellies limping in the void
Peter demanding "pigs feet sticking out of boxes like strawber-
        ries" be noticed
A 5 foot huge brown basket full of brains
I thought it was a prehistoric six-feet hairy skull
Horns sticking out of naked goat heads
Who little boys holding hands peering at the flowers
O the rumble! two shiny pigs heads snouts to Heaven
O the roar! wide eyed head of truck charging at my pen
High Halls
A man in beret feeling up the assholes of hanging pigs he's an
        official
O the Fish smell! O the Liver stink! O itchey nosed butchers of
        Paris!
Bicyclists balancing boxes of breasts
Ox breasts jiggling up and down like great rubbery jokes at dawn
Burlap spread over the scene heavenly burlap for curtain
Cows rise up dancing
A whiff of mammal smell in the atmosphere a peep of blue gowns
        of angels' bloody aprons.
Fellow conspirators, Eat!

\* \* \*

"Not like that glorious day when I summoned up all my
power and put down all of Mexico" —Gregory

\* \* \*

## Sitting in the Bar in Amsterdam

        Dumps, nothing to do
        I want to be home in bed
            with a fiery Book—

But the be bop xylophones
      hissing on the phonogaph
   followed by nasal sax
     whimpering out of the wall
remind me of you, my Dollar.

I got no money
ain't even got the blues
all I got is Amsterdam
and a red lite on the table.

Watcha gonna do
When the skeleton runs out?

O Baby!

Gimme that Dollar again
Sweet Mistress Poverty, Love me.

Sitting here calm in my nerves
afraid of a paranoiac shower of gold

Ariadne in the bar
Corso's at it again—But is it

    Poetry or Money—he's
    bleating like a lamb.

Got somebody up in a corner
with the cobwebs
gabbling about fiery princesses.
O fiery Princesses and books
Save me from boredom of empty
               purse

Gabbling about Prussia
Hoaxes and Princes
Change of sex
Lesbian saxophones.

Skeletons claim the limit
Death Darkness eats us all
Skeleton singing in the closet
Is that all you got to say?

Gimme a cigarette.

Clean your glasses, Skull
There's nothing happening
Who *wants* something to happen
said a little squeegy
voice.

## Rembrandt at Rijksmuseum, Amsterdam

*Lazarus*—Life spirit snapt out—here entering him again, he rises
up pulled by pulley force. Red human faces watching.
*Jewish Bride & Groom*—Golden & Red—Tenderness hand to
breasts, her hand over his—both hands look real—her gaze
nowhere—he worn but still a little sexual not much—

*Self portrait as Paul*—Read anything you can in the face—eyes
arched looking away, neck turned, towel around head—a
parody?—looks too clownish to be the Master of Dark
Rembrandts—Sad look in his face, in Vienna Saskia by his side
shares the look.

*The Syndics*
Great red solid paint tablecloth.
Rembrandt is the center of the picture. He's sitting 6 feet
away painting them. They're all staring at him, the hypersensitive
eye, with their own personalities—he's subjected to their ridicule
& coldness—the observer of the picture, substituted for Rembrandt by Rembrandt, is the one these judges are examining. You
have to defend self from their gaze, as R. did by disappearing &
leaving the onlooker to judge them back, frozen in his eyeblink
canvas.

* * *

[Draft of "Man's Glory," CP 260. Its later version was mistakenly
chronologized in *Collected Poems* and *Journals Early Fifties Early Sixties*
as 1960:]
Gods glory shines on top of mountains where a greystone
monastery sits and blinks out at the sky . . .

* * *

## Moon Prevention

**Excerpt From Collaboration Poem by Allen Ginsberg,
Peter Orlovsky, and Gregory Corso—Amsterdam,
Oct. 1957:**
Mankind shall inflict the planets—
mining operations on the moon—
Does the aged Texas prospector
        dream his great source of radium
                on the moon—
No gold-diggers allowed on the moon—
No baptism on the moon—
bring nothing to the moon!
little children shall be permitted to take
        their balloons to the moon!
What will he say:
        "The moon is made of green
                cheese and Gregory's
                        stolen prunes—"*
Will they allow poets to claim their planet—
        moon is theirs—
Moon doesn't belong to scientists
        but to poets
Who will be the first lovers on the moon—
Will the moon know its Raskolnikov?
I want to get drunk on the moon,
        high on the moon,
        rock 'n' roll on the moon
No death on the moon!
What jazz the man on the moon hear?
I want to have moon windows,
        moon umbrellas
        moon shoes,
        moon hats,
        moon underwear—

*This is our great
epic, you're in it
now, Peter, this
is going to
Measure†*

---

* See the ending of "This was My Meal," in Corso's *Mindfield*, p. 39.
† John Wieners' magazine.

Can I be allowed to piss on the moon?
Who'll smoke first fat cigar on the moon?
Will some Senator from Iowa drop the first
        Coca Cola bottle on Moon
Who'll shed first virgin blood? Who'll argue
        over Negroes?
Moon will explode at the first pistolshot fired?
If a knife is raised, moon will go into eclipse,
If some poison is poured, no matter how secretly,
Moon will flip & throw itself into Sun.
            No, Not at all.                          *Man, it's a*
Big Caverns will appear.                       *long mad thing!*
Who'll be the first fairy of the Moon? Cinderella?
Who'll be the first bedbug, the first Cockroach,
        the first elephant, on the moon
Mosquito, Crocodile, Warthog?*
Will the moon be at least the beauty parlor for the warthog!
Oh!
The world owes the Moon to the warthogs!          [*Silence*]
What great restaurants in what Cities?
I want to ride on the Metro! What will the name of the
        Stops be?
Artaud, Apollinaire, Marlon Brando
        Sophie Éluard, Maybe we think so
Moonshine Shampoo Stop. First stop.
Moonshine Dragstrip? Lush Stop?
War Stop? Suicide Shit & Piss Stop?
Moonshine Sunshine Lovedove Stop?
Moonshine pickelbarrel Stop?
Moon-Shine Ketchup? Amsterdam? Moscow?
Who'll grow the first tomato, Brussel Stroup† Moon?


What'll the sound of the first Ambulance be?
        Like eating peanuts.

---

* As in Corso's "Don't Shoot the Warthog," *Mindfield,* p. 34.
    † Sprout. We kept errors of typing because they were delightful.
—A.G., May 23, 1992

In what year will the first Chinaman appear on the Moon?
And Christmas? Will it snow on Moon?
Who'll become Nostalgic on the Moon?
Will Brando? Is there road enough for his motorcycle?
Did Whitman Predict it? Will there be Neon lights—
Will some girl, 20 years after the moon, sign Jimmy Dean's name in
                the great Moonglow diary visitors book
Or will she sign 1716 Elm Street something Iowa—
But now it's no longer America
        Will the Pimp of Afghanistan
Stand on some mooney Street longing for banana?
Will Auntie be able to make good sauerkraut          *Certainly,*
        on the Moon?                                  *I would*
Who'll be the (first) Christ of the Moon. Christ Again!
Who's going to wear first hat on moon Billy Graham.
Can we conjure up a Kerouac on moon? Peter, Allen, Gregory,
                Neal?
Rogozhin? Alyosha? Jean Arthur? Guillaume? Dmitri? Walt?
                Edgar? Emily? Hart? Ezra?
Will the moon make demands?
Will it insist on ice cream,
Will it want its hollywood stars?
Can I throw my garbage on the moon?
Is it true each step will bound 20 feet on moon?
Will moon know a dead Garver?
Can I scream inside moon?
Will the moon want me? You?
Will they tell me I'm ugly?
Will it give me new vision of sun?
Supposing I commit crime on the moon, what will the moon do
                me? Give me to Mars? Throw me into the sun? Can I eat
                the moon? Is all possible on the moon?
Is god on the moon?
Is there a Tibetan restaurant on the moon?
Will I be scared on the moon? Yes?
Will there be anybody to talk to?
We know we're on the moon!
Ah, hm, is it possible to return to earth? Fortunately not.
Does my sad sad lonely father look up to me?

Is he looking tonight?
How strong be the pot of the moon?
Can I finally get rid my Meyers optic clene eyeglasses on the moon?
Will they send us girls!
I want squatters rights on the moon!
I want the old life!
I want to make drill sizes on the moon!
I want a bunch Cambodian laughing disease on the moon!
Laughter on the moon!
Wax light on the moon!
I want no pimples on the moon!
Will we finally meet and have high talks with the man on the
   moon?
Will we rub our lips on the Jersey belly of the cow?
Our manifesto! the Law! For the first man that goes up to hang?
Who'll be the first Wherewolf?
O I got the first Scheme now?
Will Dracula stay up all day Now?
Will we all be perpetually looney?
Will dogs weep and make up & Cry and become intelligent?
  All these because of a Russian satellite
Will the Coyote laugh at the earth?
Can I bring back a hunk of moon to the attic?
Will my father appreciate my gift of the Moon to him?
  At last?
oh! Dracula was always right.
Oh Music! Is the Spirit of Luna Park haunting the Moon?
The apparition of Rhygel's Roller Coaster? Be shuddering trans-
   parent tonite?
owl piggyboat, Kurt Weill, O Alabama,
  Is there a Little Rock on Moon?
Will I be Constant (as ever)?
Now finally will Moonface the Goof of Toledo be happy there?
Will we all be given automatic tuxedos?
on the Moon! on the Moon! Will we get hung, it was the easiest
   relay.
Moon I'm afraid of you? Moon I close all my windows! Moon you
   did me up wrong. Moon you're a ghost to me . . . always in
   my dreams, an antagonizing revoltist
Moon will I lose my appendix because of you?

Where you freeze my amputations?
Will that lady in Amsterdam with Black dog & her Rotterdam fur
    round her neck, and she's fat, will she be the first on the
    Moon—
or will that empty handed waiter be first?
What Color will the ticket man on the moon have?
Will he be a mysterious origin?

There must be no newspapers or empty beercans, no garbage stalls.
    Not in beginning.
Will Thelonious Monk belch on the Moon:
Candles & Fignewtons! What will you have?
Pabst Blue Ribbon? No that too corny?
There must be no interstate olfactor Intercontinental 3 Penny
    Opera on the moon—
We better stop writing what we're writing now and Pay homage to
    the Moon?
What kind of Jazz—Blue or yellow?
    Is monday called moonday (because in Dutch it's Moun-
        duch for Monday)
Will Sinatra be beautiful on the Moon?
What Color Ashtrays? oh god will it all be different?
Do wars grow old? We don't read on the Moon?
Is madness Prolific? Keep literature out of it, the Moon!
Let's not desert poor old Earth! Come back & see us sometime!
Let's not put all hope in the Moon because it could all be a big
    Mistake?
Maybe we'll never get to the Moon?
Women want babies on the Moon? Don't they want em here?
How many people are going to have to write automatic on the
    typewriters of the Moon?
The third front on the Moon will be the best?
The dark side of the moon hides grandmother's lost quarter on
    which is the face of god on reverse Praeger's cat*—
Is the Moon personally hip?

* An anecdote, told by Carl Solomon, about a madhouse inhabitant
obsessed with one "Praeger's Cat" which appeared to him in enormous-
scaled movie theater-screen green hallucination.

How high is the Moon? Does it have long dark Curls.
Is in love with Venus? Just a hole in sky? Is fairy?
Is only left hermaphrodite? What dirty pix on moon.
Does moon write pornographic Films,
      do Moon police take Bribes and
Will we destroy the Moon?
Did the moon have an abortion?
Got the Moon Clap? Does the Moon have to go home?
Is it a dunce? When is it going to fry eggs again?
The moon is as human as the sun
The moon is Pariah, square, untouchable, beat, stinks!
Is it named in Police Gazette?
Does it carry its identity Card around universe?
Can you describe it with eyes!
Does the Moon know the alphabet?
Would it be taken in Color?
Is red as black as green?
Who'll murder the Moon?
Can I buy a rifle there? We'll take all those Cans there & Pay for
      it—the Moon.
Will we marry cycle repairmen & own greatest repairman store on
      Moon?
Loony Pierre—Das Kranke Lune—
Will I put on someone else's coat on the Moon—
Can't wait till when I get to the moon till I see the neon the round
      plain the naked human gazelle crying with long hair and
      high Cheeks, running hill & dale 50 m.p.h. like a kangaroo
      like a jeep over nowhere land after trout.
Nor can I wait to see the sad angel of streets in his own personal
      alley, hands to face, wings covering all, weeping his heavenly
      woe, for lack of Ebbets Field scream.
Nor can I wait to see my picture, Painted by imaginary Railroad
      Conductors, laid flat along the Million-miled Track-way to
      the starry Cockroach!

The moon has got to accept us. The moon forgets Russia.
This is our Missile! We sent up our own! The poets launch our
      own!

Like a Jeep chasing Trout, See?                    *This would be the*
Quietest thing on the moon will be steps!          *weirdest poem*
loudest thing on the moon will be hair-do!         *possible if we were*
sweetest thing on the moon will be pink pasties!   *on Tea!*
Sourest thing on the moon will be unwarranted rockets & Yehudi
      unaccompanied.
And also violin orts! Her Majesty's technique will be accomplished
      on the moon!
There is no end to the madness of the moon!
Jan Vermullen of the moon! Hoar Vermullen, his crangy coat,
      before the absinthe gates of the moon!
Moon tour will count buses of Australian atoms!
There will be big deals with Ali Khan, his tie filled with diamonds
      on the moon,
            all his father's horses will be his on the moon—
he shall sell more horses on the moon! both here and in England
Five cents a toothpick on the moon!
There will be one crumpled hand on the moon!
Mummies in the sand—
Four desires! Moon!
Dreams of the moon on the moon!
Winter, I am on the moon, dreaming of the moon! . . .

* * *

## Oct. 17, 1957—9 rue Gît-le-Coeur, Paris

Hello . . .* are you there?—Where—In Paris What's happen-
ing . . . Hello, Hello?—Yes I can hear you—There—No I said
diamond Crystal Cadillac engine giraffe Bullseye Central light-
house ocean monster beefsteak poem bone. Alone? No with two or
three? What are their names? Peter and Peter. And Peter's friend?
Here. No I mean yes. Well speak up. Well that's a fine friendship.
Where will it lead? To the grave. Mercury shining lining the coffin.
Why be vulgar? A photograph of shit on a curbstone like a dead

---

* Ellipsis periods in this passage appear in the journal entry.

bird on a grey California rock.* It might as well be spring, I saw leaves falling under the streetlamps at night in Paris before it rained, it being October. And the room, the furnished room with 2 gas burners and the dingy mouldy yellow coverlet—the bed had two mattresses—it sagged a-middle—and Gregory sat writing at the round table by the black window hung with washed shirts, nylon and corduroy, we were neat, not like rats in nest. Over the roof, a large grey bird with rat's eyes looking for a piece of cheese—eater of holes—always went hungry. All the cheese was lost by the time the holes appeared.

Where do I stand in relation to

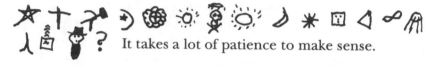

It takes a lot of patience to make sense.


Always went hungry, that's the ideal rule to follow—at the Crillon, at the Mills,† stay hungry. Spiritually hungry, growing old. The vines curl around my skull. I could not speak, for shame. My voice sounded too *me*. I leaned out of the window and implored the sky to take my consciousness away. But jump? I couldn't—too sudden and brutal, even to think of, when high—

And Dachau? How to escape the Seriousness—I want to confess to a secret confessor and not to the wide world. I'd be misquoted, I'd misquote myself, like a fool. I'd want to be a Hitler. I'd persecute Ubangis.

The whole house of cards would fall. No more gas, no more flies. Sandwiches would go hungry, hams would starve to death, the pavement would be littered with half-eaten corpses, the dogs

---

* A photograph aged Edward Weston, hands trembling with Parkinson's disease, brought out of a drawer to show author & G. Corso, who'd knocked on his door at south of Carmel, seeing his name on a sign on the coast highway down which they were hitching. —A.G., August 4, 1984. Ginsberg's account of his visit with Weston appears on p. 174

† Hotel Crillon—Expensive hotel—Paris? Mills Hotel—once flophouse on Bleecker St., N.Y. Author stayed there working in market research early 1950s. —A.G., August 8, 1984

proliferate with long hair—orangoutangs in Place de la Concorde, and Times Square full of runaway rats. I'd be given the boot quick. Some smart newspaperman would take over. Just in time, let the bomb come. As long as I'm not responsible. Nor there.

Well, Peter needs a shave. I need a bath. Gregory needs a new personality. The room needs a thicker wall—so we could yell at night and eat green butter on the wall. Is that a spider on the ceiling? A snail?

A snail that leaves a silver track behind. Peter looks like a great lousy bum. But don't make great monstrous noise eating those snails lest the neighbors who work all morning wake and gnash thru the paperthinwall.

I do not know, nor stop. Three small leaves at end of a branch. An iron foundry choked with soot, I only imagine words not visions of the inner eye. And the visions of the imagination?

* * *

## Oct. 20, 1957

Up to Sacre Coeur, standing on the balcony—rode up funicular, then walked up stairs glimpsing white domes, singing and happy—crying at first ascent to Montmartre—up Utrillo-veined avenues—Overlooked Paris a little after dusk, finally, it looked sunk under smoky dark river of 19th century, with gaslights and Balzac roofs poking out of the murk.

## Oct. 28—Paris Dreams

Downtown—Broadway—Paterson, the Lunch-shoppe of yore—however reinvented since it never existed, that lunch shop on Broadway—You go in, prices cheap—I'm given to understand it's expensive for lunch—2 or 3 goofy proprietors, an old woman on her magic uppers, an old man on his tragics, and the boys they hire to scrub the floors—which are all so wet I'm afraid to walk on them. But layer on layer of shelves full of delicacies, a super deli-catessen. Charcuterie best features of 1890 Yiddish Lower East Side, with rich Left Bank eat herring place. I walk in among grey barrels of herring juice, choose my meats, eat it, a sandwich and a few tidbits, and want more, but they say it is closed anyway soon and though they're going to give me more I go out, it's all dreamy and a drag, and

Next scene, the outside of a private home, black cats, babies, & some humped monster that would eat me up. It's moving around the building. I retreat at a crawl and watch thru binoculars afraid, get home to my 2–family Newark type house & knock for Louis to open, he does I go in, still watching down the block the tiger black monster appearing & pacing & disappearing—and other

areas and dreams—The hill in winter Haledon Avenue, the road to the little northern mts. for communist picnics.

*Later Dream:* Jack Kerouac enters living room, Lucien's, we're all there—except aint no rug, bare floor shiny, I'm sitting on it when he comes in all hale and robust and self confident—sits on bed, we talk ask about TV and radio—he looks blank but says "6 times" when asked how many radios he'd been on—I think well sure, he then explaining money, says he makes 2,000 a month, and part of contract ripens every 2 months, and he collects another 2,000, so his mother can collect and settle down whenever old loot runs out, he's set—she's set, I think certainly he's earned his perfect domestic scene, with his mother, a little living room and bedroom and nice house to live in, year after year dreaming and writing down his recollections of time and of America with and without his mother so now he has it all straight, he's won thru by his immense brown Rembrandt Industry—I sit there on the floor, on stool, looking down at my yellow thin shoes, feeling useless & a failure, I'll never have 20,000 for a book of poetry because I'm too lazy to write big millions of words of prose & be great artist. I wake depressed.

# Nov. 3—Junk

A dwarf approaches, appearing before curtained footlights, announcing "Dream of Dalí in Rags!" . . .

Exhibition, vernissage of Dalí's new creations in fur—on a Paris stage, Gorgeous hollywood Blondes, green haired, purple haired, illuminated in changing X ray dream-brite arc-lights, models parading in new surreal styles colored malachite green, neon chartreuse, shocking pink, very fine hairy furs delicate in the lights, artificial dyed longhaired fluffy lightweight, not smelly Dog Fur coats: Dalí's New Frisson.

\* \* \*

## Dream

With Natalie—we seek to wake Neal's corpse—can he be resurrected?—I find her in a hotel room in a building in Paris where we live—small grey room with small bed, phonograph, papers, books.

Saw Natalie-like girl in small room top floor Hotel—who sold Herald Trib. on streets—great job for dead Natalie.

\* \* \*

I been ill a week Asian Flu, Peter depressed putting down my cough, which keeps me up night after night irritated in left lung and throat, a raw spot that fanned by intake of breath, makes irritant cough till I cry. Once thrown up, my nose fills w/ water, my belly hurt first, now a strain in my right leg groin. Taking pills, Junk, sleep tablets. Fight it down & sleep dry mouth. Been in bed a week.

\* \* \*

Meanwhile Sputnik I and (today) II

Such a grand task, task of bitter onion.

And Spengler warned against pen and paint brush—in favor of slide rule & sea.

The new age more vast than Renaissance, Columbian, Elizabethan— ". . . each mild spirit,/New worlds to inherit."\*

American Destiny takes a fall—we all disoriented, since Whitman's prophecy defining American possibility, that America

---

\* From Blake's "Night" (*Songs of Innocence*).

surpass in beauty or else fall by wayside, be warned, among "the fabled damned" of nations.

Whitman (& Kerouac) full of cosmic references too.

We be downhearted in America as all along we were up-hearted.

It seems unimportant that it be America to surpass the earth, to moon, now that Russia has begun—As if America already had betrayed its promise of great spiritual victory—so now already's beggared materialistically.

What promise? To lead world to Fraternal Freedom full of comradely hip judgment. With this, as we surpass in poetry, to enrich world.

But Russia writes poem of moon first, a world even newer than America—and when the Chinese scientists get their hands on the sun? and weigh the Dao?

What betrayal? By not being free enough, & generous enough, and magical enough, by not going mad for joy in the world—the unsolved problems of the Blackmen South, all our eggs & wheat hoarded, all our science secrets kept, no Russian poetry printed, no Chaplin returned to Hollywood.

How write big universal psalm taken off from ideal promise of América when America now no longer the great hope of Mankind?

And if America is not that America, what is she?

* * *

[Lines following are a transcription of the draft of *Kaddish*, Part IV ("Litany"), written at the Café Sélect, as copied into Ginsberg's November 13, 1957 typewritten letter to Kerouac:]

Farewell
with long black shoe
Farewell
smoking corsets & ribs of steel
farewell
communist party & broken stocking
O mother
Farewell

with six vaginas & eyes full of teeth & a long black beard around
        the vagina
O mother
farewell
grand piano ineptitude echoing three songs you knew
with antient lovers Clement Wood Max Bodenheim my father
farewell
with six black hairs on the wen of your breast
with your sagging belly
with your fear of grandma crawling on the horizon
with your eyes of cxcuses
with your fingers of rotten mandolines
with your arms of fat paterson porches
with your thighs of ineluctable politics
with your belly of strikes and smokestacks
with your chin of Trotsky
with your voice singing for the decayed overbroken workers
with your nose full of bad lay with your nose full of the smell of
        pickels of Newark
with your eyes
with your eyes of tears of Russia & America
with your eyes of tanks flamethrowers atombombs & warplanes
with your eyes of false china
with your eyes of checkoslavakia attacked by robots
with your eyes of America taking a Fall
O mother O mother
with your eyes of Ma Rainey dying in an ambulance
with your eyes of Aunt elanor
with your eyes of Uncle Max
with your eyes of your mother in the movies
with your eyes of your failure at the piano
with your eyes being led away by policemen to ambulance in the
        Bronx
with your eyes of madness going to painting class in night school
with your eyes pissing in the park
with your eyes screaming in the bathroom
with your eyes being strapped down on the operating table
with your eyes with the pancreas removed
with your eyes of abortion

# LIBRAIRIE - PAPETERIE
# JOSEPH GIBERT

## SÉRIE
# STANDARD
## VELIN

*Paris*
*First Notations of Kaddish*

96 PAGES

## PAPETERIE SCOLAIRE
### TECHNIQUE - COMMERCIALE - GÉNÉRALE
### 30, BOULEVARD SAINT-MICHEL, 26
## PARIS-6ᵉ

Cover, Paris journal for poetry composition.
Inscription was added later.

with your eyes of appendix operation
with your eyes of ovaries removed
with your eyes of womens operations
with your eyes of shock
with your eyes of lobotomy
with your eyes of stroke
with your eyes of divorce
with your eyes alone
with your eyes
with your eyes
with your death full of flowers
with your death of the golden window of sunlight. . . .*

## Nov. 24, 1957

> How many mirrors assassinated in America
> Assassination of Poe, Crane, Lorca, Mayakovsky

* * *

## Elegy for Mama

Call Peter to come to the door! Open the Gates of Gold! X down
        from the Cross! Call Mary out of her Ivory Cloud! Call
        down the god out of heaven! Feet on the thundering
        Floor!
Call down the Trembling Lamb! Call on the Seraphs and Horns!
Call on the Horses of Heaven to drag out the Fiery Chariot and
        raise her on high in the palace of Glittering (absolute)
        (alabaster) Joy!
Greystone Greystone risen from New Jersey, lifted bodily the hos-
        pital up into the sky.

Her mouth is a radio
        Paranoia grandma

---

* Ellipsis periods appear in Ginsberg's letter.

# Elegy for Mama

Call Peter to Come to the Door! open the
Gate of Gold! X down from the Cross!
Call Mary out of her Ivory Cloud! Call
down the God out of heaven! Feet on
the Thundering Floor!

Call down the Trembling Lamb! Call on the
Seraphs and Horns!

Call on the Horses of ~~the~~ Heaven to drag out
the Fiery Chariot and raise her on
high in the palace of Glittering (absolute)
(alabaster) Joy!

Greystone Greystone risen from New Jersey, lifted
bodily the hospital up into the Sky

Page one, Paris journal.

Climbing up the outside
    apartment walls at night.
Mother, what should I have done to save you
    Should I have put out the sun?
    Should I have not called the police
    Should I have been your lover

Should I have held your hands and walked in the park
    at midnight for 60 years?
I am a poet, I will put out the sun.

Mother, after your death
    what can I do for you now
Come bearing armfuls of magic roses?
    Come visit your grave
and stare at the winter sun?
    Come visit your paid piece of earth
come visit your cunt in the dirt?
    Come visit the shades?

Down there, Aunt Elanor with feeble voice
    thin arms imploring
Sings arias from Norma by Bellini.

Down there Uncle Max
    Runs pharmacy of Moonlight
peddles dope of Styx
    worm antibiotics,
Silence hypnotics

Down there Aunt Tillie
    Will join you
With her loud voice
    Raucous laughter
Screaming at underground cabbage

Down there Louis, Eugene, Pinkus
    grandma 3 generations
I will come too, don't worry
    already I'm 31
Bald, mystic, my heart full of Cocks
    Death in the palm of my hand

—and find you?
    Naked, singing folk songs among the
    smelly tendrils of roots of trees?

We'll all be filthy angels,
Can't get the smear out of our mouths
going mad again underground

Will you have paranoia of walls
    where there are no walls
Will I write Metamorphosis
    with my heart eaten by ants?

"We become a leaf, a carrot, a cabbage."
I will become my imagination.

Bardo Thodol—were you screaming
    at a vast apparitional
        foamy mouthed giant
        at the end of space?

Mother Mother let me begin
    I'll explain in 6 languages
Dearie Cherie Amanti etc.
    Mother Mother!

Whenever I see the sea
    When I see the sea
O mother O mother
            Issa said

\* \* \*


Abraham laughing with his face in the dust

\* \* \*


All hail! All hail Heart! All hail home! All hail hallowed
    hallowed heaven!
King! Christ! Angel! Receiver! Savior! Comforter!
All hail high! All hail low! All hail hallelujah like the Lord!

Jacob—"How dreadful is this place! This is none other but the
house of God, and this is the gate of heaven." —Genesis 28:17

* * *

Jazz Mass for Mama

* * *

Song of Naomi
4 Big Sticks, 4 big sticks, 4 big sticks in my back
Wires in my head the ceiling is a radio

FDR is my mother-in-law Crawling in the window
I saw the Key, the sun in bars, sun is the key.

Now all is changed for me
and all is changed for thee*

Naomi

Worry until the brain breaks down
cerebral hemorrhage
I hear the heart torn out of the world.

* * *

Three of us lying in iron bed in dark night Paris December I awake hear them breathing the troubled souls unshaven, moneyless Gregory Peter sweating in nightmare—both to return to States to home—Gregory to what desire for apartment lamps evening books and music on the wall radiophone Bach—peace.

All breathing in bed troubled by time and by their birthdays the slow passage the boredom.

Is it a search for roots—for a home—I have no mother's belly left to crawl back to under the covers she's in the grave, she's a void—a longing for what was once not void but trembling weepy insane flesh.

All of us caught on the hook of the world, grasping in time for love for food for poetry for glory—love's cold poetry of glory.

---

* See Samuel Greenberg's "To Dear Daniel" in *Poems by Samuel Greenberg* (New York: Henry Holt, 1947), p. 45:
          Again the stain has come
          To me;
          Again the stain has come
          For thee.

And the world so small, the passage so fast, the grey rain, the wrinkle around the eye of the grave.

Should I go beyond Paris to the East in search of what—the drug of crowds and light of cities—

Yet back to Paterson I would be bored with the dentist next door the politician in gothic City Hall the days the babies the Morning Call and Evening News & slow watching die my neighbors myself and even love a slow burial of a glory.

What draws them to foreign cities, drugs, heroin cocks Marijuana the vision of satori of poetry or the grandnames of immortals the living tomb of books.

Illusory inspiration passed on to a youth in Chicago college or bum on the rocks in the West or a Desert Saint?

All sleeping in bed under the weight of Time wherein Fame is sought or Gold or love or imaginary Babe—but the soul aches for deeper pleasure than Time.

But there's no escape from Time but Death & no escape from the burden of Desire in Time.

The boys Gregory and Peter sleep I lay awake I rise and write but there is no escape from Time.

To take up the burden the poem return to Paterson wait out the years with enthusiasms of trees with poetrys of roofs appreciation of autos

But there is no escape from Time aging Dan Feitlowitz the Neighbor aging Dogs the agony of trees the change of buildings

The burnt library the old school the passage of Father the passage of Mother the passage of books of Jack of Bill

The passage of love of Peter passages of arms the passage of hair

No escape from the cats and dogs of emotion and motion in politics art.

\* \* \*

Allen Ginsberg, Gregory Corso, Corso's friend Ed
Freeman, Peter Orlovsky, Pont St. Michel, Paris.

Peter Orlovsky, Allen Ginsberg, double-sided bench,
Odéon, Paris, 1957. Photo: Harold Chapman

Peter Orlovsky, Allen Ginsberg, rue St.-André-des-
Arts. Photo: Harold Chapman

Gregory Corso, with "magic wand," Louvre post-
cards tacked to wall of his attic room, 9 rue Gît-le-
Coeur. Photo: Allen Ginsberg

Peter Orlovsky, Rimbaud portrait and Ginsberg
mirrored, chambre 25, 9 rue Gît-le-Coeur. Photo:
Harold Chapman

Cafe Bonaparte, Place St. Germain, Paris,
December 1957.

*"Ce Sadinet"*
Assis sur grosses fermes cuisses,
Dedens son petit jardinet?

\* \* \*

Shorn of birds & leaves the branch sticks out over the city

Eternity is a well in which a fool sees his own face.
(Yelling my poems down the hole.)

[First of two drafts of "Squeal," CP 165:]
He gets up, he liquefies he stretches, he is humiliated . . .

Now's time for prophecy
I do not shudder at the chill that
        passes between laughter and death
The wall . . . is too high, Apollinaire
        the vanished dead from . . .
        and my . . . curiosity,
I waited, pere Lachaise to see the remaining Apollinaire
The day the US. Resident vanished from France

after Grand confluence of phalanx state & plot
Confusing bomby tactics of the future war.
                Tobacco
Left it only Airport into blue winter day
a springtime clarity into the air . . .
                over boy Paris
& Let it be the airport of Blue only in the winter day
. . . grave'd, as . . . as an asylum smell
But the . . . illusory . . . buried
my foolish grave.

Paris Journal, beginning of what would become
Part I, "At Apollinaire's Grave."

[Draft of "Wrote This Last Night," CP 166:]


Listen to the tale of the sensitive car
Who was coughed up out of the earth in Kansas . . .


Not nature that torments us, it's man. The Dinosaurs are gone. Not death the torment—but the inachievement of Life— Chaplin holding the rose of poverty—and China tormented by our plenty.

* * *

# Now Time For Prophecy*

[Draft, of which the first ten lines are reproduced below, of Part I "At Apollinaire's Grave," CP 180–81:]


I do not shudder at the chill that passes between laughter and
      death
the wall is too high, protecting the vanished dead from my curi-
      osity.
I visited old Père Lachaise to see the remains of Apollinaire
The day† the U.S. president vanished from France
after Grand conference of Heads of state to plot

$\begin{bmatrix} confusing \\ confusy \end{bmatrix}$  bomby  $\begin{bmatrix} tactics \\ tobaccos \end{bmatrix}$  of  $\begin{bmatrix} the \\ some \end{bmatrix}$  future war.

Left at Orly Airport in the blue winter day
a springtime clarity in the air over bony Paris

So let it be the airport at blue Orly in the winter day
    and Eisenhower winging home to his American graveyard
But the illusory mist as thick as marijuana smoke buried thy
      freakish graves . . .

---

* This phrase, used in variation in "Death to Van Gogh's Ear!" (CP 168), is a fragmented quotation from a verse in Apollinaire's "Les Collines" ("The Hills").

† Eisenhower left Paris December 19, 1957, after meetings with NATO leaders.

* * *

# Images on Junk

Green walks on graveyard
Grass lives by graves
    Money lies in charnel

* * *

Green walks on Graveyard
Grass lives by graves
        Man lies in charnel
Day dreams bones
Bird sings in Heaven
Worm works in Earth
        Man smells of air
Truth is a worm.

Green walks the ground    green walks graveyards
Grass eats graves    grass eats ground
Man lies in charnel
Bird sings in heaven
Truth is a worm

* * *

Truth worms its way into the grave
Truth worming into the skull
Truth wormed its way into Apollinaire's thoughts
Where are you now Apollinaire, Apollinaire, Apollinaire?
It's very obscure. What World War Canticle?
Composed underground with Baudelaire in communication
        thru the sewer system & do you meet him there
is Max Jacob still amazed by you?

* * *

I cut off the ears of the bathtub
to make a poem.
I put on the multiple opera hats of Suicide
to make it rhyme.
I'll cut the ears off your grave

and the bathtub of mortality

a bathtub full of ears.
Eternity like a vast popsicle on the sea at Coney Island
and the great ice cream of heaven melting in the heat of summer
        graveyard.
Sand dunes of ferris wheels
bicycles of ice        white Bathers of Salt
dogs of flowers        Boardwalks of ice cream
    Stripes of consumption
        Come Union

\* \* \*

# The Fall of America

Wilson watched in a secret mansion across the street from the
    White House, dreaming in paralysis of the Fall of
    America—

and the battle over League of Nations, the clamor of politicians,
    apathy of the Mob—

Depression and the vast horror of Machinery stilled, an apple
    peddler one leg and Daemonic crutch in the Christmas
    snows of N.Y.'s canyons.

Dust bowl and Academy, Depression and the stark Red Skeleton
    preaching to intelligent crowds—

Einstein in America, sleeping in a cottage in Princeton, dreaming
    of bent light [bent Eternity] in the inevitable curve of
    Time ($E = \infty$)

Movies with rachitic dancing and famished Jazz—the creaky
    horrors of Frankenstein—New Year's in Hollywood

\* \* \*

1. Races—to be mix't
2. Wealth to be shared
3. Government to be international
4. No boundaries
5. No tariffs
6. No passports

America has fallen! has fallen!

\* \* \*

Scencs of Paris 1910—Was water the same grey, the Seine running
      onward in her medieval banks,
The lacy iron balconies in high apartments, mansards in the rain
      carriages and creaky taxis on the street
The Bateau Lavoir old rheumy and dark studios where you walked
      like a dandy to Picasso Jacob, Cendrars, Cocteau . . .
Did Andre Billy invent a new chic raincoat for your eyes?

Apollinaire Paris has changed over your body her wars sordid &
      desperate battles with Algerian beggars
Poetry dead only the flame of Artaud blows fitfully from the Char-
      nel lighthouse of Rodez*

It's to us where America falls into the same early century fright-
      ened drunkenness as France
That poetry passes with its sane compasssion for the vast pink
      marvelous pig of politics
and the marriage of the Bourgeois with a historical skeleton
And the manufacturers of politics with their Charnelhouse of
      perjured statistics
And the fat mob stupefied at television's cranked mirror held in
      the hands of mathematicians of illusion,
Celestial physicians making bombs as if the crazyhouse of matter
      were indestructible

\* \* \*

[Draft of "Death to Van Gogh's Ear!" CP 167–70:]

The poet must be priest because now the prophets of money have
      destroyed the soul of America
broken thru Congress to the precipice of Eternity
And the president has built up a war machine which will vomit &
      rear up Russia out of Kansas
And the American Century has been taken over by Franco mur-
      derer of Lorca and the mad Generalissimo Chiang Kai-
      shek who no longer sleeps with his wife . . .

---

* Rodez Asylum, where Antonin Artaud declared he had died during
electroshock.

* * *

I am the pavement you walk on unknowing unconscious
The pavement you tap with your red banded cane.

I hear the roaring of airplanes
        awful barking of the bombs
Barking & thundering race of fire
The wind that devours the windmill in its blast
The giant smoky radiant cloudy head of God
Bright blaring in the photographic smoke.

Two dogs barking in front of the store Xmas
Paris Mistral Bookshop Evening Candles

* * *

Smoke & songs & junk & wine
Hair and turkey & saddest
dogs of weekend overplus—
in Christly Science

## Sun Flower*

The "Sun-flower weary of Time" (soul's imagination rooted in material body) i.e., weary of its roots & bending on its roots to follow the foot steps of the sun walking across Time ("who count-est the steps of the Sun")

Time = footsteps of the Sun = motion of the sun in matter

"Seeking after that sweet golden clime/Where the traveller's journey is done"—the journey of the steps therefore the place where the sun's steps are going.

Youth & virgin desire *each other* (or maybe both desire other than matter)

---

* On William Blake's "Ah! Sun-flower":
  Ah, Sun-flower! weary of time,
  Who countest the steps of the Sun,
  Seeking after that sweet golden clime
  Where the traveller's journey is done:

  Where the youth pined away with desire,
  And the pale Virgin shrouded in snow
  Arise from their graves, and aspire
  Where my Sun-flower wishes to go.

* * *

The pure dark, good for soup.

* * *

## Dec. 31, 1957

My sink—long chain
       hanging over the side like broken
            neck of swan.
   Two toothbrushes, one sanitary paste
          yellow soap, a fork
   a grimacing mass of black abrasive pad for pots
       —noise of the cat of the hall
       lapping a can full of fish—
Sink in which I've washed my dishes
     of organic stew
my flowery salads, oils and cigarettes
      garbage of my eyeballs in the morning
      in which I've pissed
      and coughed up tars of mad tobacco
      and spat my bleeding gums
      and doused my burning feet
          and dipped my stinking hand
and washed my fat black balding hair
    —regurgitated ecstasy
      and thrown up junk and wine
      and washed my dirty underwear
O sink my sink white mouth of god
     Porcelain white coffin of the year—
And one day maybe yet will deliver
a final golden dream issuing from my mouth
the vision of eternity
for you to pipe back down
    to the faraway ocean of a New Year,
with fishhead nausea heroin mermaids bedsheet Ecstasy come of
     midnights
& Peter's fingernails & Gregory's hair onions of solitude
all but the bones I gave to the dog flowing toward the Poles.

* * *

## August 1956 (through December 1957)
## Reading List

Damien the Leper—John Farrow
Goethe—selections ("Wisdom & Experience" Pantheon 1949)
"John Custance"—Wisdom, Madness & Folly (The Philosophy of
        a Lunatic)
Bible—Old Testament, Genesis to Kings
Bible—all Old Testament & Apocrypha (parts of latter)
Henry Miller—Tropic of Capricorn
    ”      ”    —2nd pocket book on Morpion or whoever
Alfred Guillaume—Islam
Wicksteed, Joseph—Blake's Innocence & Experience
F. S. Fitzgerald—The Last Tycoon (& other stories, ed. by Ed.
        Wilson)
Ezra Pound—Selected Literary Essays
Poetry by—Creeley (If You); Olson (Maximus II); Ray Souster
        (Selected Poems); Frank O'Hara (selections from his
        mss.) John Wieners etc. etc. Joel Oppenheimer (Prod-
        igal Son)
J. L. Kerouac—Desolation Angels
            Tristessa
Burroughs—150pp. Interzone
Shakespeare—Romeo & Juliet
Lorca—Poet in New York (Bellitt, Grove)
Mayakovsky—Selected Poems—ed. Herbert Marshall Pilot Press
        London, 1945
Evergreen Review #1
Louis Simpson (1 of 3 Scribners—his 2nd bk)
Donald Hall—Poems; R. Wilbur—Things of This World
John Ashbery—Some Trees (Yale Poets Series)
John Hollander & Richard Howard—mss. poems
P. B. Shelley—Alastor
Thaddeus Zielinski—The Sibyl (Edge II)
Nahm—Selections from Early Greek Philosophy (Fragments)
Anacreon—Interlinear, reread
Horace—Book I & II, Interlinear

Paul Goodman—Break-up of our camp (parts)
                    Red Jacket & other Poems & mss.
Beckett—Waiting for Godot
Carl Sandburg—Selected Poems 1945 (Modern Lib)
L. Zukofsky—55 Poems; parts of *A* in mss.
                    Objectivist Anthology, etc.
Gary Snyder—complete mss. Myths & Texts & Riprap & Han-shan
Whitman—Democratic Vistas (Tangiers)
The Koran—parts

**France, Europe:**
Portable Melville (Jay Leyda), Typee
Beckett—parts of Watt & Malloy
Pound—Pisan Cantos
Mayakovsky—poems (translated to French, E. Triolet, 1957)
Esenin—French Translations (Confessions d'un voyou tr. by
          Miloslawsky & Hellens)
Shakespeare—Coriolanus
Blake—French Revolution & America
Williams WC—Kora in Hell
Jules Laforgue—Selected writings (W. J. Smith translation)
Prévert—Paroles (selections)
Artaud—Voyage au Pays du Tarahumaras
Penguin Book of French Verse
Apollinaire—Debauched Hospidar
Corso—Poems & Gasoline
Peggy Guggenheim—Out of This Century
Miller—Black Spring
Fowlie's Translations, Mid Century French poets
transition 1948
Turgenev—(a few from) Sportsman's Sketches
Evergreen II, III, IV
Pasternak—Selected Writings (ND)
Balzac—Cesar Birotteau
Chou Yang—China's New Literature & Art (Peking 1954)
The Biology of Schizophrenia—Mao Tse-tung
Khrushchev—Addresses on Literature
Peace Thru the Ages (translations of Chink poetry) Rewi Alley
Basil Bunting poems 1950 (Texas—Square Dollar)

Subterraneans—Kerouac
Baudelaire—Poems
Olson—Maximus Poems 2 vols
Creeley—The Whip, & All That is Lovely in Men
Pound—Active Anthology
Balzac—Cousin Bette
Oblomov—Goncharov (Parts)
Shakespeare—Timon, Coriolanus, Pericles, Cymbeline
Meditations in an Emergency—Frank O'Hara
Denise Levertov—Overland to the Islands

\* \* \*

But for the Millionth Time, Time and Eternity are only *words*.
Whatever concepts they once represented escape my Memory.
Much less the sensations that evoked use of such language.

\* \* \*

Last nite fucking Peter twixt the legs with his spit
 & mine, kissing him softly on the mouth
 over and over with each spasm as I came.

This notebook having become too unspontaneous
 I transferred to crazy writing in blue
 schoolbooks and will continue probably
 henceforth with loose poems rather than
 formal journal—which is now too narrow a habit.

\* \* \*

SUNSET OVER TURKEY

The gaiety of working on a poem

The gaulty of working one poem.

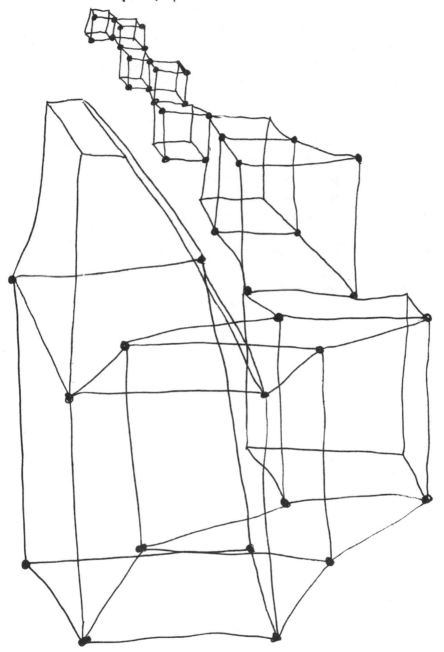

Journal page, January 1958.

* * *

When the typewriter with its unholy racket is silenced by the voice
    of angels
When we blow off the dust from the buildings of the great red
    volumes of history
When we are melancholy in the basement knowing the accom-
    plishments of 6 Centuries of Monkeys
Not even as satisfying as a fine sniff of profound junk or a long
    bath in the cocaine of finance—
Even in Mexico the vast statues gape wearily at their world of palm
    fronds and bananas
Even in Guatemala the natives have little enough chicken with
    their ecstasy
O exquisite negro of politics give back your ultimate towel of
    thoughts
And renew in my questionable beard the unquestioning absolute
    Black

* * *

"Celestial din"—dream or read it somewhere "Celestial din &
rattle."
    The expressions of Woe of bestial suffering on others' faces
in moments of my illumination were concomitant physiological
symbols of separation and division of consciousness

* * *

Naomi's white bones in a box digested by the graveyard.

* * *

        Funeral momma
        God National Anthem
        Greek lacklove bedsheet
        Scream dragon asshole
        Indian screech owl hoot
        American starry galoshes
        Black rhinoceros postbox

Monkeys is tables
Bedpans of vomit guitar
Moon library
Red beard building
Whoosh up scatter
Stars sparks thunder
Cranks of apocalypse rafters
burn burn burn burn

\* \* \*

## Jan 17, 1958

Peter Orlovsky sailed to Americay. Gare St. Lazare with Bill
5:35 Friday Evening—pernod & chocolate in café—Peter and I
kissing at station.\*

\* \* \*

## Adaptations of Sergei Esenin's Poems†

Song of the Bitch Dog
One morning in a barn
Where the hay was goldened
A bitch gave birth put below
Seven little red dogs

Till Evening she caressed them
Combing them with her tongue
And the snow melted
Trickling away under her warm belly

And that evening when the hens
Climbed up to sleep on their perches
Came the gloomy somber farmer
Who put all seven in a sack

---

\* In a 1979 note in SHD (p. 130), Ginsberg recalls: "Peter left me . . .
with tears in his eyes thinking of his brother Julius. . . ."

† Poems that follow are Ginsberg's rough literal translations from
French versions of Esenin's Russian poems as found in Franz Hellens and
Marie Miloslawsky's *La confession d'un voyou* (Paris, 1922).

The mother ran in the snow
She tried to run after him
Longtime longtime the water trembled
Under the broken ice

When she dragged herself back
Licking the sweat of her sides
The moon under the eaves
Seemed to be one of her pups

And she looked into the blue height
With loud howls
The crescent glimmered thin
And hid behind the hill

And heavily, as when
Someone throws a stone at her for a laugh,
The eyes of the bitch roll
Two stars of gold on the snow.

*  *  *

All that lives with a particular sign
Is marked too soon
If I were not a poet
I'd be a bandit or thief

Thin and small
Always hero among the boykids
Often often I came back
Home with a broken nose

Meeting my frightened mother
I muttered, mouth full of blood,
"It's nothing I was hit by a stone
It won't show tomorrow"

And now that it's frozen over
The boiling of that day
A restless crazy force
Marks up my poems

Words group in heaps of gold
In each verse and no end
To reflecting the old boldness
Of daredevil and dirty mouth scamp

Like always I'm nuts and proud
Only my approach is new
If once they busted me in the mouth
Today it's my soul's bloody

Now I no longer tell my mother,
But a foreign jeering mob
It's nothing I got hit by a stone
It'll be gone tomorrow.

\* \* \*

I am tired of living in the land I was born,
Wheaty space enorms in my desire
I will leave my cabin there
I'll make myself barefoot a thief

I will go on the curly hair of day
Look for my poor domicile
And on me my beloved comrade
Sharpens the blade of his knife

The yellow road, by the plains,
Is surrounded by sun & springtime
Someone whose name I'll keep quiet
Will chase me from his doorstep

I'll come back to the fatherly roof
I'll console myself with other's joy
And by a green dusk, with my sleeve
I'll hang myself under the window

The grey willows near the hedge
Will lean their heads more tenderly
And they'll bury with hounds howling
My body which won't have been washed

And the moon'll float out
Letting its beams fall on the lake
and like before, Russia'll continue to live
Dancing & weeping near the hedge.

\* \* \*

On the water the reddish pond
Whirlpool of golden leafage
Like a light flock of butterflies
Flying timidly toward the stars

I am amorous of this twilight
Near my heart is the yellow plain
The adolescent wind has lifted up
To the shoulder the birch tree's dress

In the soul, in the valley, a fresh chill
A bluish fog like a flock of sheep,
Behind the door of the calm garden
The little belfry stretches up and rings

Never again with so much economy
Will I listen to reasonable flesh
How good to be like the willow with its branches
Hanging over the roses of the pond

How good it would be smiling on the haystack
To eat the hay with the mouth of the moon.
Where are you, where are you, my tranquil joy
of loving all without any desire?

\* \* \*

I'll go like a humble monk, in skull cap
Or like a yellowish vagabond
There where the milk of birchtrees
Runs in the valleys

I want to reassure the corners of earth
Confiding in a problematic star
And believe in the happiness that'll follow
In the furrow swishing with grain

The cool hand of dew
Cuts down the apple of morning
Raking the hay on the prairies
Mowing machines sing me their songs

Happy who in a humble joy
Without friends without enemies
Will make a path between villages
Praying before the shackles of wheat.

*  *  *

## Feb. 1, 1958

**To London***


*I*

    Leaving Paris train Calais Dover, Gypsy musicians with tambourines & violin in the civilized green carriages, outside thru the foggy windows—a white mist over Northland and frost on the winter bushes—passed the gray stations in the woods, where ancient battlefields sleep & bones freeze under no foot walker now the brown leaves of winter have fallen in midcourse along the track bushes upstarting knee & waist high in front whitening their tips and tendrils.

    The white placid sky. Clack of train. English beardboy sleeping (Hugh Grace, the Grove, Fair Mile, Henley on Thames, Oxfordshire), Australian and Espanol dozing, High bridge, a thin river foggy below. Zigzag of the violin in the next compartment.


O Blake! Blake! Blake! the yellow sun spangling spanning the
        green winter channel
the Fog—how sad you'd be to see the dense human fog o'er
        London now,
the winter of Mankind

---

    * Part I of this entry contains a draft of an untitled poem published only in SHD, pp. 138–139.

Green water, Dover's cliffs, houses above. Silence boat motor stops, squeal of gulls afar, as if the cliffs squeaked. The long green dusty 2nd class train at Dover.


I am (not yet these properties) Allen Ginsberg arriving enchanted
          in England
weeping at the foggy earth of England's Blake
a body and a consciousness with the roar of Babel
and groan of armor round my head & thighs
clanking in the railroad car amphibrachs of misery
destined for London—where my bliss in all the smoke
may shine brightly like a sudden sun
If I walk around naked minded in the yellow horned traffic
as one with Shakespeare and dead Shelley & bright Blake
Remembering the cankered geniuses of sidewalk history
mortal & mindless in the maze of ancient cranes and girders
faces glaring with the broken consciousness of roofs, smoke,
          chimneys, windows, churches, rows of lights
faces of historied propertied war—and the great bleak acrid fog of
          lacklove mindstrain
reddening eyes with rusty tears and twisting mouths like iron.
—but bah why strain the dream on that bleak skyscraper—
Worldsmasher, smash yourself!


## II

Here in Worcester
my mind alone in the dark
with all other minds
          alone in the dark . . .
drest in red underwear
          barefoot on a Persian rug . . .
I am alone and
          want (make) music . . .
Being alone—Might
          be the music itself? . . .
Nervousness
          as 3 cups of coffee
               awaiting the loved one . . .

There are no monsters here . . .
         —but myself
am I a monster?
         morbid question
I   FEEL   LIKE   A
         MONSTER

Feeling the silence
         Tick of my Ingersoll
         watch on the table
         loaded with books . . .
         motionless, stationary
                  rug and a wall
I stare at my pants
         my body

         the floor . . .
     the floor thinks itself out flat in squares of brown cork
stretched out like a flat cat . . .

Like looking at the sea,
         or Shakespeare's grave.
or Hamlet with a skull
         puzzled sitting there
         three centuries,
                  iron statue in Stratford
         staring with brass eyes
                  into the bony eyesocket.

What is he waiting for?
         Figuring out the Universal riddle—
like worker with pipe who stares at
         the endless British sewer.


## III


         I dreamed to be here
                  (the great dream of space)
         from a sky tower looking out over London—
                  St. Paul's black dome
                  at my feet
         floating over the iron-burnt river.

A clear day:
The glassy Thames, the Bridge piers
        black & small below me
        with catwalk between towers
        white crowned at the top.
Red and white cars creeping down
        Fleet street by the new
        curved building
        and holes in the city floor
           where the bombs
                10 years ago, 15—

One clear hammer far below repeating
        its blows, iron girders
        half finished squat office buildings
        sticks of lumber, toothpick
crowds of cars on asphalt fields, green grass
           asymmetrical parks & sundial concrete walks
Haze
Fading into the Haze
        clouds, blue sky, a stream of smoke
        from a faraway factory
        or steel Locomotive—
high empty smokestack
           tower on the
    East End horizon
        haze & oblivion.

Millions of miniature churches
        peaks, weathervanes, roofs,
flats, construction skeletons

    across the river—
Another square smokestack
        with a head of white steam
        boiling out & flooding the
        sky, disperst in hazes—

Barges on the river, docks
        crown'd at water edge
Cars passing over London's Bridges, boat

whistle and Brakes' screech hammer
thump, roar of tram across
Thames far down like a worm
crawling out a hole in the
                    building side
Bonk & crack of hollow wood
            construction
Vast clear sun
            above blue smoke overhanging
            the crystalwork myriad
                        black roofs
A star gleam reflecting off the steepletop

Houses of Parliament, the little baby British
            Flag aflying its height,
graduated spires clustered nearby
The sun above glimpsed over the
            whole spreading city
Raying down, burst of clock
            bells over St. Paul's Dome
over the city

The sun slanting down
            against the flat front
            modern white building
                Daily Express Fleet Street.

                    *  *  *


Therefore I prophesy the Fall
                of America
Bitter bitter tongue
                to tell thee,
Divinity in us that
            survives the temple
            of Athens & Forum of
                Rome & waste
                of Halicarnassus
                & Palenque—

the Fall of America accomplished
     in peace or ruin
Fall of Love, Inundation of Flood,
     of starvation
agony of outsized automobiles
     Jeeps bewrayed by necessity
Anger seeking a bone of machinery
China, Persia, India, Greece, Afghanistan
America where art thou in the Mighty
     wrack of the world?

\* \* \*

[First draft of "Europe! Europe!" (CP 171–73) appears in original journal, with numerous additional drafts of its last verses. One sample of the latter is included below, following the three opening lines. Included as well are two of several drawings by Ginsberg of Dover Channel seascape, illustrating the main visual image.]

World! World! World!
I sit in my house
and imagine the future . . .

It is that death comes
before life, that no man
can love perfectly, can get
his bliss in Time that new
Mankind must be born
to herald the millennium
that comes like the giant sun
rayed down from a vast cloud
at Dover on the sea cliffs
tanker size of ant heaved
on shiny oceantop beneath
the cloud a seagull flying
thru god light's endless
ladders streaming in Eternity
to ants in the myriad fields
of England Dolphins in
Mediterranean Rainbow

* * *

Last nite after I wrote
this poem I slept
with cat all night
and saw a vision in dream
I looked down on Earth
at night from a steep mountain
I wandered among farms
met boy his parents were
down below in the valley
I saw the sides of rivers
Thames or Hudson eaten
by gleams of fire the
Cities of Man burning
Far down below me
Fire and Brimstone nibbling
The banks of the gleaming river
Thin streaks of fire inland
amid forests where cities lay
That I had known before
The night of Apocalypse
But there was no Christ
Myself and the farm boy
in paths on the steep
side of mountain no memory
of the world on the other side.
We have had this dream before
Tho I look out my window
in the afternoon dark alley
a man loads a coal truck
There's no dread correspondence
yet I believe my imagination
tho it be my doom—
there was mental dream
which this poem incarnates
into a prophetic nut
to crack open for light.

* * *

# Feb. 29, 1958

Last nite I dreamed of T. S. Eliot
welcoming me to the land of dream
Sofas couches fog in England
Tea in his digs Chelsea rainbows
curtains on windows, fog seeping in
the chimney but a nice warm house
and an incredibly sweet hooknosed
Eliot he loved me, put me up,
gave me a couch to sleep on,
conversed kindly, took me serious
asked my opinion on Mayakovsky
I read him Corso Creeley Kerouac
advised Burroughs Olson Huncke
The bearded lady in the Zoo, the
intelligent puma in Mexico City
6 chorus boys from Zanzibar
who chanted in wornout polyglot
Swahili, and the rippling rhythms
of Ma Rainey and Vachel Lindsay.
On the Isle of the Queen
we had a long evening's conversation
Then he tucked me in my long
red underwear under a silken
blanket by the fire on the sofa
gave me an English Hottie
and went off sadly to his bed,
saying ah Ginsberg I am glad
to have met a fine young man like you.
At last, I woke ashamed of myself.
Is he that good and kind? Am I that great?
What's my motive dreaming his
manna? What English Department
would that impress? What failure
to be perfect prophet's made up here?
I dreamt of my kindness to T. S. Eliot
wanting to be a historical poet

and share in hi finance of Imagery—
overambitious dream of eccentric boy.
God forbid my evil dreams come true.
Last nite I dreamed of Allen Ginsberg.
T. S. Eliot would've been ashamed of me.

\* \* \*

## Hypnagogic Automatic Writing Shakespeare Junk

"Berowne is like an envious sneaping frost"\*
that holds the fields in fief and never bears
one harvest of the snow to trickle thru the dirt
and sow the grass of industry between the rocks.
The mounts the seas the rivers and the springs
conjoin in water to bear up the flood
and there is not one petrel down from heaven
to whom the worm will turn in Daisylike desire
tho Sunflowers do seek suns, yet suns sun sons
of roses, bats and snotnose children of the ground,
daughters of violets and Empire's cousin chrysantheme
all crystal, crownly, golden tinged and sere
wise natures all spurn heaven at the price of Blood
So blood blood bothers and the progeny design
betrayals in the incest back and forth on hallowed sheets
Let Sheba be prepared to give accounting sweet
to Solomon of all the murderous parents she bore out
Before her throne was sat on by as royal pair
of buttocks as on Egypt's seat have shone.
Let cockcrow crown the buttocks of my Pete.
Repeat performance dream alone of that
Sweet death has nothing to repair
This life has seen the ass millennium
If could I but come at pricking of his breech
All would be heaven, but the joint's accursed
Cops paw in the windows of the eye, the skull rebels
and sets its thought out in the prowl cars of illusion

---

\* See *Love's Labour's Lost*, 1.1.100.

the streets resound with gunfire, windows
flash with knives, bombs go off in the office
of the soul: rebellion murder, incest power
rape authority, blood whips and mocking,
starving tears and meat of victory are mine.
Is this confession earned in sight of God
by me whose eyes have witnessed the final bliss
Can I have been mistaken and gone mad
or lost my path to beauty in such way
that now I cannot separate the strands of gold
from strands of wool or haircloth punishment
from my own robe, my flesh is torn and bald
my aches my body but my brain is reeled
& know not what I am or meant to be
nor know the future that I thought would be
the shining livid action of eternity
to rescue me to rescue me the broken
phonograph record of the soul the faded
photograph destroyed by too much light
the brain conceived and unconceived and
loosed on the swell of Time. I cannot
follow thought no longer—I am broke
apart my effort is not enough I am
lost I cannot write a poem I am
Judged for Judging toppled from my pride
bewrayed betrayed by my own stupe ambition
wanting to pine in El Morocco envying
Sinatra in the ballroom of the Ritz
Cursing Herbert Hoover in the Waldorf's top
isolation—I am gooned, gone, high
bright handsome dying blank & slow
not like F. Scott Fitzgerald but eccentric
XXth century jewboy gone against the grain
and mad in Jersey I repent, repent, have lost
beat down can't sing can't think cant even
make a line lite or conclude with a ryme.

\*   \*   \*

Yesterday Heisenberg's development of Theory of Matter was announced in papers.

\* \* \*

You America, Faggot, Pimp, whore, drunken soldier, America,
        you bitch
Thief! Exploder of Bombs! Idiotic panhandler of sympathy! Ad-
        vertising man!
Drunk, braggart, Lyncher, still haven't got rid of your Gas Cham-
        bers and Capital gallows—
Well might the negroes uprise and tear apart your electric chair,
        inspired by Chinese poets—
Much to answer for—betrayal of Whitman, the fate of Garcia
        Lorca, death of Hart Crane the murder of Poe
        bereavement & lacklove of Melville
The Frosty countenance of Emerson & frigid pond of Thoreau,
        Longfellow driven mad with anapestics—

Ach! Where to begin to list your crimes! The blood on Franken-
        steen's torn white shirt in old photos* in newspapers
Innumerable sharpers, skinflints graspers lambless meateaters
        elected & rolled into office, Congress, Army, poor-
        house, women's institutions, Presidency,
The worst of them Eisenhower maybe a soldier accustomed to
        the abstract thought of blood.
Ah! Ah! You have much to answer for and I will ask all the ques-
        tions.
I am no scared criminal witless and unsympathetic weeping in
        the precinct chair under yellow light
stared at horrified by idiot Italian detectives of reality
Jew bums with clubs, niggers drunk with revolvers of Niggerhood

---

* Pulitzer Prize-winning *Detroit News* photo of Walter Reuther & Vic-
tor Frankenstein, beaten by Henry Ford's strikebreaking goon detectives
at gate 4 of Ford's Rouge plant May 26, 1937. A Mr. Harry Bennett was
head of Ford's "Service Department," "The world's largest and most
brutal plant police force." See the description of the "Battle of the
Overpass" in John Barnard's *Walter Reuther and the Rise of the Auto Workers*
(Boston: Little, Brown, 1983), pp. 51–52.

Pure blood anglandaises in sexless stupor of Right and Wrong!

Brandishing official machine guns, rulers, tape machines charts
    and whiskey & chocolate eclair, mad virgin spinster high
    school teachers All!

Traumatizers! Perverts! Mayors who rub their cocks with money!
    Automobile Salesmen who kick bums in the dark

Trickle of urine from doorway plate glass to the curb, moonlight
    shining on the spatter of blood

and some poor soul in the summer night ain't got no old ghost
    house to home in,

You might as well be dead as sell your soul down the river to the
    Parent-Teachers organization

What do you think I'm complaining about? What do you think of

America, you who run America, make Foreign policy, School board
    schedules, appoint aldermen or football coaches—

you who therefore are America, the land that opens its mouth to
    speak

With 40 billion dollars armaments and mere piddling saliva 4
    billion Foreign aid

and most of that Bombs and horror for South Korea! Fraud and
    Chiang Kai-shek Formosa's lost cause fear!

Leaving perhaps 200 million dollars in all the world to feed India

stabilize the industrial metabolism of China, help Russia goof
    behind the Urals, irrigate Sahara, etc. etc.

And what money will be spent this year on Heisenberg's discovery
    of the flash of God!

Or will you, having free will, conspire with Russia to destroy God too?


Answer! Answer! I demand answer! I speak in the name of Him
    who didn't start World War I nor win it, nor won World
    War number III,

in the name of Him who gave his mercy to India while the West
    held on to your photo potatos & wheat

In the name of him who didn't give France half billion to continue
    the war in Algeria!

Him who didn't fear McCarthy nor Madison Avenue!

Him who owns neither automobile refrigerator nor cheap gold
    house fake rug fake China fake

underwear fake marriage and fake fuck!

I never heard such bullshit as spews out of the newspapers radio
        television
lying and cheating billboards, commercials, censored movies, fat
        politics, screaming and anguish of money!
Production for money! Work for money! houses, food, art for
        money! Money instead of love!
Dollars above love! Anguish trembling ulcer, knives and evil
        memos for money money money
Crime against nature Contra naturam and Pound in the madhouse
        knows about money!
There is no money in Eternity and no man who is holy has money
and if no man is holy it's because of god damned money
Worship of Baal-Zeebub, Moloch, gold Satan, divided conscious-
        ness
broke motive, abstract value, gathering of inequality and pride
in the evil green dollar that all men in America break their hearts
        for or die.
Poe! Crane! Sacco! Vanzetti! Abominable black murder of con-
        sciousness.
There's but one soul in America and that's the soul of the Ancient
        Lamb
and all else is riot and bullshit, revolvers and gangsters, politics and
        war,
And virgins of fear with blue laws, laws against fairies, & criminal
        laws against junk
Conformists in clothes with alcohol jobs, prestige stars in Holly-
        wood not excepted
Even poetry is perverted by mad seeking bought betrayed news-
        paper reporters asking mundane loaded questions—

Ah! I am sick of talking of these, and will turn my face to the
        Angels.
For there are boys of sweet delight that stand on corners with no
        revolvers and a flower in hair and nothing to do,
and there are poor paid bureaucrats who work hard & go home
        weeping over red tape that's destroyed a woman a week,
and there are criminals in jails penniless that know the suffering of
        Peter at Cock Crow,
and attendants in psychiatric Institutes that have care for the
        damaged soul of Brooklyn Joe,

—and a few good Hollywood stars who have nervous breakdowns
     for sincerity reasons.
This is a sample list I could name a million
but the good jobs are hard to find as a dollar paid for useful work
     that gives the poor an ear of new corn
Sure, millions of alrightniks making it, trying to pursue a life
Tho they subscribe to capital punishment, adjustment psycho-
     analysis, schoolroom lies about sex
But think of the Cops! and the Army! and Politics! And the whole
     auto industry making breakable cars! and I repeat the
     damned ad business!
And think of the F.B.I. and all the queer Senators and mad repre-
     sentative & constituents
approving the Chinese Exclusion Act, bans on erotic literature, the
     Japanese concentration camps in California,
death penalty for drug fiends, cold war on communist growth,
     helping hand to Arabic Spanish and South American
     monster dictatorships!
thus've helped cultivate mad mental dictatorship in Russia
by our capitalist adamance, merciless misery of consumption pro-
     duction and property
—Why years ago we should have opened the gate of Freedom and
     Milk and Honey
Partaken with negroes and chinks manufacturing foodstuff de-
     lights & autos in Nigeria,
Lhasa should have received our emissaries of algebra & relativity.

It's a long long list to come but I'm only beginning—
It voids my mind to think of the break of the future bomb.
America is fallen, is fallen—ah the horror wreck of all that ego
     money in its mad black structure toppling into the night

\* \* \*

Mental cancer—homosexuality

\* \* \*

[From letter to Gregory Corso:]


London Under the Sun: I saw the whole
    City under a blanket of fog and
    the smokestacks huge four towers
    on the horizon boiling out steam and smoke
    into the atmosphere
        & above all that

the yellow sun steadfast raying a mile below
    one down on a modern building front
    leaning out in Fleet St.-Bend
Streams of light reaching the building—
I saw both sun and city floor in one vast eye
    (glance.)


\* \* \*


And now the Bureaucracies of Russia and China squatting on the
    horizon shitting on the sun.
Vast hordes of doubletalking mental cowards, souls gnashing their
    teeth at the voice of dawn
hands that "do not tremble at the pistol," voices that brag a pre-
    conceived mental system
Steel cold eyes, humorless, 2000 years of starvation in that poem of
    mechanical corn,
Mao Tse-tung the Sender, Khrushchev the Sender Stalin the
    Sender of Black Horns of Siberia
Communists of the next world which will be overthrown with the
    Squeezure of a million bodies
and an endless river of weeping blood over the rocks of the Mind
and who will be the next Dictator of the Soviets to announce the
    mass shift of Consciousness to a crosseyed Messiah Dam?
What hydroelectric fraud will sphinx the characters of 200 million
    red lovers?
How much loveliness in Russia! What lacklove in China! What
    solitudes for the great poet of Green Dynamo!
Enough that america in the grip of refrigerators will crucify a black
    man or a red—

Enough two parties here that worship a fake god in a human church
that America beams and blares in the night in a car of thin metal
              that'd collapse at the touch of the shyest birch tree,
America brainwashed in solitude, peddled 3¢ ideas in newspapers
              writ by cigarette ulcer reporters
Crusading for tariff the crown of thorns Chinese exclusion act the
              heart of Christ
Left hand the nail destroying the League of Nations right hand the
              nail invasions of Communist Russia
Spike in the foot 600 million dollars French aid to continue the war
              in Algeria.
Enough television sets in foreheads, mechanical crucifixions, Mass
              starvation of India
an item buried back page in John Q. Public's last year's comic book

Surplus value goes to heaven in an autocar driven by John F. Dulles
              in raiment of shining fallout
300 billion dollars in 10 years to obsolete bombs, Arabian
              slaveholders, cigar smoking Geeks with blue cocks
They want everyone in on the act, robots, no wonder the teenagers
              riot in movies
and scream at their death-rates toothy imprecations of switchblade
              jazz
Fuck you! America once more, and Fuck you Russia
Bourgeoisie of America and Bureaucracy of the land of forgotten
              Dostoyevsky
And fuck you China too I will not be brainwashed
though 400 million solitaries daily receive the holy rice and bloody
              sandwich of official religion
God knows what solitaries stink on the banks of the Yellow River
              not yet shot
Grubbing in the mud of humanity for one single toad of honest
              embarrassment
What few eyes flash in China longing for Reprieve
from the palefaced executioner with his excuses learnt from books
mouthing propaganda against Soul, frightened of shadows,
              naked in winds of Northern Doctrine,
while disgusting literary garbage of Mao Tse-tung's taken for glo-
              rious Aurora Borealis and plasmological one manna.

Yenan Literary Conference be damned! If your society made that
        mistake, I put you down, I stamp on you
I don't care if you solve your food problem, your citizens are a
        bunch of hungry beasts
feeding the maw of Self with dialectics for lightless Blakeless war,
Warlock Zombies you are, Satan of Chinese boredom without
        mystical opium laughter
Down sex! Up work! Down mad! Up fear! Down love! Up necessity!
20 million frightened shriekless souls in the Gobi of Unreality
        preparing for the wrath to come,
Ah for the bomb! that you will set yourself to blow up China with us
        400 million coolies of the abstract
16 hundred million arms and legs flying upward like flies or the
        words of Marxism-Leninism raining from the sky in
        cheap editions.
Ah for the bomb—it will destroy the lamb too—ah for the bomb!

* * *

There is no hope in the future for peace between countries
nations races man and man.
        Where selfhood cancers soul god stays up on cross—bullet
knife or bomb or economics.
        Ugh—what social fantasies

        In the beginning is one man, myself, to change or ruin—joy
or death.
        I have a friend: faithful and kind and just
        and in my friend I find my peace & kind.

* * *

        The joy of two boys in a bright garden
        —a shrunken skull buried under the grass

* * *

        Ghostly Mussolini in an enormous room of Palazzo Vecchio
        Sad Hitler walking in the crags of Berchtesgaden with his
head wrapped in dynamite
        Six million Jews melting into the soil of Europe

Dachau, now the ash strewn walks green grass and rusted ovens and solitude.

* * *

Green banks of dynamos, smoke boiling into the sky
Arcades of steel transformers, brick labyrinths enclosing a radium pit
Jet planes ribbons inching a mile long in Tangiers sky,
Electric meadows, spools, stakes, wires, red and blue lights in the fields outside L.A.,
Silver gastanks floating at the edge of the hills by the haunted water,
Tankers tied up at night on a narrow pier with green light feebly blinking at the railroad track's end
The sadness of God to exist in that green light in San Pedro,
No human voice singing blues, soul in the soulless harbor-side silence,
I remember many industrial landscapes flashing by the years,
many docks and shipyards, long walks by huge silent anchors strewn out on the asphalt, rusty for repainting.

* * *

The yellow dirty bedspread,
          my red socks
hanging over iron head frame,
          a soiled blue towel,

Time, Shakespeare, Oblomov
          Zigzag, shirt & Observer
on the delicate thin legged
          bed table by plaster wall—

I lying in bed, rotten
          sweet sadness at heart,
alone, a grippe in my chest
          —ah, Paris, Tomorrow

if I should meet the boy I love
          or see bright face of sun
over the silver overflowing river
          I'd go out of my skull.

\* \* \*

## Making the Lion for All It's Got—
## A Ballad

I came home & found a lion in my room . . .
[First draft of "The Lion for Real," CP 174–75.]

\* \* \*

A lion met America\*
in the road
they stared at each other
two figures on the crossroads in the desert.

America screamed
The lion roared
They leaped at each other
America desperate to win
Fighting with bombs, flamethrowers,
knives forks submarines.

The lion ate America, bit off her head
and loped off to the golden hills
that's all there is to say
about america except
that now she's
lionshit all over the desert.

\* \* \*

The publicity loud blares
the magazines repeat my name
I am a hero of the Abstract.
Should I sit on lilypads?

---

\* A little imitation of Stephen Crane's "In the desert/I saw a crea-
ture, naked, bestial." —A.G., April 21, 1987

Failure failure drunken failure
Idiot ego brays in my ear
but having no soul to hope with
all I can do is listen to the radio.

I wish I could write great poem
Examining the flight of sun ray
between heaven and the human face
and prove that we're constantly watched.

But I've seen not birds but humans
fall in fields of shining blades
and stainless steel cut the neck & back
of my mother as well as tender kitten.

I would I were not that harvester, machine
I hate so much; but cities must eat
Someone must work & kill the worm
the great Industry of harvest must smoke

Back to my own face in the mirror
Bald head & lacklove, screwing men
afraid of terror or boyish excitement

Behold me in mirror bald head lacklove
screwing boys scared of marijuana
afraid of terror or boyish excitement
dreaming of poetry year after year.

* * *

# First Day of Spring in Paris 1958

The zonked sky was blue, clouds waggled over the roofs
We walked out—Bill and I, glen plaid and turtleneck, to the post
        office at 2 PM
met Lee, sober, he's always drunk at 3 AM—asking for money at
        the International window from Denmark

also there the rose cheeked german gestapo boy who just picked
             up on T and Lee & lush and Leather Jacket
and a Turk from Minneapolis—and Egyptians from Indonesia
             sneezing dice.
Then down St. Germain to the old navy, Gregory sitting inside
             talking to some new French girl bluecoat red hair with a
             big pocket book,
Outside a group, Iris* with raincoat and notebook of Olympia
             pornography
Louis with mustache who's leaving for America next week Chicago
A negro named Money who's leaving tomorrow
Al Levit "The Shades" drummer who saw *Shane,*
Someone else someone else,
Then took off for Luxembourg gardens
             and met the cowboy guitarist† (old lover
             from Helen Parker) who got left on the boat
                           when Ansen went to Europe—
I had the spectre of homosexuality walking with me on the street
I kept catching myself making sly references to men-women con-
             soling the Greeks in the sunlight
                           listening to pederast Burroughs
                           expatiate on schizophrenia
             he walking shy hand-a-pocket
Talking to Man I am mad I can't even remember their names
             Maurice upstairs the one called "Foggy Hipster"
                           who argues about sanctity also wears shades—
I talking with Iris was distant, worried she'd mistake my motives
a miserable spring afternoon—
No wonder I horror to write—
Found dumb dull Balf, everybody high, nobody had nothing to
             say—the high trees—the sky
Myriad crowd of mustaches on St. Michel hurrying past Sorbonne
             bookstores
Lonely at this and irritant empty, I shifted my gaze in the traffic

---

   * Iris Owens, author (as Harriet Daimler) of *Innocence,* Olympia
Press.
   † Ramblin' Jack Elliot.

Bill talking to one and another or walking aslant silent with me.
In Luxembourg after we had pink candy, met Mason* walking with
        clock & books to the library to look at pix of machines—
                Multiple advertisements
Bill & he talked about Junk, I went for 8 ice creams
then table facing park in café, the white lipped Harvard boy who
        edits Paris Review and quibbles about giraffes
After Mason sighed over America and called for a new
        civilization—
at last at Baird's,† the beautiful young french Arab from Meuretius
who drew fine lines—cap black hair, a boyish wisp of mustache &
        no hair a-chin
Soft eyes, & corduroy blue pants, tweed coat, sports shirt dirty,
opening door a doll & Angel—I am queer.
It's like a madness all nite long I couldn't talk.

* * *

Bill—Garver—Natalie Peter Jack Huncke Neal Kammerer
Lucien—Joan—Cannastra Chase—Carl S. Gregory Dusty‡


Carl, Chase, Lucien, Neal, Huncke, Peter, Jack, Dusty Gregory &
        Bill are still alive
and Allen Ginsberg seer of them all is still alive, I've slept & loved 9
        out of 10—
It's some accounting of my life, a cycle of sex and immortal friend-
        ship, or Death or oblivion—
I've nothing to show for it, no babies, no marriage, no business
        firms
a handful of deaths & a river of Tears, and in the end perhaps a few
        isolate drunks when we're 90
but here is a handful of poems or novels or saints, we've created
        out of that friendship a new literature perhaps,

---

* Mason Hoffenberg, coauthor with Terry Southern of *Candy*, minor
ribald classic.
    † Baird Bryant, filmmaker.
    ‡ Draft of "The Names," CP 176–79.

at least have named an Age and given it the secret dharma of Amity
       Pity Friendship
on which perhaps a nation or a heaven could be founded—or at
       least No war.
I have no moral except these Friendships were till this year as
       sacred as life—
That if they were imperfect, was less because we had no desire to unify
But more that we were torn apart by family, money, war, abstract idea
differing periods of jail or bughouse, coercion of different moral
       professions—
and now to see them, still alive, be able to say, I've survived to this
       day to take accounting
Number & name them as final, my own saints and gods, each of
       whom I've loved & has accepted me & given me a rose of
       sex or deeper than sex family sacrament or beer all night
       ashcan binge
Then I can rejoice and look back to the hedges of childhood with
       sighs and fondness
Saying, This suffering then, this ache in the breast, was for this,
       which life has given
as if it were a miracle that love should be revealed, that dreams
       come true, that humans are for Death
That what we want for deepest most we must get, and do
And that if I dream of God, and see him, know that the bliss that's
       promised is all too well to be revealed also,
That the highest & final attainment of pure desire, the oldest ache
       in the beast, the last music of the mind
will be found someday Incarnate in this very world—awaiting only
       our unfolding like a flower to receive the sunlight golden
       manna food—
But, turning aside from this crank pantheon, can I herald these
       gods universal
and say to Greasy Joe or drippy Minnerbia* or Slick Phil in the
       Diplomatic Corps

---

    * See "Poems from Subway to Work," part 3 ("Fantasy of My Mother
Who's Always on Welfare"), in Peter Orlovsky's *Clean Asshole Poems* (San
Francisco: City Lights, 1978; Orono, Maine: Northern Lights, 1993), p. 60.

Let down your overalls, your bloody bloomers or your high striped
        intellectual pants
come join our deathly beer party & be one of the Final Gang?
Can I answer starvation in India with this fragment placebo family
        milk & tit?—my own cock gratification?
Only that each had for me a star on his forehead, a willingness to
        seek sacred light
Each carried a cross of death, or art or mystic beat or alcohol
        desire, one love apiece
moved then thru life & set them apart & made them recognize me
        in time
We found each other brothers at first sight, an instant jump of soft
        flame brain to brain
Each was hip, each understood the others alcohol or cock or Mad
Like follows like, seeks like, and makes it like—are all these likes
        too mad for Universal America to dig?
But tho it's hard to say, I still presume the most of Mercy, stick my
        neck out, say
We knew each other when—In Time—knew time Sacred in life
        before death
Whether we killed each other or not—at least found that light and
        expected more
—always constantly seeking new brothers of the fold, like cracked
        religious ministers
afoot in strange vast Africas, expecting to find the crazy stranger of
        God
in every village, one man set apart for Shaman, frenzy, drunken-
        ness or love
Who out of his own soul raised up eyes and laughed to say the great
        hello of Death
as if tradition handed on from Adam, secret lumination all the
        same—
as if all we knew one identity in far mid-cities or television anten-
        naed childhood homes
Suburb to suburb, one perfect wondrous monster child in each
        city uprose with light in his breast
and went out seeking in the folds of the world for fellows that he
        knew were there

or pining away alone, and ignorant, yet prayed in inmost secret
soul to Fantasy—

great Army of light marching to sex music in a hidden continent,

another world where lovers stroll metal electric gardens with rare
eye telepathy lowered glance & laugh under palmfrond
glare

or dreams of Angel hosts descending from impossible heaven to
the chamber chosen Dreamer

as if his desire created this Myriad of Heralds—O what of the
electric chair!

Yet weep with joy on a crowded street in Amsterdam to see another
ancient-once-known-face in the crowd of passengers on
the trolley

Whom we may never see again—or jump on the trolley with a rose

and fly excited to the pants of the new stranger & drop on our
knees and begin the eternal lovetalk—

Relentless Hades, Orpheus can go back & find Eurydice—The
possibility is there at least

Despite the bad example and the dangers indicated by the myth—

Thus Jack and I are known to each other as ancient strangers of the
golden race

That know each other in eternity—and thus we speak of Angels

as every angel knows—as every angel knows—As every Angel
knows

& this is the context of Angelcy—and this is how we're angels—

Are marriages Angelic, or am I just sad queer looking for another
pathetic one

who moans the same as I in cupboards—Sometimes I wonder,
when I hear them talk, or when—

\* \* \*

Say My oops, etc.
Bust my dust
Flip my wig
Flap my rib
Wipe my fig

\* \* \*

In life or Death forsake me not Lord Elohim
Light, years—a spoke of radiance sparkling
In the Imaginable Ezekiel hell—or ladders
of angelgown—What rest what rest O Momma
Art a skull that speaks imperfectly soon, soon
as sure as steps of a stairway—or a path in the
Cemetery the blank flats of graves in the communal
faraway Long Island Cemetery—"O come to the grave
my children—and see me there at last—
There you shall be, yes you'll be there alone
like me."

* * *

Eleanor of Aquitaine in sepulchre Louvre
The worms crawling out of the belly, her chin purified
in dreaming swoon—alive still after Death
the bowels ringed out, what cunt is this!—
Death is there, and you've already seen it
in Europe & Newark
Naomi
I shall come
to the same grave
where we were born and died
And will we meet again

* * *

Nothing to eat for the cat—The yellow dirty bedspread
A piece of old cheese—O the great mountain
of my knees in the bed the battles all over with soldiers
as a child—my lost tin soldier collection—sold?—
And what's left of my mineral collection—those boxes
in the attic—letters, notes—cats gone—
and my folders of pictures & writing in old trunk,
Robt La Vigne's pictures—Iris Brodey* too was very good,

---

* Iris Brodey was a Lower East Side painter, addict, early died, her paintings peeled from canvases unhandily prepared, 1950s. —A.G., May 25, 1992

Denise Levertov in NY now—Peter marry Joy*—
A rainy April night—the day been warm—
And love from the other side, amazing—and "I
trusted it"—will trust it in 10 years—Maybe
on vile deathbed—trust the light—"the key is in
the sunlight," next the snake of Never Born lashes
thru the space of thought, Rabble in my Square
—a Place de Concorde threatened by blue lights & clouds
—Lightning over Seine—the boatmotor or night truck's
whistle—raindrops on the window-curtains—
                    Goodby Naomi
not much time left for me to pray to your shade
Would you were there to see the moon—or Russia again—

                    * * *

The Arabs race thru streets of Tangier screaming against the police
        of Spain
Politicians scream and finger the air over the Bourse & wave
        imaginary money at each other
Is the world ruled by old madmen? Who else would run it. Not
        me—
Who's Henry Luce to exercise influence? A sincere poet? An
        ulcerous powerful man on top a big building?
How many minds he owns!—Take poverty, Henry Luce, follow
        Christ, abandon the world you created
There is a Great Sneak in your magazine—I am offended—Maybe
        you're trapped in the world
Untrap yourself & untrap many—
                    Take the cloth of Beauty
                                        —Change Time
Make some heroic failure
                            —a strange imaginative magazine—
                                It must be different
Let my people go
            —or I die
                    Be a failure
as Melville, as Whitman, as Poe, as Pound,

—————————

* Joy was Orlovsky's Indonesian girlfriend in Paris.

as Christ—
Be Henry Luce not the voice of the machine.
            There's no voice necessary but that of Soul
And Soul has no politics
            though it might have a magazine
Revelation! Revelation! Haven't you had
            Revelation yet? Don't you believe it?
God wants sincerity
                Not iron
God wants Charity
                Not Judgment
God wants kindness
                Not the oppressed hangman
God doesn't want your reason
                he wants your heart
He wants *you* Henry Luce
                not your magazine—
Holy be to Henry Luce, as to poor Huncke
                Holy equally to all
That great building of lighted windows
                Rockefeller center—
                    Hive, stone, elevators, ahoys
—I once worked there too—
            that it should lack a soul?
            Alas alas who's home there?
                Charms & forgiveness in the Art
                                Department?
        No Fright No Fright
                No national put-down
Adoration to everybody trying
            glory to the heart of the poor old farmer
                    who reads the news
What strange reporting of the news
                Benevolent, Indifferent, sentient
                    To both Frenchman & Algerian
Murderer & murderee
            Demo & Republican
                Communist & camp —and girl friends too.

* * *

## Letter from Paris*

The poem is open on the page
Understandable, you understand me?
Tomorrow perhaps I'll sit at a table
          and work myself
                    up into ecstasy.
Now I do what I can—talk straight.

When you're not high, when you're low
              dragged, blank, unwelcome,
Look in your heart for the love you want
          —not at the sun, not at the wall
                    or the ceiling—
Close up your eyes and look at your poor dying hand.

\* \* \*

Get rid of your reprobate back
Escape the face of cunning

It's he the son of the jailer
which is now mad.

\* \* \*

## Crossing Channel to England

[Metric Paradigms]
down to the doom down to the loam
down to the lone down to the ground
down to the bone done to the groan
down to the bloom down to the root
down to the foot down to the gloom
down to the tomb dust bone gloom loan

\* \* \*

---

\* Published in *Beatitude* 1959; re-edited by A.G. 1986.

Under the ground into the loam
Wove in the loom drunk in the ground
Mad in the coffin sad in the gloom
She goes down without light her body is bone

Into the engine throbbing the deck
Passes the air, passes the air
Into the sea the ship bounds
Into the air, the bird flies into the air.

Excellent excellent
                Minister sweet
Delight
                Fiery Joy
over the boat to England—
Boat rolls, last time over I got sick
Now bombed over the channel
                red wink
An idiot Cypriot boy howls in his
          black-hooded mother's arms.
And we discuss the Morning Star.

* * *

[Entries below constitute exchange of written comments between Ginsberg and Gregory Corso at their Oxford reading in the second week of May, 1958. Corso's notations appear in italics:]

Let's walk out, get a train & go
    To London right **Now!**

*I ran out—promising to contribute difficulty*

What to what?

*By saying (shaking hands)*
*good bye to Aaron*
*and Mims*

O.K. but after so? What difficulty have you promised to contribute to what grape?

*with difficulty one can evoke the grape into wine—*

Yes, yes but why not take a train

another night in this vale of Boredom & I will eat shit. Can you imagine spending 4 **years** here?

<u>NO</u>

*But I can see that we are invited to eat after show!*

Food is not enuf of a bribe to sit thru another nite of this—

\* \* \*

## Viewing Eiffel Tower

and met my own gaze from the
    pinpoint of Allen's eye
    up there on the Tower
    that overlooked all the green
    Champ de Mars and the water
    of rooftops.
Eiffel's like a god standing on four legs
    with revolving machinery in its
    soft belly of crosswork steel
Rising up swooping up stolid with
    a head filled with people and
    restaurants
—I am in Paris dreaming of Paris
    in white sneakers
Sitting in a 20 franc iron chair in
    the center of Champ de Mars
crosslegged facing my equal the
    Eiffel Tower
Box hedges of trees perspecting down
    the green Park Avenue grass
    like a long box down to the
    monstrous
Eiffel Minotaur at the end
    upstriding triumphant
in the grey sky which blinks
    over it's my skull.
A branch of pink & green balloons far
    down the alley of vision under
    the box trees

Trocadero symmetrical under the
round crotch of tower
        Napoleon's tomb behind my
back—he couldn't care less I
        had no hundred francs to get in
and see him—his red tomb in
        the blue dome light
        filled with Sunday
        worshippers—what
        Aetnas and Tilsits already
        survived, & he died &
        left that behind
—I thought of F Scott Fitzgerald
(as he thought of Daisy?) Climbing
        the Eiffel drunk
A loose balloon's floating up the
        first platform
a few birds zooming to the second
        platform
and the mad movie monster*
        who climbs up to murder
        the Nazi spy on the iron
stairway—
        Eiffel is reddish brown & huge—its ankles above the Mansards—
        And Mayakovsky alone, uplifting it in his mind and carrying it
back to Russia over his shoulder
        Why put it to work like that?
        it stands is indifferent like
God—blank—blind—
        eternal—red—silent—
So sitting down on the grass a
        a mile away
I imagined an eye in the
        Tower
an Eiffel eye looking down
        over Paris
Sweeping past the Butte and

---

* I.e., as in Carol Reed's 1949 film, *The Third Man*.

Sacre Coeur church & Picasso's
bones & old studios
over the rooftops & domes of Invalide
& Pantheon miles away
St. Sulpice corner breaking the
waves of the rooftops
Under the yellowing dusk
an eye that stared down finally
& picked me out on the ground
and our gaze met
in mid-air—a
flash of Dizziness in the
center of the Universe—
and I woke & picked up my pen.

\* \* \*

I have the secret to life
I come forward in pants & shirt
with 10 fingers
My hands outstretched scattering
goodies of air, earth, death
Fake Fire engines, doves, revolutions,
peace
All my friends are sad
they are become businessmen they handle
the actual guns and money
their arms are grey and they dip
their bodies in death
their faces are ashen their hair is white
Tears redden their eyes
But I have died and have nothing
to weep for
but them
I have the secret of life—
the leaf doesn't return to the branch.
the fire engine screams down the street, Broadway
But the building is burnt to death
the infants of flowers wither after

# Spring

the old men of winter
freeze their hands in the Rhine
One is saddened by the change
But I have the secret of life
I saw it was a vision it doesn't come to all
I am sad for my friends
their lips wither with worry & talk & anger
I have the red giraffe
assist at my feast
my voice calls faster and mumbles
Eat my body it's made of candy
Fats Domino sits at my piano
I am calm, tho yesterday I was
    depressed and walked
       to the Eiffel
            Tower to think
Scratch the moon.


# What Lies Would You Tell?

I stuck a fork in Peter's back
covered him over with newspaper
bled to death died of me

Gregory a knife chopped his head
he talked too much

Jack his guts all over the sidewalk
Bill ripped right up the stomach
Joe cut his balls off

I attacked them all savagely
with bare hands
    punched their eyes bloody
    orphan bastard left for dead
    in front of his car
      by the RR shack
    —the bridge lifting open

I got them all and took off to Russia
I destroyed her with one bomb too
Went to Mexico
                    Glad to get off this scene
when local mentality takes over like that.

* * *

This material is depressing this material is amazing I know it all
I'm finished I'm at an end I can't write my position is too violent
too unreal too much publicity too much flattery too much ego too
        much people
I have to go to a far Isle
where the breadfruit call
                    and recover my sainthood
                        no use writing if not writing for
the solitary god the solitary god I repeat
who hides me
protects me makes me work keeps my feet from chilblain . . .

* * *

The cops on Utopia Boulevard
chased me with sirens ascreaming
I posed for my picture in the papers
with weeping face & television

I couldn't eat my bread right
I spilt all the milk
my father came & complained of his tears
my brother's hand shook like a bone

## Au Tombeau Apollinaire

[Draft of "At Apollinaire's Grave," Part III, CP 182:]
Sat here with bearded Beson* on a tomb & stared at your rough
        menhir
—a tall grey ragged stone 8 feet tall—and a flat square piece with
grooves for little flowers

---

* A fellow American expatriate, who lived near rue Gît-le-Coeur.

—Someone placed a jam bottle
full of water filled with daisies,
    Someone else a red cheap funeral 5&10¢ surrealist typist
ceramic rose with artificial flowers
    a cross fading into the rock,—under a fine mossy tree
neath which I sat—with snaky trunk
—2 poems—one the Coeur Renversé other
      Habituez-vous comme moi
      a les prodiges que j'annonce
—Guillaume Apollinaire de Kostrowitski 26 aout 1880–10 no-
      vembre 1918
—a piece of rough thin granite like an unfinished phallus—
    he'd taken opium & taken the light
—boughs of the tree, leaves & branches
umbrella over the menhir—and nobody there—
             La voix ulule
    —Guillaume que tu devenu—
his next door neighbor is a tree
    happy tomb with little flowers and overturned heart—

    one must have felt the shock in St. Germain when he went
out—Jacob and Picasso coughing in the dark—a long procession
winding thru the flowers. Fauns, nymphs disappearing in the
leaden glade—a bandage unrolled & the skull left still—on a bed,
outstretched pudgy fingers—the mystery & ego gone— . . .

                     * * *

        Since we had changed . . .
        [Draft of "Message," CP 183]

                     * * *

          Scratch the moon
          who ate that grave
          Refrigerator soup
           & Fried Shoes

                     * * *

Vachel, the stars are out . . .
[Draft of "To Lindsay," CP 183]

\* \* \*

Dreams—Creeley gives me BMR\*—I am afraid—what to fill it
with—what subscription list? I ask Claude for an old poem, kiss
him—
—Don't change the colors of the old French Flag
—I take a stand in Algeria

\* \* \*

## I Was Walking Down the Street

on Times Sq.
Beside two giant naked white plaster statues
of a man with no cock & a woman without a cunt
when a beggar outstretched his brown cap
from a doorway in Nedicks
                amid the smell of fried frankfurters
        floating above the heads of a man in a top hat—
and when I dropped my dime in his ragged headpiece
a billow of yellow smoke leaped up
I stared down & saw a building on fire inside the hat
a crowd collected around the corner, swaying masses, police lines
            the scream of yellow ambulances
                long snakey water hoses to the pipes of Broadway
The fire trucks lifting their enormous ladders
        and antlike men in silver helmets
            climbing up the endless rungs to the building's
                                        20th story

A scream—and a woman leaped into the air
        and fell on the heads of the crowds
        which scattered
            droplet fallen into the swaying pool
A billow of red flame leaped into the air
        out of her window
and retreated into its lair
        after licking the air with its arms

---

\* Robert Creeley had recently edited the seventh and final issue of
*Black Mountain Review,* which included pieces by Kerouac, Burroughs,
Huncke, and Whalen, and a review of *Howl.*

Explosions of dynamite stored in the basement
Typewriters bursting like scattered nuts
            the arms of secretaries and hair, ears,
                    scalp of bosses
Hands flying thru the air
Legs dropping 20 stories
O how I hated that Employment agency and the 20
            years I slept over its typewriter
The toilet bowls cracked and fell apart with clanky porcelain
Elevators crashed down molten cages in the basement
            The operator's eye came out the back of his skull
Old Lady in Mink with Pekinese
            visiting her lawyer
                rushed down the corridor
            her hands flying round her head
                like Sealo the Seal Boy*
                Or a jazz girl doing the Charleston
                    rubbing the air face of the audience
And the janitor screaming in the broom closet on the 13th floor
Trapped with his masturbation—
            a long dry mophandle
                with burning head—
The desks began to move like rollercoaster cars
            across vast offices' polished floors
Rugs burned & curled up
All the faucets in the building turned on, hot water steaming by
            the cold—
Little French girl Cheri, walking naked out of the ladies' room
            holding her breasts—
A female writer in the movie floor typing on her script
            unconcerned—
And a beggar standing in front of the building with a burning
            hat, making money,
Old man, I said, you blind old man, your hat's on fire,
—I shouted this down into the hat to the miniature beggar on the
            corner—

---

    * Impressive comedian in freak show, no arms but hands like flippers
on his shoulders, who sold souvenir box containing miniature toilet bowl
& paper, Revere Beach or Coney Island 1930s. —A.G., May 23, 1993

He looked up at me the 20 stories and nodded, as if he could see—
      pissed in his hat
           A burst of steam
      and disappeared—I found me walking down the street
along Times Square alone—
      suddenly I spied a beggar in a door

* * *

I have found myself, Hope! long ago,
Farewell, France! I'm going back home
To Americay where they halter servants
           on the negro trees
all over the generation turns, wild boys
We are one, Liberty! Tho I despair—tho
      I lie on my bed and stare at the ceiling
      dreaming of Fame, of bars in the Village
      shouting my name
           Tho I dream
of the future hero of bright Nebraska
      repeating my name, and laughing at me
      100 years hence, as if I had
         groped him in a school's corridor, corny
         and blushed—he forgave me
We became fast friends—we walked in the moonlight together
talking, of friends, of that tenderness
      The cornfields in the moonlight
         holding hands
—never to flash knives, never to vote with bayonets,
      never to suffer separation—
always to clasp hands in the moonlight of imagination—
Later, great executives, we might ride
      on ski lifts in Switzerland
      or clomp rag-legged up desperate snows
               of Tibet—
or walk the streets of New York in White shirts, in
      the summer—
What sadness, laughing thru time—
      Hold hands before we die

Before we die—dear world, dear Williams,
This is the message:
                              we are in love.


Alas, to be done with that, the Buddhists say.
                    Into the night, into the night
          the coffin lowered in Père Lachaise grass,
Tho we have sat around the table, Paris, talked . . .
—That I have eaten a sacred monkey,
          That I have lain with the man hairy woman
                    That I have knocked on the black door
                              That I have eaten the meat of flies
That I have eaten my shoes with naked savages
That I have been educated in the gaunt highcheekboned
          University—
Tho I have been demoted to a centipede
That I write poetry:
                    That I hold hands to that
because secretly I believe that poetry is the hope of God—
Because secretly I believe in god
Because I have seen what god looks like
Because I can claim this, in words
                              and know I am right
Because I know rightness does not matter
Because I am
                    Because I can describe god
Because people will believe me
                    Because others have seen god
Because I hope in his mercy
                    to make me make sense
Because I cannot say I still remember his face
Because I have forgotten
Because I have forsaken my god.
Because god has hidden himself away
Because he has his work to do which I trust in
therefore becuz I lie here in bed dreaming with unhabitual junk
          scribbling some kind of stanza
as horses are stupid and divine, to jump right off a cliff when
          the stable starts on fire—

I am sensitive as a horse—I could eat myself to death—
      I begin with my mind
      I proceed with my left foot
          My cock, my asshole, bellybutton
             hair, teeth, fingers
          Finally I'm swallowing my own intestines
It makes no sense
Now I will give a complete description of myself
                feet, nerves, tit
Number my days & what I do, every day,
                   especially the big days
                   when I do something beautiful
Like inspire myself by some wild statement of lilies to a
stranger on the hill of neon Montmartre
or the time that I talk for hours with Bill, and we become
        tender—in the kitchen
              our last time on earth together
                 over cups of tea
or talk to a cow in Oregon
        or take off my clothes & lay a girl who likes me
or realize, walking in reverie downstreet
        that I love my mother, and she put me down
          all thru my childhood, with her paranoia
or know I still bear the cup of mercy when
        I'll have no hands—
or stand in the street waiting for the great dream to unfold
or say nothing but mystery! mystery! and
        go away confused—or buy an orange tart—
                     —consolation
Or do I hate my mother and not know it . . .
—So I lie down & record my dreams—

                       * * *

    Just think of all the sweet Negroes there are in
    America willing to talk to the whites—
    and I've tried the best I could, god
        to make others aware—
    and followed the road happy wherever it led

Stern Jawheh, gentle Jesus, wise Buddha wild Mohammed
unknown Zoroaster and Kali—"This way, Allen Ginsberg,"
says a voice in reverie—I'll listen.
       Nature God loves us, not judges—
Death is not judgement
       it is a mechanical process to close
       up the flower shop—
          like 7 PM the bells ring
          The workers go home to sleep—
and it's judgement that's awry
          and screws up the reception
          in the mind

* * *

It is a matter of
courage—no—it's love
& to maintain
The breast naked and pure
for the head that would
lie there & weep it's been
weary and wants delight
For the head will come seek the open breast in time.

We're drawn by our thought
to Distraction—tobacco brokers
and poets—to work for a living
to fight with the enemy
believe in the battle and win the war
But the heart is alone in the breast
and we only want to be loved
The heart is a father in us who knows all our woes

We can do nothing by study
by work, even the bricklaying
sweetest in Italy built for the poor
by saints, or Industrialists
building in ulcerous city
If we are not silent an hour
in our bodies till we kneel on the floor
Only a man kneeling in his mind has done the right work.

Rave, scream, build jokes
Broadcast laughter on the radio,
dance on television for the world
get paid, buy a limousine, go
home to a magic apartment and child
marry a beautiful pink wife
marry a mighty and wild man
Because we all die look at the great house of Time.

Freeze, blow, judge, ennui
confounded with apples or sputum
Amazed in New York
Aroused in India, whipping
the naked blacks Smoke opium
Be served by servants, serve
uselessly great silver trays of tea
Last week I saw an empty grave house in the cemetery torn down

we are nameless, we are not
Allen, Jack, Hepzibah, Max, Willie
We will not last on earth here,
The long days pass in empty rooms
The night sets over vast crowds in Plazas
The sun downs over mobs of babes
The myriad old men trace their beards in parks at noon
One thing, we are all alike, we have one hidden Father.

Paterson, Atlantic, Paris
Youth by Tin Can River
Vast waves of green from the ship
the sea of roofs and rocky towers
What next, soul, over ocean
and new continent—to a true America
and beyond to the black mob in India
O that Americans all kneeled under the moonlight and prayed for
     a flower.

But one day I walked dreaming
By a football practice field
at the far end of the universe
and looked up at the blackening sky

I was alone on a wooden catwalk
in a field of bones where stars died
To see the Old Father nearly scared me to Death.

* * *

Aunt Rose—now—might I see you . . .
[Draft of "To Aunt Rose," CP 184–85. Lines that follow came
separately at poem's end in journal and were not published.]
          Aunt Rose, for Honey's sake
     I have remembered your black heavy shoe
     Your dark & Chinese eye
               your little hanging breasts
     Your teeth, your thin pained happy smile
          And time that eats us all.

     For Honey's sake to make Aunt Honey cry.

* * *

          Hey you—I
          Can't see eyes
          Can't hear your ears
          Can't taste your tongue
          Can't smell your nostrils
          You must be someone else
                         Not me.

## Poem Written in Green Pen Ink*

Goin home
     goin home
The gas fume smell of the Paterson-Manhattan Line Red bus
riding along the fields of Weehawken. Toward
          the safety Kleenex† Neon sign
     on Route 6

---

     * That is, written with a green-ink pen given the poet by Orlovsky.
     † Marcal (not Kleenex) factory near shores of Passaic River in Elm-
wood Park, New Jersey.

Moonachie road
stars overhead—
I've been drunk in the village
and rolled on the floor of sawdust café St. Remo
in imitation of Christ.
[I'll be] Sitting on the bus
as once six years ago,
I saw a boy with blonde hair
and blue trousers who sat next to me
in the leather seat, we settled down
Our knees touched, we rode forward in the night
together, and never spoke.
Goin home
to my Father and his lamp & desk.
—how lonely my face in the bus window
I've returned, from Mexico
From Alaska and the west
and rode that bus on weekends to New Jersey
and now from Europe, come back older
a genius with a new suit
Tired and hollow
going home in the Manhattan bus
I'll remember this green penned prophecy
of a Paris room 6 weeks before
and dream back at Europe,
all the noise of time past silverware
Cookstove & the great brown pot,
Bill downstairs, Gregory in the attic
of Rue Gît-le-Coeur,
I must be kinder to B.J., to Françoise, to George*—
must say farewell to all—
Will I ever see Bill again?
alas to leave him in tears—distinguished saintly

---

* B.J., Françoise: Neighbor friends of Peter & Gregory. George
Whitman, now of Shakespeare & Co. bookshop, crashpad hangout for
international hitchhikers thru literary-political Paris 1950s–1990s.
—A.G., February 22, 1991

Bill I tried to give you all I could you needed
and my mission in Europe is done.

Alas I haven't seen Warsaw, nor writ poems in the snow below the
        Kremlin wall
Nor wandered alone with knapsack to Berlin
never took that ship thru blue water to Greece
        and found a naked statue of oblivion's boy familiar—
nor trainride to Istanbul, no long nights on Sicily & Crete, nor
        afternoon sun bathing on rocks at Nice
Nor found the Angel of Europe, or the inspired wormy poet of
        France
Nor written the elegy of my Mother, nor the Fall of America
now must go home & face the television mob and radio fireworks
        announcer
and lay my head in Peter's arms, and lay my body along his tender
        thighs.

* * *

Dream—June 28—Going toward a long hall, into an old house,
behind the house an old garden with woodshed mausoleum as an
Egyptian tomb, I went into the stone hall of the tomb, to the upper
back room—my body was there in coffin—I thought to look at my
body, to be able to see the dead face of Allen—but when I opened
the top dust board, I saw myself wrapped like a mummy or Giotto
Christ baby in swaddling bands with face hidden—nor could not
see my face in Death—afraid to go thru all trouble unwrapping
the corpse just to see my own face, it would disturb everybody, at
midnight, in the garden—
        Remember how beautiful it was that you could have chance
to see your own face in Death—

The sky is too huge
a sum to be rolling around earth
Remember if we die, we've died ourself,
Nobody made us die,
We've done it all ourselves—
Imagine,
        Gregory said,

Six millionaires became the King of France & Spain
all Rothschilds—and the Jews made Hitler
"You can do anything you want"
          Said Pound in opium haze
          Complaining about the Jews—
The facts are too huge
          to believe, like
          a Communist lie—
Only poetry will save America
I have the message,
          Here is the Non Repulsive acre of atom bomb—
It's all up to Khrushchev's mistress and digestion—
It is not god's iron hand
          They're making big mistakes—
          ——

The Tribune is big mouthed
          & stupid—they are all—
          Bigmouthed & stupid

\* \* \*

July 2—I looked at myself in the mirror at the Hall of Mirrors in Versailles—my face, grimacing behind the heavy glasses taped because broken—balding—black coat weighted down with 1924 red Baedeker in left hand, torn pocket, white lunchbag eggs hamburgers in right.

Square blue shirt, frizzy bald hair thin, as too much cocaine & walking with dirty feet—guidebook (to Eternity) in hand.

—Thought at last, to be seeing my colored image in this mirror—the millions of other images that had flashed by this mirror before—and I pass bright image, feet on the Versailles famous hall—and others after follow the future—

Liberté Leave Thurs 17 July
arrive 23 A.M. (9am or so)

\* \* \*

## Last Poem There

The room in Paris as I leave it
          a rose in a beer bottle

Chair, cigarettes, handkerchief at my
       bed
Brown teapot shining in the lightbulb
       on the table
by the silver can of sugar once a
       can of peas
Olive oil & Vinegar near the ceiling
       atop a double eggbox on the
       cupboard, grey & old—
Aster margarine, all the fruits
       of the grocery accumulated
       a year
Pepper, chili powder in transparent
       celluloid capsules,
Myself crosslegged on the bed
       observing—
A calm entering the dark window
       open to the breeze,
the curtains rustling, six month
       new clean curtains replaced,
Battery of pothandles of pots full
       of chicken under the stove
My box of books marked Europe
       and American knapsack
Waiting by the wall
a picture of Theodore Roosevelt
       jeune & old Genet pinned
       on the mirror,
Myself again, in the mirror
       This time sideways noting
my posture bent back, blue
       shirt, bare knees clean
       feet, bald hair & heavy
       eyeglasses
Old hand-kept calendar (Peter's)
       now in disuse
The new strangeness of the
room about to be disoccupied,
The freshness of such walls,
       that the last time turning out

the light
I realized my final sight of
            this room at night
plunged into darkness
opened the light again and
sat on the bed to write this
note to read in future.
                —Perhaps I'll dream tonite
leaving Paris
            perhaps on the Liberty
on the ocean
            I'll arrive in America
and find no New York
            The blasted rock of Manhattan
smoking on the horizon
            —Startling news, 3 days
at sea, perfectly possible—
            "Slight change in plans
Security reasons
            Ship will dock in Baltimore"
or arrive in New York in
            Perfect calm—

For now to Begin, at last, to meditate
            in perfect calm
My work is over, it was never necessary
            Poets, magazines, languages and all
—Begin in Dying NY to sit in a room
            as last nite
lying in bed my body began to rock
            in silence as in a cradle,
The first petty miracle of
            contemplation, sign from
            the body—
Look in the mind and
            eat the monster there—

                                        Paris July 1958

# Index

Page numbers in *italics* indicate illustrations.

# Index of Titles and First Lines

Page numbers in *italics* indicate illustrations.